Dear George,

How'd you like to do a review of this book, or run excepts?

[signature]

BARRY BONDS

BASEBALL'S SUPERMAN

By STEVEN TRAVERS

Foreword by Charlie Sheen

Sports Publishing, LLC
www.sportspublishingllc.com

Director of production: Susan M. Moyer
Art director, dustjacket design: Kenneth J. Higgerson

ISBN: 1-58261-488-1

Printed in the United States

SPORTS PUBLISHING, LLC
www.sportspublishingllc.com

This book is dedicated to my parents,
who put up with me;
to my daughter, Elizabeth Travers, who loves me;
to my best buddy, Kevin McCormack,
who believes in me;
and to the Lord Jesus Christ, who saves me.

—Steven Travers

What They Are Saying About
Barry Bonds—Baseball's Superman . . .

"Because he is one of the big names in our pro sports scene today, and since he has shattered a record that was only broken three years ago, it's appropriate that my good friend Steven Travers has chronicled Bonds' amazing season. But hopefully the reader will find even more interesting, Travers' rare look at this reluctant superstar.

"Bonds trusted Travers enough to open up and share some private thoughts with him, about his life as an athlete, as a kid growing up and watching his dad Bobby play in the Majors, and some of his opinions regarding our turbulent society.

"Rare . . . is the opportunity to read firsthand about the man who authored such a feat. Read and enjoy this book about an unusual athlete and an incredible season. I think you'll not only enjoy yourself but learn a few things that you didn't know about Barry Bonds. And perhaps you'll come to realize as I have, that he's not only a great ballplayer, but a most interesting person."

BRUCE MACGOWAN,
KNBR RADIO/SAN FRANCISCO

Acknowledgments

I would like to thank Mike Pearson of Sports Publishing, Inc., for believing that this book could come to fruition. I also want to thank Maurey Williamson of Sports Publishing, Inc., for his efforts in promoting this book. I do not want to overshadow the rest of the Sports Publishing family: Director of Production Susan Moyer, marketing guru Nick Obradovich, and the rest.

My thanks also go out to Steve Hoskins, Barry Bonds' media representative, and to the great Barry Bonds himself, for their cooperation on this project from June to October 2001.

I also wish to thank the San Francisco Giants, a class organization if ever there was one. In particular, I want to thank Bob Rose, their former vice president of communications, who is now doing a fine job at the University of California-Berkeley. Thanks also to Maria Jacinto, Blake Rhodes and Matt Hodson. They did the tireless, behind-the-scenes work at Pacific Bell Park that make it possible for journalists like myself to do our jobs.

I want to thank the two agents who represented me at various times during the course of this project; Basel Kane of the Kane Literary Agency in La Jolla, California, and Mel Berger of The William Morris Agency in New York City. Thanks also to my manager, Lloyd Robinson of Suite A Management in Los Angeles.

I also thank Maureen Regan.

I want to thank my parents, Donald and Ingeborg Travers of Marin County, California. They put up with me and taught me to never quit.

I want to thank my daughter, Elizabeth Ashley Travers. She gives me inspiration.

I want to thank my two best friends. Kevin McCormack always believed in my writing career, and gave me encouragement that I value. Bradley Cole of New York City (who portrays Prince Richard on the CBS daytime drama "A Guiding Light") gave me advice and insight.

I want to thank Marc Samson of MAS Marketing in Santa Monica, California, and Jake Downey of Studio City, California, for their help in this project. I also want to express my gratitude toward John Shea, the baseball columnist at the *San Francisco Chronicle,* who pointed me in the right direction regarding some research, and to *Chronicle* sports editor Glenn Schwarz. Thanks also to PR lady extraordinaire Cherie Kerr of Cherie Kerr Public Relations Santa Ana, California.

Thanks also to Kevin Donahue, the athletic director at Bonds' alma mater, Father Junipero Serra High School in San Mateo, California, for the photo content he provided me. Thanks also, to Charles Scott of Novato, California, currently a scout for the Arizona Diamondbacks, and a one-time teammate of Bonds at Arizona State University. I also want to extend my gratitude to former USC pitcher Randy Robertson.

Thanks also to the man I predict will eventually be the Chairman/CEO of Coca-Cola, Terry Marks, for his ideas regarding the marketing of this book.

Thank you to Mark Brand, the sports information director at Arizona State, and to his assistant, Jeff Evans. My gratitude also is externded to Bob Nachshin, Barry Bonds' attorney, for his cooperation in this project.

I wish also to thank Beverly "Blake" Young, who gave me love that I cherished. I want to extend my gratitude to Fred Wallin of *www.businesstalkradio.com,* Oakland Raiders' and A's announcer Greg Papa, and to veteran San Francisco sportscaster Bruce MacGowan of KNBR, the "Giant 68." I wish to also thank Zach Beimes, who to this day remains the best sports editor I ever had, from my days at *StreetZebra Magazine.* I want to thank Jeff Ballard, the publicist for Charles Sheen, for his great work in helping us get Charles to write the foreword. Thanks also to Charles "Wild Thing" Sheen. Dig your work, man.

—*Steven R. Travers*

Contents

Author's Note

I first came up with the idea of writing a book about Barry Bonds in May 2001, when Bonds went on a particularly impressive home run tear in Atlanta. I told my agent right then and there that I predicted Bonds would break Mark McGwire's single-season home run record. I cannot say if my prediction came before his teammate Shawon Dunston, who bet Bonds—also in May—that he would break the record. When Bonds did accomplish the feat, he had to buy Dunston a Mercedes Benz. I will take mine silver-colored with black trim, thank you!

I approached Bonds about writing a book in May. Over the course of the next six months, many things came to pass. In June, Bonds gave me the go-ahead to begin negotiations with publishers on his authorized autobiography. I learned a great deal about the New York publishing industry. Bonds broke the record. The autobiography became a biography, and I wrote this book.

This was the most enjoyable writing experience of my career, which also includes screenplays, newspaper columns, sports reporting, songs, and political speeches. The essence of what writing can be, which is to transport one's self to a different place, occurred during this process. The book was written during the cold-weather months of fall and winter, yet I was transformed as if by magic to the beautiful, magical summer of Barry Bonds, a summer that will live forever.

My college roommate, who now holds one of the foremost marketing positions in the country, suggested the following title: *Barry Bonds Is An Asshole.* I have researched this subject, and determined that Barry Bonds is not an asshole. So what is he? Well, he is many different things. Barry Bonds is . . . well . . . what is he? He is different things to different people. I thought about calling this book *Barry Bonds Is A _____,*" and let the readers decide. This would have been grist for the talk shows. The hosts would ask me, "So what is Barry Bonds?" The truth is, I cannot call myself such an authority on the man as to provide the definitive answer. What I have done is give a fair, balanced view of this man, and present the results to you, the readers.

I love history, and not just baseball history. I felt that what I witnessed first-hand in 2001 was more than just baseball history. Rather, I felt that I was chronicling events of a tumultuous year that will live with us for generations. I hope those generations will keep turning to these pages to get a glimpse of a very special time in the history of America.

I welcome any commentary, good or bad.

STEVEN R. TRAVERS
Marin County, California
January 1, 2002
(415) 455-5971, (603) 658-0612 fax
STWRITES@aol.com

Foreword

by
CHARLES "WILD THING" SHEEN

I imagine I was asked to write this not because I once met Barry Bonds in the visiting locker room at Dodger Stadium in 1996 (after a game where he hit a shot off of Hideo Nomo that only recently landed), but because of my roles in baseball movies like "Eight Men Out" and "Major League."

I was also a pitcher in high school (sneaky fast, decent floater, worked the corners), so I thought, "Okay, what would I do if I were facing Barry Bonds?" Then I realized that for the most part, I'd be turning and admiring the arc and distance of balls sailing high over the right field pavilion and into the parking lot. I doubt my fastball would be sneaky enough. This is why I act.

I've met dozens of major leaguers, taken BP at a few different stadiums, and I count several players as good friends, so I'm no stranger to their world. But when I met Barry, despite what I'd read and heard, he was as gracious and down to earth as he could be. I was struck immediately by his presence. He has that "thing," a quality, a way of carrying himself. In the moves it's referred to as the "X factor." In sports, it remains nameless . . .

I'm a fan of baseball's superstars, but I've always had an appreciation for the non-marquee players—the journeymen, the fourth outfielders, the late-inning defensive replacements. Names you'd never find on a candy bar, faces you'd never see on a box of Wheaties. Guys who know they're never going to the Hall of Fame, just playing the game is enough for them. Barry encompasses both; one foot in superstardom, the other on the sandlot.

In a year that tested our nation's resolve, we found ourselves looking for heroes. We found many at ground zero, on the front lines, and in the trenches. We also found heroes in government, entertainment, and witnessed tremendous generosity from all 50 states. We were gratefully reminded that heroism is never seized, only earned.

When President Bush asked us all to resume our lives and go back to work, Barry certainly did just that. His pursuit of the single-season home run record had been interrupted, yet his focus had not. And once play resumed,

Barry united a grieving nation in more ways than one. This was about more than baseball. It was about America. Breaking this seemingly insurmountable record was certainly magical. To step up and do it during this time was heroic.

Sure, throughout his career Barry has had his detractors. But right now, it would be hard to say you were a baseball fan without also being a fan of Barry Bonds.

Prologue

The baseball world was both shaken *and* stirred in 2001 by Barry Bonds, who broke the greatest record in sports—the all-time single-season home run record held over the years by Babe Ruth, Roger Maris and Mark McGwire. Unlike 007, Barry did his thing in a very public manner, taking his game to a new level that astonished the baseball world with the greatest slugging percentage of all time, the most walks in a season, and an unreal .500 on-base percentage. The names of players whose records Bonds surpassed tell the tale: Ruth, McGwire, Ted Williams, Willie Mays, Mickey Mantle. After winning his fourth MVP award, his story is not just the biggest in sports in the new century. Bonds, in fact, had the greatest season in baseball history.

The son of baseball great Bobby Bonds and the cousin of another baseball legend, Reggie Jackson, as well as the Godson of Mays, Bonds is the greatest athlete in the world, the best baseball player in our lifetime, and when it is all said and done, he will make a serious bid for the title All-Time Greatest Baseball Player!

Nothing compares to breaking the home run milestone. But there is more to life than just chasing Mark McGwire's record, and Bonds had an opportunity in 2001 to get some things off his chest. He does not verbalize things with writers as well as he would like to, but he improved in this regard.

There is no doubt that to most fans, Barry Bonds is a man of mystery. A misunderstood superstar who has long engaged in a running feud with the Bay Area media, Bonds in 2001 broke new ground. His relationship with The City By the Bay finally blossomed, not unlike his Godfather, Willie Mays, who found Orlando Cepeda and Willie McCovey to be more popular for several years.

Bonds is approaching 40. A happily married man with three children, he has matured into an elder statesman of baseball. In this book, the very kinds of inner thoughts, demons and joys that the press and public have long wanted to hear from this often enigmatic, yet intelligent player are revealed.

The greatest single-season mark in the game is his. There was something primal to Bonds' season, and in fact his career. Long considered the game's best player, Bonds' ascension to greatness has taken him into truly rarefied air, and one gets the sense he accomplished all of this through some form of extra-human will and determination. It is this aspect of both his personality and physical ability that separates him from even the great stars who are and were his contemporary rivals: Ken Griffey, Jr., Alex Rodriguez, Cal Ripken, or anybody else.

This was the year that Bonds hoped to command a salary that approached the amount garnered the previous year by Rodriguez. It was felt that he would have the opportunity of signing in New York, Los Angeles—or returning to his hometown of San Francisco. This is a man whose intentions have been discerned and speculated on by the sporting press, and this book talks about the role of money in an athlete's life, and how dollar signs determine the pecking order of greatness as much as homers, touchdowns or even World Championship rings.

In the end, Bonds remained a Son of San Francisco!

Bonds' claim to sports immortality has gone beyond even the "ESPN 50 Greatest" category, or *The Sporting News'* Player of the Decade for the 1990s. The 37-year-old Bonds, a marvelous physical specimen whose training regimen and lifestyle are the epitome of dedication, now embarks on the next quest: Henry Aaron's all-time career mark of 755 home runs.

The first player in Major League history to hit 400 home runs and steal 400 bases in a career, Bonds will soon make that the 500/500 Club. He is also an eight-time Gold Glove winner, a member of the exclusive 40 homer/ 40 stolen base club and a multiple member of the 30/30 club. His goals include 3,000 career hits, and lifetime records for runs batted in and walks are within his range.

These are breathtaking achievements and place Bonds alongside Mays, DiMaggio, Ruth, Aaron and Ty Cobb. It allows his name to be mentioned in the same breath with Michael Jordan, Bill Russell, Jim Brown, Wayne Gretzky, Pete Sampras and Pele.

Bonds has long received plaudits for his on-field performance. Now this book gives fans an exclusive look at the man they all have longed to know more about, on and off the field. It follows Bonds throughout the 2001 season as he defied the very bounds of conventional logic and reduced the art of long-ball hitting into his own personal art form. As Bonds came closer and closer to the record of 70 home runs set by McGwire in 1998, we examine the reactions of McGwire and Arizona's Luis Gonzalez.

This book also details one of the most exciting, down-to-the-finish pennant races in the annals of baseball history, concluding with a September stretch in which Bonds carried his club like no player—Carl Yastrzemski of Boston in 1967 possibly comes to mind—concluding with an unbelievable final-weekend series at Pac Bell Park vs. the arch-rival Dodgers. In the first game of that series, Bonds broke McGwire's record with his 71st round-tripper against Los Angeles ace Chan Ho Park.

Although the excitement of the 2001 season is the highlight of this book, it also describes Bonds' storied career, beginning in Riverside, California, the hometown of his father; playing ball in the San Carlos Little League (where Bobby hid in the car to avoid distractions, although Barry still does not believe he was actually there); his playing career at Serra High School in San Mateo; his All-American performance at Arizona State; and his eventual superstar status.

This book describes what is it was like being a black kid growing up in privileged surroundings on the Peninsula and attending mostly white private schools. Unlike most African-Americans, he did not get a taste of life's more unpleasant realities until he became an adult. Bonds has close friends who are both black and white, and herein is discussed his relationships with his teammates, white, black and Latino. The attendant resentment, jealousy, and envy he has experienced in the area of racial politics are explored.

This book delves into the intensely private, proud mind and ego of a man who understands baseball history and his place in it, and who had the biggest season of any player in a free agent year ever. The Player of the Decade certainly is a big story.

Bonds lives in a world of luxury, the epitome of the big-money athlete's lifestyle. We see the strain of training, practice and diet; the pressures and grind of professional sports. This book looks back at his record-breaking home run production, fourth MVP, free agency, off-season publicity, and observations of his future.

The book opens with Bonds breaking the all-time home record on the final Friday of the 2001 season. After retracing the steps of his life, we begin a chronological look at his record-breaking season, starting with Spring Training and the early part of the regular season, right through the end of the season. The text is peppered with candid, and sometimes controversial opinions of Bonds, his teammates, opponents, the game, and life in general. Finally, this book allows us to look at baseball history and to examine his contribution to the game.

Barry Bonds is not who you think he is, and if he is, is he sorry? He has stepped on some toes. Some guys are better at dealing with the media than he is. Tony Gwynn is a natural at it. Bonds is not perfect. He does not run out every ground ball. He never meant to hurt any one's feelings, and yet. . . .

Once he told a writer to "get the hell out of here." As soon as he said it, did he know he was wrong, or is he in such a high place in our unbalanced society that he did not realize it? He has feelings. He cares about other people, but he also has a basic shy side. He has pressures and time constraints to deal with. He know he looks arrogant . . . or does he? Given the chance, would he apologize for it?

Within these pages are discussed:

- The Rick Reilly *Sports Illustrated* criticism, David Halberstam's "hit piece" on ESPM.com, and Tim McCarver's incendiary remarks about Bonds.
- Women in the media.
- Religion.
- Modern American politics.
- Important players in baseball history.
- Homosexuality in sports.
- His divorce.
- His college coach, Jim Brock, at Arizona State.
- Family values.
- The World Trade Center and Pentagon disasters.
- His relationship with his father.
- Jim Leyland.
- Dusty Baker.
- Playing defense.
- Teammates.
- The "Sid Bream Incident."

These, and many other subjects and views of Barry Bonds, Man of Mystery, are revealed. Prepare to take a fascinating walk through history.

CHAPTER ONE

"He hits it high. He hits it deep. He hits it outta here."

"Can you embrace this?"

The question came on national television from ESPN's Roy Firestone.

Barry Bonds, the greatest athlete in the world, having the best season in baseball history, and about to break the most hallowed record in all of sports, seemed unable to grasp the enormity of his accomplishments.

"My goal is winnin . . . what if it ends today?" he responded. "Am I the same today as I was yesterday? Am I put on a pedestal because of this achievement? 'He's handling himself so right.' I'm the same as I was last year."

But he was not the same. Nobody could be. Bonds now belonged to us. He now belonged to history, and if he could not grasp it at the time, time will allow him to understand this concept.

"People are still fascinated . . . " continued Firestone, who knows that the role of the media is to document history.

"I can embrace it, but I don't want McGwire's home run record, I want his ring, that's what we play for," replied Bonds. "I can't figure this out, you have to ask God, I've never been through anything like this, if I knew what I was doing I would have done it a long time ago."

Later, Firestone moved into familiar territory.

"Do you define arrogance?" he asked.

"I don't know," answered Bonds. "There's no lack of confidence. I'm good. I don't deny I'm good. I know I'm good."

Firestone, a man of color himself, could not refrain from going to the proverbial "race card."

"Does the American public want you to do it?" Firestone asked, and the implication, as understood by the interviewee, was that he was asking if *white* America could *stand* him doing it!

"That's reality, sure, the KKK still exists, whaddaya gone do about it?" was Bonds' answer. "It ain't gonna stop me. I still tell my son to shoot for the stars, to strive for his goals."

So, the stage was set. ESPN had become All Bonds All The Time, and as Bonds was approaching Mark McGwire's single-season home run record, the network was asking fans what the greatest single home run ever hit was. The candidates were:

1932	Babe Ruth's "called shot."
1951	Bobby Thomson's Shot Heard 'Round the World off Ralph Branca.
1960	Bill Mazeroski's World Series winner over the Yankees.
1961	Number 61* in '61 for Roger Maris ("Holy cow, Maris did it," said announcer Phil Rizzuto).
1974	Hank Aaron's 755th home run.
1975	Carlton Fisk's game-winner over the Reds.
1978	Bucky Dent's home run over the Green Monster for the Yankees.
1988	Kirk Gibson's home run off Dennis Eckersley.
1991	Kirby Puckett's extra-inning home run off the Braves in the Series.
1993	Joe Carter's shot off Mitch "Wild Thing" Williams for Toronto.
1998	Mark McGwire's 70th homer.

27.2 percent of the fans said Gibson's was number one. Would Bonds' 71st out-do that one in their minds?

Pacific Bell Park is the jewel by the bay in San Francisco. When Journey performed the classic rock anthem to their hometown, "Lights," this is what they had in mind:

"When the lights go down in the city
"And the sun shines on the bay…"

It has meant a great deal to The City, a place of duality that is both arrogant and beset by an inferiority complex at the same time. Pac Bell is something that San Francisco did right, finally. At the same time, it is something San Francisco did right, of course.

Pac Bell Park has been a source of pride and excitement for the Bay Area over the past two seasons. In a town where many would not watch a baseball game at dilapidated Candlestick Park even if they were paid to do so, Pac Bell became a Mecca of baseball and the "in" place to be. A place for the cool cats, the hipsters, those who feel the need to see and be seen. The trendy restaurants and waterfront bars that surround the stadium have become hot spots in a part of town, China Basin, that was once a blue-collar wasteland.

Pac Bell Park was built after decades of angst in and around a city known for its angst. Mainly, it was built to accommodate the heroics and histrionics of a single man named Barry Bonds.

Friday night, October 5, 2001, was the night everything would be worth it. The politics, and the money that went into building the world's best baseball stadium. The enormous contract that lured Bonds home from Pittsburgh to play for the San Francisco Giants. The locker room dissing of the media by the misunderstood superstar. All of it would be overshadowed and made right by events of this fateful night.

It was chilly at Pac Bell on this evening, certainly not a surprise in a town where Mark Twain once said he had spent the coldest winter of his life in the summer. Of course, October is different, the best time of the year, a freaky weather occurrence in a place where freakiness is the norm.

Warm autumn days do not mean warm autumn nights, however, and San Franciscans know this well. They were wrapped and bundled appropriately for a night game, and they were getting precisely what they came to see.

Now, the time was 8:15 p.m. Half a continent away, a big huckleberry of a man named Mark McGwire went down on strikes, and at that very moment an African-American slugger who is a walking contradiction took a mighty cut and made McGwire the *former* home run champion.

Barry Bonds sent a 1-0 pitch from the Los Angeles Dodgers' hard throwing right-hander, Chan Ho Park, *deep* into the arcade in right-center, 442 feet away for his 71st home run of the 2001 season.

Thanks to Bonds' heroics, Giants announcer Duane Kuiper's trademark home run call had become well known.

"He hits it high," Kuiper says. "He hits it deep. He hits it outta here!"

The greatest record in all of sports had fallen, and it had fallen as the result of a personal crusade of excellence by a man who had taken the art of long ball hitting to a new level. Bonds in this magical season had elevated his game to a place in the stratosphere, above and beyond what anybody had ever seen. His efforts had a superhuman quality to them, as if he had the will of the gods and the lightning touch of Zeus at his disposal.

Sports, perhaps more than any endeavor, allows people to observe on occasion man at his absolute primal best. One can admire the genius of Albert Einstein weighing the practical applications of the theory of relativity, but understanding it is beyond the ken of most. A great speech by Winston Churchill or Abraham Lincoln is worthy of praise, yet still abstract as a political act, rather than a thing of pure weight and substance in and of itself. Those who see it as almost a dream sequence view a Medal of Honor-worthy charge up a wartime hill, that results in taking out a vital enemy pillbox, to be the essence of courage and manly purpose, but its retelling only trivializes it to a John Wayne movie.

No, the arena of sports is the truest, best place to display human excellence. Those who pursue these arts are, of course, flawed people like the rest of us, which only adds to the duality and mysterious conundrum that makes it so beautiful and human.

Pele controls a soccer ball as if it is attached by magic string to his feet, the stirring of over 100,000 Brazilians acting in concert and as impetus with the perfect grace of his inevitable winning goal.

Joe DiMaggio races down a fly ball in the farthest reaches of Yankee Stadium to save a game while a town accords the greatest tribute of all celebrity status. Those are the cheers directed to a true New York sports star; cheers of adulation that the Marilyn Monroes of the world could never quite contemplate, no matter how hard they have tried.

Michael Jordan defying gravity while dunking a basketball is more exclamation point than two points. Joe Montana is the Master of the Universe with a minute left to drive the field for a winning touchdown. Jackie Robinson carries the burden of society's desperate battle between right and wrong, while hustling out a daring steal of home plate.

Oh, many see sports as a vainglorious parade, chafed by money and corruption, but the true believer only feels pity for the timid soul who never grasps its meaning. Surely, on October 5, 2001, the meaning of sports was as apparent as it ever is. Flashpoints of irony and incident served to permeate the consciousness of the thinking sports aficionado.

Less than one month prior, the United States had suffered a blow so devastating in nature that it seemed a bad dream. A nation was so repulsed as to put the event someplace else, like the repressed memories of an abused child. Yet, it was real and the reminders of its reality were constant.

Baseball meant nothing, but some ongoing history lesson in the back of the national mind told us that there is heritage at stake. So, the games, after a week's delay, went on. Slowly yet surely their meaning served to tell us we are Americans and we persevere.

A crowded athletic stadium is an ancient reminder of man's love of spectacle. Its roots go to the Roman Empire and are part of the Greek ideal, and it has become a place of worship not only for athletic events, but in America it is evidence of our greatness.

In the second half of the twentieth century, sports venues in Europe and Latin America have too often become places of riot. Drunken soccer hooligans failed to separate sport from religion, politics, and national pride.

In the U.S., crowds have learned their place in the greater scheme of things. Nobody can deny the rowdiness of the Georgia-Florida college football game. In the 1970s, Yankee Stadium had a criminal element to it that reflected the difficult times that battered city experienced, before its eventual Renaissance.

By 2001, however, the post-championship game tearing up of the field had become passé, replaced by a civilized perspective of events. This was the view that was held, on this night, by 41,730 baseball citizens representing a city known for its cultivation and refinement.

The reality of the crowded arena now held a new meaning in a world in which terrorists seek ways to kill as many people as possible at the same time. Part of this reality was a growing sense of defiance in denying satisfaction to an enemy thirsting for evidence that they had changed a nation through fear.

No, Americans would fill their stadiums as if to announce to the world that they were better than those enemies were. On this night, Bonds and San Francisco would embrace the meaning of baseball.

All in all, the events of October 5 captured all the emotions of sports. A record, of course, fell. The breaking of a record like the single-season home run mark is something that has a life of its own, and Bonds had built this one in an inexorable way. In April he had hit his 500th career home run, an event that seemed to change him and the way San Francisco felt about him.

In quick succession after that Bonds would pass Giants legends Mel Ott (511) and Willie McCovey (521). In May, Bonds would put on the greatest home run display of his career in Atlanta. Bonds kept hitting homers, all the while passing a laundry list of Hall of Famers on the all-time career chart. At the All-Star break, despite a slump that had lasted several weeks and dampened enthusiasm for his chances, he still remained ahead of McGwire's record pace.

Experts, acting on some kind of natural instinct of negativism, consistently rejected the notion that Bonds could break the record even after he regained his form. His homers, however, came regularly, almost as if scheduled. He carried his team like few players in the game's history, and not just with his power. With his expert eye, he drew walks at a record pace. He reached base over half the time. His swing had an efficiency to it that was downright ruthless, and his slugging percentage would be the greatest ever. Bonds would probably have a greater positive impact on his teammate, a journeyman shortstop named Rich Aurilia, than any player other than Mickey Mantle on Roger Maris.

The Giants, a decent team with decent pitching and a great manager, Dusty Baker, would stay afloat in the National League West by virtue of Bonds' heroics all season. As Bonds approached the record, the Giants thus stayed alive. However, for weeks the Arizona Diamondbacks, an average team with little firepower and a shaky bullpen, had stayed a couple of steps ahead of San Francisco. They had done it on the strength of a righty/lefty pitching combination that was the most devastating since Sandy Koufax and Don Drysdale's glory days in Los Angeles.

Curt Schilling and Randy Johnson matched Bonds in an epic stretch run, and now, on the final weekend, it all came down to an orgy of record-setting baseball and scoreboard watching that included the Houston Astros, St. Louis Cardinals, and the D'backs.

Bonds had arrived at Pac Bell Park tired and emotionally spent after coming home at three in the morning from Houston, where he had tied Big Mac's record on Thursday evening.

That day, he laid to rest his friend, Franklin Bradley, who had recently died young from complications during minor surgery. At a press conference before the game, however, he revealed that he feels more relaxed at the plate when he is sleepy.

The rival Dodgers, a team that had contended for the play-offs until recent elimination, had no intention of simply fading into that good night. They pounded away at pitcher Shawn Estes early and often for a 5-0 first inning lead.

The question in everybody's mind was whether Park would pitch to Bonds. In Houston, Astros' manager Larry Dierker had made a virtual mockery of the game, ordering his men to avoid pitching to Bonds at all costs. Consistently, Dierker's moves backfired. San Francisco second baseman Jeff Kent, hitting clean up behind Bonds, lived up to his 2000 MVP status. He powered his club to a three-game sweep that not only kept the Giants alive, but reduced Houston from their confident perch atop the Central Division. Now, they were in a death struggle with St. Louis that would not be decided until the final day.

Bonds finally got a pitch to hit in the series finale, taking advantage of it to tie the record. In their last series at Dodger Stadium, Jim Tracy's pitchers had not given Bonds much, and while Bonds had hit one, Los Angeles' strategy had helped them to stay alive in the race.

Some controversy had ensued during that series when the Dodgers, once baseball's classiest outfit, announced that they would not halt the game to allow any on-field celebrations if Bonds broke the record on their turf. The organization had somehow morphed from the team of Jackie Robinson, Vin Scully and Peter O'Malley into a petty corporate tax write-off for Rupert

Murdoch. They were peeved because recent revelations had shown that the 1951 Brooklyn Dodger-New York Giant Play-Off had been manipulated by a scoreboard-sitting spy relaying what pitches the Bums were throwing to Giant hitters.

One could not tell what was odder, the "revelation"—which had been common knowledge and the source of barroom braggadocio by Leo Durocher for years—or the fact that these Korean War-era events had occurred 50 years earlier and 3,000 miles away! As if this ancient history was not enough, the club dredged up memories of the Giants' watering the Candlestick base paths to slow down Maury Wills in 1962.

Aw, but therein lies the beauty of this, the greatest rivalry in sports. The Dodgers and Giants go farther back and involve more hard feelings than any two teams. Sure, the Yankees and the Red Sox have it in for each other, and the intensity of their fans is greater, but in reality the Bambino's Curse has rendered this a completely one-sided affair. The Red Sox play the part of the IRA against the manifestly imperialist Bombers, who deal with them in the manner of the British army.

Southern Cal and Notre Dame? Those who delve deep into the meaning of college football's greatest inter-sectional rivalry will find, in reality, a mutual admiration society.

There are many other fine rivalries, most of them regional in variety. The Dodger-Giant rivalry has successfully traversed this great nation and succeeded over time, political and social change. In New York's early days, the Giants ruled baseball under manager John McGraw while the Dodgers were considered daffy incompetents. The Yankees floundered under the name Highlanders and were the Giants' Polo Grounds tenants until the 1920s.

In the 1930s, Giant manager Bill Terry was asked about playing the last-place Brooklyns in the season finale, while battling for the pennant.

"Are they still in the league?" joked Terry. Terry was not laughing after the Dodgers knocked New York out of the race.

In 1941, Leo Durocher, an utterly amoral man who was not joking when he said he would lie, cheat, steal or knock over his grandmother to win, took over as Brooklyn's manager and started a 15-year run of success at Ebbets Field. Over time Durocher would be eased out after stepping on too many toes. He played fast and loose with gamblers, and the team would transform itself, first under Branch Rickey (who broke the color barrier by bringing Robinson to the team), and later under the O'Malley Family, into an organization of class and dignity.

Durocher took over the hated Giants, whose ace pitcher, Sal Maglie, was a headhunter who infuriated the Bums with his inside work. The '51 pennant race, of course, was the epitome of the rivalry. Durocher made the Giants listen through paper thin clubhouse walls to the Dodgers celebrating a victory next door, and New York came from 14 games back in August to tie it up, winning a three-game Play-Off on October 3 when Bobby Thomson hit the "Shot Heard 'Round the World."

When the teams came to California in 1958, the New York subway system was replaced by Highway 101, winding 400 miles from San Francisco through San Jose and Monterey; past Big Sur and through Santa Barbara; along the coast and through the hills; into the sprawling San Fernando Valley, and into the smoggy, tantalizing land of dreams that is L.A.

Drysdale and Koufax matched up against Juan Marichal and Gaylord Perry. The Dodgers won with pitching and defense, frustrating McCovey and Willie Mays while enforcing the age-old truism that good pitching stops good hitting. The Giants' frustrations came to a head, literally, in 1965. Marichal took a bat to the noggin of Dodger catcher John Roseboro in an event that Los Angeles still used when they wanted to play the victim game.

Big crowds packed a gleaming Dodger Stadium, while San Francisco's attendance shrank at the horrid Candlestick Park. A sense of inferiority pervaded the Giant side of the rivalry, with their fans resorting to mean-spirited epithets thrown at Los Angeles manager Tommy Lasorda.

In the 1970s and '80s, the Dodgers won consistently while San Francisco usually wallowed in mediocrity, and the "rivalry" had become a one-sided match-up. The Dodgers shifted their attention to meaningful opponents like Cincinnati and Philadelphia. The Giants' supporters resembled The City's left-wing politics, resorting to have-not "beat L.A." chants and drunken acts of class-enviousness.

San Francisco managed to get back into contention under manager Roger "Hum Baby" Craig, winning the West in 1987 and advancing to an earthquake-divided World Series in 1989.

Safeway magnate Peter Magowan purchased the club a few years later, and in 1993 signed Bonds for $43.75 million, the largest contract in baseball history at the time. The dynamics of the L.A.-San Francisco divide changed in the 1990s. Los Angeles suffered a fire in the Malibu Hills, riots in Watts, and an earthquake in Northridge. San Francisco and the Silicon Valley became the fast lane of the Information Superhighway, with dot-com startups giving splash and *panache* to the region.

No longer did Los Angeles dominate the sporting scene. The 49ers' pro football team had long been the standard in the NFL, and by the mid-'90s both the Rams and Raiders had deserted Southern California, leaving the area with no pro teams while the Bay Area has two.

USC and UCLA had long owned Stanford and California in football and basketball, but parity found its way into the Pacific-10 Conference in the 1990s and early 2000s.

The Dodgers and Angels have become poorly run corporate sideshows, while the Oakland A's and Giants combined to give Bay Area fans some of the best thrills of the new baseball century.

California politics, once dominated by Southern California with a conservative tilt, had given the country Richard Nixon and Ronald Reagan. That shifted in 1992's "Year of the Woman" elections, when two Jewish San Francisco Democrat women, Dianne Feinstein and Barbara Boxer, were elected to U.S. Senate seats that they still hold today.

Bonds was the motivating force behind the building of Pac Bell Park, which opened in 2000 and sold out every single game of its initial season. Suddenly, San Francisco boasted the finest facility in the game, while Dodger Stadium's age had become noticeable. An entirely new aura has manifested itself in this era. Gone are the drunken louts throwing garbage and beer bottles at Lasorda and anything wearing Dodger blue. Well-heeled preppies and corporate executives, many of them season-ticket holders, have replaced that class of "fan." Almost every seat has sold out for every game in two years. Fans drink imported beers in exclusive seating areas and eat delightful, diverse international deli items in a family-friendly environment.

Located walking distance from The City's thriving downtown financial district, and not far from Joe DiMaggio of the San Francisco Seals had fashioned a 63-game hitting streak in 1935, Pac Bell is built right up against the bay. Beyond its right field fence, past the bleacher seats and a concrete walkway, lies McCovey Cove, where many of Bonds' homers (including number 500) have landed. Several parking lots dot the area, and a magnificent view of the Bay Bridge, Treasure Island and the East Bay beyond, dominates the scene. Ferries and yachts drift around the water and dock in the nearby harbor, creating an atmosphere of sun 'n' fun.

Old warehouses have been replaced by ritzy condominiums and fun eateries where the young and attractive meet and greet. One walks into Pete Osborne's Momo's (Bonds loves their food) or Johnny Love's new drinking establishment around the corner, and is reminded of a college frat party. Johnny Love is in fact an old Cal-Berkeley frattie who would bring in local names like Mark McGwire of the A's to be "celebrity bartenders," while hot chicks under the influence would do *faux striptease* acts down to their g-strings on the bar counters. There are worse ways to spend an evening.

The park has also helped maintained the economic value of an area hard hit by the 2000-01 dot-com disaster. Many startups and the young entrepreneurs behind them also lived in the bay-view residences that went up in the late 1990s, and today high-end properties lie vacant while real estate value plummets.

On this first Friday in October, however, real estate prices and Internet failures were not on the minds of Bay Area baseball fans. All the history of the two franchises seemed to have been built up just for this moment. Two factors gave hope to the capacity crowd that Bonds would make history. First, the Dodgers had been eliminated from the race. Therefore, they would be less disposed to pitching around Bonds under all circumstances (despite the fact that Aurilia and Kent had consistently made teams pay for this strategy). Secondly, L.A.'s five runs in the first provided Park some level of comfort.

Despite Park, one of the league's toughest hurlers, this game would not be a pitcher's game in any way, shape or form. It would be a bittersweet fireworks display for the ages, and in the end a sense of melancholia would pervade the Giants and their fans.

San Francisco, being on the West Coast, was playing a late game. This, among other reasons, affects national notoriety and is the leading reason behind the so-called "New York bias" that works against West Coast athletes when it comes to awards, endorsement deals, and publishing contracts.

On this evening it would also be the reason San Francisco was playing under added pressure, as if they could possibly have any more to deal with. Arizona had already beaten Milwaukee, and shortly after Bonds' record-breaking big fly at 8:15, Houston had rallied for runs in the eighth and ninth at Busch Stadium to win an unlikely victory over the surging Cardinals at 8:44. This meant that the Giants had to win in order to stay alive for a postseason berth. No ifs, ands or buts about it.

Bonds came up in the first after the Dodgers had exploded for five runs. With nobody on base, he took a pitch, as is his custom, low and away. The next was to his liking. Bonds ripped away, and the record was his.

There were more than a few mixed feelings. The fans, of course, went bonkers, and Bonds exulted at home plate with his son, Nikolai, dressed up and acting as the team's bat boy. The bomb gave the Giants hope that they could rebound from the four-run deficit, but being down 5-1 against Park in a game you *have* to win is unsettling, to say the least.

Four hundred forty-two feet from home plate, 49-year old Jerry Rose, a season ticket holder from Knights Landing, California, came up with the ball after a mad scramble that was far from a shining moment.

Perhaps because the man was operating on just a few hours' sleep and one of his best friends had been buried that day, Bonds' body language was less exuberant than it had been when he tied the record at Enron Field. He did not raise his arms in jubilation, even though it was obviously gone from the get-go. He watched it fly out and trotted the bases amid a mad roar.

Nikolai led the Giants out of the dugout, and Bonds pointed to the sky, a custom he had adapted as his personal paean to God, and lately to Franklin's memory. When he got to the dugout, Bonds took a phone call from his father, ex-Giants slugger Bobby Bonds. He had opted to travel to his own golf tournament, which he had long ago committed to, rather than be there for his son's big moment.

Bonds did not make much comment on this matter, but the look on his face while talking to his absent father showed, perhaps, some irritation. This was not the first time.

The fact that it was the Dodgers who served up Bonds' big homer was apropos, and a repeat of his 500th hit off L.A.'s Terry Adams on April 17 at Pac Bell. The Dodgers by this time must have been tired of standing around watching a repeat performance of the Barry Bonds Show.

One Dodger who no doubt felt some joy at that moment was left fielder Gary Sheffield, a great slugger in his own right. Sheffield is one of Bonds' best friends in baseball. Despite having grown up in the Bay Area as part of the Giants' "family," Bonds has never shown any antipathy for Los Angeles or the Dodger team.

Another Dodger who was an interesting side note was catcher Chad Kreuter, dubbed the "Forrest Gump of Baseball" because he seemed to be a witness to history wherever it happened to be. Kreuter is a Bay Area product who had starred in baseball and football at Marin County's Redwood High School, on the other side of the Golden Gate Bridge. He eschewed football at Cal-Berkeley to concentrate on baseball at Pepperdine, and while playing in the Alaskan Collegiate Summer League had met and married the daughter of USC baseball coach Mike Gillespie. A journeyman at best, Kreuter nevertheless had displayed a flair for the dramatic and a talent for being near it.

In 1988 he announced himself to the league by homering off Oakland ace Dave Stewart. In 1989 he was the catcher when Texas' Nolan Ryan struck out Rickey Henderson to record his 5,000th strikeout. He was there through Ryan's remarkable late-career run that included a no-hit game, and it was Kreuter who stirred controversy with the Dodgers in 1999 when he went into the stands, Ty Cobb-style, to attack a fan at Wrigley Field who had stolen his glove in the bull pen. Now he was again the "man behind the mask" in the photographs of history!

Bonds made his curtain call and jogged to the area behind the backstop where his wife, Liz and mother, Pat, were sitting with assorted friends. When asked prior to the game what attributes he drew from Pat, Bonds had smiled and said, "I'm not as ugly as my dad. I'm better looking. That's what I've drawn from my mom." After five minutes, Kent stepped to the plate and flew out.

Two massive banners were unfurled. One read "Bonds," the other "71." Mark Gardner entered the game for the home nine and gave up a run to add to San Francisco's pressure.

Eric Davis, a veteran and one-time star with a Hall of Fame future, who had seen his career stymied by injuries and cancer, batted for Gardner and hit a three-run double to make it 6-4. Pac Bell Park went bonkers.

Lord Almighty, can we do it?

Marquis Grissom sunk San Francisco hearts with a home run in the third to make the score 8-4. Bonds now came up in the bottom of the inning.

Was it possible? Nothing seemed to be for Bonds. He was in full superman mode, riding high in that zone of athletic excellence that marks the most special moments in sports. These are the moments of the Chamberlains, the Unitas's, the Ruths.

Now, they are the moments of the Bonds's.

Park pitched him to 1-1, and then it was Bonds II. Number 72 flew just over the fence in center field, glancing off a fan's hand. The fan must have felt like the Laurence Olivier/"White Angel" character in "Marathon Man" who watches aghast while Dustin Hoffman lets his rare diamonds drop into the New York water system.

Grissom picked up the sphere and decided to have a little fun with it, first pretending to throw it back into the hungry stands, then feigned shoving it into his back pocket, before throwing it toward the dugout.

Again, Nikolai was waiting with love for dad at the plate, but by this time Bonds was unable to even believe his own feat. What could happen next? The score was 8-5 and some serious work was still necessary if his team wanted to wake up tomorrow still alive in the pennant race. After all, winning was still and always is his first priority. To set the record yet lose? This was still an intolerable prospect.

How much more could the man take? He had almost no sleep and was burdened by a young friend's sad demise. He was desperate for the elusive ring that he had never earned, a ring he needed in order to cap a career in the way that true greatness must be made complete. On top of all this, if anything was left to clutter the weary Bonds psyche, Barry might be playing his last series as a Giant.

The average person cannot comprehend the kind of emotions that Bonds must have been experiencing. Are his problems the problems we all should have? Of course they are, but handling them requires poise and focus that few of us possess. Bonds' ability to perform with all of this swirling around him is the very essence of his greatness. To say that it compares to the grace under pressure of a military hero performing valorous work under fire may seem a stretch to some, but it says here that such a comparison is not a stretch. Not with this guy, not under these circumstances.

Greatness has a way of showing itself in unmistakable terms. Here was not just the greatest baseball player, but the greatest *athlete* in the world, on top of his game. Here was the greatest star of his era having the best season in history, and bidding hard for the title World's Greatest Baseball Player of All Time.

Hyperbole? Read on.

By the fourth inning, Park was probably as weary as Bonds, but he had to face the man again. This time he walked him intentionally. All season fans at home and away had booed when Bonds would get the free pass, but now it almost was a relief. Certainly, nobody was blaming Park.

Bonds' intentional walks were the lesser of two evils all season for teams stuck between a rock and a hard place, and Kent made this premise stand up in a big way, again. With the score 9-5, Bonds' walk loaded the bases, and Kent's double to the right-center field gap cleared them to make it 9-8.

As if there was not enough joy, disbelief and mixed emotions coursing like lightning bolts through Pac Bell Park at this moment, Kent was thrown out at third on a controversial call, trying to stretch it into a three-bagger.

In the sixth inning, after Los Angeles had added another run, Aurilia stepped up with a two-run homer, his 37th of the season, to tie it at 10-10. That allowed him and Bonds to pass Babe Ruth and Lou Gehrig and become the second-greatest home-run duo in baseball history. They trailed only the 115 by Maris and Mantle in 1961. Tim Worrell took over for San Francisco and allowed the go-ahead run to score. 11-10, Dodgers.

By this time, the game was off the charts. It was shaping up to be a marathon, and the emotional roller coaster that the players and fans were experiencing was becoming something surreal, not of this world. One expected the ghost of Rod Serling to appear on the scoreboard:

"Mr. Barry Bonds, a man who thinks and thereby gets things done. A man and a team, the San Francisco Giants, who otherwise might be known as 'prime movers' in that cold, gray, shadowy area known only as . . . the twilight zone."

Despite the run off Worrell, there was one thing the San Francisco's did not think would happen. Nobody thought the scoring for the evening was done (although one could not account for the gay crowd "hooking up" in the Castro District).

Surely, Bonds would hit another homer. Runs on this night were cheap. The last team standing, or in this case the last team to bat, the home Giants, would walk away with the victory. That is a script that Bay Area fans can relate to after years watching Ken Stabler or Joe Montana leading a drive after the two-minute warning. In this, Barry's Year, San Francisco would ascend to the postseason, and once there, anything could happen. The National League was weak this season. They would have as good a chance as anybody to run the three-play-off gauntlet into the World Series.

That would be a different story. The Yankees, Mariners or A's, juggernauts all, would stand in their way, but on this evening anything seemed possible. That is why what happened next seemed so incongruous.

The Giants shut down. So did Los Angeles, but they had scored last and had the lead. It seemed impossible that the Giants would not score again, but they did not. Jeff Shaw, the Dodger closer who had been selected for the All-Star Game ahead of the Giants' Robb Nen, did his job. The game ended four hours and 27 minutes after it started.

Long games between the Giants and Dodgers are the norm. The final game of the 1962 season, a Play-off between L.A. and San Francisco at Dodger Stadium won by the Giants when Walt Alston's bullpen imploded, was a marathon, too.

This was not the first time one team knocked the other out of the race, either. The Dodgers had done it to Terry's Giants in 1934. They got some West Coast revenge for 1951 when the SoCals sent the NoCals packing in 1959, on the way to their first World Championship in Los Angeles.

A late-season run by the Koufax-Drysdale Dodgers included key victories that eliminated San Francisco while elevating Los Angeles to the 1965 pennant. The Dodgers pushed San Francisco right to the last day before bowing out of the 1971 West Division chase. In 1982, the Giants' Joe Morgan homered in the last inning on the final day at Candlestick Park to give Atlanta the division crown over Los Angeles.

The game also held an eerie similarity to the 1993 season finale, when the Dodgers again proved to be the Braves' best friend. On that day, Salomon Torres had started for rookie manager Dusty Baker in L.A., but the Mike Piazza-led Dodgers rocked him hard on the way to an 11-1 win that ended the Giants' season at 103-59, one game back in the West. In the final season before introduction of the wild-card berth, it meant that they had to go home.

In the 2001 version, it was Estes who carried on Torres' dubious tradition, and he faced an uncertain future because of it (eventually ending in a trade). Torres, a hot prospect until his '93 failure, never recovered. Others have seen their careers falter after they lost with all the chips on the line. The Angels' Donnie Moore eventually committed suicide a few years after giving up a game-tying home run to Boston's Dave Henderson in 1986. That same year, the Red Sox's Calvin Schiraldi folded under the heat of a Met rally in the World Series. Now he is a trivia question. Mitch "Wild Thing" Williams of Philadelphia in 1993 wanted nothing to do with the baseball in the World Series, and it showed when he served up Joe Carter's winning homer.

Dusty Baker's Giants had set Los Angeles' title hopes aside in the late 1990s, and now it was payback time. The huge crowd was unsure what to do. Of course, they cheered the team for their valiant effort. There was something Quixote-like in their windmill-jousting final, dramatic loss to their fiercest rivals. Los Angeles had proven to be worthy adversaries, living up to their proud history instead of giving way to the mediocrity that had swallowed them since their 1988 World Championship, and especially since their abysmal purchase by Fox.

San Francisco Chronicle sports columnist Bruce Jenkins' headline the next day said "Dodgers do the right thing—pitch to Barry" and gave kudos to Park for having the guts to challenge the great Bonds. This was despite his team harboring resentment over the Giants' request (which was turned down) to have them wear replicas of the 1951 Brooklyn club.

Recalling the on-field, game-interrupting celebration the Giants gave Bonds after number 500, Jenkins quoted Dodger pitching coach Jim Colborn as calling it "really unprofessional." Orange County Register sports columnist Mark Whicker had written, "the Giants basically played 'This Is Your Life' with Bonds" on that occasion.

Tracy had given an indication of what to expect prior to the contest.

"If our game has ramifications around the league, we have an obligation to honor them," he had told the *Los Angeles Times*. "It's about the purity of the game. Somebody who has done what he's done, well, you've got to challenge him."

Despite the Astros' refusal to do that in the preceding series, National League pitchers had not proven an entirely cowardly lot. Yes, Bonds would set the Major League record for walks, and of course many of those were intentional or of the "unintentional intentional" variety. That said, Bonds was responsible for many of those bases on balls. The man is perhaps the most disciplined hitter of all time. Certainly, along with Tony Gwynn, he is the most disciplined since Boston's Ted Williams. Mark McGwire could be had with pitches out of the strike zone, and even Bonds' Godfather, the great Willie Mays, occasionally took his free-swinging stickball mentality to the plate.

If Bonds ever had an undisciplined streak, age and experience had made him, at 37 and in his 15th season, the George Patton of big-league hitters. He had reduced batting to the margins, eliminating shades of failure. He was still a human being and therefore not immune to failure, but there was as an automatic sense to his approach. His failures never seemed to be the result of any letdowns.

It may be this very essence of his game that frustrates those trying to favorably compare Bonds to other great players. Mays had played the game with pure cap-flying *joy de vivre*.

Roberto Clemente's athleticism reminded one of a linebacker laterally pursuing a ball carrier with abandon.

Bonds approach more closely resembled a briefcase-carrying businessman boarding the 8:00 a.m. from Greenwich. The camera did not detect the twinkle in his eye like Mays, or the defiance that was Clemente's driving force. Seemingly emotionless, expressionless, a picture of confident concentration, Bonds more closely resembled a shark pursuing its prey.

Pitchers are an interesting lot. Most of them, if they are good enough to pitch in the big leagues, might think of themselves as shark hunters who can knock the eyelash off a fly at 60 feet six inches. They are big and strong, or to use a *nouveau porn* term making the rounds of late, they are "young, dumb, and full of cum." They know how dangerous Bonds is, but most of them were high school superstars, or collegiate All-Americans, and Big Men on Campus in one way or another.

"Bonds will not beat me," they say to themselves, and they mean he will not beat their best stuff. Pitchers do not talk like this to the press, but they say it to each other. They are duel-challengers and every one of them has a mentality in which he thinks he has what it takes to take a shot at the title.

In "Bull Durham," pitcher Nuke LaLouche, played by Tim Robbins, tells his catcher, Crash Davis (Kevin Costner), "I want to announce my presence with authority." They all do.

So, yes, they do pitch to Barry. In July, when Bonds went on his only so-called slump of the 2001 season, he got a lot of pitches to hit, but his timing was off just a little bit.

The best of the best amongst them, the Schillings, the Johnsons, the Parks and the Kevin Browns of the league, approach their jobs like Navy SEALS. Give in to Bonds? Afraid of Bonds? They respect him, but they are there to beat him and they have the stuff to do it.

Good pitching beats good hitting. That is what they have been saying forever, and the 2001 World Series proved it. After a season of offensive fireworks, two teams, the D'backs and Yankees, dominated with pitching because they both had it in spades.

Throughout much of the season, Bonds seemed locked in a race for the Most Valuable Player award with Arizona's Luis Gonzalez and Chicago's Sammy Sosa, but just as he had done in his three previous MVP seasons, he had locked the award up for himself with September heroics.

"I don't see how you can deny him," said Tracy.

Bonds' two homers off of Park made him 12-for-39 lifetime against the Korean flame-thrower. Park had wrongfully been accused of grooving a fastball to the retiring Cal Ripken, Jr. in the All-Star Game. Al Downing, another Dodger, had been accused of doing that to Hank Aaron when the Hammer hit his 715th home run in 1974.

In 1998, McGwire had hit five home runs in his final three games against Montreal to supposedly put the record away at 70. With both teams now out of the race, talk turned to what Bonds could do against James Baldwin on Saturday and Terry Mulholland on Sunday. Baldwin had surrendered Bonds' 67th on September 24 in Los Angeles, and Mulholland ranks third on Bonds' all-time homer list at seven. The Braves' Greg Maddux and John Smoltz, two of the premier hurlers of this era, are tied at the top with eight.

"I can't stand here and say how I'll pitch against Barry Bonds," Mulholland told the press. "Has anyone asked Barry Bonds what he's looking at from me? Has anyone asked Barry Bonds if he's going to swing or take pitches off me?"

"If you get totally preoccupied with just focusing your attention all night long with worrying about Barry," Tracy remarked in summing up the dilemma of all opposing managers, particularly Houston's Dierker, "more times than not, you're going to walk out of here with three losses handed to you."

Bonds' two Friday night homers took away some of Tracy's courage. Houston, showing no concern for Kent, walked Bonds three times on Wednesday and he scored each time. On Thursday, Kent followed a walk to Bonds with a homer. In the sixth inning, Houston was still so paranoid that they intentionally walked Bonds despite trailing 8-1.

"Because of other guys in front of Barry or behind him, you subject yourself to big innings," Tracy said. "I think it happened a couple of times in Houston."

Tracy let history repeat itself with his fourth-inning intentional walk to Bonds that loaded the bases, and Kent had followed with his three-run double.

The day after the record-breaking home run, the *Chronicle's* Glenn Dickey addressed the question of who was better, Mays or Bonds. Dickey theorized that at one time such a question was unthinkable, that Mays represents baseball excellence above and beyond any other contenders, but that Bonds' latest feats had elevated his career status to the point where it was now a fair question. Dickey rated Mays the best outfielder he had ever seen, able to play a shallow center field and still make catches at the wall. Bonds plays a less important position, left field. Dickey rated him the best at that position he had ever witnessed, a high compliment coming from a man who had seen a lot of baseball over the previous 30-plus years.

Dickey noted that Bonds' throwing arm is not strong, although he makes up for it through smart positioning. Mays had a truly great arm, as evidenced by his quick, accurate throw after making "The Catch" of Vic Wertz's drive in the 1954 World Series at the Polo Grounds.

However, as Dickey pointed out, Bonds is a great base stealer and the charter member of the 400/400 Club, with the 500/500 Club soon to come. Mays had stolen 40 bases in a season early in his career. Durocher had instructed him to "cool it" in order to avoid injuring his legs, and he never approached Bonds' numbers.

On the other hand, as Dickey noted, Mays was a better base *runner*.

"The only time he [Mays] remembers being thrown out at third trying for an extra base came on a bang-bang play in a 1962 pennant play-off with the Dodgers," wrote Dickey. "Willie insists the umpire blew the call, and he's probably right."

Dickey concluded by saying that Mays should still be rated the better player, but Bonds is very close in every area of the game. He also gives credence to the age factor, which in the end may be where Bonds surpasses Mays by the end of his career. Mays' skills diminished rapidly in his mid-30s, while Bonds is getting *better*.

Of the intentional and unintentional walk issue, Dickey wrote "when Tuffy Rhodes faced the same treatment in Japan as he went after Sadaharu Oh's home run record, the Japanese baseball commissioner issued a statement saying the walks were 'completely divorced from the essence of baseball, which values the supremacy of fair play.'"

Dickey felt that the American Commissioner, Bud Selig, should have made a similar public statement, particularly after the Astros series.

"Incredibly," wrote Dickey, "Bonds was able to maintain his focus and zero in when he finally got his pitch. Smart baseball people like Joe Morgan had said earlier in the year that Bonds would get so impatient because he was pitched around that he would chase pitches out of the strike zone and disrupt his swing. But he hasn't, in part because he was advised by Mays, his Godfather, not to."

Bonds, said Dickey, is like Willie, a student of the game. He compares the way Mays altered his swing to adjust to the Candlestick Park winds with the way Bonds sits in on meetings of his own pitchers to know how to position himself. Dickey concluded in the piece that Mays was still better, but he worded it in such way as to consider that some day this view would no longer prevail.

For Jeremy Rose, October 5 was a night of big excitement. It takes a couple of hours to drive from his Yolo County home, cross the Bay Bridge, find a place to park, and work his way to his seat. It was barely warm when Mr. Bonds launched a rocket into his waiting glove.

He and his wife went bonkers like everybody else around them, until police officer Matt Rodgers moved them through a gauntlet of beer-spilling fans to a place where they could be safe. Major League officials verified that the ball in his hand was, indeed, the historic one. As they had three years before when McGwire went after Maris, MLB had marked each ball used in Bonds' at-bats leading up to, including, and beyond the record-breaker.

"It was kind of like moving the President," said Officer Rogers. One man actually grabbed Rodgers, who pushed him off.

"*I just wanted to touch him,*" said the man.

The cheap seats where Rose sat were the most sought-after on this night, going for $150 for standing room only that normally sell for $9.

A couple of die-hard Bonds fans, Todd Thiede, 25 and Mitch Weitz, 24 had flown in from New Jersey to witness history.

"This is really worth everything we did to get here," Weitz told a *Chronicle* reporter. "You never get another chance like this."

Another fan, Ben Abrams, did what many San Franciscans did, going to the cell phone.

"I was right there," he told his girlfriend.

She was no doubt thrilled that he had left her at home.

Charles Seames of Vacaville actually traded his prestigious club-level seats behind the plate so he could stand in the cold with his brother, who paid $75 to a scalper for an SRO, and a chance to catch the dinger.

"The two gals I traded the tickets with were bombshells," Seames was quoted in the *Chronicle*. "One took my hand and said, 'You know where we're at.' But I chose Bonds over babes."

The numerous surfboarders, boaters, kayakers, swimmers and rafters floating in a waiting McCovey Cove (which probably will be renamed Bonds Bay sooner, rather than later) were left, literally, in the cold. Fireworks lit up the water while hundreds of fans on the port walk shouted and celebrated.

Most went home after the homer was hit.

"Back to Burlingame," said one fan.

"Don't drown yourself, man, it isn't worth it," Bonds had said in reference to the cove dwellers. "That water is so cold. I didn't think anyone could even go swimming out there."

Not everybody was a Bonds supporter. Danny and Bennet Gill were cousins and Dodger fans who were booed as they made their way to their bleacher seats.

"He's my second-most-hated player," said Danny, while being pelted with sunflower seeds.

On the radio side of the broadcast booth, legendary Giants' announcer Lon Simmons did a very classy thing. Even though it was his turn at the mic, he gave it over to partner Ted Robinson. All season, Giants fans had been lucky to hear excellent broadcasting of their games on radio and TV. Jon Miller was well known nationally for his accounts of games with Joe Morgan on ESPN's Sunday night telecasts. Miller, a former Baltimore Orioles announcer who had witnessed much of Cal Ripken's career, had landed a dream job in his hometown. Kuiper had developed his familiar refrain for home run calls. Earlier in the season he changed it up on occasion with the interesting moniker, "Adios, mother."

Simmons, the voice of the team for many years during the heyday of Mays and McCovey, had developed the Giants' "style" with his well known "You can tell it good-bye."

Simmons had come up under the wing of Russ Hodges, famous for his call of the "Shot Heard 'Round the World."

"Branca throws," Hodges had said. "*There's a long drive. It's gonna be it, I believe! The Giants win the pennant. The Giants win the pennant. The Giants win the pennant. The Giants win the pennant...*"

Hodges would also proclaim, when Mays and his free-swinging teammates hit one out, that it was "bye, bye, baby." A song by that name was even made.

"Oh when the Giants come to town

"It's bye, bye baby

"Always when the chips are down

"It's bye, bye baby."

When Mays caught Wertz's 1954 drive, Hodges wondered out loud whether what he witnessed had been an "optical illusion." You have got to love baseball.

In St. Louis, McGwire was facing pressure and emotions, too. The Cardinals had put up a phenomenal second-half run to come from nowhere not only to challenge for the wild card, but with Houston's sudden demise, the Central crown was now for the taking.

The Astros continued to be cold at the plate on Friday until a late rally took the air out of St. Louis and their fans. McGwire had been asked about Bonds.

"I'm very realistic about things," McGwire, who had played at USC with Johnson when Bonds was at rival Arizona State, told the *Associated Press*. "I've said since Day One, records are made to be broken. It was just inevitable."

When Big Mac broke Maris' 37-year-old record of 61, he had tacked on nine more to reach 70, and seemingly put it out of reach.

"After I hit 70, I pretty much was sure it wouldn't happen again," he continued. "But when I came back to hit 65 the next year, that was pretty much a re-evaluation, saying 70's going to be broken."

McGwire admitted that he was rooting for Bonds and predicted he would hit 73.

"He's doing it routinely," said McGwire. "His pace is unbelievable. He's totally blown away what I did."

The Cubs' Sammy Sosa, who earlier in the week became the first player to reach the 60-homer mark three times, said he planned to send a congratulatory note to Bonds.

"If you sit back and relax in your house and you say to yourself, 'Ah, 70 home runs,' before you go up there and you chase that, that's a big number," Sosa was quoted saying by R.B. Fallstrom.

"But when you have a chance to hit 60 early in the season and you keep swinging the bat really well like the way he was this year, you're going to have some hard times, but he's in a zone. When he's in his zone, there's nothing you can do about it."

Cardinal manager Tony La Russa is a hero to some in the Bay Area after having led Oakland to a World Championship in 1989. He is not a big Bonds fan, and sounded a sour note, because the media had not attached themselves to Bonds the way they had to McGwire.

"I watched every day what Mark went through from the first day of Spring Training to the last day of the season, and that was a real special burden he had to carry," La Russa told the *AP*. "Sammy didn't have it the same way because Sammy caught it about midseason.

"And Barry hasn't had it the same way, maybe because Mark's shown the way, whatever."

McGwire had said the same thing earlier, but was criticized for it and shifted his tone as Barry got closer. While the media circus around McGwire was definitely more intense in 1998, the Cardinals had dropped off the pace early. He had not had to deal with the extra burden of a pennant race, which Bonds obviously had. For that matter, so had Sosa, who led Chicago to the wild card in 1998. So had Maris, whose Yankees won a tough race over Detroit in 1961. Babe Ruth's 1927 Yankees won by so many games that the race was likely not much of a factor when he broke his own record—again.

Over in the Dodger clubhouse, Friend of Barry Gary Sheffield was unable to contain his feelings over Bonds' record-breaking effort.

"I don't want to tip my hand on how I really feel," he said before tipping his hand on how he really felt. "I was the first one jumping at the TV [watching Bonds in Houston]. It was ridiculous. They didn't even try to throw strikes. A couple of times they called strikes that were off the plate. I was thinking they're going to make it a long day for Barry."

Bonds' two-homer game was his tenth of the season and 56th of his career, passing Hall of Famer Jimmy Foxx for sixth on the all-time list.

Dusty Baker spoke about something that still hung over Bonds' head, despite his individual accomplishments.

"When you've had everything in your career, if you don't win it all, what else can you yearn or desire for?" said Baker before the game, referring to his star's great desire to win a World Championship. "He's had MVP awards. He's going to have a home run title. After a while it's like a very rich man. What does he want when he has all the riches he wants?"

Unfortunately, the loss to the Dodgers meant that the coveted ring would elude Bonds at least for another season. With the loss hanging heavily over their heads, an on-field celebration was set up for Bonds at 12:27 a.m. that had all the tragic, ironic elements of Shakespearean melodrama.

"It felt like celebrating Christmas on December 26," wrote *Marin Independent Journal* sports columnist Dave Albee.

"We've come a long ways," Bonds told the fans who chose to stick around. "We've had our ups and downs."

Then he started to cry. Superman's cape had been removed.

"Salvador Dali could not have painted a more surreal scene," wrote the *Chronicle*'s Giants' beat writer, Henry Schulman. Along with the rest of the Bay Area press corps, he must have realized that he had just experienced something that sports reporters usually just dream about. Schulman had painted a colorful picture of Bonds' momentous season all year.

"To my teammates," said Bonds, his voice cracking, "we worked real hard, and we're going to work real hard again."

A cheer went up from the crowd. Was this tidbit an indication that their hero was planning to re-sign with the home team? In succeeding days commentary would indicate that Bonds said this because he, well, could not think of anything else to say about it. On this evening hope sprang eternal in the human breast.

"It's an honor to play with a bunch of guys like this behind me," he continued, and then he added another ray of hope. "I'll play for you any time, any day of the week, any hour, any year."

Magowan was then serenaded with chants of "Sign him!" and "Four more years!" If this was a movie, Magowan would have handed Bonds a contract and the player would have signed it right there.

This is a book, not a movie, and the tears rolling down Barry's face reflected uncertainty as much as joy.

"I have two more games and I know what my future is," he continued, switching to reality mode. "I've seen a lot of changes out there this year, you guys [the media] and the fans of San Francisco enjoyed me. It's very hard. Things start turning around for the good and you don't know where you're going to be. It's tough. Everybody worked hard here to mend some fences together."

Willie Mays then told the crowd that he wanted to see his Godson put the record out of reach and get to 75. Also at the podium were Bonds' teammates, family and Hall of Famer Orlando Cepeda. Baker, however, left because he could not bear the emotional toll of it any longer.

"I was in here," Baker told the writers in his office later. "I should have been there, but it was too hard emotionally to be there. I was kind of down. I don't get down too much, but I was real down."

Baker is a real man's man but a real honest man, and if he said he was too emotional, you can believe he was. It had to have been a very heavy moment for him.

There was, however, a "cathartic" quality to the postgame celebrity, which seemed like a bad idea to have been held during the game considering the team was losing at the time, after Houston and Arizona had won, according to Schulman's account.

"When Barry was a kid I remember saying to him, 'Boy, get out of my locker,'" recalled a smiling Mays.

"I just want to thank everybody for coming out and supporting the Giants," said Shawon Dunston. "Barry really loves you, and he really does want to come back, Peter.

"What do you think? I'm coming back, why not Barry?"

Dunston's good humor was explained in part by the fact that he had just won a $100,000 Mercedes from Bonds, who revealed that he had made a "stupid bet" with Dunston in May.

"Rich Aurilia was there, and the whole team was stretching, and he just looked at me like I'm crazy, like he always does," Dunston said. "I said, 'If you do break the record you can buy me a new Mercedes-Benz.' He did break it, and he *will* buy me a new Mercedes-Benz."

"I'm happy I lost," admitted Bonds.

Paul Beeston, substituting for Commissioner Bud Selig, announced that Bonds would throw out the first ball at the World Series and receive the same lifetime achievement award given to Tony Gwynn at the All-Star Game.

"You couldn't dream of it," Bonds later told the media. "You couldn't dream of putting up a kind of year like this. When I look at all the numbers eventually and see what I really did this year, I just hope 30 home runs or 40 home runs won't be a bad year for you guys" in the future.

Bonds, unfortunately, must not have been aware of the reception given Maris, who put up those kinds of good but not spectacular numbers in New York in the years after breaking Ruth's record. He was drummed out of town.

Then again, Bonds, a fan of the game, no doubt knows the story. In his tired state, he was engaging in wishful thinking.

On Saturday morning, the *Chronicle's* front page completely ignored the War on Terrorism with a full-page spread of Bonds, in his black Friday night home jersey, shot from center field, slamming the record-breaker with a headline—"BARRY BONDS 71 AND 72"—in letters the same size as, say, "OSAMA DEAD."

Because of the late hour, the final results of the game had not made deadline, so most of the *Chronicle* coverage had to wait for Sunday. Sports columnist Ray Ratto addressed the business of Bonds, and questioned whether the team should pay for him when they could use that money to get four other players. The big question on Ratto's mind was whether Bonds was calling the shots, or his agent, the notorious Scott Boras.

Magowan had said that the Giants' decision on Bonds would hinge on how far the team made it in the postseason. Of course, Magowan had said that before Bonds broke the greatest record in sports, and had the greatest season in baseball history.

Columnist Scott Ostler, a funny writer and ex-protégé of the legendary *Los Angeles Times* wordmeister Jim Murray, made note of Bonds' McCovey Cove flotilla. He surmised that Bonds was the only athlete he could remember with his own navy. He also mentioned a strange statistic: Babe Ruth, eighth on the all-time single-season home run list!

One letter writer from Marin wrote in that if the team got rid of Bonds, he would never watch or listen to another Giants game . . . ever.

Another *Chronicle* sports columnist, John Shea (the *Chronicle* is burdened with too many columnists, and they have to be creative in writing something different from one another) addressed Dierker's defense of his constant pitching around Bonds. Dierker broke it down to an equation of pure math, and Giants' color man Mike Krukow, a former pitcher, had laughingly admitted on the air that "Dierker's right." No matter how many times the man was walked, and despite the success of those hitting around him, when he got his pitch he was so deadly that the "lesser of two evils" choice of walking him actually was the smart move.

Bonds' momentous final weekend had overshadowed the work of another superstar, Rickey Henderson of the Padres, who would finish the year having broken the career records for walks and runs scored, while nailing his 3000th lifetime hit. Another Padre great, Tony Gwynn, retired in near anonymity compared to Bonds.

Bonds' best friend in baseball, Bobby Bonilla, who had come up with him in their early days at Pittsburgh, was thrilled for his man.

"The best player ever," Bonilla told Shea. "And I'll argue with anybody on every stat you might want to bring up—when it's all said and done."

Just as McGwire had donated the jerseys worn by him and his son, a batboy when he set the record, Bonds donated the jerseys that he and Nikolai had worn, to the Baseball of Fame. A new Bonds exhibit would be going up in Cooperstown, New York.

McGwire himself was at a crossroads and clearly no longer at the apex of baseball glory. After striking out four times on Friday night, he told the *AP* that he was "tired and embarrassed," and was considering retirement. It turned out that he was serious.

Bonds claims that former A's and Yankees' slugger Reggie Jackson is his distant cousin. After some confusion over the issue, Jackson had said it "came out wrong. Yes, I am. I'll take it and I'm proud of it. And I'm happy and thrilled for the man."

As for Bonds' season, Jackson told Shea, "It renders me speechless. I've called Barry about 25 times this year on his cell phone, and all I can really say is, 'Wow, I'm really impressed.' He's been oh-my-God good. To think he's been hitting a home run every other day, all I can say is, 'Enjoy it, my friend.'

"When I called him after his 30th, I told him to remember my name when he passes me."

Jackson was the last Hall of Famer Bonds passed when he hit number 70 at Houston. After Friday he was at 566. In 2002 he will go after Harmon Killebrew (573), McGwire (at 583 and wondering why he deserves this specter), Frank Robinson (586), Willie Mays (660), Babe Ruth (714) and Hank Aaron (755).

In 2001, 10 all-time greats had fallen like Eastern Europe under Stalin: Eddie Murray, Mel Ott, Eddie Mathews, Ernie Banks, Ted Williams, McCovey, Foxx, Mantle, Mike Schmidt and Reggie.

"He's one of the greatest players of all time, and he could finish with more than 650 before he retires," gushed Mr. October, but like Dickey he did not go so far as to say Bonds was better than Mays.

A professed baseball fan, Jackson said Bonds was, along with Alex Rodriguez of Texas and Ken Griffey, Jr. of Cincinnati, the cream of the current crop. While these two players are great, Bonds left them both in the dust with a performance in 2001 that neither one will ever approach.

"I'm almost disappointed with the one-year turnarounds," Jackson told Shea, somehow forgetting about his 47-homer season in 1969, followed by an atrocious 23-homer campaign in 1970. He got so frustrated that he had flipped owner Charles O. Finley the bird during a game in Chicago. "Players hit 10 one year and 40 the next. Only three years after McGwire's 70, we've got a record again. It's such a special record, I'd like to see it stand for 30 or 40 years."

In that 47-homer season of 1969, Jackson set the record for most home runs at the All-Star break with 37, and the media went crazy speculating over his chances of breaking Maris' then-eight-year-old mark. McGwire had 38 at the 1998 break, and in 2001 Bonds had 39. In the second half of 1969, however, Reggie completely slumped under the strain of press attention, and he played in Oakland, far from a major media center. Over the years, many were called, and few were chosen. Sluggers like Willie Stargell, Schmidt, Griffey and even McGwire would start hot. Newspapers would run the obligatory "Maris Watch," followed by the equally obligatory fade-out. Memory of great hitters who completely missed the mark after a promising hitch had added to the legend of the record, giving it a mystique of unassailability.

Until now.

CHAPTER TWO

Prodigy

Barry Bonds was born on July 24, 1964 in Riverside, California. He has three siblings. His father, Bobby Bonds, and Dusty Baker, the manager of the Giants during all the years Barry played in San Francisco, were also born and raised there. Bobby and Dusty were great pals during their youth. The serendipity of Barry's life includes the fact that his father was a Major League All-Star and a teammate of the great Willie Mays. He befriended Mays and asked Willie to become Barry's Godfather. Willie accepted. Fine.

Then there is the fact that Reggie Jackson, another all-time great with the Oakland A's, is his cousin. This is unusual, but one can figure the kid came from good genes spread far and wide. His being related to various sports stars is believable.

However, the Baker connection is just stretching this thing too far. His father, being a fine athlete, was bound to grow up with other fine athletes, some of whom would go on to a certain degree of fame. After all, Riverside has a decent population, good weather, and a reputation as a place where excellent athletes come from. It is a suburb of Los Angeles, where more great sports stars grew up than any other metropolitan area in the world. Fair enough.

But what are the chances of the following?

•One of his dad's childhood pals would not just go on to play in the Major Leagues, but would be a teammate of Hank Aaron, the man whose lifetime record for home runs may very well be broken by Barry Bonds?

•Baker would become a manager, not just of any old big league squad, but the team Barry would play for?

This guy was so close to the Bonds family that, when Barry was an infant, he changed the kid's diapers. Now he is the manager of his team? In all the years that Dusty Baker has managed in the Majors, Barry was the star of his team. In all the years Barry played in San Francisco, Baker was his only manager, one of two he has played for his entire career.

Eventually, young Baker had moved to Carmichael, near Sacramento in central Northern California. It is the hometown of Olympic swimming great Mark Spitz. However, he would stay in touch with Bobby, and they would be reunited as opponents throughout their careers.

What are we going to find out next about Barry, that Babe Ruth (who was reputed by some in his early days to be part black) is a distant relative, too?

When Bobby was born in 1946, Riverside was a lot different than it is today. Being African-American, that statement means a lot more than to say they did not yet have their first McDonald's, and that the "trip" to Los Angeles was not merely a highway commute.

On the other hand, this was probably as comfortable a place for an African-American to grow up in the post-World War II years as any part of the country. Jackie Robinson broke the color barrier in Brooklyn in 1947. Adolph Hitler had been defeated, and an entire nation had gathered themselves to overcome his racist ideology.

Riverside was not a place rife with seething racial hatreds. It was the kind of place where the "experiment" could flourish. Blacks and whites could mix it up, play on the same teams, and go to the same schools. Date each other's women? Well, that was still taboo.

A young athlete like Bobby Bonds, however, could make his way up the ladder without running into stiff opposition from the forces of hatred and bigotry. Riverside was a darn good example of why America is a great country, which spends a lot of time thinking about and trying to correct its mistakes.

It was a place where the ball fields were teeming with kids all year around. Children could play freely without the criminal threats of a big city. It was a place where a youngster can find a natural swimming hole, and spend an afternoon catching fish. It was a place where people would gather at the barber shop and gossip. It was not the California Dream of the Beach Boys, but the post-war suburbanization of a rural land.

The Riverside of Bobby Bonds' youth was not segregationist Jim Crow, but black families generally lived in their part of town. White families lived in their section. Mexican families lived in their area. Over time, these neighborhoods would merge.

One thing that is timeless are the hormones of young men. Bobby lived down the street from his childhood girlfriend, Pat.

"They lived close by," said Barry of his father, smiling, "but my mom's family put restrictions on when he could see her, so he started sneaking in her bedroom window at night to 'get some.'"

Barry was born when Bobby was only 18 years of age. He and Pat were married early, and Bobby had the responsibility of a family right from the get-go when he entered professional baseball.

The 6-1, 195-pound Bonds attended Riverside Community College for awhile, and his brother, Robert V. Bonds, Jr., was a 13th-round draft choice of the Kansas City Chiefs of the American Football League in 1965. His sister, Rosie Bonds, once held the women's record in the 80-meter hurdles, and was a member of the 1964 U.S. Olympic Team competing in Tokyo.

Bobby Lee Bonds was a handsome, happy-go-lucky kid who liked singing, dancing and listening to music. One of the best athletes ever to emerge from the fields of Riverside, he signed with the San Francisco Giants. In 1965, he hit 25 home runs, scored 103 runs, and batted .323 at Lexington of the Western Carolina League. He tore up the California League with his defense in 1966, throwing out 15 base runners trying to test his arm, while slamming 16 homers at Class A Fresno. In 1968, at Class AAA Phoenix of the Pacific Coast League, Bonds was hitting .370 when the call came. He would never see the bushes again.

Aside from playing in Lexington, it is not readily apparent where Bobby played facing great prejudice. That did not stop him from making a point of it when interviewed by ESPN for the "Sports Century" feature on his son.

"They said what it was, they just used to call you a nigger," said Bobby. It is not known whether he brought the subject up himself, or was specifically asked to address it.

In June, a few tumultuous months after Martin Luther King had been assassinated, and in the same month that Robert Kennedy was killed by Sirhan Sirhan, he made one of the biggest splashes in big-league history.

He hit a grand slam home run in his first at-bat to lead a 9-0 victory over the Dodgers. In 81 games, he hit nine home runs and stole 16 bases, establishing himself as a starter on a veteran club that challenged Bob Gibson's Cardinals for the National League crown.

The comparisons with Mays were obvious, evident and immediate. Few young players have ever faced so much pressure in this area. Mickey Mantle following Joe DiMaggio comes to mind, and also in the late '60s, another Yankee rookie, Bobby Murcer, was trying to walk in Mantle's large footsteps.

Both Bonds and Murcer would have star-crossed careers, and in fact they would be traded for each other; Bonds to the Yankees, Murcer to San Francisco, prior to the 1975 season.

The Bonds family settled in San Carlos, a middle class, mostly-white-yet-mixed suburb of San Francisco located on the Peninsula. The Peninsula is a stretch of land, extending approximately 40 miles from San Francisco in the north to San Jose, where San Francisco Bay finally runs out of water and becomes land, to the south.

Before Manifest Destiny, native Indian tribes populated this area. Occasionally a hiker will discover an artifact. The Spanish eventually came. Father Junipero Serra established Catholic missions up and down the coast and inland. The weather is mild, not as foggy or windy as San Francisco, which is not as protected from the coastal breezes by mountains.

Two freeways traverse the north/south corridor. There is the heavily traveled 101, which will take one all the way to Los Angeles, and the 280, with far fewer cars, that ends in San Jose. The east part of the Peninsula is well populated by pleasant small cities. To the west lie mountains, forests, reservoirs and untrammeled land, much of it in pristine condition. Beyond those mountains lies the famous Pacific Coast Highway (PCH), overlooking the blue ocean and the mythical Golden West. A day at the beach is a half-hour drive from where the Bonds family lived.

Funky surf towns dot the coast where the rocky bluffs yield to pockets where people can habitate. The water is cold and the fog hugs the coast, yet surfers come from all over the world. In the winter, huge waves rock San Francisco along the Great Highway, to Pacifica and Half Moon Bay and Mavericks. This is where surf legends are made, and paralyzed victims of nature's fury can be seen in their wheelchairs, contemplating it all. Further south is the sunnier, world-famous Santa Cruz Boardwalk, and beyond that lies Monterey, the golf course at Pebble Beach, and Big Sur.

Two bridges connect the Peninsula to the East Bay. The San Mateo Bridge crosses the bay, a white row of lights in the blackness as seen from airplanes on approach to San Francisco International Airport, connecting San Mateo to the blue-collar Raiders town of Hayward. At some point, around Palo Alto, the Peninsula becomes the South Bay. This includes towns from Redwood City to Santa Clara and San Jose. The Dumbarton Bridge crosses a shorter, marshy stretch of water from Redwood City to Fremont.

When Bobby Bonds first moved his family there, the Peninsula and the South Bay were merely quiet bedroom communities of San Francisco, where people who "know the way to San Jose" lived. Beginning in the late 1970s, and continuing ever since, this area became the famous, or infamous, Silicon Valley. Steve Jobs, who founded Apple Computers there after leaving the University of California-Berkeley, is blamed for starting it in his hometown. The fact is it really began in 1935, when two Stanford graduates, David Packard and William Hewlett, formed Hewlett-Packard in a Palo Alto garage.

Two airports make travel convenient here. San Francisco Airport is really not in San Francisco, but rather in an unincorporated stretch of land along the bay between South San Francisco (which is also not San Francisco) and Burlingame. San Jose has its own airport. As the lowlands near the Bay give way to the plateaus and foothills that lead towards the 280 Freeway, the cost of housing goes up, too. Those who live in San Carlos, Burlingame and Redwood City want to live in Atherton, Belmont and Hillsborough. Here are mansions with million-dollar views of the water, surrounded by the lands of the Peninsula; the lights of the East Bay beyond, San Francisco to the north, all interspersed by bridges. It is every bit as spectacular as it sounds, and a big reason why so many love living in the Bay Area.

Right in the middle of it all is Stanford University. The San Francisco 49ers train in Santa Clara. Now, the San Jose Sharks hockey team represents the area. It is not considered as leafy or artistic as Marin County, home to enough entertainment players to be called Hollywood North. However, the Peninsula's convenience to The City, the airports and training facilities, has made it the residence of choice for many top athletes and corporate executives. 49er legends Jerry Rice, Joe Montana, and Bill Walsh all live in the area.

When Bobby Bonds played for the San Francisco Giants, some Major League players made $7,000 per season. A big leaguer like Bonds made a nice living, but could not bank it for the rest of his life. The pension was very important to his generation. Except for the highest-paid players, like Mays, who could afford to live in Atherton, players' housing was more modest. They were likely to live in places like San Carlos, Foster City and Burlingame.

The politics of the Peninsula has steadily progressed from moderately conservative to moderately liberal. It is not, however, as left wing as San Francisco, or as solidly Democrat as San Jose. Liberal Democrat Tom Lantos represents the area in Congress, but the state Senate and the state Assembly are more middle of the road, and strong Republican contenders have a chance. Local city and San Mateo and Santa Clara County officials are elected based on personal attributes more than political affiliation. There are no major "machines," such as existed and still exist on the East Coast and some Midwestern cities.

There are racial tensions here, but it is not a major problem. East Palo Alto, however, is an almost entirely black city located adjacent to almost all-white Palo Alto. It has one of the highest crime rates in the country. Gang activity is rampant, and there is a good deal of resentment toward the whites who live in comfort only a few miles away. The area is "contained," like a small Communist country surrounded by NATO allies, by the constant vigilance of the police. They patrol the streets as if in a kind of Belfast. For the most part, however, the people of the Peninsula range from doing well to well to do.

San Carlos was a place where Bobby Bonds could raise his family without the fear of waking up in the middle of the night with a burning cross on his lawn. It was a place where the white neighbor kids gravitated to his house, not just to get his autograph and be near a celebrity, but to be friends with his children, who because they were great athletes were cool. It was an environment where Pat could go next door to borrow sugar, and the people next door would come to her when they needed something, too. Getting a babysitter was not hard. Outside of a little grumbling, there was not a lot of talk about housing prices going down because "the coloreds" had moved in. It was California suburbia; free, easy and friendly.

At the same time, it was a place where a black kid would grow up amongst white kids, and the sense of self-pride in his race would not be emphasized. The efforts at becoming aware of African culture had not taken the full form that it has today, with the Martin Luther King, Jr. federal holiday, and Black History Month every February.

A black child growing up amongst white children may be happy and well adjusted, but it is impossible for him or her not to be aware that his skin is a different color. That makes him different. It is an unavoidable fact. For some, it leads to a search for roots.

Barry and his family always had Riverside, however. They visited often, and it was here that they stayed in touch with who and what they were all about.

In his first full season, 1969, Bonds looked to be Mays' heir apparent. He scored 120 runs, with 32 homers and 90 RBIs. On a team with Mays and Willie McCovey, manager Clyde King utilized his new star's tremendous speed in the leadoff spot. The Giants had never been a "speed team," instead going for power with the two Willies. The Dodgers were the club that played "little ball" in the 1960s, preferring to manufacture a couple of runs and let the tandem of Sandy Koufax and Don Drysdale, followed by Claude Osteen, Don Sutton, and later Bill Singer, make it hold up. San Francisco had two solid pitchers of their own, Juan Marichal and Gaylord Perry, but through the second half of the decade they were "always the bridesmaid, never the bride."

In 1969, Bonds stole 45 bases and McCovey won the league's MVP award. But Mays had been sliding since he was the MVP in 1965. Aaron and the Braves pulled out the championship in the National League West in the first year of divisional play.

In 1970, Bonds hit .302 with 26 home runs, but he also established a new Major League record of 189 strikeouts. During a nationally televised Saturday Game of the Week, he and Mays collided going after a fly ball against the chain-link fence at Candlestick Park. They both barely evaded serious injury in a spectacular, photographed confluence of youth, age, talent, potential; and of the past with the future.

Two things were beginning to influence Bobby Bonds around this time. One was racial politics, and the other was alcohol.

"Bobby was more serious," recalled Nick Peters, who covered the Giants in the 1970s for the *Sacramento Bee,* on ESPN's "Sports Century" feature on Barry. "He wasn't the affable clubhouse guy like Mays and McCovey. He was kind of the 'new breed' of black athlete. Bobby was kind of militant. It was the time of John Carlos and Tommy Smith."

Carlos and Smith had raised black-gloved fists during the playing of the U.S. National Anthem at the 1968 Mexico City Olympics.

"Bobby was not an easy teammate to have," said John Rawlings, the editor of *The Sporting News,* "and he wasn't easy to coach."

It was also the time of the Sexual Revolution, and an age of experimentation with drugs. Ballplayers were subject to temptations like anybody else. Alcohol, however, has always been the "drug of choice" among big leaguers. Babe Ruth was said to be a libertine and an alcoholic of, well, Ruthian proportions.

Drinking became Bobby's off-field recreation. Politically, he saw what black athletes like Carlos and Smith were doing. Curt Flood of the Cardinals, rather than accepting a trade to Philadelphia, had declared himself a "high-priced slave" and challenged the reserve clause, opening the gates to eventual free agency.

In the Bay Area, the Black Panthers were active, and a Berkeley sociology professor, Harry Edwards, was organizing black athletes against the "establishment." Bonds, the kid from Southern California, did not see himself the way the two older Alabama natives, Mays and McCovey, saw themselves.

He began to maintain a taciturn presence in the clubhouse and with the mostly-white press corps. Lines were drawn, divisions created.

"There was always racial edginess in big league clubhouses," recalls former *New York Post* sportswriter Maury Allen, the author of playboy pitcher Bo Belinsky's biography, *Bo: Pitching and Wooing.*

In 1971, Bonds led senior circuit outfielders with a .994 fielding percentage, while hitting 33 home runs, driving in 102, and batting .288. Assuming the power role on the club that was being ceded by the aging Mays and McCovey, he cut his stolen base total to 26, while making better contact. He only struck out 137 times.

During the years that he was a leadoff hitter, Bonds changed the nature of that position in the order. In some ways, he was a revolutionary, the way Lawrence Taylor changed the dimensions of a pro football linebacker. Bonds was a combination power/speed threat at the top of the order before Rickey Henderson came along.

The '71 Giants held off a furious, late-season Dodger run to capture the division title, but they lost to Pittsburgh in the Championship Series. It would prove to be a last hurrah of sorts in San Francisco. Mays was traded before the next season to the Mets. Gaylord Perry went to Cleveland for an alcoholic Sam McDowell. Juan Marichal ceased to be effective. McCovey would succumb to his many aches and pains, and the team would sink into mediocrity in the 1970s. It was a decade dominated by Cincinnati's Big Red Machine and the Dodger teams of Steve Garvey.

Bonds and McDowell were symbols of lost potential. Both were tremendous athletes who gave glimpses, in fact much more than glimpses, of Cooperstown-level greatness. Both were unable to sustain that greatness.

Barry Bonds was seven years old in 1972 when he saw Mays traded to New York for a bad knuckleball pitcher. Bobby had admired Willie, tried to emulate him, and tried to follow in his footsteps. He had asked the superstar to be the Godfather to his son, Barry, and Mays had accepted the role. But being the next great black outfielder to follow Mays in San Francisco had its share of pressures. At first, however, the move seemed to spur his father on. In 1972, Bobby slumped to .259, but he stole 44 bases for a club that never contended. In 1973, he had his greatest season, and yet it was a year that symbolized the frustrations of his career.

The Giants improved under Charlie Fox to 88-74. Cincinnati won the West. A young Los Angeles club demonstrated that they would be a future force to be reckoned with, at 95 wins. Bobby hit 39 homers, drove in 96, batted .283, scored a league-high 131 runs, and stole 43 bases. He was involved in five double plays defensively, and his 11 leadoff homers set a new big-league mark. In the All-Star Game, he was 2-for-2 with a homer. He was named to *The Sporting News* NL All-Star Team, and was the league's Player of the Year, although he lost to Pete Rose for MVP honors.

Despite all his accomplishments, however, 1973 was disappointing. By Labor Day, Bonds was assured of 40 stolen bases, and had 39 home runs. No player in history, not Mays, Aaron, Clemente, DiMaggio or anybody else, had ever gone "40/40." He was a shoo-in.

Instead, he tanked. Some said the pressure got to him. What did happen was that his statistics went from gaudy to good. Instead of a season that would place him in the upper echelon of the game, he remained ever so suspect.

He hit .256 for a dismal Giant team in 1974. Attendance at Candlestick Park was poor, and it was during these years, the mid-1970s, that rumors about the club being moved to another location—Toronto was often mentioned—ran rampant. Bonds had become reticent with the media and surly with the fans. He had loads of talent, but his potential remained largely unfilled. He had not made anybody forget Mays, and he had not taken his team to the next level. He had, in short, worn out his welcome.

On October 21, he was traded to the Yankees for Murcer. He had dealt with many of the same problems, namely unfulfilled high expectations, with the difficult New York media.

The New York that Bobby Bonds found was an economically depressed place, considered unsafe at night, a place with little moral focus. The Yankees were at the end of what fans have called the "Horace Clarke Era," after a decent, but not great, middle infielder.

The Oriole dynasty of the late 1960s/early '70s had grown old. Yankees owner George Steinbrenner had recovered from his conviction for illegal campaign contributions to the Richard Nixon presidential campaign. He had built a contender. Bonds was expected to provide some "National League speed." Bonds had a good season, knocking 32 home runs, but it was not enough. Boston captured the East. After one year under Steinbrenner, enjoying the Manhattan nightlife, he found himself back near his hometown in 1976. He was traded to the Angels.

Injuries turned 1976 into a wash, but at 31, Bonds expected big things in 1977. Owner Gene Autry was one of the first to spend big money on free agents. California had a line-up that included Joe Rudi, Don Baylor and Bobby Grich, to go with flamethrowing pitchers Nolan Ryan and Frank Tanana. Preseason pundits were predicting a Freeway World Series between Norm Sherry's club and first-year manager Tommy Lasorda's Dodgers.

They were right about Los Angeles, but there is a curse that hangs over the Angels, and it was there in '77. Or maybe they were just plain mediocre. Either way, the season was a microcosm, in some ways, of Bonds' career.

With 37 homers and 115 RBIs, he came close to the greatness always predicted of him. Close, but not quite, and on a 74-88 doormat, his performance went virtually unnoticed. So, the Angels tired of his act the same way San Francisco and New York had. The trade of Bonds to the Chicago White Sox for Chris Knapp, Dave Frost and Brian Downing helped complete their puzzle, resulting in division titles in Anaheim in 1979, 1982 and 1986.

So what did Bonds do in 1978? He languished. He drank. He complained. He used race as an excuse. He also played some excellent baseball.

If you see parallels between Bonds' career and Jose Canseco's, it is an astute observation (although Canseco is not a drinker). The White Sox had enough of Bobby's act by May 16, when they unloaded him to Texas for Claudell Washington and a minor leaguer. The Chisox and Rangers were both also-rans in 1978. Playing in obscurity, Bonds still hit 31 home runs, drove in 90, and stole 43 bases. Had he been on a contender in the spotlight, he would have been considered one of the most dynamic players in baseball. His greatness, however, was being wasted. Was it his fault, or the fault of "the establishment," the "good ol' boy network," the "white power structure?"

The answer is, Probably somewhere in between. The fact is, a look at the players considered at the top of the game during this period—Keith

Hernandez, Willie Stargell, Reggie Jackson, Dave Parker, George Brett, Mike Schmidt, Jim Rice, Fred Lynn—indicates that Bonds, statistically, was very close to that elite. Certainly, had he been playing with inspiration for contenders, his record would have been better. Had he been training, dieting and concentrating the way his son did years later, he may have eclipsed all of them.

The reality is, he did none of these things.

About five and one half minutes after the 1978 regular season concluded, Texas unloaded him, like a used car during a last-weekend-in-business-blowout. He was sent to another nowhere team, the Cleveland Indians, for a couple of nobody players, Larvell Blanks and Jim Kern.

In 1979, he had another good season—.275-25-90—scoring 90 runs, stealing 34 bases, and playing his usual good defense when he felt like it in 116 outfield appearances. Bobby Bonds put up numbers that compare with Rickey Henderson. That season, however, was his last gasp.

Cleveland traded him to St. Louis (.203 in 86 games), and the Cardinals unloaded him to the Cubs. He was ill suited to handle their all-day game schedule so few hours after the all-night Rush Street bars closed shop. He unceremoniously called it quits after a .215, six-homer performance in 45 games for another also-ran, in a strike-shortened season.

There was no fanfare, no farewell tour, no comparisons with Mays, Cobb, Williams, and Mantle. In 14 years, he hit .268 during an era of tough pitching. He squared off on a regular basis against the likes of Tom Seaver, Bob Gibson, and Ferguson Jenkins in the National League, then Jim Palmer, Gaylord Perry, Catfish Hunter and Ron Guidry in the junior circuit. He went big fly 332 times and stole 461 bases. He played the outfield with skill and speed. In his prime, he had a great arm and earned three Gold Gloves. He was a member of the 30/30 Club five times. He never played in the World Series!

In Elia Kazan's "On the Waterfront," Marlon Brando's Terry Malloy tells his brother, Karl Malden, "I coulda been a contender." So could Bonds, who was not a bum, but he "coulda been somebody" grander than he actually was.

Barry admired Mickey Mantle, Kareem Abdul-Jabbar and Tony Dorsett growing up. When he was a kid, he could hit a whiffle ball hard enough to shatter glass. Pat became the best customer of a local glass store.

Beginning in 1968 when he was four, Barry became a regular visitor at Candlestick Park. Pat would drive him, and later his brother, the relatively short distance from San Carlos to the stadium on game days. They hung out in the clubhouse, played catch with Mays, and shagged flies during batting practice. It was here that he began his practice of choking up on the bat, because the big league bats he used there were so heavy for the youngster.

"Willie was the best because he was the most fun," recalled Barry. "Willie would throw balls to us a lot." Pat was always there when his father was on road trips.

The San Francisco part of his fantasy life ended for Barry at age 10, when his father was sent to New York for a white center fielder who did not run as fast, throw as well, or hit the ball with the same power or consistency. But Bobby Murcer was accommodating with the press.

The Sigmund Freuds of the 2001 press corps all tried to psychoanalyze the Importance of Being Bobby on the Meaning of Being Barry. They all said that it must have been traumatic for young Barry to see his father shipped to seven teams in eight years from 1974-81. Surely, he was impacted by the fact that his father was a "black militant" who did not get the respect he deserved; who was "dissed" by every general manager he played for; who toiled for white field managers who did not understand the special needs of the modern African-American athlete.

Oh, the misery.

"I thought it was wonderful," said Barry. "To me, I got a chance to travel around, see different cities like New York. I loved it."

He is not just saying that. Barry did love the experience. Who would not? It was a chance to become a Citizen of the World at a young age, to visit new ballparks, and meet a variety of stars that were his father's colleagues.

There are many, many, many worse ways to grow up. That is not to say that friction did not develop between father and son. It did.

"My father and I were never really close when I was growing up," Barry recalled on "Sports Century," "because he was never around. I wanted my dad at my little league games, because everybody else's parents were there. My parents weren't there, just my mom."

"I went to his little league games," Bobby countered. "I went to his high school games, and the most amazing thing about it was he says I never went to a game."

"He said he was there, but I never saw him," said Barry. "I think that was why I was mad at him for so long. My mom was always there; my mom was in the snack bar with all the other moms. My mom did all the car pooling. That's why I was more of a momma's boy."

Could Bobby's memory of these years be hindered by the progressive disease of alcoholism?

"Barry's a sensitive person and wants to be loved," said former teammate Matt Williams on "Sports Century."

"He looked up more to his mother than his father for some reason," said Nick Peters.

"When Barry was 18, he and my dad got in a fight, and he just ran across the street, and he was crying and he said 'I'm never gonna be like that'" recalled his brother, Bobby, Jr.

"I don't think he'd risk harming anyone at the time," recalled one of Bobby, Sr.'s friends, Phil Lewis, of Bobby's drinking. "I know I kept his car keys a lot."

He did not grab them enough. The elder Bonds' had publicized run-ins with law enforcement on the Bayshore Freeway, a stretch of highway that separates Candlestick Park and The City from the Peninsula. He became a running joke. There seemed to be a sense of inevitability to the news reports of his drinking escapades. Drunk driving was not the taboo that it is today in the age of Mothers Against Drunk Driving. Penalties for DUI were not as severe, the stigma not as bad.

"What I was doing when I was young was probably no different than Mickey Mantle or a bunch of 'em," said Bobby.

"I think when you wake up in the morning and need a drink, you have a problem, and I think in time he did realize that," said Lewis.

"I didn't stop because I thought this was the best thing for the family," said Bobby on "Sports Century." "I stopped because I woke up one morning and saw a damn fool."

"I remember talking to him once after his recovery," recalled Bobby's sister, Cheryl Dugan, "and he said, 'Gosh, if I'd known then what I know now I wouldn't have wasted six years of my life."

"I think Barry saw all this potential that my dad had, and it was just wasted," said Bobby, Jr.

Barry was not about to waste his talent. He was the best player in every sport he played—and he played them all—from the time he started participating in them. He was usually either the only black kid, or one of just a few. His friends were often white kids, but sometimes other kids were not his friends. This inevitably led to racial conflict. This is the unfortunate reality of life. People can disagree, but if they are a different skin color or religion, it is made out to be something bigger than it is.

Barry was spoiled, selfish, and narcissistic; traits that describe millions of youngsters every day. Some people envied him, some disliked him, some wanted to be his friend and were rebuffed. Some wanted to be just like him, or were intimidated by him. Nothing about his formative years was unusual, except for the fact that he was a well-to-do black kid in a white environment; who possessed world-class athletic skills that he was happy to show off; he hung out with Hall of Fame superstars; and his playground was a big-league stadium. Other than that, it was a normal childhood.

Religion is very much a part of the black experience. It emanates from the days of suppression in the Deep South, and it is about Christianity, of the

Evangelical Baptist variety. Roman Catholicism has never been the preferred religion of African-Americans. It is a religion that has deep roots in the Latino, Irish and Italian communities. Blacks were Baptists because the Protestants of the South were Baptists.

Basketball legend Kareem Abdul-Jabbar grew up Roman Catholic, but he could not reconcile its teachings with the piercings of prejudice he felt from neighbor Italian and Irish kids growing up in Manhattan and attending Power Memorial Academy.

At UCLA, he reevaluated himself, and converted to Islam, which was when he changed his name from Lew Alcindor. In the revolutionary days of the 1960s, when Malcolm X rose to national prominence and martyrdom, many African-Americans chose to become Black Muslims.

Abdul-Jabbar has always been one of the athletes Bonds has said was a favorite of his.

"I used to get in fights at school because I was black," recalled Barry on "Sports Century." "I'll never forget, I came home one day and I said, 'I don't like white people right now.' And I'll never forget, my dad said, why don't you go out and get the mail. And I came back and tried to open up the door, and it was locked, and I was like knocking on the door, and he said don't ever come in my house like that again. He said be proud of who you are, but regardless do not allow their stupidity to make you stupid."

Barry Bonds would have gone to Carlmont High School of Belmont, in the Peninsula Athletic League. It is a nice school in a nice town that plays in a solid conference that includes Westmoor of Daly City, Skyline of San Bruno, and San Mateo High School. Instead, he went to Junipero Serra High School, where he got a full dose of Catholicism. Serra is located in San Mateo, a few miles to the north. A private school, they are able to recruit athletes and students from outside their district, unlike public schools.

This is why Catholic schools usually dominate the preps. De La Salle of Concord, located in the East Bay, currently is riding a 125-game football winning streak, and has firmly established itself as the Notre Dame of high school football. In Southern California, Mater Dei dominates in every sport. Before Mater Dei, it was Bishop Amat, where Pat Haden threw touchdown passes to J.K. McKay. In the 1960s and '70s, Verbum Dei of Los Angeles offered discipline, a good education, and national basketball power to the ghetto kids who went there. In the Washington, D.C. area, Cardinal Gibbons of Baltimore and DeMatha of Hiattsville, Maryland were hoop champions. In New York, it was Power Memorial, until the school closed.

Serra has a proud athletic tradition that includes Gregg Jeffries, Lynn Swynn, Jesse Freitas, Jim Fregosi, and New England Patriots' quarterback Tom Brady. Dave Stevens, one of the most respected high school baseball coaches in the nation, coached at Serra when Bonds entered there in the late 1970s. They play in the West Catholic Athletic League, a geographically spread-out conference that includes St. Ignatius, Sacred Heart Cathedral and Riordan, all of San Francisco; St. Francis of Mountain View, and Bellarmine Prep and Mitty of San Jose.

California is too large to host a state tournament, so they break it up into sections. The WCAL is in the Central Coast Section, which runs from San Francisco south to Monterey, and is considered the best in Northern California.

At the time Bonds entered Serra, the top baseball power in the area, if not the country, was Redwood High School of Marin County. Coached by Al Endriss, who was National Coach of the Year in 1976, they captured the North Coast Section championship in 1977, 1978 and 1981. The catcher on their 1981 team was Chad Kreuter, who would be behind the plate when Bonds hit his 71st home run in 2001. Redwood was notorious for recruiting, and had gone as far south as San Jose to find pitching help. Bonds was known to Endriss coming out of the eighth grade, but Barry stayed local.

The North Coast Section runs from the Fremont-Union City area in the East Bay, up to the North Bay, and includes Marin and Sonoma Counties. Other sections are the Oakland City Section and the San Francisco City Section, which consist entirely of public schools in those cities. The Sac-Joaquin Section includes Sonoma County, east to Sacramento, and runs south with Interstate 5 to include Fresno and Bakersfield.

Further south, and west, is the Southern Section, which is the largest and toughest. This section covers an area from San Luis Obispo to Santa Barbara and Ventura, the San Fernando Valley, all of Los Angeles' private and Catholic schools, and Riverside, San Bernardino and Orange County. The section is divided into numerous divisions, as many as 10 for football, based partly on school size.

In the middle of this section is the Los Angeles City Section (all public schools). To the south is the San Diego Section, but that includes both the city and county (private and public schools). By the early 1980s, the state had started a basketball tournament, widely divided by divisions to accommodate the various school sizes (which does not always mandate what division a small, yet powerful, school might play in). The California Interscholastic Federation (CIF) has never created a statewide baseball tournament.

Now, the San Francisco championship game is played at Pacific Bell Park. The Oakland title game is held at the Network Associates Coliseum. The Central Coast Section, or CCS, plays its marquee games at Police Athletic League (PAL) Stadium in San Jose. The top power in the CCS prior to Bonds' years at Serra was El Camino High of South San Francisco. That town is usually called South City.

In the Southland, the games have long been held at Dodger Stadium and Anaheim Stadium (now Edison International Field). The best California high school players compete in an annual North-South All-Star Game, usually at one of the big league sites. Traditionally, the South is stronger. Then they team up to make a California All-Star squad that travels and plays all-star teams from places like Oklahoma, Texas or Florida.

Bonds was one of the few blacks at Serra, but his sports reputation preceded him, and of course he had name recognition. He was accorded instant celebrity status, which was not exactly of his choosing.

"Bobby would come to the ballpark to pick him up, and all the kids would just hover around trying to get autographs, and I think this kind of affected Barry, who closed himself off at an early age from the kids around him," Serra teammate Mike Roza told "Sports Century."

"You want to be my friend because I'm Barry Bonds or because my dad plays in the big leagues," is the way Bobby characterized it. Bobby, the all-star athlete, was demanding of his son.

"If I scored three touchdowns in one day in football," recalled Barry, "came back [the next game] and scored one, something was wrong with me." That did not stop him from establishing himself as a phenom.

"Bonds as prep; Signs of a Superstar," read a *Chronicle* Sporting Green headline. Bonds was a three-sport star at Serra. He wore number 34 playing hoops for the Padres.

"Because he was so darned good, and made things look so easy, people looked for a chink in his armor," Dave Stevens told "Sports Century."

"Barry had a certain sense of cockiness and maybe they [teammates] got rubbed the wrong way about the way Barry carried himself," said Bobby McKercher, a white guy who is generally felt to be Barry's best pal. "He used to steal bases in high school and get everybody upset because he would never slide. He'd say, 'Why? I don't need to wash 'em.' We're sprinting on and off the field, caught up in the old school style of ball, and Barry was on a different cruise level."

"He liked to showboat a little bit, you know, show a little flair," said Roza.

"On the way out to the field he'd be puttin' his gloves on and fixin' his hat," said Ray McDonald, who played with him at Serra.

"My coaches always wanted me to excel, and they'd all yell at me, 'You can dribble around this person, why aren't you?'" said Barry. "And then you'd have friends who weren't at this level, and sometimes I held back a lot just to stay in the group."

He was already an individualist.

"When Barry wanted to have fun, he'd have fun," said Rosa. "If Barry didn't want to have fun, he'd hold back. Barry would be in his own little world, and it was like, 'Don't bother me.'"

"I'd separate myself some times because I didn't want to deal with people always wanting to talk about me," said Barry.

"I've been around him when the switch will turn and he becomes very quiet," said Stevens.

Bonds was once quoted by ESPN.com recalling what it was like growing up who he was.

"My father and I have always been very close," said Bonds. "Even today, I don't do anything without talking to him and my mother first. He's always been there when I need him. As a child, I loved being the son of a baseball star. How many kids do you know whose dad would take you to the ballpark to meet stars like Catfish Hunter and Thurman Munson? And, of course, he was always giving me advice on how to play. One thing he especially didn't like was when I would get angry at striking out. He'd yell at me and say, 'Throwing down your helmet is not going to get you a hit.' His theory was that you should be more concerned when you were doing well than when you were in a slump. 'Panic when you're hitting well, because you'll soon find out that it's only for a short time.' It's funny but that's exactly how I feel today about hitting. I am much more worried when I'm in the groove than when I'm having a bad day.

"And it wasn't just my dad who criticized my play. Willie Mays kept his eye on me constantly and would often tell me I wasn't concentrating enough. Then there was cousin Reggie, always ready to get his two cents in, too. One thing all three had in common: They would never accept excuses. I obviously appreciated their love and help, but it did leave me in a difficult position of being compared to all three. It seemed to me that the media thought I was competing with them."

Bonds hit .404 in three seasons at Serra. He was a prep All-American as a senior, hitting .467. The Giants drafted him. Bonds rejected their $70,000 offer. He wanted $75,000, so he accepted a scholarship to Arizona State. It was the best of times and the worst of times. The younger Bonds' star was on the rise. The older one was now a has-been, deeply mired in the throes of alcoholism. These were the days in which Bobby's drinking occasionally made the news.

Barry made an immediate splash when he arrived at Tempe.

"He came in a nice new car, and everybody and everyone was talking about the fact that Barry Bonds was coming here," recalled Patsey Brock, the widow of the Sun Devils' coach, Jim Brock, on "Sports Century."

Arizona State is located in a suburb of Phoenix. Needless to say, it is very, very hot there. Baseball is played in perfect conditions all year round. The school is not known for its academics, but rather its sports. It is also known for its party atmosphere, close proximity to hot nightlife, and the beautiful, tanned girls who walk the campus. This fact was accurately depicted in a TV movie about a gambling scandal that occurred there some years ago, in which the main character says going to school here was like "landing in a Coppertone commercial." It is as close to paradise as it gets for a college jock.

Frank Kush had built the football program into a national power by the early 1970s, and in 1978 ASU and the University of Arizona left the Western Athletic Conference and joined the Pacific-8 (now Pac-10) Conference. Kush, however, was fired for getting too physical with his players.

The top college baseball program in the country is the University of Southern California. Coach Rod Dedeaux led the Trojans to 10 National Championships from 1948 to 1978. His 1978 College World Series winners were considered by some to be the best collegiate team ever. However, the NCAA instituted scholarship restrictions after that season. That supposedly made it more difficult for expensive private schools like USC to bring in "walk-ons" and partial-scholarship players.

This gave rise to schools like Cal State Fullerton, who began to emerge as top programs. Both Arizona schools, however, already shared the status of major powers by the early 1970s.

Jerry Kindall developed Arizona into a champion in Tucson, where the Wildcats captured the 1976 and 1980 National Championships. Arizona State, however, was the big kid on the block when Bonds was being recruited.

Bobby Winkles, a kindly disciplinarian, developed ASU into a champion in the 1960s. He recruited the likes of Reggie Jackson, Sal Bando, Rick Monday and Gary Gentry. The Sun Devils won their first National Championship in 1965. Bando, Jackson and Monday became the nucleus of the Oakland A's championship clubs of the 1970s. They all came up through Charlie Finley's farm system to the Major Leagues together.

The first amateur draft was held in 1965, and the All-American Monday, a Southern Californian recruited away from Dedeaux by the father-figure Winkles, made history as the first player selected, by the A's.

Jackson was the second player selected in 1966 and would recommend the program to his cousin 16 years later. Winkles captured another National Championship in 1969, then was lured by the California Angels in the early 1970s. His rah-rah college style did not fit with the big leaguers, however.

When Winkles left, the job went to Mesa Community College coach Jim Brock. In his first year at the helm, Brock led the Sun Devils to an incredible 64-6 record, but it was not enough to overcome Dedeaux's Trojans, who would win five straight national titles from 1970 to 1974.

In 1975, it looked like it would be Brock's year. His club went 61-13, and Augie Garrido's upstart Cal State Fullerton Titans knocked out USC in their regionals. It was Cliff Gustafson and the Texas Longhorns, however, who would emerge from Omaha, the site of the College World Series, with the brass ring. It began to look like Brock was star-crossed in 1976. The Sun Devils were a gaudy 65-10, but Kindall's Arizona Wildcats, who were dominated by them in WAC play, came on strong at Omaha to win it all.

Finally, in 1977, Brock's team went all the way. They finished second at Omaha to Southern Cal in 1978, and joined the Pac-10, along with Arizona, in the 1978-79 school year. In actuality, the baseball portion of the "sun belt" portion of the Pac-10 was divided, for purposes of weather, travel and competitive balance, into the Southern Division, or Six-Pac. The Northern Division at first consisted of Washington, Washington State, Oregon and Oregon State, but over the year's teams dropped out and others were added.

Joining the Six-Pac gave the Devils exposure to California players who could check them out when they visited USC, UCLA, California and Stanford. Bonds was one of those players.

In 1980 and 1981, his sophomore and junior years at Serra, the College World Series was won by Arizona and Arizona State. USC had fallen on hard times, blaming the scholarship limitations. The new rules did not affect Mark Marquess, who was building a top program down the road at private school Stanford. Bonds was no academic whiz, and his acceptance at Stanford would have been questionable, although the proximity of the school to his home was attractive.

California, under new coach Bob Milano, had experienced a Renaissance. In 1980, the Golden Bears finished third, barely falling to Arizona, in the College World Series. They went after Bonds, too. UCLA had just built their shiny new facility, Jackie Robinson Stadium. They had previously played at a dilapidated field near the Veteran's Administration in Westwood, and were as much an enigma then as they are now. Despite great weather, a huge population to draw on, and an attractive college, coach Gary Adams has never lifted the Bruin baseball program into the upper echelon.

Bonds looked at the aging Dedeaux, considered to be "old school" in terms of his approach to modern players, and rejected that program. Besides, cousin Reggie had been a Sun Devil, so it was off to Arizona State, where he would play his games in the gleaming Packard Stadium, one of the top facilities in the country.

When Brock recruited Bonds during his senior year, he had the imprimatur of the 1981 National Championship pushing his sails. At 55-13, the Sun Devils had been led by pitcher Kendall Carter, who was 19-1. Alvin Davis would go on to play for Seattle. Kevin Romine would play for the Red Sox.

The adventure and experience of college enticed Bonds, too. Bobby and Willie could tell him that the minor league life was not a glamorous one, and the chance to be a college man was attractive to him.

Bonds' large family has always made a habit of seeing him play. Many of them would make the trip to Arizona, or watch him when the Sun Devils came to play at Cal and Stanford. His "Riverside folks" were regulars when ASU visited USC and UCLA. It was not always sweetness and light, however.

"My dad would call me in college, and I'd just pray he didn't show up," recalled Barry on "Sports Century." "I never knew if he'd be sober or not."

Bonds, the "showboater," the "big leaguer," had his way, and it was not always about giving it the "old college try."

"There were some of us who felt like he might have coasted just a little bit when he got here," recalled ASU play-by-play announcer Tom Dillon on "Sports Century." "I think Coach Brock recognized the greatness in him and tried to impress upon Barry to do his best all the time. Jim Brock got the best out of everybody who ever played for him. He may have been tougher on the most talented players than he was on the less talented players."

"I really didn't think he had that much fire inside him when he got here," Charles Scott, the Sun Devils' ace pitcher during those years, told "Sports Century." "Talent-wise, there was never any doubt."

"He [Brock] would ride me for anything," recalled Barry. "If I didn't run to the batter's box, he'd sit me down."

"He and Barry got along at times very well," said Scott. "There was lots of joking between those two, whereas Coach Brock rarely joked with anyone else."

Bonds was suspended for missing curfew during a road trip to Honolulu in 1984.

"When you go to Hawaii in college, you are not gonna stay in for curfew," Bonds recalled, laughing, on "Sports Century."

"To say he was the only one staying out past curfew is probably an understatement," said Scott, recalling the event with less levity. "Brock called the captains in his office and said each guy would have to run five miles, and Barry spoke his mind and said it wasn't fair because there were other guys who were out, and basically he was just being 'Big Mouth Barry,' talking when he should have just shup up and did what the rest of us did."

"Well, you didn't talk that way to Coach Brock," assistant coach Ed Yeager told "Sports Century." "So he suspended him, and went to the rest of the team and said, 'I want to take a team vote on whether we should let him back on.' The team voted and said, 'forget him,' and Brock went back to them and said, 'I don't think you understood what I said,' and they voted again and Barry was back on the team."

The Phoenix newspaper responded with the headline, "Brock kept Bonds despite team vote."

On the field, Bonds was all that he had been billed to be. He was not the most-liked player, but he was not the least-liked, either. On the road, he encountered verbal abuse, much of it centered on his father's less-than-sterling reputation. I was at USC with Mark McGwire and Randy Johnson during the years Bonds played at Arizona State. USC fans called him "Bail Bonds" because of Bobby's adventures on the Bayshore Freeway.

"With regards to Barry, I really didn't know him at all when I played against him when he was at ASU," recalled Southern Cal pitcher Randy Robertson. "The only thing I remember about him was a home run he hit that hit the bed of a pickup truck that was driving by on Scottsdale Road (I think that is the name of the street that runs along the center/right field fence.) I couldn't believe he could hit a ball that far, especially since he wasn't your typical slugger, i.e., McGwire. I always thought Barry was a very good hitter, and I would always try and keep the ball away from him since he did have good power on the inside pitch."

"I remember that he was not that much of a power hitter," recalled another Trojan pitcher, left-hander Steve McGhghy. "I'm not sure he was even their best player, but he was a slick fielder, real quick with great speed."

He was good enough to have his number 24 retired after he left. It is interesting that, when he had a choice of numbers, he wore 24—Mays' number, and Jackson's at ASU, too—and not the 25 that his father wore.

In his freshman season, 1983, Arizona State was 44-24, and 17-13 in the Six-Pac. They battled USC for a play-off spot. The Trojans featured sophomore All-American first baseman McGwire, converted from being a pitcher by Dedeaux. McGwire hit 19 home runs and batted .319.

On the mound, USC had an "enigma" of their own. Mickey Meister was considered to be the best prep pitcher in the nation. He had led Redwood High to the National Championship (where he was 37-3 in four seasons). In 1979, one prep sports publication named Mick the National Athlete of the Year. His competition? John Elway of Granada Hills and Jay Schroeder of Palisades. Meister had earned the enigma moniker from the *L.A. Times* because he had not, and never would, fulfill his expectations.

On the other hand, SC featured a 6-10 southpaw from the Bay Area, Johnson, who had shown promise but had a long, long way to go. *He* would fulfill every inch of his potential. The Big Unit was 5-0 that season, but still as wild as a March hare.

ASU secured the berth in the NCAA Regionals, which they hosted. The Sun Devils swept past Brigham Young, 19-1; Cal State Fullerton, 8-0; and Fresno State, 7-2.

Unfortunately, Bonds did not compete against Stanford's Elway, who did not play that spring in what would have been his senior year. He had signed for over $100,000 with the Yankees the previous year and played in their minor league system. Of course, he quickly gave up baseball for a Hall of Fame football career in Denver.

At the College World Series, ASU met their match. After losing to Alabama, 6-5 in 11 innings, they beat the Maine Black Bears, 7-0, and the Oklahoma State Cowboys, 6-5. The Crimson Tide had their number, though, knocking them out, 6-0, before they bowed to Roger Clemens, Calvin Schiraldi and Spike Owens of the National Champion Texas Longhorns.

The Sun Devils featured two other Bay Area stars, catcher Dan Wakamatsu (who would play briefly in the Major Leagues) and pitcher Doug Henry, a reliever with Milwaukee and the Giants. Wakamatsu hit .340 for the 44-24 Devils, while Henry won nine games against seven defeats.

All-American outfielder Oddibe McDowell hit .352, and freshman Bonds put up a .306 average, a team leading 11 homers, and 54 RBIs, while making the All-College World Series team. Wakamatsu, McDowell, Kendall Carter and outfielder Steve Moses were All-Pac-10 selections.

Bonds played for the Fairbanks, Alaska Goldpanners that summer, but did not hit well. The Goldpanners are the preeminent collegiate summer team. Started in the 1960s by Red Boucher, the Mayor of Fairbanks, the team attracts top college players from around the country to play in the Land of the Midnight Sun. Tom Seaver of USC had played there, and his well-publicized success helped make the team known to others.

The Alaskan League includes the Goldpanners and the Anchorage Glacier Pilots. Teams have also been established in Kenai, Palmer and other cities in the state. A second team in Fairbanks, the North Pole Nicks, came to be formed. Eventually, the league became the Alaska-Hawaii League, with travel between the two states becoming a regular part of the schedule.

The success of the Goldpanners and the Alaska baseball experience in general, led to other collegiate summer leagues. Players found themselves playing in "exotic" locales like Kamloops, British Columbia, Canada; Red Deer and Edmonton, Alberta; in Colorado Springs and for the Boulder Collegians; and in the Jay Hawk League, where top-flight franchises have had success in Hutchinson and Dodge City, Kansas. Yes, the same Dodge City where Wyatt Earp is buried at Boot Hill.

Today, the Goldpanners are still a prestigious place to play, but the Cape Cod League has become its equal. With teams located along the New England coast, the Cape, as it is called, bans aluminum bats. Scouts feel that they get a truer picture of a player's professional potential when they see him hit with the lumber. Many a collegian has seen his .355 collegiate average drop to .255 on the Cape. Aside from the "wood effect," the collegiate leagues also offer competition that is perhaps stiffer than the college season.

Teams like the Goldpanners are virtual college all-star teams. The players usually live with local families and are given easy "jobs" to keep them in spending money. They are able to concentrate on baseball like professionals, playing every day without the encumbrance of classes.

At the end of the summer, the champions and at-large selections from the various summer leagues make a tour of tournaments. At one time, the Kamloops International Tournament was a prestigious event that featured top teams from Canada and the U.S. (including Alaska and the contiguous 48). The one event that has lasted is the National Baseball Congress, held in Wichita, Kansas each August. The winner is crowned as National Champions.

In 1983, Bonds hit only .222 for the Goldpanners. McGwire had led the Alaskan League with a .403 average the year before, when Dedeaux had decided to have him make the permanent switch from pitcher to position player, and sent him north in the summer to work on his swing.

In 1984, USC again featured McGwire, the college Player of the Year, and Johnson, whose wildness hindered his effectiveness. USC went to the West Regionals in Fresno but lost. Brock's Sun Devils were talent-laden, going 55-20 and 23-7 in conference play, good for first place. Ranked number one going into the postseason, ASU again swept through a regional that they hosted.

Washington State fell, 8-4, followed by Hawaii, 15-11 and Stanford, 5-4.

In the College World Series, Miami was beaten 9-6. Then Oklahoma State fell in a slugfest, 23-12, but Texas took them 8-4, followed by eventual National Champion Cal State Fullerton, 6-1.

Wakamatsu hit .311. McDowell batted .405 with 23 home runs and 74 RBIs. On the mound, Henry was 11-2, and Carter was 6-4. Bonds hit .360, and along with McDowell made the All-CWS team again. McDowell was the star of the team, named by Baseball America as the Player of the Year, and he also won the prestigious Golden Spikes award. He repeated as a First Team All-American, while outfielder Todd Brown was a Third Team selection.

Bonds, Brown, Wakamatsu, McDowell, and pitcher Dave Graybill were named to the All Pacific-10 Conference team, with McDowell sharing Co-Player of the Year honors with McGwire. Brock was named the conference Coach of the Year.

The junior McDowell was the 12th pick of that year's draft, going in the first round to Texas. Most good college players leave after their junior years. The rules are different for baseball than other collegiate sports. Football players were bound to play four years until that rule was relaxed in the late 1980s. Still, only the very best players in the nation come out after three years.

Basketball players used to be held to the same limits, but Spencer Haywood, who played for Dick Vitale at the University of Detroit, challenged the practice. Thus, the "hardship rule" was established, and now hoop stars routinely declare themselves for the draft after their freshman and sophomore years.

Many baseball players sign out of high school, because of the minor league system that other sports do not have. There are two drafts each year, one in June and the other in January. The January draft is mostly for junior college players, who are free to sign after their freshman or sophomore years. If drafted in January, a juco player is bound to that team until draft day in June. He can sign with his winter team, or resubmit for the June draft.

A player who goes to a four-year college is ineligible for the draft until his junior year is completed. If he wishes to go pro before that, he can drop out of school, or transfer to a JC, then be eligible for the next draft after that.

The best juniors almost always sign, because they have the most leverage. However, they do not have to make any decision on the matter until the first day of school in the fall. They can hold out while playing summer ball in places like Alaska, threatening to come back for their senior years. In recent years, agents—namely Scott Boras—have taken the "junior year leverage" concept further. While a top player like Bonds turned down $70,000 in 1982, nowadays he would be offered a multimillion dollar signing bonus. Boras holds these players out, squeezing every penny from the clubs who draft them. Many times, he puts the word out ahead of time that a player does not want to go to certain teams, usually in small markets or towns without much marquee value.

Occasionally, a high draft choice does return for his senior year, and sometimes a kid will bide his time in an independent league until Boras, or his Boras-wannabe agent, extracts the deal he is looking for.

In 1985, his junior, draft-eligible year, the Sun Devils had lost too much talent, and fell to 31-35. They played .500 in conference play, and failed to make the regionals for the first time since 1982.

Bonds was a Second Team All-American selection, hitting .368 with 23 home runs and 66 runs batted in, with 91 hits. Wakamatsu batted .294, first baseman Luis Medina hit .379, and outfielder Mike Devereaux, a future big leaguer, batted .296. Pitching killed the Sun Devils, who had lost Carter, Henry and Graybill. At USC, McGwire was gone, but Randy Johnson was completing his last season. Still wild and largely ineffective, Johnson did not help his team rise from mediocrity. He was drafted by Montreal, but was not a first-round selection.

Bonds, Wakamatsu and second baseman Rick Morris were all-conference picks. A look at Arizona State's all-time leaders indicates that Bonds, the greatest player ever to come out of the program, put up good statistics, but not spectacular ones. His 23 home runs in 1985 are second all-time to Bob Horner, who hit 25 in 1978. His name does not appear among the leaders in any other Sun Devil records for a game, a season or a career.

Arizona State "legends" like Hubie Brooks, Paul LoDuca, Chris Bando, Alan Bannister, Mike Kelly, Ken Landreaux, plus pitchers like Eddie Bane, Floyd Bannister, and Larry Gura were great college superstars who put up gaudy numbers in Tempe. Their names appear in the Sun Devil record book more than Bonds.

The numbers, however, can be deceptive. Take Johnson, who had a losing a record and an earned run average north of 5.00 at Southern Cal. He became the most dominant pitcher since Sandy Koufax. Reggie Jackson, whose own name is scarcely mentioned among Sun Devil record holders (except for his 62 strikeouts in 1966), was one of the most sought-after players in the country.

Bonds hit .347 in his three years, with 45 homers and 175 RBIs. He tied an NCAA record for consecutive hits in the College World Series.

The Pirates made him the sixth overall pick in the 1985 draft. What kept him from being number one? Certainly, he was a well-known commodity. He had the Bonds name, of course. He had the great high school record. He had shined in the spotlight of the College World Series. He had made All-American playing in what was still probably the premier program in the nation.

He also had exhibited a bad attitude, an occasional lack of hustle, and an unwillingness to be coached. In this regard, Brock was a good coach for him. Brock, who passed away, the untimely victim of cancer in the mid-1990s, was more of a public relations man than a bona fide coach. Arizona's Kindall was considered a much better teacher of fundamentals.

Aside from "standing up" to Bonds after his Hawaii curfew violation, Brock had tried to get along with his temperamental, moody star. Had Bonds played for a real disciplinarian like Frank Kush, or Jim Leyland, at that age, it might have made him grow up and be prepared for what he would face in Pittsburgh.

Instead, at 20 going on 21, he had absolutely no idea that the axis of the world did not revolve around him.

THREE

" . . . He was probably somebody that everybody in the clubhouse wanted to beat up . . . "

Barry Bonds' professional career began at Prince William of the Carolina League in the summer of 1985. He was an immediate splash, being named Player of the Month for July.

"Every day it was the talk show fodder in the papers, 'When's Barry going to Pittsburgh?'" recalled John Perrotto of the *Beaver County* (Pennsylvania) *Times* on "Sports Century."

In 71 games he hit 13 home runs, and stole 15 of 18 bases, while batting .299.

"He had just been signed and they were gonna send him to the minors for a while, but he was gonna take batting practice in Pittsburgh," ex-pitcher Rick Sutcliffe told "Sports Century." "Don Zimmer and Jim Leyland were standing in back of the cage, and he probably hit 10 of 15 swings out of the ball park, but he pulled every one. So Leyland made the comment, 'Hell, anybody could do that,' so two out of the next three pitches he hit to left field. So he turns around and says, 'Ya wanna see one to center field? Watch this,' and the next pitch he hit one out to center field. So Leyland and Zimmer are walking together, and Zim's looking at Leyland, and he says, 'What in the world are you doing sending this kid out?'"

The next season, he was assigned to Hawaii of the Class AAA Pacific Coast League. Bo Belinsky used to flat-out say that playing in Hawaii was better than a lot of big-league towns. Young and single, Bonds no doubt enjoyed the surf, the sun and the island girls (without Jim Brock's college rules). It did not affect his play, for sure. In 44 games, the young phenom was hitting .311 with 30 runs scored and 33 walks. He stole 16 bases. His power was modest—seven homers—and he struck out 31 times.

"Of course, right away we heard of comments he made about how people making decisions didn't know what they were doing," said former pitcher Bob Walk. "He was right. Before the season was over he was up there, starting in the outfield."

To compare Bonds then with Bonds now is like looking at the United States and Mexico. There is no comparison. In this regard, Bonds is more like Aaron than Mays and Mantle.

Mays and Mantle were huge celebrities before their first games, particularly Mantle. He was dubbed the Commerce Comet. Mays made his name in Minneapolis, where he was hitting almost .500 before Leo Durocher brought him up.

Bonds was one of the biggest minor league talents in baseball. He was an absolute can't-miss prospect, but nobody can predict MVP awards and Hall of Fame plaques. After all, the Giants, of all teams, had passed on him when they could have had him for $5,000 more.

The comparison with Aaron speaks to the long-ball prowess of the two players. Both showed power early, but neither would have been considered sluggers. They just kept coming.

On May 30, 1986, the Pirates brought him up.

"When he first came up, he was probably somebody that everybody in the clubhouse wanted to beat up at some point in time," Sid Bream, a Pirate teammate before going to the Braves, told "Sports Century."

"If they got into a fight on the field, it might be 49-1, and it was pretty obvious who the 'one' was," said Paul Meyer, who covered Barry for the *Pittsburgh Post-Gazette.*

"He rubs people the wrong way, but he's respected on the field," said Eric Davis.

"You don't have to be everybody's buddy," was Bonds' assessment.

"Baseball's not always played on the field," Willie Mays had told Bonds as a piece of advice. "It's also played off the field."

"He could play that role," said Bobby Bonds, "but he wouldn't be playing himself."

"Smiling and waving is just not me," said Barry Bonds.

No, it is not. At least not until 2001.

Bonds hit .303 in 115 minor league games before arriving in Pittsburgh. This was right after the 1985 "cocaine scandals," in which a clubhouse manager in Pittsburgh had been found to have been a drug dealer to many National League players. The franchise needed something new, fresh and exciting.

"We were all sure Barry Bonds was gonna be a great ball player, particularly in the mid-1980s here in Pittsburgh, where we were all fearful that we'd lose the franchise," recalled broadcaster Larry Frattare on "Sports Century."

The Smoky City is a blue-collar town, although some wealthy suburbs such as Mt. Lebanon exist outside the city limits. It is not a great night life town. It is not a city known for the arts, museums, or the theatre. It is a "shot and a beer" city, filled with union steelworkers whose livelihoods are affected by the large companies they work for.

In periods of distress, recession, or major change, Pittsburgh is subject to bad times. The city generally votes moderately Democrat, but there is a strain of conservatism here. Its citizens are no-nonsense types, family people, and they tend to be religious.

Pittsburgh is located in Western Pennsylvania. This is football country, and not just the Pittsburgh Steelers. Great quarterbacks seem to rise like steam from the plains of Western PA. Their names include Johnny Unitas, Joe Namath, Dan Marino and Joe Montana.

Pittsburgh has a football mentality. The people work hard during the week, and save it up for Sundays. They let it all hang out when their beloved Steelers give them something to live for on cold, gray afternoons.

However, a little history lesson is in order. The Steelers were the joke of the National Football League until 1970. Their teams in that decade were among the greatest in the game's history.

The Pirates, on the other hand, had given this town many thrills going back to 1903. They played in the first World Series against the Boston Pilgrims (their name before Red Sox) that season. Honus Wagner was with the franchise when they arrived from Louisville around the turn of the century. Paul and Lloyd Waner starred on championship contenders in the 1920s. After a down period, Pittsburgh won the 1960 World Series.

Oakland manager Art Howe was growing up in Pittsburgh, and he, like the rest of the city, was rabid in his enthusiasm for the team. Colorful broadcaster Bob Prince told fans to "beware of the green weenie." In the next two decades, the Pirates probably did more to introduce "National League baseball" and provide opportunities for minorities than any team in baseball.

"National League baseball" is a code phrase for the kind of exciting, hit 'n' run, make-things-happen game that was played in the old Negro Leagues. Jackie Robinson brought it to the National League, which evolved into a more aggressive league. Pulitzer Prize-winning author David Halberstam made an interesting study of this in *October 1964.*

In that book, Halberstam looks at American society through the prism of baseball. On the right were the Yankees, who symbolized the Republican Party—conservative, rich, white, country-club types. On the left were the Cardinals, who symbolized the Democrats—a mixed group of blacks, whites and Latinos who represented a changing America.

Because the Yankees dominated the game, baseball people in the American League failed to recognize that their brand of baseball, which was to wait for the long ball, was something only the Yankees could sustain. The rest of the league could not. American League clubs were slow to bring in minorities, but these kinds of players starred in the National League. The difference between the two leagues became obvious over many years, in which the Nationals dominated the Americans in All-Star Games.

Eventually, the Yankees and the American League modernized their approach, and experienced a resurgence, much like Ronald Reagan and the Republican Party did.

The Pirates, the team of Roberto Clemente, Willie Stargell, Manny Sanguillen, Dave Cash, Doc Ellis, Dave Parker, and Al Oliver, were typical of the New Breed.

In the 1970s, they became the first Major League club ever to field an entirely non-white starting line-up. Their teams won, including World Championships in 1971 and 1979.

The "We Are Family" Pirates of 1979 were a team, led by "Pops" Stargell, that played to the utmost of their abilities. They had chemistry and team unity, and despite wearing some of the ugliest uniforms and worst hats in Major League history, came from behind against the powerful Orioles to win the Series.

The fans took to the Pirates, and the team interacted with them. The fans of Pittsburgh are knowledgeable and have an appreciation for the kind of good, clean hardball their teams always played. The spirit of Clemente, who died tragically on New Year's Day, 1973, trying to fly rations to earthquake victims in Nicaragua, had helped to maintain the club's winning tradition after he was gone.

Stargell had taken over as their spokesman, a symbol of the team. On the Pirates, you played to win. You played for the team, even if that meant personal sacrifice. Pittsburgh fans expected this.

"When he first came up, he was just full of talent, and had an energetic attitude, he was a guy who just wanted to conquer the world," trainer Kent Biggerstaff told "Sports Century," speaking of Bonds.

The young hotshot was better than Stargell, maybe even better than Clemente, but the impression of him was that he was not selfless in the Stargell-Clemente tradition.

"He had it from day one," broadcaster and former Pirate pitcher Jim Rooker told "Sports Century." "You'd hear rumblings in the clubhouse, 'he already has his Hall of Fame plaque ready.'"

"He knew he was gonna be good, and I hate to use the word good, but he wasn't using the word good, he knew he was gonna be great," said Bobby Bonilla, who came to the Pirates around the same time, after having been traded during the 1986 season by the Chicago White Sox.

Bonds' first Major League hit was a double off the Dodgers' Rick Honeycutt on May 31. On June 4, he hit his first home run off Craig McMurtry of Atlanta. He led all National League rookies in home runs (16), runs batted in (48), stolen bases (36) and walks (65). He still struck out too much (102) and hit only .223 from the leadoff spot. Todd Worrell, a hard-throwing relief pitcher with St. Louis, was the league's Rookie of the Year.

The Pittsburgh press, however, was still replete with writers who had recalled his father and the Giant-Pirate rivalry of the early 1970s.

"I think there was a little bit of a chip on his shoulder about being confused with his father the first couple years," said Walk. "It was unbelievable how many people would call him Bobby Bonds. He wanted out of that desperately."

"He really resented that, " said Paul Meyer of the *Post-Gazette*. "He'd stop the interview and say, 'I'm Barry, Bobby's my father.'"

"'Are you as good as your father?' they'd ask me," recalled Barry.

The fact is, however, that Bonds enjoyed talking to writers when he arrived. He was brash, good-looking, intelligent and charismatic, with something to say. In this respect, he and Bonilla were cut out of the same cloth.

"When I first came up I was talking to the media too much, but I was hitting like .205 or something, and I did all the interviews, and Leyland said if you don't concentrate and do things your supposed to do, you're gonna sit down," Bonds says now (as quoted on "Sports Century"). "He said, 'You have to leave these reporters alone because these people are not your friends.' So I cut out the media."

"I think sometimes they take advantage of that, and there are times you need some private moments," former manager Jim Leyland told "Sports Century."

Leyland was in his first year at the helm. If being just like the city you work in makes one perfect for the job, Leyland was perfect for Pittsburgh. Born in Toledo, Ohio in 1944, he came from a big, clue-collar family. Leyland had a special appreciation for the working men and women—truck drivers, waitresses, construction workers . . . and those who toiled on the steel.

He was a career minor leaguer, gruff and plainspoken, but smart. He did not take any crap. He demanded respect, but gave it in return. On the surface, it would seem that he was the worst possible first manager of Barry Bonds.

Here was an outspoken black kid, full of himself with a lot of hot dog in him. Nobody had ever really stood up to him before. Leyland did stand up to him, and to Barry's great credit, he was smart enough to recognize in his manager a man who deserved respect. Leyland got it from him.

The importance of Leyland on his career must not be underestimated. If Bobby Bonds had a manager like that in his early years, instead of a steady stream of baseball hacks like Herman Franks, Clyde King and Charlie Fox, his career might have turned out differently.

Bonds instinctively liked and respected what Leyland was trying to do in rebuilding the club, which was 64-98 in 1986. Bonds and Bonilla bought into Leyland's aggressive philosophy.

Barry was less respectful of the Pittsburgh media, and when his manager told him to stop accommodating them, he took the message to heart.

"His problem is, he didn't treat people with as much respect as they wanted to be treated," Jim Lachima, the Pirates' publicity man at the time, told "Sports Century."

The New York Mets under Davey Johnson had won 108 games en route to the 1986 World Championship. The Eastern Division in 1987 was the toughest in baseball.

New York, after spending the off-season reading their press clippings and hitting the New York party scene, got off to a horrendous start. The Whitey Herzog-led Cardinals went on a terrific run, but by late August, early September, the talented Mets had crawled back into contention. A late-inning home run derailed the Mets in a head-to-head match-up with St. Louis in September, providing just enough momentum for the Redbirds (95-67) to win the division by three games.

Laboring in the shadows, out of the race, the Pirates were the real story in the National League that year. Leyland had led his charges to a 12-game improvement. Pittsburgh boasted one of the best young outfields baseball had seen in a long time.

In right field, Bonilla, the kid from The Bronx, hit .300 with 15 homers, and 77 RBIs. In center field was Andy Van Slyke, who .293 with 21 home runs and 82 runs batted in. In left field and batting lead off was Bonds, with 25 homers, 59 RBIs, a .261 average, and 32 stolen bases. He still struck out more (88) than he walked (54). They all played great defense.

The pitching staff showed promise in the form of a young Texan, Doug Drabek, who had a "drop-and-drive" motion reminiscent of Tom Seaver. He was a right-hander who brought it three-quarters, and he had a heavy, dipping, sinking fastball like Don Drysdale's. Jim Gott, a reliever with moxie and a willingness to pitch inside, had a 1.45 ERA out of the bullpen.

Pittsburgh finished at 80-82, tied with Philadelphia for fourth place. Minnesota would win a strange, back-and-forth World Series with St. Louis, but knowledgeable baseball people knew the Bucs were comers.

In 1988, New York regained their footing, winning 100 games with such marquee names as Daryl Strawberry, Keith Hernandez, Gary Carter,

Dwight Gooden and David Cone. St. Louis forgot how to win. The Pirates were learning how to do it. At 85-75, they were still 15 games off the pace, but nobody wanted to face their lineup.

They were a typical Pirate club, and in this regard that made them a typical Leyland club; scrappy, fast, aggressive. They stole bases, hit-and-ran, and took chances on defense. They featured names like Lind and Belliard, role players who fit Leyland's mold by playing hard and staying prepared.

Bonilla moved over to third base, and drove in 100 runs with 24 homers. Van Slyke added another 100 ribs and 24 homers. Left fielder Bonds hit 25 homers, and drove in 59 from the leadoff slot. After being named National League Player of the Week in April, though, he only stole 17 bases after injuring his knee in a June game with the Cardinals.

It is interesting to note that Kirk Gibson of Los Angeles, that season's National League MVP, hit only 25 home runs and drove in 76. Bonds' numbers, hitting leadoff and playing hurt, were comparable.

Nineteen eighty-nine was supposed to be the year that the Pirates emerged as a major contender, and Bonds would become a big-time star. Both would have to wait one more season. The Chicago Cubs, a team that emerges from nowhere every few years to contend, were led by a young sinkerballer, Greg Maddux, winner of 19 games. Don Zimmer's club won 93 to take the East by six over the Mets. St. Louis (86-76) and Montreal (81-81) finished ahead of the disappointing Bucs (74-88).

Bonilla produced another 24 homers to go with his 86 RBIs and .281 average, but the other two that round out the Big Three—Van Slyke and Bonds—were not in a groove.

Van Slyke hit only .237 with nine homers. Bonds played in 159 games. He finished second among NL outfielders in assists with 14, and stole 32 of 42 bases. He also struck out as much (93) as he walked. Bonds' average was a pedestrian .248 to go with 19 home runs and 34 doubles.

One bright spot in Pittsburgh was shortstop Jay Bell, who showed signs of emerging stardom. Drabek, John Smiley and Bob Walk all posted winning records, but Leyland's team never got off the ground and played to their potential.

The next season, Pittsburgh put it all together. The Mets were getting old, Chicago found its usual water level (77-85), and Herzog's Cardinals, who had survived with speed in the 1980s, lacked a step.

Buck Rodgers' Montreal Expos had talent in the form of Andres Galarraga, Tim Wallach and Rock Raines, but the Pirates had all engines firing. Leyland's team demonstrated the power of the Mets and the aggressiveness of the Cardinals. Drabek came into his own to win the Cy Young award with a beautiful 22-6 record to go with a 2.76 ERA. Leyland's bullpen did it by committee, however, and despite their 95-67 record, this was considered their weak area heading into the Championship Series. Jim Gott had left to pitch for his hometown team, the Dodgers, and when the game was on the line, the Pirate skipper had to go to Bill Landrum, Stan Belinda or Ted Power.

Bream hit 15 home runs playing first base. Bell played fine defense. Third baseman Jeff King contributed 14 homers, and at the hot corner, Bobby Bo became a star. He hit .280 with 32 homers and 120 runs batted in. Van Slyke hit .284 and played excellent defense in center.

The real reason the team won the East Division was left fielder Barry Bonds, and the biggest reason for the surge in his performance was his being moved from the lead-off spot to an RBI position in the order. Bonds had been lobbying Leyland for this opportunity for a couple of seasons, but it was only now that the manager felt it was an appropriate move.

"I put him in leadoff because most young players aren't ready to knock in runs, it's good experience for 'em," Leyland told "Sports Century."

"I thought my ability was just being wasted, it was ridiculous, to lead the team in home runs hitting leadoff," responded Bonds. "I went into his office, and he said, 'Sink or swim, son.' I said, 'Sir, I've been swimming all my life.'"

The result was his first MVP award in 1990. That was the year that Bonds made the National League All-Star team for the first time (0-for-1, one run scored). He joined Cincinnati's Eric Davis in 1987 as the second player in history to hit 30 homers and steal 50 bases (third in the league) in a season. He led the league with a .565 slugging percentage and threw out 14 base runners testing his arm, which was stronger, and just as accurate, in those days.

Bonds was the league's Player of the Month in July, the Player of the Week for April 23-29, and the Major League Player of the Year, according to *The Sporting News.* He came on strong down the stretch, along with his team, finishing at .301 with 33 home runs and 114 runs batted in. One of the most important, yet overlooked, statistics was his strikeout-to-walk ratio. For the first time in his Major League career (and the only time other than his 44 games at Hawaii in 1986), he walked more (93) than he struck out (83). While Bonds' statistics in his Pittsburgh years do not match up with his record in San Francisco from 2000-01, it should be noted that, while weight training was in vogue by then, the players had not honed it into the efficient, strength-gaining, supplement-induced practice that it is today. Bonds was lean and mean, but not the monster that we see today. Offensive numbers were not as impressive during this period in baseball history. There were a lot of good pitchers in both leagues, and expansion was still three years away.

Oakland was the defending World Champions, and with the Bash Brothers, Mark McGwire and Jose Canseco, along with two 20-game winners, Bob Welch and Dave Stewart, along with the great Rickey Henderson, all in their primes, they looked to be a team for the ages, a dynasty. They swept Roger Clemens and Boston in their Championship Series. Whatever team emerged from the National League would have their hands full.

At first, it looked like the Pirates. Their opponents were another young, aggressive club, the Cincinnati Reds. Manager Lou Piniella's club had started out hot, and after weathering a slump, held on to win in the West.

Cincinnati and Pittsburgh had startling similarities. Both were established franchises with proud traditions. Both moved from old ballparks with character to cookie-cutter, all-purpose Astroturf monstrosities in 1970. Both had dominated the National League in the 1970s, when their play-off battles had been the stuff of legend.

In 1972, the Pirates were three outs away from the World Series— where they would have played Oakland—when Cincinnati catcher Johnny Bench hit a home run to tie it. The Reds did not stop there, winning it on Bob Moose's wild pitch. They met each other in 1970, 1972, 1975 and 1979, with the Reds winning the first four times. The "We Are Family" Pirates beat Tom Seaver in the '79 NLCS opener in extra innings, en route to a three-game sweep.

Both clubs had experienced down years and scandals in the 1980s. The pre-Leyland Pirate clubhouse had been a drug bazaar. The Reds were battered by allegations that their manager, the legendary Pete Rose, had bet on baseball, an issue that still hangs over the game to this day.

Like Pittsburgh, the Reds had regrouped with a new manager and young, exciting players like Davis, shortstop Barry Larkin, outfielder Paul O'Neill, starting pitchers Jose Rijo (Juan Marichal's son-in-law) and Danny Jackson. They featured a tough bullpen that compares with the one Joe Torre has had in New York in the late 1990s and early 2000s. They called them the "Nasty Boys," a term apropos to the high, inside heat they threw, and the attitude behind them. Left-handers Randy Myers and Norm Charlton were tall, strong left-handers who brought it in the high 90s. Rob Dibble was the same dose from the right side. Charlton and Dibble are actually nice guys off the field. Dibble has even carved out a successful sports radio career for himself alongside ESPN's Dan Patrick. Myers was a different kind of animal, prone to wearing Army fatigues with hand grenades, which nobody really could tell were live or not, hanging from his sides.

The two teams met on the plastic grass of Riverfront, where Reds owner Marge Schott employed lackeys to scrape up her dog's frequent bowel movements, in the opener. In a classic game, Cincinnati tagged Bob Walk for three first-inning runs, but Bonds kept his club's attitude up. No Jim Leyland team ever gave up. They were scrapers and clawers, and young Bonds had materialized into a classic Leyland prodigy in his first MVP season.

After picking up a single run in the third and two more in the fourth on Bream's homer with a man on, Pittsburgh knocked Rijo out in the sixth, then went to work on Charlton in the seventh. The usually reliable Davis mis-played Van Slyke's fly ball in the top of the seventh, allowing what would prove to be the winning run to score. Belinda, Bob Patterson and Power, the bullpen by committee, held the lead.

With Doug Drabek going in game two, Pittsburgh looked to be in good shape. O'Neill, who along with Larkin was a Cincinnati kid, drove in both runs off Drabek, who went the distance in a 2-1 loss against Tom Browning and two-thirds of the Nasty Boys—Dibble and Myers.

Three Rivers Stadium, which sits on the banks of the Monongahela, Allegheny and Ohio Rivers, had a rock concert atmosphere in those days. Baseball had picked up on the music and emotional crowd exhortations of the NBA, where Michael Jordan was emerging as a superstar at that time. Their fans were excited after an 11-year play-off drought.

Unfortunately, good Cincinnati pitching stopped Bonds and the good Pittsburgh hitting. Danny Jackson went 5 1/3 innings for the Reds, allowing two runs to pick up the win, with all three Nasty Boys closing it out from there.

Rijo beat Walk in the next game to put his team up, 3-1. This time, Chris Sabo's two-run homer broke a seventh-inning tie, and Davis threw out Bonilla trying to stretch a double into a triple in the bottom of the eighth. Dibble closed out the 5-3 victory with a scoreless ninth.

Drabek was up to the challenge in the sixth game at Cincinnati, going 8 1/3 innings to fend off the Reds, 3-2. The offensive star for the Pirates was not Bonds, who continued to flounder at the plate, but Van Slyke, who drove in a run with a triple and then scored himself.

Pitching again dominated the final game, a 2-1 Reds victory to win the series. Jackson went six, and Myers earned the save in a one-hitter. Glenn Braggs saved the day by making a brilliant ninth-inning catch of a ball that looked to be a homer, and just like that, the season was over.

In six games, Bonds was 3-for-18 (.167), scored four times, drove in a run, had no extra-base hits, walked six times but struck out five times, and stole two bases.

That off-season was one of mixed feelings for Bonds. He was named Most Valuable Player in November.

"He's coming of age," Leyland told the press when the award was announced, but the player wanted a contract that would put him in the pay scale of other superstars of that era.

He also had to fend off nagging doubts and catcalls from the press and fans about the discrepancy between his regular season and postseason performance. When he showed up for Spring Training in Bradenton, Florida, in February, he was filled with attitude. He had taken Leyland's advice to avoid the press to extremes. He did not simply avoid them, he disdained them.

Bonds would use his glove to shoo people away from him like flies during practice sessions. He would see cameras, stop, stare at the photographer, and ask, "Is this candid camera?"

The media wanted to know about the MVP—his marriage to an exotic Montreal beauty of Swedish descent (Sun), his star father, superstar Godfather, where he and the flamboyant Bonilla went at night.

"He was a young boy, and he felt like when you are on the field, if you give 100 percent, that should be it, and what you do off the field should be irrelevant," Bobby Bonds told "Sports Century."

"Some newspaper people were hard on his dad, and at times that bothered him," former Serra Coach Stevens, shedding some light on Bonds' early feelings about the press, told "Sports Century."

"If you think that's gonna breed a son whose open to the media and fans, that's not gonna happen," Thomas Boswell of the *Washington Post* told ESPN, in reference to Barry's awareness of his father's press dealings.

"There might be two or three days from Spring Training to the end of the season when Barry would be as good and open and as frank as anybody I've ever been around," Paul Meyer told ESPN, "and the next day, nothing again. Bottom line is I don't think Barry really cared what we thought. He just wanted to go out on the field and hit, run, throw."

"Barry brought a lot of this on himself," said Rooker. "He never went out of his way to be accommodating."

On the heels of acrimonious contract negotiations, in which Bonds did not engender sympathy from Pittsburgh's fans or writers, an incident occurred involving press liaison Jim Lachima.

"He was involved in some drills," said Lachima, "and he didn't want cameras in that area."

Bonds let the cameramen know that, loudly.

"He told me that he would decide who took his picture, not me," recalled Lachima.

Bonds showed the photographers the baseball he was holding, as if threatening to throw it at them. Bonds then got in Lachima's face, swearing at him and telling him to keep the (expletive deleted) away from him.

"I'll decide who'll be in my face," said Bonds, all the while waving his arms and causing attention, with all the media standing around watching, taking notes, and capturing it on camera.

Pirate coach Bill Virdon saw what was happening.

"I was working with the outfielders, and right out of the blue Barry's yapping and yelling and causing a big hubbub, raising hell, ranting and raving," Virdon said on "Sports Century." "He says, 'Nobody's gonna tell me what to do,' and of course that hit me wrong."

Bonds got in Virdon's face, yelling and swearing, all pissed off, showing no respect.

By this time, Leyland saw what was going on. He saw Barry yelling at Virdon, and just snapped. He got in *Bonds'* face, swearing, yelling, pissed. Leyland can have a very short fuse.

At this point, there is no doubt what Bonds should have done. Jim Leyland is not a big man, but when he gets mad it can make the hair stand up on the back of your neck. He is fury. Bonds should have waited until Leyland was finished, bowed his head, and said, "I'm sorry, Skip. You're right. I lost my head. My bad."

Is that what happened? Uhhh…

Barry yelled back at Leyland, which was definitely not his best move at that point.

"*Don't fuck with me*," Leyland kept saying.

"I'm not fucking with you," Bonds tried to reply.

"*I said don't fuck with me*," Leyland repeated, getting madder by the second. "I'M THE MANAGER OF THIS TEAM AND I'M GONNA TELL YOU WHAT TO DO AND YOU'RE GONNA DO IT AND IF YOU GODDAMN DON'T LIKE IT YOU CAN GO SOMEPLACE ELSE. I'M THE MANAGER OF THIS FUCKIN' TEAM."

When Leyland said that, Bonds made a waving motion with his glove, as if to discount Leyland. Another bad move. It was left up to co-star Bonilla to rescue Barry from the situation and separate the two. He then put his arm around Barry, and led him away to cool down.

"It was just a reaction," Leyland recalled on "Sports Century." "My temper got the best of me and maybe his got the best of him." However, when the writers and cameras caught up with Leyland later that day, he was still steaming.

"*I'm the manager of this fucking team, and anybody who doesn't like that can go someplace else*," Leyland repeated to them in his office.

Bonds' explanation was that he was mad because a friend of his was on the field taking pictures, but the team had told him he could not be there, even though Barry was paying him to take the photographs. There were others photographers on the field, and his friend was the only one they told could not be there.

Some say this was the best thing to happen to Bonds. Leyland was the first to ever stand up to him, at least since becoming a star. Brock had tried to stand up to him at Arizona State, but his efforts at discipline seemed to be more for show.

If his performance, and the performance of the club is any indication, this analysis is right on point. In 1991, the Pirates were the class of baseball— during the regular season. This was a year that ushered in a new era. The powerful A's slumped badly, and out of no where, the Minnesota Twins won their division. In the National League West, the Braves came from last place and, on the strength of an exciting, young pitching staff that included Tom Glavine, John Smoltz and Steve Avery, held off Los Angeles by one game to win it.

If one were to ask pundits prior to 1991 who the Team of the '90s would be, however, the consensus would not have been the Braves, but the Pirates. The Bucs were loaded.

The Persian Gulf War had been fought and won during the off-season, and the country had experienced a great patriotic fervor. President George Herbert Walker Bush had been riding 90 percent approval ratings in February, but a nation's attention span is fickle and short-lived.

Once the parades ended, Americans began to realize that the economy was in a recession. Economists will tell you that economies are cyclical in nature, and a President's policies cannot really change this inevitability. That, of course, does not deter the loyal opposition from playing the blame game.

Some U.S. cities are affected by these cycles more than others are. Pittsburgh and its steel industry is one of those places, and the town went through hard times during the 1991 Recession. If out-of-work steelworkers were looking for somebody to blame, they were not finding fault with their Pirates.

By this time, Leyland's reputation was assured. Here was a guy who knew how to "handle" black players. Bonilla, the kid from the inner city, and the spoiled son of baseball royalty, Bonds. He handled the Latino players who did not speak English and the Southern boys who went duck hunting in the winter. The fans loved Leyland, who came from a family of people who were not afraid to tackle the hard, unglamorous jobs that count to the hilt. The media respected him because he told them the truth. He did not care about a player's religion, sex life or choice of music. He cared only that they come to the park prepared, did their work, and gave him 100 percent in the games.

One example of the Leyland Philosophy came after Bonds left Pittsburgh. Al Martin is a flawed man who went through elaborate gyrations to cheat on his wife. He "married" one of his groupies in a ceremony in Las Vegas, but later claimed that he did not think the Elvis-type ceremony was legal. Apparently it was, and so bigamy allegations were leveled at him. He was accused of sticking a gun in the mouth of one of his "wives," telling her "I'll O.J. you." *Niiiice.* Martin told writers that he made a tackle for USC in a Rose Bowl game, but he had quit the Trojan football team before ever playing in a game. On the field, however, Martin played hard and with intensity. When he replaced Bonds as Pittsburgh's left fielder beginning in 1993, Leyland loved him for his hard-nosed style—on the field.

Leyland also was not a grudge-keeper. Once a player aired his feelings, Leyland would close the issue and move on. Consequently, after the Spring Training flare-up with Bonds, the issue was resolved and forgotten.

Sid Bream was gone to Atlanta, but Jose Lind and Jay Bell made a strong double-play combination. Bonilla was moved back to right field, and he hit .302 with 18 homers and 100 RBIs. Van Slyke's statistics were almost the same as the year before, unspectacular but, by 1991 standards, productive at .265-17-83.

Drabek slumped to 15-14, but left-hander John Smiley picked him up with a 20-8 record and a 3.08 ERA. Zane Smith won 15, while Stan Belinda and Bill Landrum combined for 33 saves. The division race was never in doubt, with Pittsburgh winning it with baseball's best record, 98-64, over St. Louis (88-74).

Bonds threw out 13 runners from left field while committing just three errors, was Player of the Week (with Will Clark) at the end of July, was second in the league in sacrifice flies and intentional walks, and drove in a run once every 4.4 at-bats, the best in baseball. He had 116 RBIs and hit .292 with 25 home runs, stole 43 bases in 56 tries, walked 107 times against only 73 strikeouts, scored 95 runs with 149 hits, including 28 doubles and five three-baggers.

Bonds should have been named National League MVP. Instead, the award went to Atlanta third baseman Terry Pendleton, a good ball player who will never be mistaken with a Hall of Famer. Did Bonds' personality cost him votes? Probably, but the fact that he had won it the year before also hurt him. Writers often tend to dole out the "goodies" in a manner they consider to be evenhanded. This theory helps explain why Oakland's Jason Giambi did not repeat as AL Most Valuable Player in 2001.

Pendleton, a third baseman on a team that won with pitching, outhit Bonds by 26 points, but his 86 runs batted in paled next to Bonds' 116. Pendleton's numbers in their frantic seven-game Championship Series with Pittsburgh failed to answer any head-to-head questions, as he batted only .167 with no homers.

Just as they had the previous year, the East Division-champion Pirates started the proceedings in fine fettle when Drabek beat Cy Young winner Glavine, 5-1. Van Slyke's homer and double drove in two runs.

The rest of the series was gut-wrenching and filled with nail-biting pressure. Pittsburgh and Bonds simply did not hit, and while it is easy to condemn Bonds for this, one has to acknowledge the dominance of the Braves' tremendous pitching staff. They stuffed bats up all Pirates' butts, if you will excuse the quasi-sexual connotation, giving it to them from the left side, the right side, up and in, hard and soft.

In the second game, southpaw Steve Avery, a hard-thrower with a sweeping curveball thrown from three-quarters overhand in the manner later seen by Mark Mulder of the A's, quieted the Three Rivers crowd that had started the night in the usual rock concert manner. Atlanta scored a single run in the sixth, and Avery made it stand up, 1-0.

With the series tied 1-1 it was back to Atlanta, where Smiley was ineffective. Smoltz won the first of many big postseason games over the next decade, 10-3. The next day, the Pirates evened things up when pinch-hitter

Mike LeValliere's single drove in Van Slyke, who had walked, then stole second, with the game-winner in the tenth, 3-2.

Zane Smith, who had lost 1-0 to Avery, outdueled Glavine in a classic fifth game, 1-0, to put Pittsburgh up heading back home.

Avery, a blazing young star whose ascent to Cooperstown would be derailed by nagging injuries, was again phenomenal in the sixth game. The game was tied, 0-0, until the ninth, when Ron Gant walked, stole second, and scored on Greg Olson's double.

It all came down to the seventh game, which can be described in two words.

JOHN SMOLTZ.

The hard-throwing Atlanta right-hander tossed a fabulous six-hit, complete game at Leyland's club to send his own team to the Big Dance with a 4-0 shutout.

Bonds was 4-for-27 with no RBIs. People were focusing on him not producing in the play-offs for the second straight year. Van Slyke was no better at .160, although he did have three RBIs and made things happen enough to score three times. Bonilla managed to go 7-for-23, and Bell hit .414. It was not enough.

"He just tried too hard to hit three-run homers with nobody on base," Braves ace Tom Glavine said. Glavine was a "nibbler" who took advantage of Bonds' overexuberance.

"I'm not trying too hard," Bonds told reporters who relayed Glavine's comments to him.

Teammate Jeff King was injured during that series.

"He made public statements about Jeff King not playing with pain, when maybe he should have been," said Jim Rooker.

The next day's headlines had read, "Bonds Royally Rips Kings' Absence."

"It's awful hard for any athlete to look at another teammate and question his heart, or his gut," said Andy Van Slyke on "Sports Century."

Bonds was all of 1-for-20 at the time. "I may be hitting under .200 but it's a hard .200," he had said.

The economy had still not turned the corner in 1992, when Leyland's team returned from Florida ready to do it again. The economy of baseball had reared its ugly head in the form of free agency, too. On December 2, 1991 Bobby Bonilla signed with his hometown team, the New York Mets. The great Barry Bonds was heading into the last year of his contract, and he was devastated. Years later, he would say that this occurrence, the "loss" of his best friend, would change his entire outlook on the game. From this point on, all future teammates would simply be "temporary colleagues."

If part of Leyland's strategy was to motivate his star and his team into winning the division because it would be their last time together, it worked.

For the third straight season, Pittsburgh won their division handily. In this era of free agency, such a feat almost makes this a dynasty.

Don Slaught hit .345 splitting time with Mike LeValliere behind the plate. Van Slyke, coming into his own, hit .324 with 89 RBIs. Drabek, a 15-game winner, again led the pitching staff with a 2.77 earned run average.

The 96-66 Pirates found the 98-64 Braves waiting for them in the NLCS again. Again, Atlanta did it with pitching, particularly in the form of the crafty Glavine at 20-8 with a 2.76 ERA.

In 1992, Bonds hit .311 with 34 home runs and 103 runs batted in. The key to his offensive game was discipline and knowledge accumulated over seven seasons in the Majors, as exemplified by his 127 bases on balls vs. just 69 strikeouts. Speed was still part of his repertoire, as he stole 39 bases. He hit five triples and 34 doubles in 140 games, and scored 109 runs. Defense? He won his third straight Gold Glove and committed just three errors.

He was April's Player of the Month and never let up from there, except for a stretch on the disabled list in July. He was elected as a starter on the All-Star team for the first time, and in September put on a performance that would come to be seen as his patented, end-of-season run.

There are several reasons why great players tend to do well in September. For one, lesser players lose focus while great ones maintain theirs. Teams that drop out of the race may be dogging it, and a lot of younger players are given a shot, especially when rosters are expanded.

Bonds, like him or not, has matured into a player with focus, a worker, a dedicated athlete who yearns to win. In Pittsburgh, he gave everything he had to get his teams into the postseason. Did he simply having nothing left to challenge the great talents of Atlanta's pitchers?

"Here's a guy winning two MVPs, he's getting us to the play-offs, but once we're there, he disappeared," Bob Walk told "Sports Century."

The two Championship Series between Atlanta and Pittsburgh in 1991 and 1992 go down in history along with some of the most intense postseason rivalries in sports. The nature of the games, the intensity, and building pressure of these games rank with the Dodger-Yankee Subway Series of the 1950s; the Packer-Cowboy NFL Play-Off games of 1966-67; the Raider-Steeler battles of the 1970s; and the longstanding Celtic-Laker rivalry

Then there was Smoltz! Bonds must wake up at night seeing his mustachioed visage peering in for the sign; the wind-up and big kick; the horsehide traveling hard and swift to an unhittable corner of the plate. For eight innings on October 6, he did just that, in a tidy four-hitter over eight innings, for the 5-1 win. Ex-Pirate Bream, the man who once wanted to beat up Barry Bonds, was now a Brave, and he had two hits and scored twice to lead the victory.

The passions of the games, the rivalry, the pressure, were building up like the crescendo of Shakespeare's "Othello." In game two, the Bucs knew only frustration. A four-run second inning was all that Avery needed in Atlanta's 13-4 victory, forcing Bonds and his team back home down 2-0, with their backs against the wall.

They needed to rally. Staying with the Shakespeare theme, Leyland may not be a modern Henry V, urging his "band of brothers" to rally against a powerful enemy, but he does not accept losing well. He has a way of forcing his men to pick themselves up and come back, no matter how dreary the circumstances. This is one of the reasons Bonds, who also hates to lose, admires the man so much.

It would not be easy. Knuckleballer Tim Wakefield was facing Glavine at Three Rivers Stadium, but the rookie was up to the task. He went the distance, baffling the Braves with an assortment of floating knucklers. Van Slyke's sacrifice fly in the seventh gave his club the edge, and he and his mates hung on for dear life to crawl back in it, winning 3-2.

Then came Smoltz again, for six and a third innings over Drabek. Now the Pirates not only felt the wall, but also could see the Braves loading their weapons and forming a firing squad.

Bonds finally showed life in a play-off game the next day. With his team down three games to one, he, King and Lloyd McClendon hit consecutive run-scoring doubles in a four-run first inning. Avery was knocked out with only one out, and Walk went the distance in a 7-1 victory that sent the series back to Atlanta with the Braves up, 3-2.

In game six, Bonds again showed up. He led off the second inning with a homer off Glavine, igniting an eight-run inning. Wakefield went the distance, the Pirates won, 13-4, and it was time for the rubber match.

There was John Smoltz standing in their way, but he had to be tired, trying for his third win of the series. The Pirates touched him in the first, 1-0. They scored another run in the sixth. Inning after inning, Doug Drabek held off Atlanta. Goose eggs.

Now, we are in the ninth inning at Atlanta-Fulton County Stadium. Last chance for the home team. The fans, standing as one, and in full Tomahawk Chop. Even Jane Fonda woke up and lifted her head off Ted Turner's shoulder.

"C'mon, baby," says Barry Bonds to himself, slapping his glove against his thigh in left field. "Three more outs."

It was not to be. The Braves rallied, had one run in, and men on second and third with one. Drabek was gone, Stan Belinda was in. Francisco Cabrera, a journeyman, was at the plate. Standing at second base, the potential winning run, stood Bream, who nobody will ever mistake for Maury Wills.

Bonds hears something. The place is a cacophony of noise, but he looks over at Van Slyke in center field. He is whistling to him.

Bonds motions with his glove, "What, Andy?"

Van Slyke uses his glove to motion, "Move in and to your left."

Bonds does not budge.

McClendon sees the exchange.

"Why isn't Barry moving over?" he thinks to himself.

Van Slyke sees Barry remain deep and close to the line.

"C'mon, Barry," but to no avail.

Belinda whips a sidearm pitch to Francisco Cabrera. Whip! A base hit, to left field. To Bonds' left. Bonds rushes in, valuable steps. Bream rounds third. Bonds reaches down and fields the ball.

Heart pumping. Clean pick. Hop-skip for momentum.

"Find the target." Look up, there is the catcher, fire it, center mass. Bream running.

Throwing a baseball is a delicate act. A slight twist of the wrist, finger pressure, releasing it at just the right or wrong point. Bonds' throw looked at first to be there, but veered slightly off, bounced, and came to the catcher a few feet up the first base line.

It was not a bad throw, but it was not perfect. Somehow, it represents the ever-so-close nature that has always tinged Bonds' career with semi-tragic imperfection. In the mind's eye, one is convinced that Mays or DiMaggio would have made that throw.

Bream, no speedster, barely eluded the tag for the game-winner.

Bonds watched Bream score, dropped to his knees, then just walked off the field.

Drabek became the first pitcher to ever lose three games in one series.

This was not Shakespeare, it was Charles Dickens. *Bleak House.*

Bonds acknowledged that Van Slyke had signaled him, but defended his decision not to do so. He said that Van Slyke, being a center fielder, could roam more, but said, "if he hits a bullet that ball's gonna go by me." Today he uses positioning to make up for the fact that his arm is not as strong as it was then.

"The ball was to my left, coming across your left to have to make that throw, across your body, the play was still close," Bonds told "Sports Century." "There were other chances for us to win that had nothing to do with me."

"Once again they focused on Barry because he was the star," said Leyland. "Barry didn't choke, and I don't think anybody should judge his career by that."

The soft crying of Bonds interrupted the stone silence of the losing clubhouse.

Now, the emphasis shifted to his future. Leyland told Bonds there was no way Pittsburgh could afford him, and the team never offered him a contract. Toward the end of his last season at Pittsburgh, Bonds was interviewed on the field by a Pittsburgh TV personality, amid fans' shouts of "Stay Barry, stay."

The Pirates knew they had lost Bonds. Bonilla was gone. They had kept it together for one more season, and came agonizingly close to going to the World Series, but now they were reconciled to facing a rebuilding period.

Other teams have dealt with the question of losing a superstar. In Minnesota, the Twins had a player, Kirby Puckett, who was not just a Hall of Famer, but valuable to the team because of his high standing in the community. The same thing in San Diego with Gwynn. Bonds?

"There were players on his own team who would go up to him and give him a baseball, and he won't sign it," Jim Rooker told "Sports Century." "I've never heard of that anywhere."

"I think Barry wants the best for his teammates on the field, but he certainly communicates that `you're not important to me, off the field,'" said Andy van Slyke.

"If you want a friend, buy a dog," Bonds once said in Pittsburgh. Such warmth! Bonds had not been happy that Van Slyke was making twice as much. Bonds called him the "Great White Hope."

"Barry and Bobby both lost arbitration cases," recalled pitcher John Smiley. "Doug Drabek and myself both won, they were trying to say it was a black thing. I don't think his agent was too prepared. How can you put up numbers like that and lose an arbitration case?"

Bonds won his second MVP award.

"He saw other guys getting taken care of, guys who were not as integral to the club as he was," said Perrotto on "Sports Century."

Bonds in Pittsburgh was not meant to be.

CHAPTER
FOUR

"It's like a dream that's come true for me."

Peter Magowan, who ran Safeway Stores, had saved the Giants from St. Petersburg, Florida. It was a masterstroke of genius, a bold move that threatened the team's shaky economic stability. It also put them on the road to recovery at the same time. Magowan outbid all the usual suspects in the free-agent sweepstakes of 1992-93. Barry Bonds never really considered any other possibility. He came home for $43.75 million for seven years, the largest contract in baseball history at the time.

When Bonds arrived in San Francisco, his first request was to unretire Mays' number 24, the number he wore at Arizona State and Pittsburgh.

"Barry is usually not deferential to public opinion," KNBR sports personality Ralph Barbieri told "Sports Century." "I think he picked up that one, then he went to his father's number." He would wear number 25.

"Every time I step on that field," Barry told his contract-signing press conference prior to the 1993 season, of playing at Candlestick Park, "I know my Godfather's in center field and my dad's in right field. It's like a dream that's come true for me."

Now 28, he was, according to Chris Fowler on ESPN's "Sports Century," a "man in full," to borrow a Tom Wolfe phrase. He had hit .275 with 176 home runs in Pittsburgh.

Bonds homered in his first at-bat as a Giant. During an early-season series against Pittsburgh, off to a good start in 1993 despite having lost many top players, Bonds said the Bucs' strong effort was not unexpected because, "Nothing about a Jim Leyland team surprises me."

Bonds has said that whenever it appears that things are going his way, something happens to keep him from fully enjoying it. Is it hard to empathize with him when he says that? Still, his arrival in San Francisco was not completely smooth.

"He was labeled as a choker on a team that had a hard inner core of established vets," said Nick Peters on "Sports Century." "He was hard to get along with, and his reputation preceded him." The main "hardcore veteran" was first baseman Will Clark.

Will Clark *was* the Giants from 1986 to 1992. He had broken in with a home run off Nolan Ryan. He had led the 1989 Giants over the Cubs in the Championship Series, and into their first World Series since 1962.

"Pressure?" he had repeated in his squeaky-Southern twang, to a question about performing in the NLCS. "This is what ya play for."

He was considered a "redneck," a good ol' boy from Louisiana, and the inference was that the no-nonsense Clark had problems with black players. He had supposedly had run-ins with the likes of Jeffrey Leonard and Kevin Mitchell in the past, although these were blown out of proportion by the media.

"When he showed up, it was suddenly Barry's show, and I'm sure they didn't take to this brash young guy coming in," said Peters of the "Clark faction." Read: White players.

"It was like if a team had a quarterback and another quarterback arrives, it's always rocky at first," recalled then first-year manager Baker.

Baker was the key. He is black and a lifelong friend of the Bonds family.

One baseball insider, a black man who wished not to be identified, had this to say about Baker.

"Dusty comes off with the white people in the media as fair, not affected by color," this man said. "Let me tell you something. Dusty Baker is *black*. He grew up with prejudice, he remembers prejudice, he never forgot it, and get him away from whites, away from the media, and he *talks black*. He doesn't want to let you know that, but he talks the jive and understands that he has to be better and play the game with the media. But make no mistake, Baker is *black*."

Whatever Baker is, he made Bonds comfortable and was in his corner, and he established himself right away with every player on the team, all the media, and with the fans. Bonds was his usual arrogant self.

"He walked into a pitchers meeting and started pointing, 'I got you, and I got you, and you,' every guy he homered off," recalled Bud Geracie of the *San Jose Mercury News*, on "Sports Century." "He immediately had problems in that room."

It was also around this time that his private life unraveled, in the form of his six-year marriage to Sun, which ended in divorce. She claimed that he had physically attacked her, but no charges were filed in court. Bonds did not like his personal life discussed in the media.

"I don't think anybody likes mudslinging," said Bobby Bonds.

"All the newspapers think I'm some crazy lunatic dude, but they don't even know the truth," said Bonds. The press loved the juicy story of the swinging bachelor athlete who married the sexy Canadian with a past. They considered that these were two tempestuous personalities, and by no means discounted the possibility that either one of them physically struck the other.

"Bonds Denies Abusing Ex-Wife," read one headline. It was not far from "Bonds Quits Abusing Ex-Wife," and it also examined her "tantrums."

"It's very easy to sit from afar and dislike him because a writer or a journalist said he's not a nice guy," entertainer Bill Cosby, who has advised Barry on how to improve his image, a practice he has engaged in with African-American athletes over the years, told ESPN.

"I thought about quitting," Barry recalled of this stressful time.

"I remember one time at Candlestick he was in the on-deck circle during a day game," recalled Barbieri, "and some heckler yelled, 'Hey Barry, where's your wife?' and he turned around and said, 'I don't know, maybe she spent last night with you.' Then he got up to the plate and hit one into the upper deck."

"He carried that team in 1993 all the way through," said Geracie.

He sure did. In comparing Bonds with Mays, Willie has gotten the edge in part because his game had a quicksilver quality to it. There was the flying cap, the head turned to look at the outfield to see where the throw was while he rounded the bases in a fury. There was the lunging swing, and the easy manner of Mays warming up before a game, throwing sidearm.

Bonds is an automaton on the field. He plays the game with cold efficiency. He is a killer, a machine. His hat stays on his head. He eyes each pitch like the guy who stares through the "Eye in the Sky" at The Mirage.

In 1993, however, the Giants as a team had quicksilver. Every once in a while it happens. In recent years, the Braves and Twins had gone from last-to-first. The 1967 Boston Red Sox and the 1969 New York Mets had made the leap.

Roger Craig's 1992 squad had finished at 72-90, playing before friends and family at the windswept 'stick. Clark hit .300, but there were few other bright spots. Baker took over, the club went to Scottsdale with Bonds, and started hot. Bonds ripped early and often. Pundits waited for the contenders to become pretenders. The two-time champion Braves, despite adding Cy Young award-winner Greg Maddux to their formidable roster, struggled.

Bonds pushed and prodded his team, in a way that few really could envision even Mays having done. Perhaps in 1962, when Mays played the game with such hard ferocity that he had to be hospitalized for exhaustion, but Mays had a lot of talent to help him.

It was not that the '93 Giants were not talented, it was just that everybody had a career year, and it would be hard to not credit the newcomer Bonds with inspiring his mates to play above themselves.

Bonds, in 1993, resembled Joe DiMaggio in 1949. Substitute the Giants for the Yankees, the Braves for the Red Sox. It may have been David vs. Goliath, but David carried a big stick.

Bonds garnered 3,074,603 votes for the All-Star Game. Batting second at Baltimore's Oriole Park at Camden Yards, Bonds started in left field and went 2-for-3 (two doubles) and scored twice.

His home run, RBI and batting average totals would have won him the Triple Crown in five of the previous seven seasons, and his .677 slugging percentage was the highest in franchise history.

This is a franchise that has seen not just Mays and McCovey, but Mel Ott and Bill Terry. He was walked intentionally 43 times, the second-highest total in Major League history. He scored five runs on August 4 at San Diego. He stole three bases August 20 against the Marlins. He was the Player of the Month in April.

Bonds took his game to a new plane in 1993, hitting .336 with 46 home runs and 124 runs batted in, scoring 129 runs in 159 games, garnered 181 hits, 38 doubles, 126 walks against 79 strikeouts, and stole 29 bases.

He was the *Associated Press* Major League Player of the Year, and a consensus All-Star (*UPI, The Sporting News, Associated Press*). His batting average was higher than 27 National League players who had won the homer and RBI crowns in the same season since 1937, when Ducky Medwick of St. Louis had won the league's last Triple Crown.

He won another Players Choice award as Player of the Year. He won another Gold Glove. He led the league in slugging percentage and on-base percentage, which are statistics he has always dominated and may tell the story of his greatness as well as any numbers in his record. He was named winner of the S. Rae Hickok Belt Award as the nation's top professional athlete. He hit .333 with six homers and seven doubles, with 21 RBIs and an .860 slugging percentage down the last 16-game stretch, when every game counted. He won his third MVP award.

By August, Atlanta had recovered and turned the West into a dogfight. It was the last year of the two-division format. Florida and Colorado had joined the league, but the Central Division would not be created, and with it the wild card, until the next season. It was winner-take-all. Clark had a good, but not great, year, hitting .283, but second baseman Robby Thompson played over his head to finish at .312 with 19 home runs and 65 runs batted in.

Shortstop Royce Clayton was a defensive whiz. Third baseman Matt Williams, a hot-and-cold hitter his whole career, was in a hot stretch, hitting 38 home runs with 110 RBIs with a .294 average. Right fielder Willie McGee hit .301 with speed. Center fielder Darren Lewis provided, along with Bonds, the best outfield defensive combo in the game.

The key, aside from Bonds, was pitching. Two sinkerballers, Bill Swift (21-8, 2.82 ERA) and John Burkett (22-7, 3.65 ERA) held opponents for set-up man Mike Jackson (3.03 ERA in 81 games) and closer Rod Beck, another career-year guy with 48 saves and a 2.16 earned run average.

San Francisco entered the final four-game weekend series at Los Angeles, in a neck-and-neck battle with Bonds' old nemesis, Atlanta. On Thursday night, Bonds' home run won it. On Friday in a tie game, he homered off Omar Daal to win it again. He led Saturday's win before the team and Rod Beck ran out of gas on Sunday, falling one game short despite 103 wins.

The club drew 2,606,354 fans to regain financial stability.

That off-season, the team faced a decision on whether to sign Thompson or Clark. They made the wrong choice, letting a star player, Clark, go to Texas. They kept a good, but not a star player, Thompson. Clark's prickly attitude and perceived problems with Bonds contributed to the decision. It is difficult to imagine that there had been anything that brought the club down in Baker's first year. They had played to their absolute potential.

Nineteen ninety-four was a year that will live in baseball infamy. It was a year in which player greed and union intransigence combined to ruin a great season and derail a great game. On August 12, Williams had 43 home runs and was in a great position to overcome Maris' home run record, when the players greedily struck. The season ended with no World Series. They struck all winter, and missed the first part of the 1995 season. It took a long, long time for people to care about baseball again.

Bonds was on his way to another terrific season, maybe another MVP year. He hit 37 home runs and probably would have finished with 50. If he misses Hank Aaron's career record by 10 home runs, 1994 can be blamed.

A bone spur in his right elbow slowed him, barely. Playing before his old fans at Pittsburgh in the All-Star Game, he started and hit a sacrifice fly. He was named to *The Sporting News, AP* and *Baseball America* All-Star teams. He earned the National League Silver Slugger award, picked up another Gold Glove, hit three homers on August 2 against the Reds, and stole 29 bases.

To further recap 1994 is simply too depressing to do in these pages.

The next two seasons were "wilderness years" for Baker and his club. The 1995 club went 67-77 in a schedule shortened by the insidious strike, followed by a 68-94 season in 1996.

Bonds was as good as ever on a losing club. He led the National League in walks (120) and on-base percentage (.431). He scored 109 runs, hit 33 homers, drove in 104, had 292 total bases, slugged at a .577 rate, had 70 extra-base hits, and tied for the league-lead in assists with 12. Again, he was the league's leading vote-getter for the All-Star Game (1-for-3 batting third with an RBI at Veterans Stadium in a National League win, having bested Mark McGwire in the Home Run Contest the previous day).

He became the first Giant since his father to hit 30 homers and steal 30 bases, and on June 28 he stole a base against Colorado to make him and his dad the greatest father/son stolen-base combination in history, with 783. Maury and Bump Wills had held the previous record.

In 1996, the club would unload Williams, leaving Bonds exposed in a weak line-up. That did not stop him from playing some of the best baseball of his career. He joined Jose Canseco on the 40/40 Club, set the league record with 151 walks, intentional walks (30), RBI ratio (4.0) and home run ration (12.3). He started and went 0-for-2 in the All-Star Game at Cleveland, won the Gold Glove for the sixth time, and was Player of the Month in April (32 RBIs). Bonds hit .308, with 42 homers and 129 RBIs. Had his team contended, he would have been a fine MVP candidate.

"Barry might make two or three mistakes over the course of the year," Mays told *USA Baseball Weekly* in the spring of 1996, "and that's when I talk to him. Other than that, he knows what he's supposed to do."

When Mays was asked to help arrange for an interview with Bonds, Mays knew where to draw the line.

"Not Barry—Barry's in his own fucking world," Mays says.

"You can't get under my skin no more," Bonds had said to a small crowd of reporters in the clubhouse. "My life is a lot different and better now."

"He's made a conscientious effort—I've seen him signing autographs more this spring," Baker said shortly thereafter. "Sometimes Barry is tough to deal with, but most of the times he's a gentleman. He ain't phony or fake about anything."

Is it phony or fake to be courteous?

"I think what happened to Albert Belle last year [surliness probably cost Belle the MVP award] made him realize that sometimes you have to open up and let people get close," Tony Gwynn told *USA Baseball Weekly*. "He fights the media off, and he does it with players in the league, too."

At the 1995 All-Star Game in Texas, which was Bonds' fifth such appearance, Gwynn, Ozzie Smith and Bobby Bonilla tried to get their friend to relax with the press.

"We were telling him, 'Man, you've just got to loosen up, you've got to relax and be yourself. Let them see what you're all about,'" Gwynn said. "I said, 'Here's an opportunity for you to let these people get close, but will you do that? No.' And he said, 'You're right—I won't.' I know what's going on up there [in Bonds' head] and I can be a little more sympathetic than most people. I still say he's the best player in our league, without a question."

That spring, Bonds was asked about hitting 50 homers and stealing 50 bases.

"No, I don't think so," Bonds said. "I'm not that strong."

However, he was by this point in his career upgrading his workout regimen, supervised by personal trainer Raymond Farriss. Farriss also trained former NFL running back Roger Craig and all-world wide receiver Jerry Rice.

In four months, Bonds had lowered his body fat to eight percent from 12 percent, and was bench-pressing 315 pounds, up from 230. He had increased his explosiveness by running sprints. He now looked more muscular, more defined, more powerful, with bulging biceps stretching his jersey's sleeves.

"I thought I was in great shape the way I worked out before because I was putting up the numbers I did," Bonds said in *USA Baseball Weekly*, "but I was out of shape. I wanted to prove to myself that I could do it, and I'm happy with the results, but it doesn't guarantee success. I don't care how many weights you lift—you can lift until you're blue in the face—it doesn't guarantee success.

"I don't put a whole lot of emphasis on my training program. I don't say that it's going to win me an MVP."

Bonds by this time was officially referring to himself in the third person.

"I'm like Tony Gwynn now," Bonds continued, laughing. "If he hits .340, it's like, 'So? That's Tony.' If Barry Bonds hits 30 home runs and steals 30 bases, it's 'So? That's Barry.' It's harder for people to recognize it now because if somebody has one good year out of his career, it overshadows what I do consistently."

"The years he didn't win the MVP," Gwynn said, "if I had those years, I'd probably win it. That's the hole you dig for yourself. If you're more consistent than anybody in the National League and you do the same thing for five years, sometime around the third year, there's no glamour to it. He's just doing what he should be doing.

"It's going to take an ungodly year. In Barry Bonds' case, it might take 50-50 for him to be an MVP again. That, and the fact that he could do that and his team would probably have to win, too."

"If I ever did try to do that," Bonds said of a prospective 50-50, "I'd hit about .220. You'd have to be willing to give up something for it and I'm not willing to give up anything. I like the 30-30 and hitting .300 and driving in 100 and scoring 100. To me, that's as complete as you can be."

"He sees things quicker than any other player except Hank Aaron," Baker said. "He sees a pitcher flaring his glove on a changeup and he'll come back to the dugout and say, 'Did you see that?' Other guys don't see that until the sixth inning, if they see it at all. And once you can see it, you'll always be able to see it."

"I just know the game well, I guess," Bonds said. "I don't try to evaluate every little thing that other people are doing. I just try to keep myself mechanically sound and if they make a mistake and put it within that square, then if I'm mechanically sound, it doesn't really make a difference what they throw."

"He's probably more comfortable in those [clutch] situations than he is with nobody on in the first inning," Matt Williams told *USA Baseball Weekly*. "Playing against him and playing with him for the last couple of years, nothing he does surprises me. The more you see, you just accept that he's a special player."

"I think it's just that I don't like to lose," Bonds said. "I want to be up in that [clutch] situation to have a shot at it, but I don't have dreams about the World Series or having the bases loaded or nothing like that. My dreams are 9-0 and we're winning in the World Series rather than having a situation where there's a noose around my neck. I try to look at things a little easier than stressful."

"It's like in hockey in an overtime game, you anticipate Gretzky will score," Baker told the media. "In basketball, you know Michael Jordan is going to take the shot. In football, you know Jerry Rice is going to catch the pass. That's the real superstar—when everyone knows he's going to get the ball and he still scores or makes the play."

Bonds also addressed his reputation.

"I feel the press puts a stamp on certain players and once they stamp you as a 'bad person,' then that's what they feed on and there's nothing you can do about it," Bonds said. "I know in my heart the type of ballplayer I am and the type of person I am.

"Every time they say, 'Well, people say,' everyone knows it's just, 'The press says.' I mean, be honest—they didn't do a survey, they didn't really ask anybody.

"As many people as they say don't like you, I have that many people who do like me, so I don't worry about it."

In this respect, Bonds hit the nail on the head. Most of his "bad reputation" has been based on his relations with the media. He is occasionally standoffish with fans, and not always available for autographs, but this can be attributed to time constraints. He does have love in his heart, and a genuine desire to help people in need.

In the off-season, he joined Baker on an eight-game tour of Japan, where he hit .292 with a homer while the Major League All-Stars posted a 4-2-2 record.

In 1997, Baker and Sabean had reorganized the club into a surprise contender again. How they did it is still something of a mystery. Second baseman Jeff Kent, who had played college ball at nearby California, was a solid fielder with pop. First baseman J.T. Snow was a defensive whiz. Their opening day pitcher was Mark Gardner.

Mark Gardner?

The club went 90-72 and beat Los Angeles by two games to win the West outright. Third baseman Bill Mueller hit .292, and Shawn Estes emerged as a top pitcher with 19 victories, a 3.18 ERA, and 181 strikeouts in 201 innings.

How did they really do it? Two words. BARRY BONDS.

The Giants superstar hit .291 with 40 homers, 101 RBIs, 37 stolen bases, 123 runs scored, 145 walks, and started in left field in the All-Star Game (stealing a base). He hit *two* inside-the-park home runs against San Diego on September 21, so if he breaks Aaron's record by one, you know where to find that margin.

The Giants were two games behind Los Angeles with 12 to play when the Dodgers came to town. Bonds hit a homer in his first at-bat, and the Giants won eight of their last 10. Bonds had seven home runs and 14 runs batted in.

"When they made the play-offs, there's a shot of Barry running into the infield, waving his arms in pure joy, and the little boy in him came out," former teammate Matt Williams, who had been traded to Cleveland by then, told "Sports Century."

In the postseason, it was the same old story.

San Francisco faced the upstart, recent-expansion, wild-card Marlins in the first-round Division Series. Florida featured Bobby Bonilla and a host of free-agent stars cobbled together for a one-year run by Blockbuster Video owner Wayne Huizenga, who spent $89 million. By midseason, he was ready to sell the team because he said he was losing millions despite a 30 percent increase in attendance.

Bonds had three hits in three straight losses to the eventual World Champions.

"I remember during the playoffs, walking into the locker room, and Barry was under a sea of microphones, and his eyes were red and it hurt," observed actor Robert Wuhl.

Barry had made a guest appearance on Wuhl's HBO comedy, "Arli$$," about a craven sports agent. In the episode, Arliss says he wants him as a client because other players of less talent get more endorsement money than he does. Arliss asks him why that is?

"I'm too nice a guy?" replies Bonds.

"From time to time, I'll wear my ring, and he's taken it off and looked at it," Bonilla told ESPN. "And he's not said much, he just won't talk about it."

"There's times I just can't take the abuse anymore," said Bonds. "Everybody expects so much, and that's a lonely place to be."

The abuse? Bill Clinton took abuse during the Monica Lewinsky scandal. A kid who comes home each day to a drunken father who beats him suffers abuse. It is quite the stretch to imagine this million-dollar baseball player experiencing legitimate "abuse."

"Barry says whatever he feels," said Josh Suchon of the *Oakland Tribune* to ESPN. "He doesn't care if the manager gets upset, his teammates get upset, and he definitely doesn't care if the media gets upset."

"He made the guy from *Sports Illustrated* wait for four days before he talked to him," recalled Mark Whicker of the *Orange County Register*, referring to the infamous *SI* cover, "I'm Barry Bonds, And You're Not."

"I said to his father, I said, 'Bobby, how come you're such a nice guy and your son's such a jerk?'" recalled Hall of Fame Chicago scribe Jerome Holtzman.

"Reggie Jackson was that way, too," recalled veteran beat writer Ron Bergman of the *San Jose Mercury News*. Bergman had covered the A's in the 1970s, and wrote a book about Charlie Finley's dynasty, "The Moustache Gang." "But Reggie loved the press and knew how to work it."

"A lot of players don't like dealing with us," added Whicker. "Barry Bonds is one of the few who's honest about it. He's got a Michael Jordan type of presence, but he doesn't have a Michael Jordan type of diplomacy."

In 1998, Bonds created the 400/400 Club.

"He comes up to me and says, 'Well, I've done it, I got you off the list,' and I said to him, The only thing you've done is make up the best father-son combination in baseball history, and believe me, father is first," said Bobby on ESPN.

Is there any doubt that the two are rivals? That Bobby, for all of his fatherly pride, still holds on to his own position vs. his son? Can one imagine that Barry sniffed arrogantly when Bobby said that to him?

"He might be the most confident individual in sports," said Bonilla. In a radio interview taped years ago, Bonds was infamously quoted saying, "I'm not arrogant, I'm good."

"Both Griffey and Bonds saw the good side and the bad side of being the son's of fathers in the Major Leagues and of being superstars," said the *Chronicle*'s Henry Schulman on "Sports Century." "I think they both would sell their souls in order to win a championship."

Nineteen ninety-eight was the year baseball came back from the 1994 strike, led by Big Mac's record-breaking home run production. Baker's club won 89 games, and after 162 regular-season contests, their postseason fate was still undetermined. Tied with Sammy Sosa and the Cubs for the wild-card berth, they had to go to Wrigley Field for a Monday Play-Off, which they lost.

Bonds, as usual, was spectacular in the regular season, but he had to go home disappointed again. Batting clean up at homer-friendly Coors Field in the All-Star Game, Bonds hit a three-run, 451-foot home run off Bartolo Colon. That made for the first-ever father-son home run combination in All-Star Game history.

For the record, he hit .303 with 37 homers and 122 RBIs. He had 44 doubles, a career high. He set a league record by getting on base 15 consecutive times during a key August-September stretch. During this run, he was 9-for-9 with two doubles, two homers, and six walks.

On April 26 he hit his eighth grand slam. On May 28, Buck Showalter walked him intentionally *with the bases loaded!* He also did something on August 2 that he rarely does, which was charge the mound after being hit by Philadelphia's Ricky Bottalico, earning him a three-game suspension.

Nineteen ninety-eight may have been the year of McGwire and Sosa, but *Sports Illustrated* still recognized Bonds' greatness:

"It's hard to talk baseball these days without having words like McGwire, Griffey, homer and Yankee dominate the conversation. But don't let the hub-bub surrounding the Maris chase and the other record onslaughts obscure the real man of the '90s. Barry Bonds. The Giants outfielder isn't having his strongest statistical season, but he still looms large as the decade's most productive player."

In April, 1999, ex-wife Sun Bonds won a state appeals court ruling that overturned their prenuptial agreement and granted her half of the All-Star's baseball earnings during their seven-year marriage.

The couple had signed an agreement the day before their wedding in February, 1988 in which they relinquished the right to community property and agreed to keep future earnings separate. That meant Sun Bonds would not share in 50 percent of Bonds' salary, which was $8 million per year when they divorced in December 1994.

Bonds' agent had warned her that there would be no wedding without her signature. The agreement included several typographical errors and appeared to be altered.

In addition, Sun Bonds, a Swedish immigrant who had been in the U.S. for only a month, did not understand English well and was only advised by a Swedish friend while Bonds was represented by two lawyers and a financial adviser, the court said.

The ruling concluded that Mrs. Bonds did not voluntarily agree to the prenuptial agreement.

Sun Bonds' lawyer, Paige Wickland, said Mrs. Bonds would not get half of everything Bonds earned during the course of the marriage, but that her client would receive half the money and property that remained from his earnings when the couple separated in May, 1994.

The ruling is "very important, because more people are doing premarital agreements and they should be fair and fairly procured," Wickland told the press.

In this case, she said, "one side had everything, had all the money and got all the benefits of the agreement. ...There was no one who was looking out for her benefit."

In 1999, Bonds experienced injuries that limited him to 102 games. He suffered from left elbow pain, groin problems and knee inflammation. The ailments actually may have been the determining factor in his future success, since it made him reevaluate his body, his workout regimen, his stretching routine, and his diet. He felt that his routine in 1996 was making him too bulky, so now he would begin to accommodate his age. The result was, literally, history.

In '99, Bonds knocked out 34 home runs in the team's last season at pitiful Candlestick Park. On October 1, he had arthroscopic surgery on his knee, performed by Dr. Art Ting. The successful procedure repaired his cartilage and removed inflamed tissue. Bonds had gone under Ting's knife in April to remove a bone spur and repair the damaged tendon in his left arm. Prior to that season, he had played 888 of 908 regular season games with the Giants, but injuries kept him out of the All-Star Game. Baker's squad played winning baseball, but it was not enough to reach the Division Series.

In 1999, Major League Baseball announced their All-Century Team.

"When Griffey was named to the All-Century team, where was the outrage when Barry Bonds was left off?" asked Steve Hirdt of the Elias Sports Bureau on "Sports Century." "Bonds had a much higher slugging percentage, a much better on-base percentage, 400 more walks than Griffey and twice as many stolen bases, yet people just said, 'Yeah, Griffey, sure, he's gotta be on the team.'"

"Barry Bonds is one of the greatest players of all time," said renowned announcer Bob Costas. "He's on a relatively short list. I don't think the public's embraced him the way they embraced Ken Griffey, Jr., but his career accomplishments place him on that list."

"They're very similar players," Seattle manager Lou Piniella said. "They're both multi-talented. Both can beat you with their bat, their glove and their legs.

"When I had Junior here, I thought that because of the more demanding position he played and the age factor that he was the one. But that's not to take anything away from Barry."

"It's unfair on my part to compare Barry to Griffey because I never [previously] played with Griffey," said Seattle outfielder Stan Javier, who had four seasons with Bonds. "Barry is one of the most complete players to ever play the game. He has 400-plus home runs and more than 400 steals—no one else has come close to that. He'll probably hit 600 home runs, and steal between 550 and 600 bases.

"To me, if you compare both at their peaks in their careers, I think Barry is the better player because of his speed."

Then there is the question, "Which is the best father-son combination, Barry and Bobby or Ken, Sr. and Junior?" Bonds and his father, Bobby, are the all-time leaders in father-son home runs, stolen bases, and RBIs. Neither Barry nor Junior has ever played in the World Series.

"I saw Barry after we won the World Series in Florida," former Pirate coach Rich Donnelly once told a reporter. "I saw his look and he was jealous. It was like, 'I have everything but I don't have that.'"

"That's got to drive him, to get to a World Series," Rickey Henderson said of him. "He's done everything in baseball except reach the Promised Land. In the postseason, he hasn't been too successful, and he wants to get there and come through when the chips are down and show that he's a money player, too."

Bonds said the same thing in an interview with *Sports Illustrated*, denying that the attention Mark McGwire and Griffey receive or any statistical milestones motivate him.

"If I never reach another milestone and the Giants finally win a World Series—that's all I could ask for," he said. "I'd be complete."

By 1999, Bonds had become a creature of habit. His regular pregame routine is to take some light batting practice, then go in the back of the clubhouse, lie down and take a nap. He wakes up about 7:25 for a 7:35 game.

"The game is easy for him," Donnelly said. "He's playing with the best players in the world, and he looks like that one 12-year-old in Little League who's better than everyone else."

Bonds has a lot of bounce back, too. He once took a swing, grimaced, took a few steps and fell to the ground in pain with a sprained joint in his lower back. He rode off the field on a cart. Everybody said he was done for a while, but after four games he was back. He hit a homer his first game back.

His ability to hit the ground running after injuries and layoffs separates him from McGwire. Big Mac almost always slumped for a time after coming off the disabled list. Bonds is not intimidated by inside heat, either.

Oakland's Tim Hudson once threw up-and-in at Bonds. He homered into the upper deck.

"All you do is wake up the lion when you throw at my head," Bonds told reporters.

Shawn Estes was asked once about Bonds' relations with reporters.

"I think Barry is making more of an effort to be liked, I really do," Estes told the writers. "But if it looks like a rat and smells like a rat, it's probably a rat. At thirty-something years old, you're never going to change who you are, deep down."

Donnelly once told a story, however, that speaks to Bonds' inner beauty.

"My daughter passed away in 1994 with a brain tumor when she was 17 years old," Donnelly said. "I remember one day when she was 15 and she was supposed to meet me at the car after the game, and she showed up late.

And when I asked why, she said, 'I just had the nicest talk with Barry Bonds. He told me how I should be when I grow up, how I shouldn't use drugs, how I should go to school.'

"And I said, 'Are you sure you were talking to Barry Bonds?'"

Donnelly said that when he told Bonds about his daughter's death, he cried.

"He can be the meanest guy a writer's ever seen and he can be the warmest, most considerate guy, too," Donnelly said. "And you'll ask, Is he the same guy? Yeah, he is.

"He's an enigma."

As more than one writer and player has said, Barry is Barry.

San Francisco has a checkered past. One story concerns a man who was born in Japan, but raised in San Francisco. He moved back to Japan while still in his youth, and was recruited by the military to return to San Francisco as a spy in the late 1930s, prior to World War II. When he arrived in The City, he was met by the site of the Bay Bridge, a span that extends from San Francisco to Treasure Island and Yerba Buena Island, where the 1937 World's Fair was held. The bridge then goes through a tunnel, and spans again from the island to Oakland across the bay.

In an apocryphal story, the man tells his handlers that they should rethink their plans about going to war with America. Any country capable of building such a structure, he tells them, is capable of "doing anything."

Candlestick Park, which opened in 1960, was another story. Vice President Richard Nixon was a big sports fan, but his analysis of stadiums was not very good. When he dedicated the Los Angeles Memorial Sports Arena, later known as the "Clip Joint," where LA's second basketball team played their games in cheap surroundings, he called the place the "best" basketball facility in the country. Up in San Francisco, Nixon said Candlestick was "the finest baseball stadium in America."

It was the worst. After playing two years at Seals Stadium, the club had moved into their new facility, which immediately looked old. What happened was a story of political graft and corruption. San Francisco Mayor George Christopher had a sweetheart deal with construction and land magnate Charlie Harney. Harney had tons of dirt, but no place to put it. They decided that they would use it to create landfill at Candlestick Point. All they needed was a buyer.

Enter New York Giants owner Horace Stoneham, who had a checkered past himself. One knowledgeable sports insider, Edgar Scherick, who helped found the Wide World of Sports and baseball's Game of the Week in the early 1960s, says it is "common knowledge" that a drunk-driving Stoneham once killed a man in Arizona in a car accident, but used his money to keep the incident quiet.

"Horace used to like a toddy," says Scherick, now a movie producer. "So did his buddy, Chub Feeney."

Stoneham had decided to follow Dodger owner Walter O'Malley to California. O'Malley did his homework, scouting out a perfect hilltop location near downtown Los Angeles, surrounded by easily accessible freeways for his projected Dodger Stadium.

Land was not as plentiful in smaller San Francisco, a city surrounded on three sides by water. Christopher and Harney decided to sell Stoneham on Candlestick Point. The problem was that the wind blows so bad there that it seems like one is making a winter passage past the Cape of Good Hope, and the fog comes in over the hills like Passover.

However, these meteorological events often do not act up until around three in the afternoon. Harney and Christopher drove Stoneham out to the point one morning, on a sunny day before the wind worked up. Stoneham liked all the land, because he was convinced that he had to have a lot of parking. That was a big sticking point. He somehow did not notice that only one freeway came close to the stadium, and that fans would have to traverse narrow ghetto streets to get to the place.

It was a big, gray concrete mausoleum. When the Oakland-Alameda County Coliseum was built in 1965, it was immediately identified as a much more pleasant place to attend sports event. Only the most die-hard Giant fan expressed any love for Candlestick. Fans avoided the place, even when the team was good. It cost the team untold millions.

Politics in San Francisco range from liberal Democrat to socialist, to be kind. Local government is slightly more organized than post-World War II Italy. Getting anything done in such an atmosphere is, at best, problematic.

Consequently, efforts to build a new stadium spelled frustration for Bay Area fans for decades. Politicians and citizens groups always brought up issues of the homeless, the schools without heat, and other social dilemmas that needed to be attended to before a stadium could be built with taxpayer funds.

Eventually, plans to build a new park in The City were scrapped. The idea was to build one somewhere in the South Bay. San Jose and Santa Clara, considered "Giants Country," seemed logical choices. So, ballot measures went up for votes. What happened? They were defeated every time.

It was left to Magowan, the businessman, to organize an effort to build a stadium using mainly private funds. The result was Pac Bell Park, which opened in 2000, and does more to wipe out the image of San Francisco as a town of bumbling politicos than any other symbol in recent memory.

So, 2000 was a whole new ball game. Barry Bonds had as much to do with a stadium being built as any player since The Babe and the Yankee Stadium (The House That Ruth Built) in 1923. In their first year, the club sold out every single game in the 40,800-seat park to finish the season at 3,315,330 in attendance.

Those who say baseball is boring and has lost fan support are out of their minds. It is the most popular sport in America, if not the world. San Francisco is not the only city that sells out every single game. Toronto had done that in the late 1980s and early '90s. Cleveland, Texas, Colorado, Atlanta and other stadiums do the same thing. Baseball games are televised every night on ESPN, Fox, and on local stations.

Pro basketball teams play 41 home games and have a hard time selling out 16,000-seat arenas. Pro football teams play eight home games, and maybe they sell out, maybe they do not. Here is baseball, played day in, day out, and they fill stadiums with enthusiastic fans over and over again.

The game is recession-proof, scandal-proof, and incredibly, strike-proof.

After getting off to a bad start in their new yard against the Dodgers, no less, the Fabulous Baker Boys went on a tear to beat Los Angeles by 11 games. Arizona had looked, with Randy Johnson, to be the favorite, but the Diamondbacks collapsed. San Francisco surged to finish at 97-65, the best record in baseball.

The starting rotation of Livan Hernandez (17-11), Shawn Estes (15-6), Russ Ortiz (14-12), Kirk Reuter (11-9) and Mark Gardner (11-7) combined with the bullpen of Felix Rodriguez (2.64 ERA) and Robb Nen (41 saves, 3.45 ERA) to propel the club to the best earned run average in the Major Leagues, 3.45.

Baker became the winningest manager in San Francisco history with 655 wins, while earning the Baseball Writers Association of America's National League Manager of the Year award for the third time.

Magowan was named "2000 Executive of the Year" by Street & Smith's *Sports Business Journal* for his role in building the park that energized a town and its team.

The real heroes were Bonds and Kent. Kent hit .334 with 33 homers and 125 RBIs to win the MVP award.

Bonds? He found newfound inspiration.

Bonds appropriately hit the first-ever homer at the new stadium on April 3 against Los Angeles. He was the league's Silver Slugger winner again, and made the *AP* and *Baseball America* All-Star teams. He was named to the All-Star Game, but a small injury kept him out of the game. Bonds hit 49 home runs (28 in the first half), slugged .688, walked 117 times (against 77 strikeouts), scored 129 runs, got on base at a .440 pace, had 330 total bases, 81 extra-base hits, drove in 106 runs and hit .306.

He hit six home runs into the new McCovey Cove, including his first one off the Mets' Rich Rodriguez on May 1. He hit in 14 straight games from September 4-20, hit homers in four straight games in June, and was 11-for-22 from May 22-28.

Then came the play-offs. Bonds did nothing, the team stopped hitting, and the Mets eliminated them in the first round, three games to one. Three hits in 17 at-bats. A double, no homers, one rib. This monumental player, this genuine superstar, this all-time great first-ballot Hall of Famer, had now played in five play-offs (two Division Series and three Championship Series). He had batted .167 against Cincinnati in 1990, .148 against Atlanta in 1991, and .261 against the Braves in 1992, for a .191 NLCS average. He had hit .250 against Florida in 1997, and .176 against New York in .2000 for a .207 Division Series average. In the one-game 1998 Play-Off with Chicago, he and his team came up short, too. He had disappeared.

"Some guys get sympathy by virtue of never having been on a winning team," said Costas on "Sports Century," referring to players like Ernie Banks. "Perhaps because he has not endeared himself to the press and public, Barry is one of those people who get a demerit for it."

Other than postseason frustration, though, Bonds seemed different at this point in his career. Maybe it was the new ballpark. Maybe it was a happy marriage and three beautiful children. Maybe it was maturity and experience. For whatever reason, the Bonds persona changed a bit in 2000.

"Barry seemed to have a personality transformation in 2000 when Scott Boras took over as his agent," said Nick Peters on "Sports Century."

"There was a concerted effort on Barry's part to become more open with the media and present a more friendly type attitude," said ESPN analyst Dave Campbell.

"There's a threat of suspicion that he's not being sincere, and he's doing it because he's gonna be a free agent," said Peters.

"Now I'm too old to fight, I don't have the energy anymore," Bonds said.

"I started covering the Giants in 2000, and that was the year he vowed to be more cooperative with the press," said Dan Brown of the *San Jose Mercury News.* "So I introduced myself and said, 'Hi, I'm Dan Brown,' and we had a great conversation, and the next day he blew me off, just to show who's in charge."

In my research of Bonds, I have discovered that Brown is off the mark. He does not give writers the on/off personality to show who is in charge. He does it, quite simply, because he is moody. We have all known moody people. Some people are moody because they have a chemical imbalance. It does not make them bad people, it makes them quite common people. Moody people are often hard to be around. It takes a certain kind of personality to understand and tolerate mood swings.

Still, for the media, it causes frustration. I once saw an out-of-town radio guy from a small market and his assistant approach Bonds in the clubhouse, like Dorothy addressing the "Wizard of Oz." Bonds did not tell them, "How dare you approach the great 'Wizard of Bonds?'" That is not his way.

He just went about his business as if they did not exist. Imagine Patrick Swayze in "Ghost." That's what the radio guy and his assistant must have felt like.

Another time, I had a normal conversation with him, and the next day I approached him to update him on the book's progress. He just rolled his eyes and said, "Can't you tell it to Stevie?" (his media rep, Steve Hoskins). On other days he would come up from behind me with a big smile and greet me with, "What's up, buddy?" So go figure.

"He's the same guy he was 10 years ago, in some ways that may be true, but inside himself, he's not the same," said Leyland, doing his best to psychoanalyze the man of mystery. "Barry's at more peace with himself than he's ever been before."

The Bay Area media is not particularly harsh. On KNBR, the "Giant 68," which has covered the team for years, the sports personalities are virtually shadow employees of the club. It is nothing compared to Los Angeles, where talk radio kills the Dodgers, Bruins and Trojans. It cannot be compared with the piranhas that make up the many print, radio and TV outlets in New York's tri-state area. Despite his supposedly more open relationship with the media, however, Bonds did not garner the votes for a fourth MVP.

"Kent deserved the MVP, but I don't think he would have gotten it had Barry Bonds not been there," said Mark Whicker.

"It was pretty much a toss-up, but Jeff outpolled Barry by a considerable amount," said Barbieri.

Whatever. It says here Bonds was the real National League MVP in 2000. Now, the press began to focus on a rivalry with Kent.

"We have a friendly relationship when we work, but we ain't that close," Bonds said of Kent. "I mean I don't need 700 friends."

"Kent has the reputation of being a leader," said Brown. "He does a lot of things the same as Barry. He's also not a guy to call a team meeting and have a rah-rah speech."

"Sometimes you get chosen to be a clubhouse leader because you're the best, but that doesn't mean you're a leader," Baker told ESPN.

It is said he has four lockers, but Bonds said he has two, one for his son. He points out that so did Shawon Dunston's son, so did Mark Gardner's son, because "We want our kids to feel like they're Major League players."

"To me, who cares?" Eric Davis said of the clubhouse arrangements.

"I have bulging discs in my back," said Bonds. "The trainer recommended the chair." Bonds said he paid the $3,000 for the chair, not the team. Bonds has been known to be sound asleep on the chair with a blanket over him, oblivious to all others in the room.

What about his play-off failures?

"I've lost five playoffs, but my son's won two little league championships," Bonds said. "I'm happy now. "

Bonds married Liz Watson in January 1998, and this marriage, which has worked for him, softened his image.

"It's gone from, 'He's a great ballplayer but a jerk,' to 'he's our jerk,' and now it's just that he's a great ballpayer," Barbieri told ESPN.

"Surely Barry will never be loved by everyone, and a sneaking suspicion tells me that's the way Barry wants it," said Lloyd McClendon on "Sports Century."

Bonds is not afraid to be lonely at the top. He seems satisfied knowing, in his own heart, how good he is. In this regard, he has changed.

"He knew when he got to a certain point he was good," Pirate broadcaster Steve Blass told "Sports Century" of the earlier version of Bonds. "Some people can keep it inside and just go about their business and be dominant, but Barry, I don't think he was reluctant to let you know he was good."

Do smaller ballparks, expansion and poor pitching inflate Bonds' recent home run numbers?

"Home runs are cheaper," Steve Jacobson of New York Newsday said on "Sports Century," about Bonds' recent achievements. He did not see the same excitement for Bonds that he saw for Mark McGwire.

Jerome Holtzman came right out and indicated that he did not admire him as a person. The question among many is not whether he can win. Rather, if he has opened up, people said he was just doing it to make people not dislike him.

The question is, will time do for Bonds what it did for Ted Williams, now considered one of the most beloved players ever? One difference between Bonds and Williams concerns the subject of reticence with the media. Williams was a good interview who gave the writers what they wanted. They just disagreed with him. Bonds consistently left the beat writers with nothing. It should be noted that, while Bonds has been more available to the media lately, he picks his spots. He is friendlier on television with a single interviewer than he is in front of assorted notepads and microphones. He is nicer to the national media than the local. He can turn it off in a second as soon as the lights go out. He favors a national interviewer like Roy Firestone, a man of color. Race is a subject he has himself said is a factor in the way he is perceived, and in this respect, unfortunately, he is probably right.

The 1995 O.J. Simpson murder verdict brought the racial divide in America to light. Who can forget the sight of dancing, cheering, celebrating African-Americans, as opposed to the somber, downcast white Americans, when a black man was pronounced not guilty by a mostly black jury for the savage killing of two white people?

Who is Barry Bonds? He is, in many ways, an average American whose favorite food is pizza, which he says he could eat every day, despite its fattening propensities. Bonds is not into rap or hip-hop music, but prefers R & B, and during football season he is an avid fan of the 49ers. Bonds has an appreciation for the old stuff. His favorite comedian is not one of the new, profane hipsters, but rather Bill Cosby, who he considers to be one of the most influential people in his life. His favorite city to play in is San Diego (how dare a NoCal express fondness for the Southland!). In his spare time, aside from weightlifting for baseball, he engages in martial arts and dancing. How does he relax? He likes to sleep.

"Sometimes I'm off at the beach, walking around, trying to take the intensity out of my body, trying to be as relaxed and as calm as I can," Bonds once said.

"You fail seven out of 10 times," he said, referring to the baseball standard of success, a .300 average. "I try to deliver 30 percent, with 100 percent effort. If I was in any other business—basketball, accounting or the stock market—30 percent and I'd be out of a job. That's why you'll never see me get mad out there. I'm too grateful."

Who is the best hitter he has ever seen? Pete Rose.

In 2000, the California Supreme Court had upheld Bonds' agreement with his former spouse in which she gave up her right to half the fortune he would earn during their marriage. The court said that Sun had understood the consequences of signing the premarital agreement the day before their wedding, voluntarily giving up all her rights to community property.

In ruling in Bonds' favor, the court suggested that requiring each side to have a lawyer would open up a flood of litigation.

"In a majority of dissolution cases in California at least one of the two parties apparently is not represented by counsel," wrote Chief Justice Ronald George. Having a lawyer is "merely one factor among several" that a court should consider in deciding whether the agreement was voluntarily signed, he said.

The justices reversed a state appeals court ruling that required each spouse-to-be to have independent lawyers.

The decision was one of the first in the nation to interpret a national law adopted by 28 states—including California—that set out the basic requirements for premarital agreements. All seven justices ruled in Bonds' favor, and he was "ecstatic" when he heard the news, said his lawyer, Robert Nachshin.

"I'm glad it's 99 percent over," he told the *Chronicle.*

The couple had met in Montreal in August 1987 when Bonds was a Pirate, making $106,000 a year. Sun Bonds was studying to be a beautician. They were both 23. After a whirlwind, three-month romance, they became engaged and set a wedding date for the following February.

On their way to the airport, where they were catching a plane for a Las Vegas wedding the next day, they stopped at the office of Bonds' lawyer. Sun signed a premarital agreement that she had seen for the first time only a few hours earlier.

By the time the couple divorced in 1994, Bonds was making $8 million a year with the Giants.

Sun had asked for support for both herself and their young son and daughter. A San Mateo judge ruled that Sun voluntarily signed it, and awarded her child support as well as $10,000 in monthly spousal support, which ended in December 1998.

Bonds then remarried.

The court said that Sun was not threatened; that she had signed the pre-nup of her own free will and without coercion. She apparently had been happy and calm. A lawyer for Bonds had discussed the agreement with her about a week before she signed it, and had even suggested she get her own lawyer. She agreed with Bonds to keep their property and earnings separate.

The wedding had been an impromptu affair that could have been postponed if Sun wanted to have a lawyer look over the agreement. The suggestion that she was naive and vulnerable when she signed over her rights to community property was not something the court saw. Instead, she was "intrepid rather than a person whose will is easily overborne," Chief Justice George said. He noted that she had emigrated from her homeland when she was barely 20, gotten a job, made friends and could speak two foreign languages.

In the Uniform Premarital Agreement Act, which California adopted in 1985, the drafters specifically rejected the requirement that each party have a lawyer, although it was noted that do so is always a wise precaution.

"The best assurance of enforceability is independent representation for both parties," wrote George.

Nachshin, Bonds' trial lawyer from Los Angeles, said he and Bonds felt "totally vindicated," and that the agreement having been upheld, he felt they would prevail in the lower courts in interpreting other provisions of the contract.

They "found Sun Bonds to be a totally noncredible witness," he said.

"I'm at a loss to imagine what facts they would find that would constitute a valid agreement," said Paige Leslie Wickland, the San Francisco lawyer who represented Sun.

In November, 2000, Bonds again traveled with a group of U.S. allstars to Japan. It was during this trip that he and Kent had apparently gotten to know each other better. All signs pointed to 2001 being his best yet.

CHAPTER
FIVE

"Son of San Francisco"

Scottsdale, Arizona is the long-time Spring Training home of the San Francisco Giants. On the surface, it makes sense to train there. The weather is great. The facilities were upgraded to first-class status a few years ago, and it is conveniently located in the middle of the Cactus League.

The Cactus League mainly involves big-league clubs who train in and around the Phoenix area. Scottsdale is the most upscale suburb of Phoenix. There are a few teams that train outside Metropolitan Phoenix, but for the most part, Phoenix is Baseball Central every March.

The Cactus League beats the heck out of the Grapefruit League, which is in Florida. The Grapefruit League gets rain and requires more long bus trips than the Cactus League. Also, a large number of big-league players make their residence in the Phoenix area—mainly in Scottsdale.

So, Scottsdale makes sense. The only "problem" is that Scottsdale, Arizona is one of the great secrets of the Western World. The nightlife in Scottsdale may be the very best in the Continental United States.

Scottsdale? It is a retirement community. Old people live there. Very true. It is also, for reasons not known but worth researching, the home of the most beautiful women in the U.S.

Beautiful girls and hot nightspots would seem to be the province of Hollywood, Manhattan, and Miami's South Beach. Ask anybody who hangs out at Sanctuary, Jilly's, Six, Maloney's, Martini Ranch or any number of bars located mainly within walking distance of each other near downtown Scottsdale. In the interest of thorough journalism, I have done just that. I can tell you that the "talent"—a code word for cute girls—is as impressive in Scottsdale as any of these glamour places.

Scottsdale can hang with any spot in the world: Ibiza, Cannes, Budapest, the Italian Coast. Furthermore, it boasts an All-American quality these other places lack. Young, fresh-faced people having fun. Drugs are not nearly the problem in Scottsdale as they are in other dens of inequity.

So what is the problem? Well, into this environment arrive hundreds of young (usually single), handsome professional baseball players. Their employers pay a lot of them large sums of money. Some of them are married. They are supposed to be there for a month and a half to buckle down and get ready for the rigors of a long season. They are supposed to be at the yard early, and this means getting to bed at a reasonable hour. It does not happen that way.

The Oakland A's, who train next door in Phoenix, made nightly pilgrimages to the Scottsdale nightclubs, led by their Master of Fun, MVP outfielder Jason "Party like a porn star" Giambi. Somehow they still had the best record in the Cactus League in 2001, but before embarking for Oakland at the end of March, pitcher Tim Hudson remarked to me they had best get out of town "while we're still standing."

Whether the hangover effect of 45 days in party town was responsible for Oakland's 8-18 start to the 2001 season is up for debate, but once the team settled down they finally turned it on and won 102 games en route to the play-offs.

The San Francisco Giants have become an institution in Scottsdale. They practice at Indian School Park and play their exhibition games at Scottsdale Stadium. They used to train in Phoenix proper. Del Webb, a local developer and one-time owner of the New York Yankees, was one of the men responsible for bringing spring ball to the desert. He used the game as a lure for upscale hotel guests staying at his resorts.

In 1951, the New York Giants and Yankees switched spring sites, giving Phoenix fans a chance to see a rookie named Mickey Mantle. The Mick terrorized people sitting behind first base. A shortstop back then, Mantle's throws would career like errant missiles into the stands.

Giants' manager Dusty Baker is a modern man who treats his players like men. A longtime big leaguer himself, he knows that boys will be boys who will get out and about at night. He also knows that they are professionals with a job to do, and he does not hector them with intrusive rules and constant bedchecks.

In 2001, Baker went to his ninth Spring Training as Giants' skipper with a veteran club, led by one of the greatest vets in history, Barry Bonds.

Bonds has never been a monk, and he certainly has enjoyed the Scottsdale nightlife in the past, going back to his college days at Arizona State.

By 2001, however, Bonds was a man of maturity and purpose, leading a team of maturity and purpose. The Giants, unlike the young A's, were a group of experienced pros who went about their tasks efficiently.

Bonds' second marriage was working out. He was a family man. He was heading into a free-agent season at age 36, and he was in the best physical condition of his life. Bonds has always been one of those guys who plays his best in free agent seasons.

Somehow, controversy and Bonds are constant, however. The kind of smooth sailing that always characterized Tony Gwynn and Cal Ripken has eluded Bonds.

The press coverage of the Giants' opening camp centered on Bonds and their efforts to retain their superstar. The Giants "unequivocally" wanted Bonds back in 2002, and there was virtually no chance they would trade him before his contract expired in the fall, general manager Brian Sabean said.

But Sabean also reiterated the team had no plans to sign the 36-year-old left fielder to a contract extension before the end of the 2001 season, when Sabean would have a clearer picture of the Giants' financial future.

That did not sit well with Bonds, who checked into camp saying he wanted to remain with the Giants as long as they stayed competitive, but also wanted to know posthaste whether they planned to resign him after his three-year, $22.9 million extension expired.

"It's up to them and my agent to sit down and talk and see what happens," Bonds told reporters during an informal, 15-minute chat. "I've got two kids from one marriage where it's really important to be able to establish some form of bond or even a closer relationship if there's a situation where I'm not going to be here. If I am going to be here, let's talk about it and get it done."

When asked whether it was possible the Giants truly did not know whether they could sign him for next year, Bonds said, "They know. I don't believe that for one minute."

Bonds was setting no deadline for an answer, but said he expected the team and his agent, Scott Boras, to start talking before the end of Spring Training.

"There has to be some form of communication," Bonds said. The Giants feared the agent would negotiate with them only to leverage a bigger contract for Bonds as a free agent in the off-season.

Sabean was caught between a rock (giving Bonds what he wants) and a hard place (trying to maintain a competitive team with a smaller budget than most contenders).

"I've said from Day One, consistently, we want the player back, but . . . we also need to look at getting other people signed for the future," Sabean said. "While Barry's the most important piece, we also need to figure out Shawn Estes: When he gets a raise, whether it's through arbitration or a long-term contract."

"I look at it this way," Bonds countered. "Why should it be any different for me than the way my Godfather was sent out, the way the rest of them were sent out, the way Matt Williams was sent out? Why should it be any different for me? It's just unfortunate, that's all. We'll see. Time will tell."

A New York paper published a projected Mets' play-off lineup with Bonds hitting third. Bonds had the right to veto any trade but said he would waive his right if dealt to a desirable team.

Sabean, however, insisted he would not move Bonds before the July 31 trade deadline, just to ensure the Giants getting something in return before he could walk away as a free agent in October.

"We'd have to end up flat on our face and literally be out of it at the trading deadline," said Sabean. "There would have to be horrific consequences to even entertain him not being here. So he will be here for the duration to help us win the division."

Wherever Bonds signed in 2002, he would earn far more than the $10.3 million he was to earn in 2001. He said he was willing to take less in San Francisco as long as the Giants committed to staying competitive.

"I don't want Alex Rodriguez's money," said Bonds.

Barry did establish something of an informal deadline—the end of Spring Training—by which he would like to at least begin a dialogue about his future.

"I'm not saying the deal has to be done," he said. "I'm just talking about some form of communication. If there's just dead silence by that time, then all my questions are answered."

Sabean responded that Bonds ought to know the Giants want him back, and that the team's wishes had nothing to do with why there was no new deal in the works.

"Unequivocally we want Barry back," Sabean said, "but as we stand here today, it's easier said than done. As I stand here today I don't have answers to the questions that need to be answered: How many years and for how much money?"

Sabean said Boras had not yet contacted him.

Boras is notorious for squeezing teams for every last penny when his clients hit the open market.

"I don't expect to talk to Scott," Sabean said. "That's not Scott's style. He kicked and moaned when we wanted to get Robb Nen's contract done. Scott is about marketability."

Sabean noted that if Bonds waited he would be perhaps the premier player on the free-agent market come winter.

"I find it hard to believe Scott Boras and Barry Bonds would contact us and do the kind of deal Robb Nen did, which, in the end, was well below market value," Sabean said.

Nen, another client of Boras, had signed the previous September with the Giants for $32 million over four years. The bargain in that deal was made clear when Yankees' closer Mariano Rivera, who was not eligible for free agency, signed a four-year deal worth nearly $40 million.

Sabean also seemed wary of making the first offer to Bonds, because Boras might simply use it as a benchmark for free-agent bidding in the winter. Boras also represented Rodriguez and Johnny Damon, two elite players who turned down lucrative offers from their former clubs and wound up playing elsewhere.

"We make offers to sign people," Sabean said. "We don't make offers to not get signings done. I know it's always incumbent on the club to try to get something done in the end, but I've said from day one consistently, we want him back. But for all people it's going to be better served probably at the end of the year, when I know exactly what we're up against for 2002 and into the future."

Bonds was just six homers away from 500, and number 600 was well within his reach. In short, his market value in this era of exploding salaries could be as much as double the $10.3 million he was due to make.

The Giants' payroll in 2002 figured to be around $65 million, probably no higher than tenth or twelfth in the majors.

Bonds said he would waive his no-trade clause, if he were headed to a contending team. Still, he would leave his heart in San Francisco.

"I have no bitterness toward the Giants," he said. "I was able to come back and play in my hometown. I was pretty lucky to have that opportunity. I don't hold grudges. I'm not a vindictive person. There would be a lot of dead people if I was."

Holding grudges? *Dead people?* There is a sense of fantasy in the athlete's world. Barry Bonds says he flunked English in high school. He went to college, but his academic credentials are short of, say, Bill Bradley's. He has a brother who has struggled like the rest of us.

If he were not a big-league baseball player, he would not be a millionaire. He would have to work for a living. He would have to keep his bosses happy and, if he held grudges against them, he likely would have to find another employer. Dead people would also not be an option, and if any showed up it would be, well, a matter for the police!

Barry Bonds' employer from 1993 to date has been the San Francisco Giants. Every two weeks, the Giants dutifully deposited huge checks in Bonds' bank. The checks never bounced. They were never late. Is there is some set of circumstances, some alternate universe, in which the very concept of Bonds holding a grudge against the depositors of those checks is anything less than preposterous?

Then there is the injury factor. Once the contract is signed, the money is theirs, even if they get hurt. There may be some variables on this equation, but by and large, the player gets paid no matter what. If the player plays lousy, which happens a lot, he still gets paid.

These guys have no business complaining or holding grudges. Ninety-nine point nine percent of them would be lucky to make $50,000 doing anything else. A lot are just plain lucky to be living in America. If not for the teams some hold "grudges" against, they would be living in squalor in their native countries.

Bonds is not unusual. Many, many pro athletes think like this. Average people cannot figure them out, but obviously money changes people. Not everyone, but a lot of them.

By the same token, some of these people, like Bonds (or Michael Jordan) are so good that they are virtually irreplaceable, at least in the short term. They do draw fans, they are franchise players, and they are responsible for fortunes being made, championships being won, even stadiums being built.

Furthermore, athletes are less the diva than many entertainers. Rock stars and movie stars are far worse than athletes, who are required to stay in top shape and work within a team framework. Tom Hanks (who is not a diva) makes roughly $20 million for one movie. Did preparing for, filming and promoting "Saving Private Ryan" take as much time and effort as Alex Rodriguez getting ready for and playing one baseball season?

Hanks and Jack Nicholson do not have to go work every day facing an opponent who has been plotting and strategizing on how to make them fail, and is loaded for bear to do just that. Britney Spears does not face 50,000 booing road fans trying to shake and rattle her into having a very bad night.

Kid Rock does not have a general manager whose purpose in life is very much about breaking down his value by exposing, in contract negotiations, that he is not worth the money he makes.

"Say, Kid, you're not hittin' the high notes like you did last year."

Somewhere in all of this celebrity status is a human being who has been elevated, like a modern Caesar, above the people. So far, we at least ask them to live within the law. Old Roman Emperors could have people thrown to the lions or boiled in oil for displeasing them. The Barry Bonds's of the world are not at that pitch, although if a guy like that so much as smiles or demonstrates normal human traits, people use this as "evidence" that they are such nice persons.

On the flip side, they do not have the privacy of going to work every day in anonymity. Instead, their failings, their worst professional, and often private, embarrassments are exposed in the papers, on the radio, and on television.

Drunk driving, infidelity, children born out of wedlock, late-night barroom brawls—if a celebrity is ensnared in these not-so-unusual endeavors, it is splashed all over the news.

At Indian School Park in Scottsdale that spring, Scott Boras, an ex-minor league player, emerged wearing jeans and a sports jacket, and carrying a briefcase. He "looked as pale as someone who spends 12 hours a day in the library," wrote Lowell Cohn of the *Santa Rosa Press Democrat.*

He said they had a good meeting, but don't they always? He said he had conveyed the feeling in no uncertain terms that Bonds wanted to remain a Giant.

"You may not know this, but Bonds is a sensitive guy," continued Cohn, a longtime Bay Area scribe with an acerbic side. "He's not sensitive to your feelings or my feelings—Heaven forbid. He's sensitive to his own feelings, and a suspicion exists among Giants players that a sensitive guy like Bonds may sulk without a contract extension. The sulking may lead to depression, and depression may lead to poor play, and before you know it, Bonds could go into the tank."

(Bonds, of course, would prove this side of Cohn's analysis to be about as wrong as any so-called professional sportswriter could possibly be proved wrong, with his 2001 performance.)

Cohn then "covered his ass" by positing the opposite possibility, that his pride had been challenged, so he would burst onto the scene like "Superman rushing out of a phone booth . . . "

So why not sign Bonds right then? Maybe the Giants thought they could get more out of a hungry Bonds than a satisfied Bonds. If this was Sabean's intent, then he might go down as the best motivator since Knute Rockne told the Irish to "win one for the Gipper."

Maybe, back then, the Giants had no intention of ever re-signing Bonds. He was getting older. He was a "pain to have around," according to Cohn. Maybe they just wanted one last season out of the guy.

The Giants were understandably leery of Boras. Some pundits said he comes off as the kind of guy who smiles at you while he is stabbing you in the back.

Seattle negotiated with him in good faith right up until the time Rodriguez signed with Texas the previous year. The same thing reportedly occurred with Johnny Damon, until Oakland stepped up.

Bonds came into the 2001 season with eight Gold Gloves under his belt, and a reputation as one of the greatest defensive left fielders of all time. His competition is not a long list. Carl Yastrzemski comes to mind. Mike Krukow, a Giants broadcaster since 1991, remembered how Bonds used to play Gwynn, one of the best left-handed hitters in Major League history, like he was some pitcher who couldn't get the bat around.

Why?

"He knew with the speed of Bill Swift's sinker or the speed of John Burkett's sinker and with Gwynn's swing type, he had to hit the ball down there," Krukow told the *Press Democrat*'s Jeff Fletcher. "He couldn't pull the ball or he couldn't drive the ball in the gap. He knew that if he tried to do that, he'd have to alter his swing.

"So the guy in left field has affected the guy at the plate, just by the way he's positioned himself. That is a smart sucker right there."

"He's one of the smartest players in the game," Fletcher quoted Shawon Dunston. "Barry's no dummy. He might want you to think that, but he's no dummy. He's got a lot of talent, but he's smart, too."

"I really don't want to discuss that," was Bonds' reply when asked to address the difficult, complex, controversial question of why he plays defense so well.

"Being around that your entire life, you are going to learn this and that," Giants hitting coach Gene Clines told Fletcher. "You are going to pick up some stuff quicker than guys who don't have that exposure."

Clines was the hitting coach in Seattle in the early '90s, when Ken Griffey, Jr. was rising to his prime. Clines said Griffey, like Bonds, seemed to be able to easily absorb the nuances of the game.

"We had meetings and we'd go over scouting reports and you'd think he was sleeping, but he was taking it all in," Clines said. "It's just his way of doing it."

"I played with Bobby [Bonds] in Chicago at the end of his career, and I marveled at the little stuff I learned from him," Krukow told Fletcher. "He knew about pitchers tipping what's coming, middle infielders tipping. Middle infielders tip pitches more than anybody does. Those guys understand that stuff. …They see the game in a different way."

Giants bench coach Ron Wotus played with Barry Bonds in the minor leagues in the mid-1980s. According to him, Bonds does little things that today's players often ignore, like watching an opposing pitcher in the bullpen, before he's even gotten into the game.

Bonds is not like Gwynn, who watches a lot of videotape, and he does not go over scouting reports on how to position himself against hitters. Defensively, he has instincts, which is what they said about Mays.

"I believe it's just from being out here and watching the game," Fletcher quoted Wotus. "Everybody talks about his talent, but he's real sharp. He picks things up that other players miss."

Bonds knows what he knows, but does not share his knowledge easily.

"I don't think he is malicious with the fact he holds back the information," Krukow told Fletcher. "He feels that other people see it, too, and he's surprised when they don't, because to him it's easy."

Bonds has expressed a desire to go into coaching after he retires, maybe at the college level. However, Krukow's observation may be what prevents him from becoming a great coach. Like Ted Williams, who could not relate to ordinary hitters, Bonds may not be able to understand mediocrity. Celtic Hall of Famer Bill Russell had the same problem, once he retired as a player and coached so-so teams. The best baseball managers are often journeymen, like Leyland and Sparky Anderson. Gwynn, who is taking over at San Diego State, will hope to dispel this "truism" of the game.

Left-handed relief pitcher Chad Zerbe had a surprisingly close relationship with Bonds because he played for Class A San Jose while Bobby Bonds was the hitting coach. He said that sometimes Bonds' advice is wasted on ordinary players.

If asked, however, Barry will help out. Once Shawon Dunston failed to make good contact when he knew a slider was coming, so he sought out Bonds. He told him that not merely knowing what kind of pitch is coming is less important than waiting long enough to see if it's going to be a strike.

The problem is that this ability to "wait long enough" is a Bonds trait that few, if any others, share.

Bonds can play 10 feet off the line because he has the speed to still track down a ball if fooled.

"It's a combination of baseball smarts and talent that make Hall of Famers," wrote Fletcher.

"There are a lot of stars, but then there are superstars," Dunston said, "and that's what separates them."

Image, as Andre Agassi's camera commercial used to say, is everything. Sammy Sosa has a good image, and he signed a multi-year contract extension with the Chicago Cubs. Barry Bonds did not have a good image, and he would play this year for the Giants without an extension.

When Ken Griffey, Jr. played with the Mariners, he had a golden image. Club executives, however, said Griffey did nothing off the field unless he was paid for it. Griffey has a beautiful smile, but when he got to Cincinnati, he let his guard down. He left the 2000 All-Star Game early, saying he had to take care of his fireplace. Of course, he needed to make sure his fireplace in the Queen City was in good working order in July. It gets about 119 degrees with humidity in Cincinnati in the summer, so of course this makes sense. Radio talk show host Jim Rome was on Griffey like a cheap suit, saying that, naturally, Junior had to get out of town because he had "fireplace issues."

Sosa had made nasty public statements about Cubs management, but he remained a lovable figure in Chicago. This, even though he had become, like Jose Canseco with the A's in 1990-91, a player who had decided that the only part of the game worth concentrating on was hitting home runs.

In 2001, Sosa rallied his game and improved defensively while having another great offensive season. The Cubs, a perpetual loser yet a popular team because they, more than any club, live on image, felt they had no choice but to extend his contract.

Bonds often contributes his time and money to charities without publicity. He actively discourages efforts to make his efforts known. His image is mostly negative, but is he better or worse than Sosa and Griffey?

This was a factor on the Giants' approach to a contract extension. The Giants get excellent TV ratings, and while fans receive Bonds well at the park, there is a core of fans that call in to KNBR and email the papers with anti-Bonds sentiments. Are these the people who do not buy tickets?

Bonds does not seem to care. He does not "work" the media. He talks on his own schedule. He is unpredictable. He may sing like a bird after an oh-fer, but retreat to the trainer's room after a two-homer day.

Sosa had public leverage that Bonds lacked. Amazingly, spring pundits were saying that despite Bonds' superb condition, there were signs that his age was beginning to catch up with him. His 2000 season may have been the best of his career up to that point. Baker's decision to occasionally rest him, however, was used as "evidence" that the man was losing it.

The Giants knew they were taking a risk by not waiting on Bonds, but they felt they had no choice. They could not afford to pay a high salary to a player who would no longer be worth it, and they were not bound by their fans' love of Bonds, like the Cubs were with Sosa. The general feeling in Scottsdale was that it would be Barry's last spring there.

Some say that when the pressure is on, Barry chokes. As Bonds prepared for the season, those who consider such things were asking whether he was one of the greatest athletes, and one of the most important people, in Bay Area sports history. Or, was he selfish, whining, overpaid, and unwelcome. E-mails from Giants fans to media outlets suggested both, and very little in between.

Some days, he is a great guy and a credit to his team.

Other days, he is mean. He does not always hustle. The universe revolves around him.

Without Barry Bonds, there is no Pac Bell Park, and the Giants probably would be in Florida. The Giants have been better with Bonds than they were with Mays. He has carried the franchise on his back.

During the regular season, he is money when the game is on the line. Bonds has to throw away at least 100 at-bats a year before the season even starts, yet he still put up his numbers while making his teammates better.

No one takes the extra base on him. He plays the wall like few before him.

He has experienced personal problems and is hassled constantly, yet he does not get the benefit of the doubt.

Is he the man?

He once came storming into the locker room calling everyone "green flies."

"Where the hell've you been all year?" he yelled at everybody within 50 feet of him, most of whom had been right there, all year.

At times like this, writers have described him as "demonic," dismissing entire groups like Nero giving the thumbs down to a downed gladiator. In 2000, this attitude, or memories of it, may have cost him his fourth MVP award. It really should have been his fifth, since his loss to Atlanta's Terry Pendleton in 1991 was a travesty, too.

Approach Barry Bonds with something, and he wants to know if it will change his life. Prior to 2001, it had been said that he does not even talk to Kent, that he would not even have dinner with his teammate. Some say he is a racist.

On the other hand, Bonds has been asked to help kids and contribute to charity, and he has done so without asking how it will change his life.

The man is a conundrum.

Bonds has enemies in the media. There are those who have examined his postseason failures like Woodward and Bernstein going after Richard Nixon. They say he is one of the biggest chokers in baseball history, and always has been, going back to little league. He has been accused of being a lifelong loser, a bum who half-steps singles into doubles or misses fly balls. They say he is a phony who turns on his act like Bill Clinton when he saw the cameras at Ron Brown's funeral.

Once, Bonds turned on the charm for the media at a press conference. He smiled. He was handsome. He was humble. He listened to every question attentively. When the cameras and the microphones were turned off, a writer approached him. The writer did not have a question for him; he just wanted to tell him he was friends with one of Bonds' teammates from Arizona State. Bonds did not say, "Really? How is he?" or "Yeah, he was a great guy, when did you see him last?" No, he turned his back on the writer without so much as gracing the man with acknowledgment. The Patrick Swayze effect.

The real test of a person's character or personality is not how they "perform" for the media, but the way they are with average people in average situations, when nothing is required of them except grace.

Hall of Fame basketball player Rick Barry has a sports talk show on KNBR. He is intelligent, articulate and knowledgeable. He sounds like a very nice guy. Once, he was given a tour of homes on the Northstar-at-Tahoe golf course, and the real estate agent guiding him said he took rudeness to a new level.

Bonds has been both nice and rude. Not everybody is like John Wooden, a legend in his time, comparable to Bonds. Wooden always deals with people in a kind, gentle, honorable way. That is what makes him better than the rest.

So Bonds hides in a fancy locker with big-priced toys. One San Francisco writer used a term typical of that town's politics, calling him "elitist scum."

These were words used to describe Bonds prior to the 2001 season. That kind of rhetoric is gone for now. How soon we forget. Bonds lives in the ultimate "what have you done for me lately?" world.

When Bonds made his spring debut, it did not come with the usual bombast. There were no bold predictions or outlandish statements. There was, however, a little sadness as he pondered his future.

Bonds may not have felt there were many big-money contracts left in his career.

"I really don't know what's going to happen," Bonds said. "But if I'm not going to be here, I should just be told so I can tell my family. If I am going to be here, then let's talk about it and get it done.

"They know what's going to happen," Bonds said of the Giants' front office. "I ran into [vice-president] Larry Baer last week, and he said he couldn't envision me not wearing a Giants uniform. But last time I looked, he didn't own the team.

"If they don't want me back, they should let me know. …What I've done for this team, I deserve that much."

In eight seasons in San Francisco, Bonds had hit 318 home runs, but he knows baseball history. He knows it is a business. He was eight in 1972, when the Giants traded Mays to the New York Mets for knuckleballer Charlie Williams.

"That's the only thing that irks me," Bonds said. "They traded my Godfather. They traded Matt Williams. It's unfortunate. But why would it be any different for me? This is my first choice. But I have a family to support."

Athletes who have enough money to support 10 families until the end of the 21st century love to talk about supporting their family, providing "security" for them. It is bogus. They want the money for various reasons. Greed is one of them, but as often as not, the money is a sign of their place in the pecking order of their profession. It is as much about pride as anything is. It is also, crazy as this may sound, about respect. It seems ridiculous to normal people to consider that a baseball company paying an employee millions does not respect him because it is not enough millions.

Consider the Rod Tidwell character, played by Cuba Gooding in "Jerry Maguire." There was nothing sympathetic about Tidwell. He turned down money from the Arizona Cardinals that was more than most high-priced lawyers and doctors make. Tidwell claimed he was not getting "love" and "respect," all wrapped up in some kind of quasi-word—*kwan*—from any and all entities that, in his warped view of the world, owed he and his a living for as long as he walked the Earth.

Bonds, who like Tidwell would not be a Wall Street banker, a Beverly Hills lawyer, a top surgeon, a hotshot advertising executive—or a top-notch writer—if he was not an athlete, insisted that he was not Tidwell. He swore that it was not about the money and that he was not trying to break the bank for one last payday.

"I just want what I work for," he said, echoing the sentiments of most anybody outside of homeless bums. "I'd even give up a little to be on a ballclub committed to winning. I'd work out anything if it was a contending team."

Dusty Baker had been in a similar situation in 2000, waiting until the season was over to sign a new contract after the Giants won the NL West.

Baker was prescient in his observations of the situation.

"It's hard to get the top, top money if you don't take a risk," Baker told the media. "You think I would have made as much if I'd signed early?"

The three-time Manager of the Year expected a huge season out of his star.

"Players become totally focused in their contract years," Baker continued. "If he stays healthy, he's going to get it."

"I've played pretty good every year," Bonds said after being told what his manager had said. "A contract year isn't going to make any difference."

Of course, playing "pretty good" and playing the way he would this season are two separate things.

In the exhibition opener at Scottsdale Stadium, the Cubs beat the Giants, 6-5, and the first thing on everybody's mind was the high strike, which the Commissioner had declared would be in force this season. Livan Hernandez opened with a fastball above the belt of the Cubs' Eric Young, and home-plate umpire Kerwin Danley called it a strike. Young stepped out of the box and gave Danley a look that said, "Huh?" They chatted briefly, smiled, then got into a mock argument.

Former Giant Julian Tavarez sent Barry Bonds a message by firing a first-pitch fastball over his head.

"I want to throw strikes," Tavarez said afterward. "I haven't pitched in a while. I was trying to pitch inside, and the ball got away from my hand. I wasn't trying to hit Barry. Why should I hit Barry? I've got nothing against Barry. I don't have any reason to hit Barry."

Bonds hugged Tavarez when they met at first base after Bonds grounded out.

"Barry didn't think it was intentional," Baker said. "He had fun with it. I'm just glad Barry didn't get hurt."

In Florida, Gary Sheffield was telling the Dodgers, through the media, that he might not play as well unless his demands were met. Frank Thomas was boycotting the White Sox camp to protest his salary. Bonds, on the other hand, continued to let his representative do his bidding.

"This reminds me a lot of the Kevin Brown contract," Boras said of the seven-year, $105 million deal he negotiated with the Dodgers a few years earlier. "The issue was a 33-year-old pitcher. Most pitchers at 33 are near or at the end of their careers. But we have situations where these players are anomalies. Their performances exceed the customary performance you see for players their age."

"I don't think it's fair to anybody that you engage in this and don't get something done," Sabean said. "Then everybody's going to take a side, people on the team, the fans, the media. Then it becomes counterproductive."

The Commissioner's office, meanwhile, ordered that Bonds' elbow protector be no longer than 10 inches. The one Bonds has worn for years is longer. How much longer?

"None of your business," was Bonds cheery answer to the writers doing their jobs. "My elbow pad is not illegal. Does that answer your question? Goodbye."

Gene Clines confirmed that the shield is a few inches too long and would be modified. The new restrictions were designed to make hitters more fearful of leaning into tight pitches, reducing hit batsmen, and cutting down on brawls.

On March 10, Willie Mays arrived for his annual visit to camp saying he was happy that Bonds soon would join him in the 500-homer club.

What about Mays' 660, a stated goal of Barry's?

"That's kind of shaky," Mays told the media. "We've talked about that. I don't think he should be worried about how many. Just go up and do it. When you start concentrating on just one aspect of the game, then you lose the game. I think with his ability, he should just go enjoy what he's doing. If he gets to that number, that's fine."

Bonds' first six homers would make him the 17th Major Leaguer to reach 500.

"Anytime you can get 500, that's a great feat," Willie told the press. "There aren't many guys up there. I've talked to him about that. That's a great accomplishment. He could have gotten it last year, but I guess 49 home runs is pretty good. I wanted him to try to get 50, because not many guys have gotten 50 in a year either."

Going into 2001, Bonds needed to average 34 a season for five years to surpass Mays for third place on the all-time list.

Over at Phoenix Muni, the A's, despite being led on near-nightly forays into neighboring Scottsdale by Giambi, had a great spring. They were favored to win the American League West, and many felt they would do better than that.

Of course, of all the cliches in sports, "It's only Spring Training" might be the truest one. San Francisco broke camp at 9-19 after their seventh straight loss, 9-8 to Arizona.

"So far nobody's hurt," remarked Baker. "But it's time to start practicing winning. The season is right around the corner."

"We haven't played worth a shit in spring training since 1997," Sabean told the Bay Area press before the team headed to San Francisco and an exhibition series vs. McGwire's Cardinals.

Picking the order of finish to a baseball season before the season starts is one of those things that seems reasonable at the time, but in hindsight it is just filling space. The *Chronicle's* Henry Schulman saw it this way on April 1, 2001.

1.   San Francisco.
2.   Los Angeles.
3.   Arizona.
4.   Colorado.
5.   San Diego.

Baker's lineup looked like this:

CF, Marvin Benard
SS, Rich Aurilia
LF, Barry Bonds
2B, Jeff Kent
1B, J.T. Snow
RF, Armando Rios
3B, Russ Davis
C, Bobby Estalella
RHP, Livan Hernandez
LHP, Kirk Rueter
RHP, Russ Ortiz
LHP, Shawn Estes
RHP, Mark Gardner
RH closer, Robb Nen

Two thousand one would, of course, be still another year of the great Giant-Dodger rivalry. The Los Angeles Dodgers had seen better days. For the first 60 years of the existence of the Dodgers and Giants, the Giants had it all over their New York rivals. The Giants were given that name, one of the best and most time-honored in sports, by their owner-manager, Jim Mutrie, who in the 19th century surveyed his troops and proclaimed then, "My Giants." Many felt they got that moniker because they played in a "giant" city filled with "giant" buildings. Not so.

The Dodgers got their name because of their fans. In the old days, Brooklyn was a suburb of New York, a city in and of itself. Therefore, one of their names was the Suburbas. Can you imagine that at one time Brooklyn was considered a suburb?

In order to get to Ebbets Field, at the corner of Bedford and Stuyvesant Avenues in the Flatbush section of Brooklyn, their fans had to navigate a difficult series of trolleys, the precursor of the current subway system. Brooklyn baseball fans would find themselves "dodging" the trolleys. Somebody started to call them "trolley dodgers." By the early part of the twentieth century the team was the Dodgers. Not exactly Giants.

In the last 16 years of their mutual stay in the Big Apple, the rivalry was intense but favored Brooklyn. Until Barry Bonds arrived in San Francisco, the Dodgers dominated the rivalry in California, too.

By 2001, the Dodgers had "gone Hollywood." Dodger Stadium had always been a meeting place of L.A.'s Beautiful People. However, despite being run by Fox and studio mogul Bob Daly—people weaned in the entertainment industry—the team and place had lost much of their lustre. The club was no longer headed by the O'Malley's, a dedicated baseball family. They had lost their touch. In a fashion typical of the go-go late 1990s, Fox just threw money at their problems like a government bureaucracy gone bad.

The team entered 2001 carrying a $100 million payroll filled with big-name underperformers. On the other hand, Kevin Brown, Chan Ho Park, Darren Dreifort and Andy Ashby made up a formidable starting staff, with All-Star closer Jeff Shaw out of the bullpen.

Right fielder Shawn Green had disappointed when he returned to his hometown after putting up big years in Toronto. Former UCLA first baseman Eric Karros was good for 30 home runs and 100 RBIs a year. None of them, it seemed to his critics at least, when it counted.

In Phoenix, manager Buck Showalter was gone, replaced by ex-Giant Bob Brenly. Brenly inherited some great names who were past their primes, among them third baseman Matt Williams and second baseman Jay Bell. Center fielder Steve Finley would still provide strong defense. First baseman Mark Grace, a free-agent signee after years of great seasons in Chicago, promised to still have something left. In left field a new star had emerged. His name: Luis Gonzalez.

Arizona, though, would live or die with Curt Schilling and Randy Johnson. Reliever Byung-Hyun Kim from South Korea had looked unhittable when he first came over with his sidearm delivery, but the question about him would be, "When would the hitters figure him out, sooner or later?"

Mike Hampton and Denny Neagle had signed for a mint to pitch at Colorado's Coors Field, but the plan was to improve on the club's 34-47 road record in 2000.

Former Tennessee quarterback Todd Helton was a budding superstar, and third baseman Jeff Cirillo, along with ex-MVP Larry Walker, rounded out a strong offense, especially in Denver's thin air.

San Diego added Mark Kotsay, the 1995 College Player of the Year at Cal State Fullerton, but the Padres had fallen far and fast from their 1998 World Series team. Tony Gwynn was past his prime entering his swan-song season. Ryan Klesko and Phil Nevin were quality players, but the Pads had very little starting pitching to set up ace closer Trevor Hoffman.

San Francisco had scored a franchise record 925 runs the year before, but that included Burks' 96 RBIs. Henry Schulman would prove prescient in his assessment of Aurilia: "Although Rich Aurilia is not the prototypical num-ber- two hitter, his homer and RBI potential gives the Giants a different look there than they had with Bill Mueller, and that's not necessarily bad."

Not necessarily.

Defensively, questions dogged the team, not the least of which was Bonds, who it was felt could not get to balls he used to routinely catch. The big problem was in center, where Marvin Benard had occasionally justified Baker's faith in him, yet he had the potential to be a bust in the field and at the plate.

Shawn Estes and Russ Ortiz entered the season considered to be, fi-nally, *pitchers*. Livan Hernandez, Kirk Rueter and Mark Gardner made up a potentially strong staff, veterans capable of taking advantage of the new higher strike zone.

Closer Robb Nen was a one-inning guy, so Felix Rodriguez and Tim Worrell would have to do the job in set-up roles.

Dusty Baker was the owner of a new two-year, $5.3 million contract with one managerial playoff win, a record of 1-6 in two Division Series (plus a tiebreaker loss to the Cubs).

Each club would play the other division teams 19 times. Bonds and his teammates would be facing plenty of Johnson, Schilling, Brown, Park, Dreifort, Neagle, Hampton, Pedro Astacio, and Woody Williams.

"You don't know until you get into competition," Schulman quoted Baker. "You don't know if you've got enough or don't have enough. Who would have guessed last year we were going to win more than anybody in baseball? If you had gone to Vegas and put that down in December, you would have won a lot of money. You don't know what's going to happen. It's all a plan. It's all speculation. It's all on paper."

Somebody once approached Mays and asked him who would win the pennant that year.

"Man, how should I know?" Mays mocked in that whiny voice of his. "That's why they play the season."

The Giants would live or die on offense with Kent and Bonds, the one-two finishers in the 2000 MVP race.

"How much more can they do?" was Baker's rhetorical question to the media. "A man can only do what a man can do. All I want them to do is what they can do, and everybody else has to do their jobs.

"And you may never make up for Ellis. . . . Like it says in the Bible, the Lord never puts more on you than you're capable of doing. I'm not the Lord, but that's how I feel about it here.

"I can't ask Jeff to hit 52 home runs and drive in 172 runs, or ask Barry to hit 68 home runs…"

Sixty-eight home runs? Now just *hoooold* on there, Dusty.

"I've had a good spring; Dusty managed me very well during Spring Training," was Bonds' assessment. "He conserved my body a little bit and it paid off. I feel good—strong and flexible."

Bonds thought about it, then scratched his head.

* *"I think I'll hit 72 or 73 homers this year,"* he said.

On opening day at Pac Bell Park, the Giants beat the Padres 3-2. Already they were doing better than the previous season, when they started 0-4 and had people wondering if the new park was jinxed.

It was their first game played in anger at Pac Bell since the play-offs against the New York Mets, and not a few among the crowd reminded Bonds that he hit all of .176 in that one.

On this Opening Day, or opening, depending on your view of things day (as Jim Bouton once said), Bonds did it with his arm, his bat and his glove, just like Mays in his prime.

In the top of the fourth inning, Bonds fielded a ball hit by Wiki Gonzalez, jamming his two left fingers in the process, yet he was able to fire it in to catcher Bobby Estalella. He made the tag on Gwynn, ending the inning.

In the fifth, on the first pitch he saw, Bonds hit a 423-foot home run to the left-center-field bleachers. 40,930 paying customers knew they were getting vintage Barry.

Bonds finished up his trifecta with a seventh-inning catch of Chris Gomez's fly ball to left center that both Bonds and Benard went for. Bonds lost it in the sun, but he recovered. He is one of the best outfielders in history when it comes to negotiating fly balls in the sun, the clouds, and the lights. After catching it, he crumpled to the ground.

Throwing, catching, hitting . . . what did he enjoy the most?

"I can't say throwing out Tony, because he's 45," said Bonds, giving him five extra years. "So I guess it would have to be the home run."

Barry's postgame comments were more than he usually gave, but this was an indication that maybe he was opening up a little more this year.

"I'll talk to you about the game and nothing else," he said. "I'll talk as long as it's about baseball."

As in baseball *playing*, not baseball *contracts*. Bonds was sensitive to his being lumped in with Thomas and Sheffield, who had hurt their clubs and themselves by not approaching Spring Training with full intensity, because

*Just kiddin'.

they were unhappy with contract negotiations. Bonds may not have been happy with negotiations, but nobody could accuse him of a lack of baseball dedication.

"We've got an older team," he said. "If you go night-day-night-day, you'll lose a lot of us. We need more recovery time."

There was one other thing Bonds was happy to talk about. His 11-year-old son Nikolai, a team bat boy, was waiting after his homer. Bonds, who was not allowed in the dugout during games as a child, gave his son a kiss on the cheek.

"That's nice," he said. "I enjoy that. I didn't have that opportunity with my dad, but there are different rules now."

Bonds still had another game this day. Nikolai had a 5:30 little league game on the Peninsula and Dad was going to be there. He would not hide in the car, either.

By April 12 the thrill of his Opening Day performance was already a memory. Bonds was approaching the longest hitless streak in his career (20 at-bats), so Baker gave him the night off.

The ever-observant Gwynn, however, said, "He's like a time bomb waiting to explode," he said. "You just hope when he does it's just solos."

When he returned the next day, he hit home run number 496 to snap his hitless streak in the Giants' 8-3 loss at San Diego.

"You start thinking about things, how lucky I am to be in the position where I am in my life through baseball," Bonds said. "I just needed to get back in the fight. I kind of got star-struck for a little while, a little nervous, trying to block things out of my mind and go back to the basic things and play the game.

"It's hard to explain the feeling that you go through. It's like you never dreamt you'd be in a position to do certain things in your life and your career. You never thought it was possible or reachable. The next thing you find out, you're knocking on the door and you're a little bit nervous. You find you're on center stage. You're out there by yourself alone."

Next came a telling remark. "Now I've probably figured out why I don't hit in the play-offs," admitted Bonds. "The spotlight. It's tough."

The Giants were 6-3 after sweeping the Padres at home to start the season and going 3-3 on their current trip with three games to go in Milwaukee.

Life is a fragile thing, and the Giants understood that after their flight to Milwaukee ended with 25 fire engines lining the runway in Chicago.

As the team plane from San Diego approached Milwaukee at around midnight, the pilots discovered that one of the flaps on the right wing would not deploy. They decided to land at O'Hare International Airport, about 80 miles south of Milwaukee, which has longer runways to accommodate speeding planes with no flaps to slow them down.

The pilots never announced the diversion until the plane landed and everyone saw all the flashing lights.

The Giants considered chartering buses and driving to Milwaukee, but mechanics fixed the flap and the plane took off again for the 16-minute flight, where they arrived about 2 a.m.

In 1971, the Oakland A's, favored to win their division under new manager Dick Williams, had started 2-4 when they ran into a close call on another plane ride to Milwaukee. Everybody fueled themselves with alcohol after that, resulting in some horseplay by the players, who stole a bullhorn. Williams, who had powered a few scotches himself, let them know in no uncertain terms that he was capable of being a "prick," and unless they buckled down on and off the field, they would learn just what a prick he could be.

The team went on a tear after that, and finished with 101 victories. Would San Francisco react in a similar manner?

Barry Bonds motivates himself. He does not need close calls in the sky, whether he finds out about those close calls after the fact or not. At Milwaukee's brand new Miller Field, he hit three homers and two doubles over his next nine at-bats.

"Don't ask me," Baker said. "I don't know. Maybe that's called greatness."

The Brewers, however, hit five off Mark Gardner in an 11-6 victory. Bonds' three-run homer in the fifth keyed a five-run rally that brought the Giants within 7-6 before they stalled.

The Great One, however, was humbled the next evening when he dropped Jeffrey Hammonds' routine line drive with two out in the bottom of the eighth to widen the Brewers' lead to 7-3, killing any real chance the Giants could complete a comeback.

A TV network was ordered to the Giants' clubhouse to get a Barry Bonds sound bite on his approach to homer number 500.

"I don't care about that right now," Bonds said softly. "If you want to ask me that question, come tomorrow. This ain't a good day. I lost this game for us, and this ain't the right time."

Bonds did not cause the Giants' 7-4 defeat, but he carries his team and feels the responsibility.

"I straight fucked it up," he said. "That's the best way I can put it. I just, wow. That's all I can say. I saw it. I just took my eye off it at the last minute. I took it for granted that I had it and made a beeline to the dugout."

"You rarely see it, maybe once on a blooper tape nine years ago when he was with the Pirates," said Hammonds of the rare Bonds mishap. "That's gold out there."

"It shows he's human," said Baker. Human, huh. Who knew?

Bonds had earlier lined number 499 over the left-field wall off David Weathers.

The Giants returned to San Francisco for their longest homestand of the season, 12 games, starting with the first of three against Los Angeles, and with Bonds one homer away from 500.

"Now, he'll get number 500 at home," Milwaukee manager Davey Lopes said. "That's the way it should be, and better yet they're playing the Dodgers, so the stage is set."

"Imagine how many home runs Barry Bonds might have if he had signed with the Giants in 1982 instead of going to Arizona State for three years," wrote Schulman in the *Chronicle*.

"We drafted him," muttered Frank Robinson, the Giants' manager at the time. "Didn't get him signed. Missed by $5,000."

Fourteen of the 16 hitters who have hit 500 homers are in the Hall of Fame, and the other two (McGwire and Eddie Murray) almost surely will be. It is one of the most exclusive clubs in the world—Aaron, Ruth, Mays, Robinson, Harmon Killebrew, Jackson, McGwire, Schmidt, Mantle, Foxx, McCovey, Williams, Ernie Banks, Eddie Mathews, Mel Ott and Murray.

"I think Todd Helton put it well last year when he was going for .400," Bonds told the media. "He said, 'I'd rather just do it than talk about it.' I'd rather talk about it after it's done. That would make it a lot easier for me, and I don't have to think about it that often. Sometimes, when things seem like they're forgotten, they're better. They happen a little easier."

Bonds acknowledged that his 0-for-21 slump came about because was trying so hard to get to 500.

"You've got your family going, 'We want to be with you when you do it,' and I'm saying, 'Wait until I get to 499,'" Bonds explained to the media. "Everybody can travel with me. I'll pay for it."

"I want my parents there. I want my wife there. I want my kids there."

The Hall of Fame contacted Boras to see about getting the bat he would use to hit his 500th, as well as the ball, his shoes and the like. Both Willies—Mays and McCovey—were on hand.

"It took awhile," said McCovey of his 500th on June 30, 1978. "There was a lot of pressure because a lot of the media was following me around waiting for me to hit it. I just wanted to get it over with."

Five hundred homers, like 3,000 hits and 300 victories, is a magic number that is supposed to assure somebody of entrance to Cooperstown. However, there have been debates. Jose Canseco needed just 54 homers for 500 in April, 2001. He has been a DH since 1994, and not a particularly complete player prior to that. Dave Kingman approached 500, but nobody thought the surly ex-Giant was Hall material.

Don Sutton had made it to 300 wins as a pitcher, mostly by compiling 15- and 16-win seasons over many years. Despite grumbling, he was enshrined. Tommy John had come close to 300 but just missed it, yet he was not generally considered a Hall of Famer. Neither was Jim Kaat.

Bill Buckner had approached 3,000 hits, but he was also a World Series goat, and not generally looked upon as an all-time great. Was longevity enough?

Five hundred home runs, 3,000 hits, 300 victories—these are a lot of homers, hits and wins no matter how you slice it, all earned at the big league level. It is difficult to deny somebody their due if they attain these kinds of figures.

Taking the argument one step further, should McGwire's 555 homers be mentioned in the same breath as McCovey's 521, for instance, given that Big Mac hit 300 of them in what is considered the modern juiced-ball era?

Barry Bonds was already a first-ballot Hall of Famer. Five hundred home runs was not something he needed to get in. By 2001, Bonds was something new and different. He was born with remarkable genetic gifts, and those gifts had carried him a long way. But now he was much more. His training regimen, his diet, his knowledge of the game, his sheer experience had elevated him far above even his own prior accomplishments.

Baseball is a game of repetition. If one does it enough, practicing every day, playing against the best; learning, observing and improving; they can become great players that way. Prognostications of their ability when they are young go out the window.

This is what had happened to Kent. He was a solid high school player growing up in Huntington Beach, near Los Angeles. He was a top college player, helping the University of California to the 1988 College World Series. He had moved through the minor leagues and become a major leaguer. He was solid, but not a star.

A smart, observant, driven man, Kent worked the game. He improved over time. His experience became as important in his approach as his natural ability, and by 2000 he had earned an MVP award.

Jeff Kent is a nice player who knows the game inside and out. Bonds is a great, great star who had not wasted an ounce of his ability, which many before him had.

Jerome Holtzman, the longtime Chicago newspaper columnist, felt that perhaps Bonds was the last classic baseball player, which reeks of the "in my day" rhetoric that old-timers have passed down since Ruth played.

"I think Bonds can classify that his 500 home runs have been more difficult to come by than McGwire's and Sosa's," Holtzman told Schulman. "Maybe he's the last one through the door." Sosa is projected to get there eventually.

"The best setting would be tonight, game-winning home run in the ninth," Baker said before the first game of the homestand. "We'd all be extremely happy." Nobody had to wait long.

On April 16, his five 500th homer came in the bottom of the *eighth* inning against Los Angeles reliever Terry Adams. With cameras flashing, Bonds' shot sailed over the right-field wall and into McCovey Cove. Almost as importantly, the home run gave the Giants a 3-2 win over the Dodgers.

"Deep to right field," Jon Miller called out from the broadcast booth. "This is on its way to McCovey Cove, number 500."

"Unbelievable," said his partner, Mike Krukow.

There was hardly any spontaneous joy, however. There was no reaction in the dugout. A batgirl met him, followed by Aurilia.

"I think there's some who had no urge to shake his hand," said Mark Gonzales of the *Arizona Republic* on "Sports Century."

His teammates "were all happy for me," Bonds insisted.

He hugged Aurilia, who scored ahead of him, then his parents and his brother. Then he greeted the two Willies.

"When I touched him, he was still shaking," Mays said. "That shows me he realizes what history is all about."

After Aurilia's leadoff triple, he turned on a 2-0 pitch and drove it 417 feet out of the stadium, over the portwalk and into San Francisco Bay, where sailor Joe Figone scooped it out.

"He threw me a slider in," Bonds said. "I couldn't believe I hit it because everything was in slow motion. I was looking up and the ball was in midair and it wasn't going anywhere. Then, when it got to the people, I said, 'Wow.'"

He got a standing ovation from 41,059 fans, the largest crowd ever at Pacific Bell Park (the Giants added 129 new seats into the club and field levels).

"I was getting kind of stressed because everyone around me was making me a little nervous, and I really was," he said. "I knew my wife wouldn't be nervous anymore, and my dad would be grateful and not in my ear saying, 'Relax, relax, relax.' "

It was his fifth homer in five games, a first for him, and his third at-bat since his 499th in Milwaukee. In those three at-bats against Darren Dreifort, he struck out, hit a fly ball to the warning track, and grounded out.

The high fly in the third, caught by Sheffield, almost got out.

"I think so, yeah," Bonds replied when asked whether he was happy the big one went into the Cove. "That was kind of nice. I'm glad the one in left field didn't go out."

The *San Francisco Examiner* gave it front section headlines: "OUTTA HERE" in big boldface, along with my article, "On this night, time to give Barry his due."

I wrote that Bonds, the "son of Bobby, the Godson of the 'Say Hey Kid,' and according to a few, a son of maybe something else" was "above all, a son of San Francisco" who had now entered the pantheon of Bay Area greatness previously reserved for Mays, Joe Montana, Joe DiMaggio, Bill Walsh. My piece also stated that Bonds' experience could be compared to Ted Williams returning to Boston after Korea, or Mickey Mantle "capturing New York's imagination" when he chased Ruth's home run record with Maris in 1961.

"Barry was sort of like Mays, when he came to San Francisco," McCovey said. "He was not universally accepted. But it turned around. Barry was the same way. I hope this home run tonight erases all that, and he's accepted in San Francisco the way he should be."

"First of all, I could care less about Barry Bonds' achievements," said Adams. "All I worry about is winning and losing a game. That's all I care about."

Nen saved it after his warm-ups were interrupted by the ceremony, striking out the dangerous Sheffield to end it.

Bonds, despite his lifelong affiliation with the Giants and The City, bears none of the usual San Francisco angst when it comes to the Dodgers.

"No," he said. "I have a lot of respect for that ballclub. I have a lot of friends there, Gary Sheffield, Marquis Grissom. We're all going for the same goal, winning a World Series."

This one was just the latest among key milestone home runs in his career, which included:

1st: June 6, 1986 off Atlanta's Craig McMurtry
100th: July 12, 1990 off San Diego's Andy Benes
200th: July 8, 1993 off Philadelphia's Jose DeLeon
300th: April 30, 1996 off Florida's John Burkett
400th: August 23, 1998 off Florida's Kirt Ojala

Bonds had now entered a new era. He found himself compared to Mays, not just as a player, but as a San Francisco icon. Mays had encountered resistance from the fans when he came with the team from New York in 1958. Orlando Cepeda and later McCovey, for some odd reason, seemed to be more popular with the fans. Cepeda and McCovey were both single, and were seen out and about in the City's nightclubs. Cepeda, in particular, liked to cha-cha-cha the night away at Latin dance clubs.

In the mid-1990s, a Wendy Finerman-produced film starring Robert DeNiro and Wesley Snipes, called "The Fan," was produced. It was based, not too loosely, on Bonds, but morphed the Snipes character with Mays. The "Cepeda character" was played, brilliantly, by the great actor Benicio del Toro.

Mays was New York's guy, and as great as he was, his occasional pop-ups with men on base seemed to reinforce the fans' ultra-high expectations of him. Through his sheer greatness, Mays had won the fans over, probably by 1962, when he led the team into a thrilling seven-game World Series against the Yankees, who won the last game, 1-0.

Now, Bonds was there, with Mays, Willie Mac, Bill Walsh, Joe Montana, and the other legends of San Francisco.

Nowadays, The City's public high schools no longer put out great athletes, but there was a time when San Francisco and the Bay Area was a gold mine of sports talent, the way Southern California, Florida and Texas are today. San Franciscans, always a fickle and hard to please bunch, had reserved some of their greatest idolatry not always for the greats who played on the local teams, but for those who came from the area and played in other parts of the country.

Joe DiMaggio was first among these legends, having attended Galileo High (where his grades were so bad he did not play baseball), then starring for the local San Francisco Seals. The Seals had played at Seals Stadium, located at 14th and Valencia, not far from where Pac Bell Park is today. Prior to owner Charlie Graham building Seals Stadium, considered one of the greatest minor league parks ever, the Seals and Mission Reds played at Old Recreation Park. There is no sign of either stadium now.

This part of San Francisco has changed over the years. South of Market Street, known as SoMa, has seen many transformations. "Alternative" night clubs sprang up in low-rent bungalows and warehouses, but it has proven to be a place of pitfalls for partgygoers. A straight man would go there on a Friday night, meeting hot chicks and having a great time. The following weekend he would return on a Saturday, only to find out that Saturdays are "Gay Night." Hey, that is San Francisco.

In the '90s, SoMa became Yuppieville, when the Internet Revolution turned computer-literate 20-somethings into IPO paper millionaires. As it says in the Bible, this too shall pass, and it has.

On Brannan Street, a convention hall became notorious for teenage rave parties and the even more notorious Halloween "Exotic Erotic Ball," a pseudo-gay-hooker flesh carnage.

Before the days of pseudo-gay-hooker flesh carnages, there was baseball, and in 1935 DiMag had hammered out base hits in 63 consecutive games for the Seals. From 1936-51, he was a legend of the first order for the New York Yankees.

Then there was Bill Russell, who prepped at Oakland's McClymond's High before leading the University of San Francisco to two NCAA basketball championships and a record 60 straight victories. He would be the leader of the great Celtic dynasty of the 1960s.

O.J. Simpson had gone to Galileo, a school that boasted one of the greatest athletes ever in three different sports; DiMaggio in baseball, Simpson in football, and Hank Luissetti, who "invented" the jump shot, in basketball.

Simpson had starred in Buffalo before ending his career, and later his popularity, when he was accused of murdering his wife and a Los Angeles waiter in 1994.

So, entrance into the special club San Franciscan's reserved for their heroes was no easy task, yet Barry was now a bona fide member. It should be argued that he deserves membership in this club even more than the others, in that he is not just a superstar there, but is from there, too.

At a postgame press conference after home run number 500, Mays and McCovey demonstrated as much humility as Don King. When asked whether Bonds' entrance into a new pantheon of San Francisco greats reminded him of his own struggle from out of DiMaggio's shadow, Mays had this to say:

"You can't compare Joe to me. None of his statistics hold up to mine. I had 660 homers, he had 363."

Somehow, Willie did not think much of the fact that DiMaggio had personally cajoled and willed his team to four straight World Championships from 1936-39, and three more from 1949-51. Plus, a few more in between. Comparably, he had led San Francisco to second-place finishes every season from 1965-69!

McCovey was asked about his winning the Most Valuable Player award in 1969, when two writers refused to place Mets' pitcher Tom Seaver on their ballots. Seaver, who carried the Miracle Mets on his back and deserved the award, would have won if two writers had placed him fifth or sixth. He only lost by a few points. The system awards 10 points for a first-place vote, one point for a tenth-place vote. Both writers had decided pitchers should not win the MVP, since they already had the Cy Young award.

"He had no bidness winnin' MVP over me," McCovey said. "In fact, I shoulda won it the year before over Bob Gibson."

Of course, that year, 1968, Gibson only pitched 48 straight scoreless innings, tossed 13 shutouts, and posted an insane 1.12 earned run average to lead St. Louis to the National League pennant—over McCovey's Giants.

Old-timers.

After the game, the Giants wrapped Mays and McCovey in mothballs, not to trot them out until Bonds' next big moment required their presence. On April 19, Schulman wrote, "We hate to break this to you, Barry old chum, but the pressure is back on.

"Thought you could exhale after hitting your 500th homer Tuesday night, did you? You can't, you know."

Next on the agenda? Dale Long, Don Mattingly and Ken Griffey, Jr., who shared the Major League record for homering in consecutive games, with eight. Bonds needed just two.

"What record are you talking about?" Bonds asked when told about the consecutive homer record. "I didn't know anything about it. I don't care about that. I don't need another thing to think about in my life right now."

Apparently, President Bush had put him in charge of a new task force to find solutions to that spring's energy crisis, so thinking about mundane things like baseball records was just too much for the man.

Twenty-four hours after beating the Dodgers with his 500th homer, he did it again by going deep with two out in the seventh inning off Chan Ho Park. Bonds followed Aurilia's game-tying, two-run shot with another water blast. It was the difference in the Giants' 5-4 victory. They were now 5-0 at home.

The "Bonds stories" were now starting to appear.

Dave Stevens, who retired after 27 years of coaching at Serra and was now spending much of his time in Chandler, Arizona, said he knew Bonds was exceptional.

"I never thought 500 homers, but I knew he could play because he could do so many things well," Stevens said. "His best qualities were speed, quickness and patience at the plate. He seldom swung at bad pitches."

The story about the Giants' flirtation with the teenage Bonds was re-played. General manager Tom Haller and Bobby Bonds could not reach agreement, so Barry headed to Tempe.

"It wasn't a big disappointment," Stevens said. "I told Barry that if he didn't feel ready yet, and didn't factor money into it, that ASU would be a good place with good coaching. Jim Brock was considered one of the best in the country, and Arizona State had won the National Championship the year before."

"I was criticized for leading off with Barry," recalled Leyland. "I thought it was important for him to learn to get on base and use his speed. I didn't want to put that much pressure on a young kid.

"We all knew that someday Barry would be a big RBI guy. Early on, it was important for Barry to get some confidence. As for 500 home runs, who could have known?

"He'd be hitting .333 and decide to hit some homers, so his average would drop. He finally put it all together and became one of the greatest hitters of all time. If he stays healthy, 600 homers is a slam-dunk."

"Jim Leyland is number one," Bonds said when asked who his greatest coaching influences had been. "He brought me up like a father. He had a flair for saying something and making you listen. He'd say that you didn't have to like each other, but on the field you had to come together and become a team.

"We took care of each other like a family on the Pirates. We felt safe as a team. Leyland could tell when you were out of focus. He saw you drifting, like, 'Get out of the playground and back to class.'"

Bonds then allowed himself to make the comparison with other all-time greats.

"I'm like Hank Aaron because I hit home runs and never hit 50," he said. "And I'm like my Godfather because I can hit homers and steal bases. I'm a Willie-Hank kind of player."

Willie Mays. Hank Aaron. Now *that's* pretty fair company, and nobody could argue the point.

At 36 years, 268 days, Bonds was the 11th youngest to join the 500 club. He did it in his 7,502nd at-bat and his home run to at-bat ratio of 15.004 was the fifth best of players with 500 homers. Bonds was the fourth player to spend the majority of his career with the Giants to reach the 500-homer mark. Willie Mays (660), Willie McCovey (521) and Mel Ott (511) also had done it.

Bonds had also begun what would be a season-long courtship, of sorts, with the fans.

"I love you and I'm proud to be in a San Francisco Giants uniform," he had told the crowd during his ceremony.

"One of the best players who ever pulled on a uniform," said Bonds' good buddy, Garry Sheffield.

"As far as being able to do it all, I don't think anybody comes close," Eric Davis told the *Chronicle*. "When you talk about hitting 500 homers, winning eight or nine Gold Gloves and possibly being able to steal 500 bases, those are things that put him in a class by himself. He's set a standard, raised the bar with his greatness."

"I'd like to see him get it out of the way real quick and go toward 600," Baker had said before the historic shot.

Bonds' bat was headed for the Hall of Fame

"Cooperstown will be at our house," said Bobby Bonds. "That bat's coming home."

Chronicle columnist John Shea interrupted the post-homer lovefest when he suggested that Bonds might not go into the Hall himself with a Giants hat on his head.

" . . . the only question is which team Bonds will represent once he's enshrined, and that's no slam dunk," wrote Shea. "Dave Winfield, who'll be inducted in August, shunned the New York Yankees last week when announcing he's going to Cooperstown as a San Diego Padre.

"So, Barry, which team's cap will you wear on your Hall of Fame plaque?" The question was posed before the game.

"The last team I play for," he said.

Shea went on to point out that Nolan Ryan played eight years with California, nine years in Houston, and his last five in Texas. He went to Cooperstown as a Ranger. Bonds was in his ninth year in San Francisco after seven in Pittsburgh.

"Is Barry going to retire a Giant? Your guess is as good as mine," Shea quoted Bobby Bonds, employed as a Giants' advisor. "Barry would like to finish his career here, but I don't think anybody knows. If you look at the history of the Giants, you'd have to say it doesn't look good."

Bonds' point was that of the Giants' last five Hall of Famers, only one ended his career in San Francisco, and that was McCovey. He was traded late in his career only to return to the organization four years later.

Mays went out with the Mets. Juan Marichal retired a Dodger. Gaylord Perry played for seven teams and won Cy Young Awards in each league, and Orlando Cepeda won an MVP in St. Louis after leaving town.

"And guess what?" wrote Shea. "All five appear in Cooperstown wearing an SF logo."

Now Bonds' place in the game was becoming a topic of discussion. Not just his place as a player, but his popularity. Fan polls in recent years had rarely shown Bonds considered the best player in the game. More popular names like Griffey, Rodriguez or Derek Jeter occupied that place. Bonds? Too many felt he was the "poster child" for what was wrong with the modern player.

This was a man who was 25 stolen bases shy of becoming the first player with 500 homers and 500 steals. No one else even has 400 home runs and 400 steals. He had three MVP awards and should have had five. Nobody else has more than three.

The Pirates have not had a winning season since he left Pittsburgh. He has eight Gold Gloves. Respected? Arizona manager Buck Showalter once intentionally walked him with the bases loaded.

Unbelievably, Bonds did not make the All-Century team, receiving less than a third of the votes Griffey received, even though Griffey trailed Bonds in every offensive category (except batting average, where he had a slight edge). Junior continues to fall further and further behind. Griffey is a great, great player, and he plays center field, the most important outfield slot, so the All-Century vote can be understood, but Bonds is the better player.

Baseball officials could have added him to the team, but they chose not to.

Pittsburgh is no media capitol, and in San Francisco, his performances often did not make the East Coast newspapers or the early SportsCenter.

Bonds has that .196 batting average in the play-offs. He has never reached the Series. Neither has Gwynn or Griffey. Carl Yastrzemski went twice, and his teams lost both of them. Mays hit .239 in the World Series with no home runs and six RBIs. Ted Williams hit .200 in his only Fall Classic. Honus Wagner outplayed Ty Cobb when they met in the 1909 Series, and that was the Tigers' third straight Series defeat. The Georgia Peach never went back.

Instead of single, incredible moments that fans could hold on to— Mays and The Catch, Williams last at-bat, DiMaggio pushing his team to victory despite painful bone spurs in a four-game sweep at Fenway Park in 1949—many fans still remembered him for asking for a reduction in his child support payments during the strike, and the *Sports Illustrated* cover statement, "I'm Barry Bonds and You're Not."

Things have a funny way of turning around, though. Bonds was beginning an ascent in terms of both his reputation on and off the field. A recent book on DiMaggio, on the other hand, had revealed what many already knew, that the Yankee Clipper had been an aloof jerk, long protected by sportswriters who paid for access to him by attributing his behavior to his "class" and "desire for privacy."

Bonds can be a jerk, but there is something else there. Ted Williams could be a jerk, too. Still, there is a sense that Bonds and Williams could *be* a jerk, but that they are not *actually* jerks. On the other hand, one finds it difficult to ignore the evidence that DiMaggio *was* a jerk, all the time. Bonds, like Williams, Cobb, and John McEnroe, is a complex person. He is hard to figure out. There is too much evidence of his religious values, his love for his family, for his friends, for kids, for a better society, to dismiss him with the "jerk" label.

People were starting to say that he was the best left-handed home-run hitter in National League history, and the retrospectives were starting.

"My mother could have managed Barry Bonds, that's how good he is," said Jim Leyland.

Richard Obert of *The Arizona Republic* wrote this on April 17:

"It was starting to rain before the 1985 Arizona State alumni game at Packard Stadium, and a fearless kid named Barry Bonds was showing off to the big leaguers.

"Bonds, starting his junior season at ASU, stepped into a batting cage, and, with the pitching machine cranked at 80-something, he moved closer and closer. Finally, Bonds was about 30 feet from the machine. Pitch. Whack. Pitch. Whack.

"Jaws dropped at the lightning in Bonds' aluminum bat.

"'He'd just turn on it,' said Louie Medina, then-ASU first baseman who is now a scout with the Kansas City Royals. 'None of the big leaguers would try it. He was a special talent.

"'He's slowed down, but he's not a slug by any means,' Medina said...

"He was three years old, running all over the Phoenix Municipal Stadium concourse, when Bobby Bonds was tearing up the Pacific Coast League for the Phoenix Giants...

"'Barry was never quiet,' Medina said. 'Barry was Barry. He wasn't the best-liked guy on the team. He wasn't the worst liked. He took care of himself. I got along with him great. He was criticized as not the hardest worker. But when he got between the lines, he always performed.'"

Diamondbacks second baseman Jay Bell played with Bonds on the front end of his career in Pittsburgh, when he was more of a singles and doubles hitter.

"His drive has always been there," Bell told Obert. "I think he's driven by the Hall of Fame and strives to show he can equate some of the numbers produced by his childhood heroes."

An odd topic also began to make the rounds during the early part of the season. There was supposed to be a gay player who was dating a prominent gay journalist, who wanted to "out" him. Jim Rome explored the issue, asking the question, "What if a gay player came out?"

At first, he would be the "Jackie Robinson of gays," but things are more accepting and less shocking than in the past. Over time, if he could hit or pitch he would do okay. The player's identity has yet to be revealed, but he would not be the first gay athlete by any stretch, just the first openly gay, active male athlete in a team sport. Billy Beane (not the A's GM, who must be *thrilled* to share this name) was a gay baseball player with the Padres. Dave Kopay was a gay player in the NFL. Glenn Burke of Berkeley was gay when he broke in with the Dodgers, a family-conscious team that constantly asked him when he was going to get married. Burke ended up with the A's, where he would make regular trips to San Francisco's gay bars, always frightened about getting recognized. Eventually, he passed away from AIDS. Ex-Cowboy Dave Meggysey, who wrote *North Dallas Forty*, hinted around in the novel that he was bi (although the darker elements of the story, and bisexuality, were not part of the film's depiction, featuring a semi-macho Nick Nolte).

It is now obvious that a large number of women athletes are gay, to the consternation of not-a-few outspoken parents. Billie Jean King broke that ground years ago.

Considering the incredibly crude, misogynistic, screw-anything-in-a-skirt ways of many male athletes, it seems odd that they should be judgmental about sexuality, but they are. Bonds' teammate, Eric Davis, said he would want to know if a teammate was gay so he could steer clear of him. Bonds, the kid who went to Catholic school, steered clear of the issue himself.

The fact is, there is not much that supersedes ability on the field. It is about winning, and talented players put money in their teammates' pockets. That is the real bottom line. Players' sexuality, criminal behavior, political affiliations—unless these matters become all-encompassing, on-the-field performance is what counts.

It has been said that Stalin could have had a job in baseball if he could hit with consistent power. It was, in fact, mainly wildness on the mound that kept Fidel Castro from becoming a pitcher with the Washington Senators (of all teams) instead of a despot. As a radical lawyer and budding *revolutionary,* he once inserted himself into a Winter League game, and almost knocked the head off of the Pirates' Don Hoak with a bean ball pitch. If the Senators had come through, and if Castro had learned control, in more ways than one, then who knows what could have happened? Maybe, established in the U.S., he would have gotten involved in politics and gotten elected to Congress as a left-wing Democrat.

The point is, baseball is a game that has seen all kinds.

In a 5-4 win over St. Louis, Bonds was not wearing any protective gear on his right wrist, which was injured when he robbed Albert Pujols of a home run. He had injured it when his wrist hit the top edge as he was coming down, causing him to miss one game and delaying a face-off with McGwire.

While Bonds was getting hot, a soap opera of sorts was taking place over his number 500 home run ball.

On May 1, 2000, Bonds had hit the first baseball ever hit out of a Major League stadium and into a body of water. Joseph Figone, 39, recreation supervisor for the City and County of San Francisco, was waiting in an inflatable raft and scooped up the ball in a fishing net.

Figone offered the ball to the club, but Magowan told him to keep it.

"The ball should have been put on display at Pac Bell," Figone told Bob Padecky of the *Santa Rosa Press-Democrat.* "Peter said because I was so generous in my offer I would be allowed to throw out a first pitch before a game."

Figone is a San Francisco native and a lifelong Giants fan who said he had seen around 500 games. Consumer marketing director Tom McDonald left a message on his home answering machine saying it would not be appropriate for him to throw out a first pitch since he "wasn't a sponsor," said Figone.

"I've seen a lot of people throw out first pitches and they weren't sponsors," Figone said. "I was lied to. That was an insult."

"We never expected any ill feelings from Mr. Figone," a club official told Padecky. "We never had any intent to mistreat him. We're sorry he misinterpreted events."

This all seemed to fall into the "no good deed goes unpunished" category.

"I know they give tours of the stadium," he said. "I wasn't offered one. Why couldn't I have taken a few photos with Barry?"

A few days later, KNBR radio sportscaster Gary Radnich asked what the Giants had done for him. Very little, according to Figone.

"Three hours later the Giants called and said I had two free tickets to that Friday's [May 5] game," Figone said. "But when I went to my seat, I wasn't sitting in the owner's box. I was sitting a half-dozen rows back of them. And during the game, without my knowledge, the Giants put my picture up on the Jumbotron. I had no clue they were going to do that to me. I knew because of what happened my privacy was going to be invaded."

So, who retrieved Bonds' 500th homer on April 17? You guessed it.

"I put myself at great risk," Figone said, in what is really not an understatement considering that the Cove, on these occasions, looks like a miniature version of the Normandy Invasion. "I could have been killed out there."

When Figone met Bonds after the game, he showed him the ball but did not give it to him.

"But Barry's jaw dropped when I took it back from him," Figone said. "He was ready to walk away with it. I just caught the ball and now it's time for me to turn it over? I should let them walk all over me and give them the ball? I wasn't prepared to do that."

It was an awkward situation.

"I really felt I was put on the spot," said Figone, once a Candlestick Park grounds keeper who had often chatted with players, including Bonds, during that time. "It made me a little uncomfortable. I would never put family or friends on the spot."

"The moment was awkward but there never was any pressure placed on Mr. Figone at all to give the ball up," a Giants' official told the press. "It was never our thought to disrespect him."

"Both home run balls are equally significant," Figone said. "So why would they let me keep one and return the other? Both should be on display at the park. I just don't think this is the way you treat people."

Figone put the ball in a safety deposit box. John Acheson, a collector who owns Card Pro in Sonoma, valued the ball at $500,000, but he believed that by the time Bonds retires it could be worth $1 million.

"Barry could come over to the house for dinner," Figone said. "Barry could call me. That would be nice. If the 500 ball is really important to him, then you would think he would have called by now. But he hasn't. So I guess it can't be that important.

"Barry needs to talk to me. We are both on the same level. We are no different. Barry went to Serra. I went to Sacred Heart.

"I guess you could say I feel a certain amount of betrayal. Why does one fan get $3.1 million for Mark McGwire's 70th homer and another fan is offered two free tickets for another home run ball? Is that fair? MLB needs to address this issue.

"Fans have been polled on what they would do with either ball. The majority said they would sell it. I have never tried to sell it."

The next step? Lawyers, of course.

"Don't you think they will bring a lawyer?" Figone asked. "I'll bring one because they know how to talk to each other. Had I not been so generous in the beginning, none of this would have happened."

One argument beginning to make the rounds was whether the Giants were a big market or a small market team. The Bay Area supports two teams, which has proven to hurt both the A's and Giants over the years.

Now, after its initial season in Pacific Bell Park with revenue of $165 million—exceeded only by the New York Yankees and Mets, Brian Sabean said, "From year to year, we're at a fixed level with no dramatic increase on the horizon. A lot of that has to do with owning and operating our own park, from the year-to-year debt service [of about $20 million] that has to be paid up front to the ticket takers and ushers and cleanup crew. You just have a lot more going out than you ordinarily would, and that's without adding in a $62.5-million payroll."

The Giants were said to require a profit of at least $1 million a year, which they achieve with a payroll in that $62-million range.

The Giants had traded third baseman Bill Mueller, who was arbitration eligible, and let Ellis Burks, who hit .344, drove in 96 runs and was a clubhouse force, offsetting the distant relationship between Bonds and Kent, join Cleveland as a free agent. The thin line between failure and success on a team like this required new blood and unexpected strong performances from certain "journeyman" players, like Aurilia. The stars, Bonds and Kent in particular, had to be at their best.

"As important as it is to bring along a younger player or two each year, it's more and more difficult to just go with kids and try to rebuild long term in this division," Sabean said.

The question of whether the team would be better off without Bonds was a double-edged sword. There was the argument that said the team had never gone to the Series with him, so why bankrupt the team to keep him? On the other hand, San Francisco is a town of frontrunners in an area with a million things to do. The thrill of the new park would fade, as it had in Toronto. A marquee name like Bonds would be required to fill regular-season seats even if he failed to produce postseason wins. The team could contend without him, but would lose too many spectators in the early part of the season, before people got serious about them.

"It's just too difficult to go with kids and fill the ballpark and pay the bills," said Sabean. "I don't know who would understand us being in a rebuilding phase in any year. I mean, people talk about the veteran players we've taken on, but there isn't one starter we're asking to play more than they have for most of their careers."

In early May, the Giants traveled to the new PNC Park in Pittsburgh. Baker, a man who thinks about such things, told the media how happy he was to see a new park there, emblematic of an economic rebirth in Steeltown. After describing the new, shiny buildings and storefronts he saw during his last visit to downtown Pittsburgh, this writer said to him, "Maybe it was a Potemkin Village."

Baseball people—writers, players and managers alike—are a cliquey group. Most who were crowded around Baker did not know what a Potemkin Village is, and what they do not know or understand, they show contempt for.

In an odd twist of reality, most baseball managers would have looked at me like an idiot for speaking about something *they* were ignorant of. Instead, Baker genuinely wanted to know what a Potemkin Village was.

He listened patiently while I explained that the Queen of Russia had been told that her country's economy was good, its people happy and prosperous. In fact, they were starving. The Queen's advisor, a man named Potemkin, derived his political power base from the Queen believing the rosy scenario. In order to con her into believing his lies, he created fake storefronts and homes depicting happy, dancing Russian citizens when the Queen toured by boat along the Volga River.

"Talulah Bankhead played her in the movie," remarked the *San Jose Mercury's* Ron Bergman, an erudite type who enjoys the theatre and other pursuits of intellect.

Bob Smizek of the *Pittsburgh Post-Gazette* waxed melancholia over the return of Bonds to the city he had once brought success to.

"Beautiful PNC Park, the pride of Pittsburgh, is graced on the outside by three statues of the players who are widely acknowledged as the greatest Pirates," he wrote. "As is well known, all three of the men immortalized—Honus Wagner, Roberto Clemente and Willie Stargell—are deceased.

"So how could it be that last night, on a glorious spring evening, the greatest player to wear a Pirates uniform was playing left field on that sweet PNC Park grass?

"Although Wagner, Clemente and Stargell had the greatest Pirates careers and are the most revered players in franchise history, that doesn't mean they're the best to wear the team's uniform.

"The man in left field last night is not a Pirate, although he played for the team for six [*correction: seven*] years. When he goes into the Hall of Fame, it won't be as a Pirate. He wouldn't want it; the fans of Pittsburgh wouldn't want it.

"But that doesn't mean Barry Bonds isn't the greatest player to wear a Pirates uniform."

Smizek went on to write that Bonds was better than the Waners, Ralph Kiner, Bill Mazeroski, or Pie Traynor, too.

Smizek said that Pittsburgh fans "detested" Bonds, but acknowledged that he was reaching for an excellence that went beyond the petty boos and catcalls that are part of the game. Bonds' sheer greatness was literally beginning to overshadow his personality.

Bonds had batted .191 with one home run and three RBIs in 20 games as the Pirates lost three consecutive league championship series from 1990-1992.

"But to judge Bonds on 20 postseason games," wrote Smizek, "as opposed to the 860 regular-season games he played for the Pirates is, to say the least, unfair. He won two Most Valuable Player awards while with the Pirates, which is twice as many as any other Pirates player and was a major reason the team advanced to those three postseasons...

"The notion held by many that Bonds is not as good as Clemente is barely worth arguing. By virtually every comparison, Bonds is a better player.

"Although Bonds, who hit six balls into the Allegheny River during batting practice before the Giants' 11-6 win, has more than 1,900 fewer at bats than Clemente, he has 265 more home runs and 122 more runs batted in. Although Clemente won four batting titles and Bonds has not won any, Bonds' on-base percentage—a far more significant figure than batting average—is 52 points higher than Clemente's.

"Bonds has scored 183 more runs, stole 390 more bases and has a slugging percentage that is 94 points higher than Clemente's.

"It's a rare feat for a player to hit 30 home runs and steal 30 bases in the same season. Bonds averaged a 30-30 for the 1990s. Clemente never hit 30 home runs, never stole 30 bases. ...

"A more convincing argument could be made that Wagner, who won eight batting titles, is the greatest player to wear a Pirates uniform. With almost 3,000 more at-bats than Bonds, Wagner has 305 more RBIs. Although Bonds will likely catch him, that's an impressive number."

Roberto Clemente? Honus Wagner? These are legends who left indelible marks on the game. All-time greats. The best of the best. Now, a writer in a provincial town was saying this guy was *better* than they had been.

Of course, everyday life has a way of intruding on even the gods of the game.

"BARRY — NICE THROW — SID BREAM," said a banner trailing a plane over PNC Park during the first game of the series. It was a reference to Bonds' throw, just slightly off, which had allowed Bream to score and give Atlanta the win over Pittsburgh in game seven of the 1992 Championship Series.

"That's a waste of money," Bonds wryly commented about the plane episode.

The Giants battled from 4-1 down with a two-run home run by Bonds en route to a victory.

When twilight arrived, the lights did not go on. The game was stopped when only two of the seven light banks were on, both behind the left-field bleachers. Several players were jammed because they did not see the ball very well before the situation was rectified.

On May 6, Willie Mays turned 70, and a celebration was held for him at Bally's in Atlantic City, where Mays is employed in an ambassadorial role.

Mays' 70th birthday occasioned the question of whether he is the greatest living ballplayer, a title that Joe DiMaggio supposedly demanded at public appearances.

"Greatest living ballplayer?" Peter Magowan said to Henry Schulman. "Yeah, I do think he is. I thought it when Joe DiMaggio was alive. DiMaggio was a little ahead of my time, but of the players I saw—Willie, Stan Musial, Ernie Banks—Willie was the best, and if you talked to most of the guys who played with him they'd say the same thing, at least in the National League."

Would his Godson take that title away? Every day in 2001, he was getting closer.

CHAPTER
6
SIX

The Pace

In May, Bonds went on an incredible tear.

On Saturday night, May 19 in Atlanta, he upped the ante in a game that ended well after midnight after twice being delayed by rain, and after 90 percent of a crowd of more than 42,000 had departed. Bonds hit three home runs to give his team a 6-3 victory over the Braves at Turner Field.

If there was a turning point in 2001, it was during this series. The images are indelible. It was hot and humid in Georgia, and one recalls Bonds playing with sweat dripping off his face, his uniform soaked.

This was also the time when Bonds' strength became more apparent than ever. He had always hit homers. He always had power. Unlike McGwire, however, a Bonds home run usually resulted from Bonds getting his pitch and driving it. In Atlanta, Bonds demonstrated that every time he swung the bat, he was capable of going yard. He tomahawked the ball. He powered the ball. He went out to all fields. High flies and line drives. Bonds himself was in full "ask God" mode, completely unable to explain himself. The look on his face rounding the bases was the look of wonder. This supremely confident player, accused by some of not playing the game with joy, was now amazing himself.

With two out in the eighth inning, Bonds hit his third of the game and his 20th of the year to lift his team after a wrenching loss on Friday night.

"If there was any doubt about who the best player in this game is, it was pretty much answered tonight," Atlanta third baseman Chipper Jones said after Bonds hit three solo homers off three different pitchers, two to right-center and one to straightaway center.

"We're lucky we got out of here with a win," Bonds said, maybe exhausted at one in the morning facing a day game in a few hours. Or, perhaps he simply was unable to believe his own prowess. The late-night heroics would be a staple of his game. Bonds has a way of staying in the game when all around him are tired, and he can be at his best when playing in a light-headed stupor after getting little sleep. His on- and off-season conditioning program was kicking in, paying dividends. It reminded one of what George Patton once said.

"This is where it pays off," General Patton said as he watched his men marching through the snow during the Battle of the Bulge. They had won a winter battle, then with no sleep and no hot food, were in the middle of a 100-mile slog against heavy German resistance, rescuing the 101st Airborne Division at Bastogne, Belgium. "The training. . . . The discipline. My God, I'm proud of these men."

So it was with Bonds, who was making history in a different way than Patton, but in its own context he was just as impressive.

Bonds started the night with 511 homers. Before it was over, Mel Ott, Ernie Banks and Eddie Mathews would fall, leaving him in sole possession of 13th place. Next up: McCovey and Williams, tied at number 11 with 521.

Ott, Banks, Mathews, McCovey, Williams. This was getting serious.

"Man, what a great night," Baker said. "All I can say is, we've got some pretty good midnight players."

Bonds hit six solo home runs in the three-game series, together traveling, according to Henry Schulman, only 128 feet short of a half-mile. The undisputed truth of baseball, which is that it is not a one-man game, was all-too-apparent, though, as the Braves took two of the three.

In the finale, Bonds powered numbers 21 and 22 in an 11-6 loss. Bonds tied a Major League record with five homers in two games, four in four straight at-bats (five times in six at-bats and six times in eight). Two errors by Russ Davis cost two runs, though, and that was more than even Bonds could overcome. When historians look back at Bonds' storied career, the Atlanta series will stand out. Comparisons with other all-time greats were inevitable.

In 1949, DiMaggio was out until June with painful bone spurs in both heels. He came back for a four-game series against Boston at Fenway Park. He had not been to Spring Training or seen a pitch in a real game in over eight months. He had taken little batting practice. His team had stayed in the race under rookie manager Casey Stengel, but the Red Sox, led by Williams, Vern Stephens, Joe's "little brother," Dominick, and a strong pitching staff, were expected to brush them aside. This would be their statement against the Bronx Bombers.

In that four-game series, described eloquently in Pulitzer Prize-winning writer David Halberstam's classic *1949*, Joe DiMaggio put on a display of courage, skill, leadership and charisma matched by few athletes in history. The Fenway Faithful rewarded him with one of the most memorable standing ovations of all time. The numbers, while impressive, did not tell the story of chemistry and hope. If ever a player lifted his team on his shoulders and carried them, DiMaggio carried his club to a four-game sweep that propelled them to an eventual pennant and World Championship. Was it a New York legend, hype? No, this was the real deal, recognized for what it was by knowledgeable, appreciative fans of the Yankees' fiercest rival. When Mays contemptuously stated, "You can't compare Joe to me," one wanted to earmark the chapter in Halberstam's book describing DiMaggio's Boston series, and hand it to number 24.

The Atlanta fans, while not as savvy as their New York and Boston brethren, have seen some pretty good baseball. A fella named Aaron did pretty well there. Over the past 10 years, their own team had teetered on the edge of a dynasty.

In the series finale, they cheered the star of the team their guys had just beaten. They had seen something so special that an entire stadium of hostile fans rose in appreciation. It was a moment not unlike DiMaggio's Fenway cheer, and yet there was something different. DiMaggio's teams won and won and won. Bonds, like Mays, played on good teams that often finished second. Like Mays, it was not his fault, just as DiMaggio was lucky to play with great teammates. Bonds, Mays, Williams—some players played their careers under the shadow of a kind of Shakespearean curse, lone wolves baying at the gods of greatness, desperate for something so close, and yet so far away.

(Mays did have one World Championship, in 1954, but played 19 years after that without a second.)

So it was that night in Atlanta, when fans used to booing Barry Bonds rose to cheer him on a night he would lose, just as he would hear cheers five months later—on another night he would lose.

Bonds declined to talk about home runs. There was a disappointment to him. For all his personal achievements, he was truly sincere when he insisted that winning, getting to the Series and emerging with a championship, was his greatest priority.

Getting back to the theme of Patton, it was like when the General announced, "If we are not victorious, let no man come back alive." The hyperbolic comparisons of an athlete with a world figure such as Patton or

Julius Caesar, or the descriptions of his derring-do as having Shakespearean qualities, usually pale. Not with Bonds. Not now. Following him was like riding with Patton as he drove the Hun out of the Low Countries, covering the Nixon-Kennedy campaign, watching the Berlin Wall fall.

For a journalist, there is no greater thrill, no better opportunity. It usually is a once-in-a-lifetime occurrence. It is history, pure and simple.

Barry would acknowledge the history in Atlanta.

"I've never done a lot of things in life," he said when reminded he had done something neither he, nor anybody else, had done. "I've never traveled over the world.

"Dude, we're trying to win baseball games. I'm tired of being on the losing end against that team. That's all. It's been like this the last 10 years. It's amazing what they do over there."

"Unbelievable," Braves star pitcher John Smoltz said of Bonds. "I've seen him do a lot of things. But the things he did in this series, that was amazing. For us to get two wins when the guy hit six home runs was amazing."

"There are no certain words to describe a thing like that," said Eric Davis. "You don't try to explain it. You just enjoy it. When you have special moments in this game from special people, you don't try to break them down. You can't try to understand it. Just ride it and roll with it."

"I've never seen anything even remotely like it," said Chipper Jones.

"That's the first time I've ever seen an individual performance like that," said Brian Jordan. "It just shows how great he is. It shows why he's a Hall of Fame player."

Bonds was on pace to hit 82 this year, and Jordan, who had played with McGwire, was asked about Bonds' chance at the record.

"I wouldn't be surprised," he said. "The type of zone he was in this weekend, unless you walk him every time up, he's going to have a chance. The guy can hit."

After Bonds' first homer, a laser into the right-center bleachers, he returned to the dugout and laughed. After his second homer, a high 436-footer to straightaway center off Mike Remlinger that had even Andruw Jones gazing skyward in disbelief, the crowd of 33,696 gave Bonds a standing ovation.

"When you get a standing ovation on the road, it's special," Eric Davis said. "You don't get claps on the road. There's not too much that compares to that."

Schulman's notebook read like this:

"Homers, homers, homers.

"— Barry Bonds' two homers made him the 23rd player in Major League history to hit five home runs in two games.

— Bonds became the eighth player to hit six homers in three games, with Manny Ramirez (then with Cleveland) in 1998 the most recent.

"— Bonds has homered in his past four at-bats, tying the Major League record.

"— Bonds leads the Majors this season with 22 home runs.

"— He has 516 HRs in his career, leaving him five short of Willie McCovey and Ted Williams for 11th place on the all-time list."

The Giants then moved on to a three-game series at Phoenix. The season was really heating up, and it was not about the spring temperatures in the desert. The Diamondbacks featured Schilling and Johnson and they promised to be the team San Francisco would have to beat. However, something else was at play here. Barry Bonds led the Majors with 22 home runs. The Diamondbacks' Luis Gonzalez had 20.

"I prefer to downplay it anyway," Gonzalez told the media, who wanted to play it up like a match between Mays and Mantle, DiMaggio and Williams. "I'm not your prototypical home run king type of guy." "Gonzo," one of the nicest guys in baseball, was just a down-home Southern boy who had been a journeyman in Detroit and Houston. He had broken out in Arizona, but now he was hitting home runs like they were going out of style. He is a wiry guy, not a muscular slugger like Bonds, Sosa and McGwire. How was he doing it? The bottom line is he was meeting the ball and it was going out.

"I just played with him every day and saw how he does it," Gonzalez said of his tour of Japan, in which he played with Bonds the previous off-season. "He's got a great approach. There's a reason why he hits 400-plus home runs and steals 400-plus bases. He's just a talented player."

"I like him a lot," Bonds said of Gonzo. "He's a good contact hitter. Right now, the contact he's making is out of the ballpark."

Bonds entered the series 10-for-21 with seven homers on this trip. His 71 homers since the start of 2000 led the Majors.

On Tuesday night, he did it again, hitting another home run (his eighth in five games) and etched his name deeper into history. Again, his team lost, this time by 4-2.

Bonds was not just a home run hitter at Bank One Ballpark. He played "peacemaker," according to John Shea. When J.T. Snow charged umpire Charlie Reliford, who threw him out for throwing equipment, Bonds grabbed Snow in a bear hug and dragged him away. Baker then stormed after Reliford and quickly got tossed, igniting Baker to fire his cap across the infield.

So Bonds hauled Baker away.

Bonds long fly ball off Schilling was chased down by center fielder Danny Bautista near the warning track, but his next time up Bonds hit a 442-foot shot to center field. Eight home runs in a five-game stretch, a National League record previously held by Jim Bottomley (St. Louis, 1929), Johnny Bench (Cincinnati, 1972) and Mike Schmidt (Philadelphia, 1979).

Bonds also tied Frank Howard's Major League record of eight, reached twice with the Senators in 1968.

"There are some things I can't understand right now," he said. Some writers wanted more out of him. They wanted to know how it *felt*.

Bonds, however, was genuinely unable to verbalize it. His training had paid off even beyond his wildest expectations. Talk of steroids was making its way into press accounts. In an odd way, these "accusations" were a compliment to him. Steroids can make a man look ripped and juiced at a bodybuilding contest. They can allow a person to recover from weight lifting sessions faster. They can give a lineman brute strength, combined with explosive swiftness. Can they make a man hit a baseball farther? The answer is maybe. However, hitting a baseball requires precise timing. It is a game not of inches but of millimeters. Home runs are about bat speed, wrist action . . . and overall body strength. Was Bonds on the juice? The answer to that question does not lie within these pages.

"The balls I used to line off the wall are lining out [of the park]," he said. "I can't tell you why. Call God. Ask him. It's like, wow. I can't understand it, either. I try to figure it out, and I can't figure it out. So I stopped trying."

The McGwire Watch was in full swing. Ridiculous? Maybe, but this writer approached Bonds about writing a book on May 25 because I predicted he would do it, and thought it would be the biggest sports book of the year. It apparently was not so ridiculous to Shawon Dunston, who around this time made his bet with Bonds that he would get the record.

"To talk about it on May 21 is ridiculous," said Bonds, but when I told him I thought he would get the record, he did not say it was ridiculous. He smiled and seemed confident that he could do anything. Bonds was giving the press time-honored cliches, the party line. "I could be hit by a truck tomorrow, then what? 'He was on his way, but, damn, he got hit by a truck.'"

True, except that he had not been hit by any trucks in the past, and there was no logical reason why such an occurrence was more likely now.

Chipper Jones came out and said Bonds could break Hank Aaron's career record of 755.

"Hell, no," said Bonds. Interesting, but when the season was over and Boras was driving up his contract demands, the agent put together a big packet predicting that Bonds would get to *800* within five years.

"I promise you from the bottom of my heart I won't be in the game that long," said Bonds, seven months before asking the Giants for a five-year contract with the expectation of breaking Aaron's mark in a San Francisco uniform. "I guarantee you that. I'm going to be on vacation."

Bonds also said he would not participate in the home-run contest at the All-Star Game.

"I'm done," the slugger said a month and a half before competing in the home-run contest in Seattle. "No home-run derbies for me."

With eight homers in five games, Bonds had 23 this season and 517 in his career, was four away from McCovey and Williams, and like it or not he was in the home-run contest to beat all home-run contests.

Passing McCovey would also make him the greatest left-handed home run hitter in National League history.

The Giants were closing out a road trip through the hottest cities in the league—Miami, Atlanta and Phoenix, but they were cold. They got colder the next game, losing 12-8 to the Diamondbacks, despite another Bonds shot.

The San Francisco media was trying to determine what his nickname should be by now. Barry "U.S." Bonds seemed like it had been used before. USC fans had called him "Bail Bonds" because of his father's publicized problems, but that was not going to fly. John Shea made his bid for Grantland Rice status, calling him Barry Ballgame. After all, Ted Williams already had three nicknames—The Kid, The Splendid Splinter and Teddy Ballgame—so why not give Barry the latter?

"It would be a lot more gratifying if we were winning," said Bonds, now with nine homers in six games, all but one losses. "Just thank God it's May. It would be nice if it was helping our team win games."

Bonds set a National League record with nine home runs over six games (homering in each). Four other National Leaguers, including Mays, hit seven home runs in six consecutive games. Frank Howard (1968) hit 10 over six, the big-league record.

One problem the team was having was that their homers were solo shots. Of their previous 20 home runs, 18 were solos. Bonds had seven solos in a row until his homer in the 12-8 loss plated Aurilia. Edwards Guzman followed with a solo homer!

Sportswriters are famous for keeping bootleg tapes of the famous sportsmen they interview going off on them. There was the Lee Elia Incident, when the Chicago Cubs' manager went nuts on Cubs fans, wondering if they all were unemployed idiots. How else could they attend all those weekday afternoon games at Wrigley Field?

A writer once asked a powderkeg called Tom Lasorda what his "opinion of Dave Kingman's performance" was, a few minutes after Kingman's homer display beat his Dodgers in a crucial game.

Lasorda managed to sound like Joe Pesci (either the "riddle wrapped inside an enigma" scene from "JFK", or the "Do I amuse you?" scene from "Goodfellas"), only with a *lot* more swearing. Writers have been playing that legendary tape for years.

One prankster observed a female groupie offer Dodger second baseman Davey Lopes, now Milwaukee's manager, a "blow job" at Candlestick Park. Lopes seemed interested. The prankster then went to a payphone and called the visitor's clubhouse, where Lopes was by now, and asked the attendant for Lopes. He made his voice sound like a woman, and taped the conversation, which went like this:

"GROUPIE": Hey, Daveee...?

LOPES: Yeah, who's this?

"GROUPIE": I'm callin' in regards to the request for a blowjob on the field.

LOPES: (brusquely) Ya, ya, ya.

"GROUPIE": Can I see ya after the game?

LOPES: Ya, ya, ya...section 23, by the bus.

"GROUPIE": Will your wife be there?

LOPES: It don' matta.

On May 23, Ray Ratto of the *Chronicle* revealed that a new "blue" tape existed. This time Brian Sabean was on stage.

"Cock your ear toward the wind and listen, listen, as that vein in Brian Sabean's forehead pounds out the gentle strains of 'My Generation,'" wrote Ratto.

"Watch and see how his eyes bulge like a Tex Avery cartoon when he is asked the question. Hear him curse in three languages, including New Jersey, as he answers. And stare in wonderment at those who saw him the last time he was asked, doubled over in uncontrollable laughter.

"In short, the Giants' general manager is about to have another Barry Bonds Moment. You might remember Sabean's last one, back in the early days of Spring Training. Bonds had just arrived at Scottsdale Stadium and held his annual 'State of Me, Mostly'...

"Armed with a small story, the reporters faithfully trooped up to Sabean's office to get his reaction. What they got was a Vesuvian oration, featuring every common curse word, two that haven't been used much, and a very common one used in a new part of speech. He blasted the writers for dredging up old news, for forgetting that Bonds' contract would not be addressed until after the season, and for behaving like small burrowing animals in Sabean's delicates.

"The tantrum was taped for posterity, and was so good (as these things go) that even Sabean asked for a copy."

Ratto went on to explain that Bonds was putting up the kind of numbers that make agents ask for "A-Rod money," and that a new Sabean explosion was predictable, only now Ratto wanted to get it on video.

Meanwhile, Bonds was above it all. After taking a night off, Bonds hit his 25th home run on May 25—his tenth in a week—before 40,856 at Pacific Bell Park. Just as important, San Francisco won, 5-1, behind Shawn Estes two-hitter.

Armando Rios joined Bonds and Kent in the long-ball party.

"He's still getting pitches," Baker said of Bonds. "You don't get many, but when you get one you can't miss it. Guys like Barry and Sammy are like lions on the hunt. They've got to stalk a guy. Their prey is not going to run at them."

Bonds hit a home run for the seventh time in eight games, the second time he had done so this season. He reached 25 home runs in the Giants' 47th game. McGwire needed 52 to get there.

It was May. There it was, the McGwire Comparison. The Home Run Watch. The Chase For 70. *The Pace.*

Ann Killion of the *San Jose Mercury News* added to the chorus of voices calling for a new evaluation of the man. Bonds' "name belongs in the same paragraph—if not the same sentence—with his Godfather, Willie Mays.

"His peers are calling him 'the best player in the game.' We tell our children to 'come quick, Bonds is up,' because we know they're seeing history, the way we stood at attention for Mays."

Bonds was still playing hide-and-seek, mostly hide, with the press.

"It's as if he has an invisible sign posted above his locker—approach at your own risk—and on a daily basis, very few do," wrote Ailene Voisin of the *Sacramento Bee.* On the field, Bonds was getting regularly summoned for curtain calls and standing ovations from adoring fans.

"A lot of games, Barry hits a home run, but that's his only hit," Eric Davis told Schulman. "If you ask him, he'll tell you. He just has trajectory going right now. He gets the ball up in the air, and as strong as he is, if he hits the ball up in the air, he has a chance to hit the ball out of the park every night."

Bonds continued to hit at a blistering pace. Could anything stop him? He injured his hand, but x-rays showed no real damage. Then there was the power shortage being experienced by California during this period.

The stadium operations manager at Pac Bell assured the media that there was enough juice to keep the lights on.

Interestingly, while the scoreboard and video boards could go dark, the public address system would stay on. Major League Baseball required PA systems to be linked to emergency power after the 1989 World Series earthquake, when the sound was knocked out and the Giants could not tell fans the game had been called.

One could just hear Sonny and Cher singing " . . . and the beat goes on" Friday night, May 30 at Pacific Bell Park, when two more legends bit the dust. Unfortunately, so did the Giants.

The night before, San Francisco played a baseball game for the ages. It was an 18-inning, 1-0 marathon loss to Arizona that would go down with the

Marichal-Warren Spahn 16-inning, 1-0 pitcher's duel, won on a homer by Mays in the 1960s. Or Vida Blue's 18 shutout innings against California the night Tony Conigliaro struck out five times, then called it quits in a post-midnight press conference in Oakland.

Bonds did not provide Maysian heroics to win the pitchers' struggle, but he did come back the next evening to go yard, again in a frustrating defeat.

"This is when the strong survive," said Baker.

In the series finale against Arizona, Bonds hit his 521st and 522nd career home runs to catch and pass McCovey and Williams for 11th place on the all-time list.

The homer that tied McCovey landed in the cove that bears his name. Bonds' second homer went over the center-field wall, giving him the National League record for left-handed hitters. It was his 28th of the year.

The Giants lost, 4-3, thus getting swept by rival Arizona, and falling below .500 (26-27) for the first time in the season.

The Diamondbacks held first place in the division, while San Francisco had lost 11 out of 15 games.

Bonds was on a roll, but could not enjoy it.

"You can't explain this," he said. "It's really hard. You don't want to take away from the objective of the team, which is going back to the postseason and winning a World Series. You have to accept this and run with it, but you've got to keep it in perspective."

What was happening was a mirror, in some ways, of his career. He was hitting better than he ever had, and his team was not benefiting. His critics would point this out and say that it was proof that he is a selfish player.

Hogwash. Bonds can be a selfish person. He is not a selfish player. Was he at one time? Maybe a little bit, but never to the point where it hurt his team. The people who count, Dave Stephens, Jim Leyland, Dusty Baker, probably Jim Brock if he were still alive, would not call him selfish.

The people calling him selfish were the people who sell news, in print and electronically, by finding and stirring up controversy in any form. Selfish in the clubhouse, selfish with the writers, selfish with his time, okay. On the field, Bonds was a team player in ways that Frank Thomas never had been. More than Tony Gwynn. More than the sainted Cal Ripken.

Bonds learned the importance of team play from Mays, the essence of a team leader. He did not possess Willie's "say hey" personality, he did not give of himself or mentor young players or "manage" on the field like Captain Mays had, but he played every inch of every game to win.

His hustle occasionally lapsed, but even this was calculated. He had seen and heard what happened to Mays, who played every inning of every game hard "because I don't know any other way," and had been hospitalized in 1962 for physical and mental exhaustion because of it.

Baseball is not, on its face, the most taxing game. To those who know it, though, Major League baseball is one of the most taxing ordeals in sports. There are the physical requirements, and they are many. Playing and practicing day in and day out from February to October results in nagging injuries that must be played through.

However, the preparation, the mental strain, the concentration, on a daily basis, including day games after night games and travel, requires extraordinary professional toughness.

Bonds occasionally jogged out ground balls for two reasons. One, he knew he would be thrown out, and two, he knew what he was saving in May or June he would have in September and October. Pete Rose might not have done it that way. It was an approach subject to criticism. Nobody could argue with the results.

Bonds had enjoyed winning three MVP awards. He did not always spout party line cliches about winning the award. He wanted to win them, those were goals of his.

So what? Baseball needs more Dizzy Deans, guys who are good and know it. They need people who will say, "I want to win the MVP award because I know if I win it, I will have done the best to help my team win."

But Mr. Bonds was star-crossed. His teams were usually good, but not quite good enough. Did Bonds leave it all on the field during the regular season? Was he too exhausted to carry his team in the postseason? The Mets' Mike Piazza faced similar questions in New York.

Bonds was a victim of his own greatness, yet the bottom line is this: He is paid to play baseball in the most excellent possible manner within his ability, he had always done it, and now he was doing it better than ever.

Leading off the second inning with the Giants down 2-0, Bonds hit Robert Ellis' first pitch into the drink. When he crossed home plate he acknowledged McCovey, who was sitting in a front row seat near the Giants' dugout. McCovey joined in the standing ovation and acknowledged Bonds with a wave.

Bonds' second home run, to center, came with first base open after Kent singled and stole second. This time, Bonds stopped by McCovey's seat after rounding the bases to shake his hand.

"I'm glad he was able to do it at home and I was able to see it in person," McCovey said. "I'm glad it's over with, so now he can concentrate on winning."

"It was great to hit 500 in McCovey Cove, and 521," Bonds said. "I really wanted to jump over the railing, give Mac a hug and say, 'I did it in your house.' The other thing is, I got to do it in Willie Mays' yard."

Bonds also set a Major League record with his 16th and 17th home runs in May, a mark that Mickey Mantle and McGwire had shared.

Watching in the stands was Kevin Mitchell, the 1989 NL MVP, who hit 49 that year.

(Author's note: In a minor league baseball game in Kingsport, Tennessee, as a pitcher for the Johnson City Cardinals, I struck out Mitchell *five times*, and whiffed 15 Mets that evening.)

"It looks like he's going to hit one every time up," Mitchell told the press. "He's so locked in right now. He's seeing everything."

"Barry Bonds' 29 home runs this year are like snowflakes," wrote Schulman. "Taken together they look like an avalanche, but each is really unique."

Against Colorado at Coors Field, Bonds hit his 29th, a two-run liner to right off rookie pitcher Shawn Chacon, igniting his team to a much-needed 11-7 win.

Armando Rios and Aurilia added homers in the thin air, and Calvin Murray, just brought up to replace the struggling Marvin Benard in center, doubled twice, walked and scored twice.

In Bonds' first at-bat, Chacon intentionally walked him. His next time up, Chacon sent Bonds two pitches nowhere near the strike zone. Bonds laid off both.

On a 2-0 pitch, a fat fastball right down the middle, he drilled it over the right-field fence. It was an at-bat typical of his whole season. Always a disciplined hitter, Bonds was now a Zen Master. He demonstrated patience and selectivity. He refused to be drawn in by tantalizing pitches just out of his sweet zone. This was his game, the mental edge gained by years and years of learning and experience. Yes, he was strong, and he had inherited genetic talents from generations of Bonds's. But more than anything, he had the head game down to a pure science.

Cobb, Williams, Gwynn, Bonds, these were the technical champions of hitting. Ruth, "Shoeless Joe" Jackson, even Mays, they relied on instinct. Twenty-nine homer runs, his highest first-half total, and it was five weeks before the All-Star break.

"When you walk as much as he does, and they're always throwing around you, and then you get the one pitch you can hit, how do you just square up and hammer it?" Calvin Murray, who had been in Fresno all season, wondered to the *Chronicle*. The young center fielder from the University of Texas must have felt like he was sitting with Abe Lincoln on the train to Gettysburg. He had not just been assigned to the big leagues, he had been given a front row seat to history, and like everybody else on Barry's ride—writers, club officials, teammates, fans—he sensed that this was not something that happens all the time. "You'd think once in awhile they'd sneak attack him. That's why he's him, and we're us."

Bonds now had 51 walks.

"I just don't take anything for granted," he said. "I'm not anticipating he's going to throw another ball. I just expect he's going to throw a strike. You can't go up there with the mind set that he's going to throw a ball. Only when you're slumping you pray they throw a ball."

Bonds, the team guy, called Murray's performance "awesome, and he ran down balls I didn't have to go after. I was loving him."

The *San Francisco Chronicle* was now printing the "pace."

"Way ahead of pace Barry Bonds is the fastest to 29 homers and way ahead of the pace set by previous record-setters (season totals in parentheses):

"— Barry Bonds, 2001: 54th game

"— Mark McGwire, 1998: 62nd game (70)

"— Sammy Sosa, 1998: 73rd game (66)

"— Roger Maris, 1961: 75th game (61)

"— Babe Ruth, 1927: 79th game (60).

"Fastest to 30

"— Babe Ruth, 1928: 63rd game*

* Ruth hit his 29th and 30th homers in the 63rd game of 1928 and finished the season with 54."

The home run pace also looked like this at the end of May:

Name, Team, Year	March -May	Total
Barry Bonds, Giants, '01	28	85*
Mark McGwire, Cardinals, '98	27	70
Sammy Sosa, Cubs, '98	13	66
Roger Maris, Yankees, '61	12	61
Babe Ruth, Yankees, '27	16	60
*projected		

John Shea, in his June 1 column titled "Going, going . . . gone?" said Bonds was on pace to hit 85, "But is Bonds slugging his way out of San Francisco?"

The Pace, naturally, could only lead to The Contract.

"I'm not a pimp to money," Bonds said, and of Boras he echoed hopeful words. "He works for me. I don't work for him."

"Barry is more than a franchise player," Shea quoted Peter Magowan. "In '93, we signed what we thought was the best player in baseball, and nothing happened since then that says it's not an accurate statement."

The Giants payroll in 2002 was predicted to go up to $68 million from $62.5 million. Add to The Pace and The Contract, The Question.

"In the final analysis, are we going to have a better chance to win with him or without him?" asked Magowan. "It sounds like a stupid question.

People would say, of course we'll have a better chance to win with him. But there's a finite amount of money, and will there be enough for everyone else?"

Boras then began to lay the groundwork for his fall argument that Bonds was not like other players. Maybe he was a freak of nature, like Nolan Ryan. His new contract would not be negotiated the way other 37-year-olds negotiate contracts. This guy could be setting records and thrilling fans in San Francisco for many years to come.

"We said all along that Barry is a remarkably conditioned athlete, and his skill level is so high," Shea quoted Boras. "He's not a customary 36-year-old. . . ."

Boras had wanted a contract similar to those of Toronto's Carlos Delgado or Houston's Jeff Bagwell, around $17 million annually. Now, however, it was beginning to look ridiculous mentioning names like Delgado, Bagwell, Sheffield, Thomas, or Shawn Green, with the likes of Bonds.

There is Danielle Steele, Tom Clancy, Robert Ludlum. Good writers, sure. Then there was Ernest Hemingway, F. Scott Fitzgerald, and Charles Dickens.

Some people make lasting impressions. Bonds would be mentioned by baseball fans in 2080 the way Ruth was revered now, maybe more so because he benefited from television.

After Bonds passed McCovey, the career Major League leaders among active players looked like this:

Home Runs
1.   Mark McGwire, 556
2.   Bonds, 522
3.   Ken Griffey, Jr. 438

Runs
1.   Rickey Henderson, 2,205
2.   Bonds, 1,625
3.   Cal Ripken Jr., 1,614

Runs batted in
1.   Cal Ripken Jr., 1,645
2.   Harold Baines, 1,627
3.   Bonds, 1,457

Walks
1.   Rickey Henderson, 2,086
2.   Bonds, 1,591
3.   Mark McGwire, 1,263

Stolen bases

1.   Rickey Henderson, 1,380
2.   Bonds, 476
3.   Kenny Lofton, 469

By June 13, it had gotten to the point where Bonds was a story if he *did not* hit a home run, as was the case when he went homerless in the weekend A's series.

Bonds reached 33 in the Giants' 64th game. McGwire hit his 33rd in St. Louis' 70th game. At this rate, Bonds would hit 37 long before he turned 37.

"I've seen only a couple of players who can turn it on and get ready," Baker told the media. "Oh, yeah, Barry is one. Rickey [Henderson] is another. I'd like to see it. It's not scary. No matter what, the whole thing is Barry's health. If Barry's healthy, he's going to get it. You can count on it. That's fact."

So there it was. Baker, who says what is on his mind, was not couching the "Can Barry do it?" question with platitudes about it being too early. He is a baseball fan. He has an opinion. He said his guy would get there if he stayed healthy. Period.

Giants trainer Stan Conte cited Bonds' genetics, training regimen and ability to avoid serious injuries as reasons for his success, adding he wouldn't be surprised if Bonds surpassed McGwire.

"He hit 49 home runs last year, and he was probably positioned and physically able to hit 60," Conte told Shea. "His health and fitness get him on the field, and then it's up to his hard work and natural skills."

Bonds has two personalized fitness consultants. One is Harvey Shields, who stretches Bonds before games and is called The Shadow because he follows him around so much. Greg Anderson oversees Bonds' weight training.

"He's more flexible," Shields told Shea. "He's not as big as he was when I got here, but he's more toned and more defined."

"Any good scout will confirm that '90s expansion has watered down big-league pitching and that most staffs have pitchers who should either be in the minors or be retired," wrote Shea. This is a "fact" of some dispute. There have always been average pitchers. The guys pitching to Ruth, DiMaggio and Cobb were not all named Bob Feller or Hal Newhouser.

Mays and Aaron probably faced the toughest pitching. They ushered in the age of West Coast travel, played a lot of night games, performed a substantial number of years before expansion, and faced National League competition that included blacks and Latins. They also faced the slider, a relatively modern development.

Probably the most important factor was that they faced pitching from an elevated mound. In 1969, after the Year of the Pitcher in 1968, when baseball had a 2.99 earned run average, the mound was lowered. Pitching statistics in the 1950s, 1960s, 1970s and into the 1980s were significantly better than today.

Aaron did not face Spahn (his teammate) just as Mays did not face Marichal for the same reason, but they both squared off against Sandy Koufax, Don Drysdale, Tom Seaver, Bob Gibson, Steve Carlton, Ferguson Jenkins, and other top-notch hurlers. Teams played each other as often as 18 times a season in the 1960s, but everybody knows that the more times a hitter faces a pitcher, the advantage is gained by the hitter.

Mays, Aaron, Mantle, Killebrew, Frank Robinson, and the like did not see the specialized relief pitchers like Mariano Rivera, "lights out" guys who can neutralize a game. They did not face the set-up men who are so much a part of baseball today. They saw a lot more of a tiring Gibson or Spahn pitching on guts in the eighth or ninth innings.

Dick Radatz was an effective reliever in the American League for a couple of seasons. So was Ron Perranoski of the Dodgers, then in Minnesota. Baltimore, however, won three pennants in a row with almost no bullpen. The 1969 Miracle Mets used whoever Gil Hodges thought was hot that day. Sometimes that was an erratic Nolan Ryan, just as likely to walk a hitter or groove a home run pitch as get a strikeout. They also did not see the split-fingered fastball that has made a success out of so many pitchers, especially since Cubs' reliever Bruce Sutter popularized the pitch in the late 1970s.

In 2001, Barry Bonds and his teammates squared off against division rivals Arizona and Los Angeles 19 times each. Schilling and Johnson are every bit as tough as any of the aforementioned pitching heroes of the 1960s. So is Kevin Brown of the Dodgers. Chan Ho Park is pretty close, and Jeff Shaw exemplifies the modern closer that was not there 30 years ago.

How about a trip to Atlanta, where Bonds had torn up the Braves in May? Facing Greg Maddux, Tom Glavine and John Smoltz throughout the 1990s was just as tough as getting Catfish Hunter, Ken Holtzman and Vida Blue in Oakland, or Jim Palmer, Mike Cuellar and Dave McNally of Baltimore in the 1970s. Bonds was facing relievers. He was getting left-handers brought in, sometimes kept on rosters, specifically for the purpose of getting him out. Heck, Jesse Orozco was probably still in baseball because of Barry Bonds.

Furthermore, he was playing against players chosen from an ever-expanding population, in the United States and around the world. This includes the many Dominican stars, other Latin American players, plus pitchers emerging from Taiwan, South Korea, Japan, Canada, even Australia.

Mays and Aaron virtually never faced American League pitchers like Hunter, Denny McLain, Dean Chance, and Whitey Ford. Now, because of free agency, a Randy Johnson brings his heat in the American League for Seattle, then in the National League for Houston and the D'backs.

The most important factor disputing the so-called "pitching is weaker" argument is the effect of weight training. Pitchers lift. They benefit from it by getting bigger, throwing harder, and giving themselves the opportunity to rebound faster and avoid injury.

However, pitching always has been and always will be about finesse—finger pressure, movement, pinpoint control. Hitters gain more from lifting weights than pitchers do.

True, the ball *may* be livelier now than in the 1960s. Baseball denies it, but it probably is. That and smaller ballparks are more prevalent reasons for increased offense than bad pitching, although the whole thing is self-fulfilling, in that pitchers will change their style and be less aggressive when they are giving up more runs.

The new strike zone was having an effect, too. Bonds knows it so well that he was able to adjust to the 2001 zone, laying off pitches other hitters went for, and making use of the higher, narrower plane.

In the Giants' 2-1 victory over Oakland on June 16, Bonds flied out twice, once to the warning track in front of the 399-foot sign in center field. He walked in the seventh and ended up on the front end of a double play seconds thereafter. He was in the on-deck circle at the end of the Giants' last at-bat. He caught a fly ball.

Bonds had homered twice in the Giants' 3-1 win over the A's on Friday night, giving him 36 homers in 198 at-bats over 67 games. Still, an interesting phenomenon manifested itself.

Most of the local writers were interested mostly in the Giants' fifth straight win and the A's third consecutive loss.

McGwire, and later Sosa, endured great scrutiny in 1998. Certainly, it had started for McGwire early and was intense by mid-June. Perhaps because the record was still only three years old, and Todd McFarlane had not cashed in on his number 70 ball by selling it, the national media had not yet invaded the Bay Area.

They would.

Scott Ostler, once considered the heir apparent to Jim Murray when he broke in with the Los Angeles Times, wanted to know more about what made Barry tick. He came up with an interesting observation, which is that left fielders are loners. He cited Bonds, Rickey Henderson, and Gary Sheffield, noting that they tended to be at odds with the media.

In Boston, Ted Williams, Carl Yastrzemski and Jim Rice mistrusted sportswriters.

"Williams spat at 'em, Yaz wrinkled his nose at 'em, Rice growled at 'em," wrote Ostler.

Writers from all around the country were hitting the phones, getting quotes from all-time greats about this new all-time great.

Ernie Banks: "He can be compared to anybody who has played any position—Willie Mays, Hank Aaron, Babe Ruth or Mickey Mantle. He can hit, hit with power, run and field."

Frank Robinson: "You can mention him in the same breath as Willie Mays right now."

"Who cares, man?" Bonds asked when told. "What's the big deal? What really is the big deal about this?"

Ted Williams batted .344 in 19 seasons with a .634 slugging percentage, 1,798 runs and 1,839 RBIs. Williams may have been the player with the most in common with Bonds. He had missed the better part of five seasons because he flew planes for the Marines in World War II, then flew jets in combat for the Corps in Korea. If ever an athlete's life would make a great movie, it is Williams, whose off-field heroics are even more interesting and admirable than his playing career.

Astronaut John Glenn was *Williams' wingman* in Korea. Another Marine pilot, Jerry Coleman, who would play for the Yankees and become San Diego's broadcaster, once listened to a harrowing radio account of Marines in a dogfight with Soviet MIGs, a common practice. It was not until Williams flew his flak-scarred jet in that he had realized the fighter ace dueling the Communists in the skies, like an aerial Wyatt Earp, was Ted Williams.

Somebody once told Williams, who was 6-4 with matinee idol good looks, that he was the "real John Wayne. Wayne played those roles in the movies, but you *lived* it."

"Yeah, I suppose so," Williams, never a humble man, replied.

So why would Williams be compared to Bonds, who never served his country in the military and might not know an F-16 from an F-7?

Well, for several reasons. Bonds, like Williams, is a handsome devil. Like Williams, he endured a failed marriage while in the public eye. Like Williams, he was at best misunderstood by the media, and in some cases downright libeled.

The Boston press was down on Williams for some of the same reasons as Bonds, and for some other reasons. The similarities were that Williams was said to be selfish, his teams did not win, and he was a bust in the clutch. Other reasons involved politics, an area Bonds avoids.

Williams was from Southern California. His mother had been a lifelong Salvation Army worker, his father a handsome alcoholic. Williams was a rugged individualist and an outspoken conservative Republican.

He criticized Franklin Roosevelt and Harry Truman, setting himself at odds with the Kennedyite liberals that make up the Boston press corps. They went after him every way they could, exposing his faults as a husband and father, and even going so far as to criticize him as *unpatriotic* for not volunteering to fight in Korea fast enough after North Korea crossed the 38th parallel in June, 1950.

Bonds, like Williams, speaks his mind. The difference is that Williams never shut up, while Bonds senses there are times to pipe down, even at the risk of further alienating the writers. Williams disdainfully addressed the writers as the "knights of the keyboard," and was one of the most politically incorrect athletes this side of John Rocker.

In the mid-1960s, *Sports Illustrated* did an article that followed the retired Williams on his fishing adventures off the Florida coast (Williams is considered one of the best big game fishermen of the 20th century). Ted referred to anything that was substandard, whether it be a poorly tied fly, hitters who do no not know the strike zone, or the Great Society, as "Chinese."

One newspaper editor who had covered Williams when Williams had managed the Washington Senators in the early 1970s, tells the story of meeting Williams for lunch at a hotel in Oakland when the Senators were in town to play the A's.

Oakland is a diverse ethnic enclave, to say the least. In a room liberally sprinkled with blacks, Latinos and Asians, this tall, overbearing, sunburned white man, in a booming voice that could be heard by everybody, launched into a tirade/recollection of his combat flying days on the Korean Peninsula.

"Everything was gooks this and gooks that, and people are looking at this guy," recalls the editor. "Waiters, people at other tables. They didn't know who he was, they probably never heard of Ted Williams."

"I'd see a bunch of fuckin' gooks on the road and I'd just let 'em have it," Williams had said. "I just mowed the bastards down. It was great."

Bonds is a cosmopolitan fellow from the Bay Area. There is no doubt that his Catholic school upbringing effects his politics, his religious views, his opinion on such things as homosexuality, but he has never maintained any of the strong, public opinions that Williams was famous for.

Like Williams, though, Bonds is a patriot. He would demonstrate that a few months later.

Stan Musial batted .331 in 22 seasons with a .559 slugging percentage, 1,949 runs and 1,951 RBIs. Musial was the polar opposite of Williams, a beloved figure who stayed out of trouble by never airing strong opinions, if he had any.

"To me," said Gary Sheffield, who may be on Bonds' payroll along with Bobby Bonilla, "Barry is not only the greatest player in the game today, but he might be the greatest player in the history of the game."

The Sporting News had put together a panel a few years ago to rank the greatest players in the 20th century. Ruth was first, Mays second, Williams eighth and Musial 10th. That panel put Bonds at number 34, but now he was on a roll, like a politician who catches fire in the primaries.

Still, there was that postseason performance. Most of the Yankees had great postseason records, of course. There was Ruth, Gehrig, DiMaggio, Mantle, Yogi Berra, Derek Jeter. But the game is filled with superstars with subpar records in play-off and World Series competition. Even Musial had a less than awesome record in this regard. His Cardinals had enjoyed mixed success in the Series, all during the war years, which almost should be viewed as asterisk seasons. Musial feasted on wartime pitching while Teddy Ballgame served overseas. The 1944 St. Louis Browns' pitching staff that Musial faced in that year's World Series was filled with a bunch of over-the-hill Methuselah's named Ned Garver.

Bonds was by no means the only great player with unimpressive play-off numbers.

"It does affect you," Bonds had conceded a few years prior in an article in *Sport* magazine. "You're human. How can you be so good and do so well in 162 games, and then all of a sudden disappear?

"You feel like you've disappeared. All of a sudden now I'm this ghost, I'm gone."

Williams' Red Sox won only one pennant, and he batted .200 with no homers and one RBI in the 1946 World Series.

"That's going to be forever," Bonds said of winning a World Championship. "People will come back and see it for a lifetime. I might put a barrier around it so no one steps on it. Might even hire a bodyguard for it."

Orel Hershisher was a Dodger pitching ace who had thrown 59 straight scoreless innings to close out the 1988 season. That one year, he pitched as well as anybody in baseball history to lead Los Angeles to a World Series victory. He was asked about Bonds when he showed up at Pac Bell as part of an ESPN2 broadcast team.

"I'm sure he hit some against me—I faced him so many times," Hershiser, who remembers *every homer* Bonds hit off him, told the assorted media.

"But how you pitched him then is different than now. He's a different hitter. Back then, he would take pitches and go to left field. Now he pulls just about everything. He's bigger than he was, and he takes that inside pitch and pulls it over the right field wall.

"I love Barry," Hershiser, Bonds' teammate for a period in the late 1990s, continued. "He was great to my kids when I was here.

"I know he's gone through some rough things with the media, but I think this is a great second chance for him, and it's a chance for America to get to know him and see him put his best foot forward. Not many people get to have a second chance. I hope he takes advantage of it. And I think he is."

The national media was starting to say attention. Bonds appeared on the cover of *ESPN the Magazine* in June.

Photo courtesy of Serra High School

"SON OF SAN FRANCISCO"

The local boy makes good. Does anybody care? He is the godson of Willie Mays, the son of Bobby Bonds, and some say a son of something else, but former Serra High All-American Barry Bonds will always be a Son of San Francisco.

"SPEED DEMON"

Bonds was an All-American at Arizona State and set an NCAA record by getting seven straight hits in the College World Series. He was one of the fastest men in the college game, and a first-round draft choice by Pittsburgh in 1985.

Photo courtesy of Arizona State University

"READY TO UNCOIL"

Bonds turned down an offer to sign with San Francisco out of high school, accepting a scholarship to Arizona State. Playing for coach Jim Brock, he faced Mark McGwire and Randy Johnson of the Southern Cal Trojans, foreshadowing his Major League career.

Photo courtesy of Arizona State University

Tim Johnson, AP/Wide World Photos

"HAVE CHEW, WILL TRAVEL"

Bonds helped popularize the "extra long pants" look that thankfully ended the "knee-high stirrups" era. Note also the can of snuff located in his right rear pocket in this May 22, 1990 photo of Barry hitting a grand slam at Houston, en route to leading Pittsburgh to the East Division championship. Bonds was wiry and not as muscular as he currently is, but the home run follow through that would launch baseball's greatest season 11 years later is most evident.

BARRY BONDS

Ben Margot, AP/Wide World Photos

"PLAYER OF THE DECADE? TRY PLAYER OF TWO CENTURIES"

In 1999, The Sporting News named Barry Bonds "Player of the Decade" for the 1990s. Little did anybody know that they "ain't seen nothin' yet." Two years later, Bonds had baseball's greatest season, and in leaving contemporaries like Ken Griffey Jr. and Alex Rodriguez in the dust, he now embarks on a quest for the title "Greatest Player Ever."

"EAST MEETS WEST"

Two extremes on the style spectrum, Bonds and Ichiro Suzuki were the top vote-getters at the 2001 All-Star Game at Safeco Field in Seattle. Ichiro's American League topped the National League 4-1, but Bonds showed his softer side when he tried to outfit former Dodger skipper Tommy Lasorda with a chest protector after a close encounter with a broken bat.

Elaine Thompson, AP/Wide World Photos

Susan Ragan, AP/Wide World Photos

"AN EXCLUSIVE CLUB OF SPEED, POWER AND BASEBALL ROYALTY"

In 1996, Barry Bonds joined (from left) his godfather Willie Mays, his father Bobby, and then-Marlin Andre Dawson, as the only players ever to hit 300 homers and steal 300 bases. Like an F-16, Barry then left the others in his shadow, creating first his own 400/400 Club, and in 2002 he will give birth to 500/500. Also a member of the 40/40 (single season) Club, Barry's accomplishments make it harder and harder to deny that he may someday be recognized as baseball's all-time greatest player.

Eric Risberg, AP/Wide World Photos

"MY HOME BOYS"

Raised in the affluence of the San Francisco Bay Area's mid-Peninsula, Barry Bonds refuses to be typecast. Here he is pictured with two of his best friends, Gary Sheffield (then of the Dodgers) and Eric Davis, a couple of guys from the inner city. Despite his lifelong affiliation with San Francisco, Bonds has never echoed the tired Bay Area mantra that "all things Los Angeles are bad," saying in 2001 that he has family in Southern California, he respects the Dodgers and "one of my best friends plays there."

BARRY BONDS

"THE MAN OF HISTORY AND THE MAN OF MYSTERY"

Bonds, Barry Bonds, is a man of mystery who understands baseball history and his place in it. His godfather, Willie Mays, is the player whose standard Barry strives to attain. One can only imagine the stories of "inside baseball" young Barry heard growing up at the feet of Mays, his father Bobby, and the other "gods" of our national pastime. Here, Mays congratulates his heir apparent on his 500th career homer.

Ben Margot, AP/Wide World Photos

"SET IN STONE"

Like Willie Mays, Barry Bonds came home to San Francisco after making his name some-place else, and like Mays, the city was slow to accept him. In 2001, Barry hit his 500th homer, broke the all-time single-season record, and in winning his fourth MVP award, established himself within the pantheon of Bay Area sports icons. Still, few really know what makes him tick. On July 1, a cement handprint honored the enigmatic superstar.

Eric Risberg, AP/Wide World Photos

David Phillip, AP/Wide World Photos

"ALL IN THE FAMILY"

To those who ask who Barry Bonds is, one answer is that he is a devoted father. On October 4, 2001 in Houston, he tied Mark McGwire's record with his 70th home run, and was met at home by his loving son, Nikolai. Considering the genes in the Bonds family, one can only imagine Nikolai's potential in baseball.

BARRY BONDS

Julie Jacobson, AP/Wide World Photos

"'YOU CAN TELL IT GOOD-BYE.' 'HE HITS IT HIGH. HE HITS IT DEEP. HE HITS IT OUTTA HERE.' 'ADIOS MADRE.' 'BYE, BYE, BABY.'"

Every description has been used to describe Barry Bonds' home runs except, "THE GIANTS WIN THE PENNANT!" *On October 7, 2001 at Pacific Bell Park in San Francisco, Bonds launched his 73rd homer. Next on the agenda: That elusive championship ring and Hank Aaron's career mark of 755.*

BASEBALL'S SUPERMA

"Bonds is now with The Mick and The Babe and Willie and The Killer and Frank and Double X and Willie Mac and Mac and don't expect for even a second that Bonds will be able to absorb all of that," the article said.

"I don't even listen to him right now because Barry doesn't even know what he's saying," Mays was quoted in the piece. "I just want to let him sleep tonight. I want to let him cry a little bit."

The premise of the story was that Bonds' 500 homers is a larger number in baseball history than 3,000 strikeouts and 2,000 RBI.

"Was Barry Bonds right this spring when he looked into an ESPN camera and said that on the day he's inducted into the Baseball Hall of Fame, he's going to stand at the podium in Cooperstown and say to the fans, 'Thank you, but you missed the show?'" asked *ESPN the Magazine*.

"Does the man have a persecution complex? Or has his career truly been tarnished by members of the press who've made the fans focus more on the things he doesn't do—like run out every ground ball like a kid just up from Fresno, or answer their questions enthusiastically—than on the things he does, like put up numbers that already place him among history's greatest all-around players?

"I think the fans only believe what they read," Bonds was quoted. "If you have a good relationship with the media, they'll write nice things about you and the public will admire you. But if you're your own person, and you just want to go to work and don't want that light in your face all the time, then they'll write that you're standoffish or arrogant. Do they really know you? No. But they think they do through what they've read. I know how I'm perceived."

Bonds, like Greta Garbo, just wanted to be left alone, which is fine, except that he has chosen a profession where you perform for others, and where the amount of money you and your team makes is dependent on fan support.

Bonds seems to fail to understand that he *owes* the press in a way. Take away the media, and the game is just a game, not The Show. Take away newspapers touting each contest, with its statistics and standings, its hype, its predictions and prognostications and opinions, and the players would perform in empty arenas, like Congressmen speaking to C-SPAN cameras in an empty hall.

Television gives glamour and *panache* to sports. Radio makes it a part of millions of everyday lives. The media gives these people the celebrity status of rock stars and movie actors. The publicity machines of Hollywood and the recording industry do the same thing for their people.

Take away the media, and you have an anonymous game played between the Fresno Grizzlies and Las Vegas Stars, just as the latest Bruce Willis, absent media hype, would play in art houses in two or three large cities.

So, yes, Bonds can play baseball without the media, but the media plays a big part in making him the marketable product, worth millions, that he is. Without the attention, he would play this beautiful game in his beautiful way, and he would make about as much money as a good college coach like Stanford's Mark Marquess.

Bonds is not comfortable with the media. That is not his fault, and he should not be excoriated for it. But he does need to understand that he has chosen this life. It is a free country and he can do something else. As long as he chooses professional baseball as opposed to, say, building houses or selling real estate, he will face down the press.

People owe other people one thing: Courtesy. Bonds owes writers courtesy, just as they owe him the same thing. He owes each new person he meets the benefit of the doubt, and vice versa. If he does not want lights in his face, there is no law, no rule, no judicial mandate, no legislative ruling or Federal order, that says he must continue to be paid millions and millions of dollars to play this game.

These are the facts.

Still, Bonds was not crediting the standing ovation he saw after he blasted his third home run in the game in Atlanta. Then there were the Arizona fans who booed their own pitcher for walking him intentionally with a southpaw on the hill, to pitch to last year's Most Valuable Player.

"It was surprising," Bonds told *ESPN the Magazine*. "It was nice." The question was not whether America had room in its heart for Barry, but whether Barry was ready for it.

History, as in "running out of the house in your underwear every morning to check the box score" history and "ignoring the wife and kids on a Saturday afternoon while you follow the GameCast" history was being made, according to the article.

Bonds continued to channel all interview requests through a personal publicist. Steve Hoskins works for a company called Kent Collectibles, and apparently has never heard of world famous columnist George Will. Hoskins is one of Barry's oldest and best friends, and a very talented artist who specializes in Bay Area sports memorabilia. His drawings usually feature depictions of Barry and Bobby Bonds, or Willie Mays or Willie McCovey, or all of them in various combinations, usually called "Legends of San Francisco" or something like that.

He is not a professional publicist, but handles Barry's media because "I'm the only guy Barry trusts," according to Hoskins.

"Stevie was a pretty good shooting guard," says Barry of his pal, who played basketball at Carlmont High of Belmont while Barry went down the road to play at Father Junipero Serra, the Catholic school in San Mateo. "He could pop." Bonds was a fine prep basketball player in his own right, and has an affinity for the game that he shares with Hoskins.

Sitting at Bonds' spacious locker with Hoskins, you see a side to him others do not see. He is among friends, or at least with a friend, and lets his guard down a bit.

"The team wants you here at Sunday at 10 for the hands-in-the-cement ceremony," Hoskins reminds Barry.

"10 a.m. on Sunday?" Bonds scoffs. "Yeah, right. I'll be here at 10 a.m. Ain't no way I'll be there at 10 a.m."

Now we see the responsible side of Bonds kick in.

"10 a.m., huh?" he asks. "Yeah, I'll be in bed by eight on Saturday." He smiles.

"My daughter still crawls into bed with us," he tells me, and the smile on his face thinking about it is worth at least a year of what he makes on his contract.

When I first thought about writing a book about Bonds, I contacted Hoskins. He ran it by Bonds, who passed on the idea. Then he hit all those homers against Arizona and Colorado, and by mid-June he was the biggest story in sports. I went back to him, and this time Bonds agreed to give it a try.

I had spoken to Bonds before, in my role as a sports columnist for the *San Francisco Examiner*, mainly in press conference settings like the one after his 500th homer.

Hoskins cleared the book idea by him, and told me, "Once Barry decides to do something, he does it 110 percent."

I was born in San Francisco and raised in suburban Marin County, where I played on Redwood High's National Championship baseball team. I was of the same vintage as Bonds, and followed his exploits at Serra.

I played professional baseball in the St. Louis Cardinals and Oakland A's organizations, and attended USC with McGwire and Randy Johnson when Bonds was squaring off against them for Arizona State. I saw plenty of Bonds during his years in Tempe.

I had been living in Los Angeles for several years, working as a sports columnist for a *StreetZebra* magazine, and also writing for the *Los Angeles Times*. In 2001, I had returned to the Bay Area and gone to work for the *Examiner*.

My observations of the "mating dance" between Bonds and the media was that Bonds ignored writers on a good day, and was rude to them on many days.

Writers treated him like the Abominable Snowman.

I had no problems with Bonds. Maybe it was because I had come over from Los Angeles and did not have any Bay Area baggage like almost everybody at the *Chronicle*. Maybe it was because I am 6-6, 220 pounds, an athletic guy who stays in shape and is around Bonds' age. As a former pro pitcher myself I could answer yes to the question athletes sometimes throw at writers, "How the hell would you know? Did you ever play?"

Mainly, I just approached him like a man. I walked around the big pillar that hides him from everybody in the clubhouse. This was No Man's Land, where writers fear to tread. None of his protectors were there, just Bonds sitting on his recliner in his underwear, watching his personal big screen TV. Roy Firestone was interviewing him on the TV. Bonds put out his hand. I thought he was telling me to leave.

We watched a couple of minutes of the interview in silence, until it broke for a commercial.

"I taped that last night," I said.

"Cool," he said. "Can you get me one?"

"No problem," I said.

When I asked him if he really wanted to do the book like Hoskins had indicated, he said "Definitely."

Other writers started coming up to me.

"You look like you've got Barry's ear," they would say, like I was Rasputin and Bonds was a Romanoff.

People would approach me in the press box with recollections of Bonds, more often than not horror stories revolving around his bad personality.

One radio guy told me he had grown up in San Carlos near Bonds, and said one time a neighbor came by to ask Barry to move his car, which he parked partially blocking his driveway.

"Fuck you," Barry said, according to this guy.

Leonard Koppett, a Hall of Fame writer who covered Maris' chase of Ruth, would meander on over and dispense wisdom. He firmly believed Bonds owed nothing to the writers. Koppett is the opposite of Len Shecter, a talented New York sportswriter in the 1960s who edited Jim Bouton's *Ball Four*.

"Schecter'd overhear guys complaining," Koppett told me, "then he'd write about it."

Koppett, as you might imagine, did not think much of *Ball Four*, which was an entire book full of overheard conversations. I told Jim Bouton I was writing a book about Bonds, and he then went off on a five-minute dissertation on why Barry is all that is wrong with today's players. This from the guy who exposed Mickey Mantle as a drunk.

Anyway, I made my first appointment to meet Bonds at Kent Collectibles in San Carlos. When I arrived, no Bonds.

"He blew me off," I thought to myself. "Same old Bonds, I guess."

When I arrived at the park, Bonds was full of apologies.

"Dude," he said, "I'm really sorry, man, but I got a call at 8:30 this morning from my daughter's school, and they need her tuition payment like, *today.* I thought it was taken care of, and I was on the road. Man, it's like $18,000. I don't just have $18,000 in checking, so I had to go to the bank and get a cashier's check and drive it over to the Crystal School. Then when I got there they said the only way I could sign her up was on the Internet. *The*

Internet?! So I had to go back and do that. It took all morning. Man, I'm sorry, buddy."

I had arrived in the clubhouse ready to think Bonds was what everybody said he was. Charming one day, a brush-off artist the other. He was not a brush-off artist on this day. Now, I had to consider that he was not viewing me like other journalists. Since we were talking about doing a book together, I guess he saw me as a business partner who was bringing him a deal.

Regardless of that, as Barry Bonds explained how he had to go through bureaucratic gyrations to get his little girl enrolled at the exclusive Crystal School, my heart went out to him.

I did not see a millionaire athlete or an arrogant superstar. I saw a fellow father who, just like me, cared for and loved his daughter the same way I cared for and loved my daughter, Elizabeth Ashley.

"I'm a member of the Bay Area media," I told Bonds. "For some reason, that means I'm not supposed to like you, but I couldn't help myself, I thought you were all right. Now, man, I'm digging you, because I'm thinking that if I had an emergency with my daughter, she'd come first, no matter what. That's what it's all about."

"Your children are just little kids for awhile," he said, "and you gotta cherish 'em."

Fans often do not realize the pressures that athletes, particularly Major League baseball players, are under. Bonds had played a late game the night before, but instead of getting a chance to sleep in, he had been interrupted by a phone call from his daughter's school. That same day, Armando Rios told me that after the team had returned from a recent road trip, he did not get to bed until 4 a.m., and had to keep a dentist's appointment at 8:30 a.m.

"I never sleep in anyway," Rios said, "because I like to get up and make my kid breakfast."

A baseball player does not just work the three hours it takes to play the game. For a 7:00 p.m. game, they need to be at the park at least by four. Many get there well before that for extra batting practice, treatment, to view tape, to lift weights, or for other reasons. Tony Gwynn is at the stadium by one to view tape, and he stays late to watch tape afterward, too.

In the three hours the player has, they have to get dressed, stretch, take batting practice, work on their defense, do their infield or outfield work, maybe take swings in the cage, hit the weight room (some do this after the game), deal with the press, deal with what the manager, coaches, and trainer want them to do, grab something to eat, change into a fresh game uniform, and get ready for battle. All with people milling about watching them (except for one hour prior to the game, when the press is not allowed in the clubhouse).

After the game, they may lift, get treatment, deal with the press, shower, and get home by 11 if they are lucky. Few are able to get right to sleep. Wives and girlfriends are often waiting, and they have the usual needs of wives and girlfriends everywhere. Not to mention a couple relaxing beers and checking out SportsCenter.

Day games after night games are extremely taxing, requiring a 10 a.m. arrival for a 1 p.m. game. Most players live at least 30 minutes from the park.

Road trips throw their routines into havoc. There are rain delays, make-up games, double-headers. Yes, they have an off-season. Nobody who plays in the big leagues has the right to complain. But there are many legitimate reasons why, on any given day, a fan will not see a player at his optimum best.

The next time I saw Bonds, a couple of days later, he was again checking out ESPN. This time, Roger Clemens was pitching for the Yankees, and he poured one high and tight to the hitter.

"Clemens with the inside heat," I remarked, "just like to Piazza."

The previous season, Clemens had hit the Mets' Mike Piazza in the head during the regular season, then in the World Series had fielded a soft grounder from him, along with a splinter of Piazza's broken bat, and thrown it at Piazza while he ran to first base.

"He don't even think about that shit on me," Bonds said defiantly. "I'll kick his ass."

False bravado? Probably. Bonds is not a "kick ass" type of baseball player, in the mold of a Pete Rose or Lenny Dykstra. He would not like the attention that being a brawler would bring down on him.

"I don't care for the attention all that much," Bonds explained in his *ESPN the Magazine* interview. "I think the more attention that gets drawn to me, the further I push myself away. Baseball is something I do well, but not something I enjoy talking about that much. I mean, Mark McGwire said it himself, over and over: This is a team sport. And the media and public accepted it. Now, I just hope they do the same thing for me. As time goes on, maybe we'll get to see if there's a double standard."

While Bonds continued to deny that he had a legitimate chance at the record, others told *ESPN the Magazine* something else.

Luis Gonzalez: "Without a doubt Bonds can do it. He's got a short, consistent swing, he can hit the ball out to all fields, he doesn't get himself out by swinging at bad balls. I wouldn't be surprised at all if he did it."

Brian Jordan: "Unless you walk him every time up, he's going to have a chance."

Dusty Baker: "The scary thing is that right now, the best is still ahead. Bonds is a second-half home run hitter, which most guys are. The pitchers begin to lose a little velocity in the second half and their ball doesn't sink or move as much, their breaking balls aren't as sharp. Historically, Barry's strong in August and September when the pitchers start to wilt a little bit. Who knows?

"The whole thing boils down to his health."

"I'm going to enjoy the ride as long as I can, but it's still going to end up like it always has," Bonds said. "I've had hot streaks before, and I've never hit 50 in a season.

"There are some things I can't understand right now. The balls that used to go off the wall are just flying out. I've tried to figure it out, and I can't do it. So I stopped thinking about it. I can't answer that question. I don't understand it either. Call God and ask Him."

At 228 pounds, Bonds was 20 pounds heavier than he was five years prior—but he said he had cut down heavy lifting in favor of flexibility. His dedication in these areas was the result of missing 60 games in 1999 with elbow, groin and knee injuries.

"He's playing with underclassmen now," Baker was quoted in *ESPN the Magazine*, and perhaps the manager had hit the nail on the head. "You get to his age, and if your body can still perform, you're like a senior playing with freshmen and sophomores. Through experience, process of elimination, he knows what guys throw him and when. Hank Aaron told me that. You get to a point in your career where the guesswork becomes easier because you've seen everything so many times. Well, Barry's at that point."

Bonds may be the only power hitter who chokes up one or two inches from the knob, a habit he developed because when he was a kid hanging around his dad at the ballpark, he played with big bats, where he had to choke up. He is able to crowd the plate like Frank Robinson used to because his hips and hands are so quick, and he is thus able to pull balls on the outer half of the plate.

Four "home run parks" have been added to the league since McGwire hit 70 in 1998—Houston, Milwaukee, Pittsburgh and San Francisco. Of his first 47 hits in 2001, Bonds had 26 homers and only 11 singles. In the history of baseball, there was only one player ever to finish a season with more home runs than singles. That was McGwire, who has done it three times.

Some National League teams, in response to Bonds, had started play- ing the third baseman up the middle, the shortstop to the right of second base, and the second baseman in short right field, similar to the "Williams shift" started by Cleveland manager Lou Boudreau in the 1940s. However, by 2001, Bonds so rarely put the ball on the ground that the shift was not terribly effective.

Bonds rarely checked his swing or had his bat broken, signs that he understands the strike zone and was seeing his pitches as well as can be done.

His talents on the field are undisputed. They always have been. The bigger question, *ESPN the Magazine* wanted to know, was "is he ready to be loved?"

"We all want to be loved," he told them.

He also understood his place in history.

"My Godfather played center field and my father played right field," Bonds told Bob Padecky. "I am having the privilege with playing with ghosts out there."

"One small swing for man, one giant moment for baseball," wrote Padecky of what it would mean if Bonds were to break McGwire's record.

Rod Beaton of *USA TODAY* continued the drumbeat of national media, imagining "Bonds on Broadway," playing for the Yankees the next year.

One of Bonds' best friends in baseball is Bobby Bonilla. It is an interesting friendship, like the one Bonds shares with Sheffield. Bonilla and Sheffield are street kids; Bonilla from The Bronx, Sheffield from Tampa, where baseball and his relationship with a cousin, Dwight Gooden, helped keep him out of trouble. Both are black.

Bonds grew up spoiled and privileged. He attended a mostly white private school, Serra High of San Mateo, and grew up in a predominantly white suburb, San Carlos.

It is worth noting that one of his best friends in San Carlos, if not his best friend, period, is Hoskins, another black man. Hoskins, like Bonds, did not grow up in a "black" neighborhood, and so he and Bonds may have gravitated to each other for this reason.

Does Barry actively seek out other African-Americans? He has many white friends, and while many take issue with him, very few say he is a racist.

Bonilla and Sheffield may offer him something different than the suburbanite Hoskins. In recent years, black athletes talk about being "real." This seems to be a need to identify with African-Americans; their music, clothing, speech, and the need to be proud of themselves and earn respect.

Another San Franciscan, O.J. Simpson, had been accused of "going white" long before he was accused of killing his blonde bombshell of a wife.

Left to his own devices, Bonds may have gone the "white" route. One can easily envision him getting into the music of Frank Sinatra. He already dresses like a preppy. On the other hand, there is the "Riverside" of Bonds—the family and history that was there before his father became a star and moved the family to the Bay Area. The family that still resides in this part of Southern California called the Inland Empire. This was where Barry had experienced Christmases that his Arizona State teammate and friend, Charles Scott, said were not "white Christmases . . . ski trips to Tahoe."

In choosing Bonilla and Sheffield, Bonds chooses other great athletes who have dealt with labels, sometimes unfairly. All three are supremely confident and can be outspoken, but are careful about who they talk to, and about what subject matter.

Perhaps the racial angle has less to do with the fact that all three have had their ups and downs with the fans, and the press. They have experienced contract hassles, and feel misunderstood.

Bonilla, who was like Bonds' older brother when they were young stars leading Pittsburgh to the gates of the Promised Land in the early 1990s, says he has "nothing but love" for Bonds.

As Bonds got closer and closer to history throughout 2001, both he and Sheffield were vociferous in voicing their opinion that their pal was not just one of the best, but the *very best* who has ever played the game.

Bonilla, a man of many travels, had not seen his career take off like Bonds. In 2001, he was a Cardinal, an interesting development, since that made him a teammate of McGwire.

St. Louis is, perhaps, America's greatest baseball town. New York and Boston fans are as knowledgeable and passionate as they get, but they can be too rude for school.

To be a New York sports star at the level of Ruth, Gehrig, DiMaggio, Mantle, Seaver, Jeter, Frank Gifford, or Joe Namath, is to achieve the very highest level of pagan idolatry in this country. Only selected short-term heroes approach the level of heat these guys generate—John Glenn right after his space flight in 1962, Douglas MacArthur after returning from Korea. Among Presidents, perhaps only Abraham Lincoln and Dwight Eisenhower were at this pitch. When he ran for President in 1968, Senator Robert Kennedy was treated like a "rock star," complained Richard Nixon to J. Edgar Hoover. No actor or real rock stars can quite get to where the New York athlete is.

Marilyn Monroe learned this when she was married to DiMaggio. After returning from a trip to Korea, where she entertained the troops, she breathlessly exclaimed to DiMag, "Joe, you've never heard such cheering."

"Yes, I have," replied DiMaggio, like a bucket of ice.

Still, ask McGwire where he would rather take his hero worship, St. Louis or New York, and he will tell you it is St. Louis. New York chews people up and spits them out, like a bloody Presidential campaign that leaves both candidates' private lives hanging like open intestines.

St. Louis fans love baseball and are just as knowledgeable as their East Coast counterparts, but they are polite. So it was with The Cardinal Nation, outwardly civil towards Bonds when the Giants traveled to the Gateway City. Whenever he stepped to the plate, he heard almost as many cheers as boos.

Vahe Gregorian of the *St. Louis Post-Dispatch* asked why Bonds works so hard to be difficult, when being a good guy would be easier. He "just has to be Barry," an unnamed "colleague" told Gregorian. Bonds perhaps sensed that St. Louis was an important opinion center: McGwire's "Mecca," home of the game's truest fans, and a symbol of Middle America that stands for what the coasts do not stand for. Bonds gave an insightful interview to the St. Louis media, saying he did not want to retire "unloved," like Albert Belle. Instead, he wanted to go out like St. Louis icons' Ozzie Smith, Lou Brock and Bob Gibson.

The St. Louis writers were comparing him with Mays, saying that to do so was no longer a "stretch." His lack of postseason success was "the only entry missing from his dazzling resume," and they were also saying something else worth noting, that he was more "fascinating" than their own McGwire. Bonds was a "spectacle," and that was what we ask of our sports heroes.

Baseball experienced a magical season in 2001. Over in the American League, Ichiro Suzuki, the "rookie" right fielder of the Seattle Mariners, had come over from Japan and electrified his team into the best first half ever. But Suzuki does not speak English.

Americans are a diverse lot, and we welcome people of all ethnicity's, races and nationalities into this beautiful land. We fell in love with Sosa, a Dominican, in 1998.

However, Americans still connect with other Americans more than foreigners. They can relate to a person who has gone to schools here, who has grown up with the music, the TV shows, and the movies of the United States.

So it was with Bonds.

Dave Stevens was getting a lot of play. People wanted to know about the kid from Serra High.

"He hit one of those long, towering drives you see him hit into McCovey Cove," said Stevens, recalling an epic homer Bonds had hit in high school, which had come to be remembered as the "homer at the beach."

"We got so excited, everybody was there at home plate, and when we got back to the dugout and looked up, all the scouts were gone. They had seen what they came to see."

"When you're a child and thinking about playing in the Major Leagues, just having that opportunity alone is special in itself," Bonds told the reporters in St. Louis. "I thought having my number retired in college and having my name up there on the board at Serra High School was pretty special."

Bonds was a "special talent" when he was a teenager, Stevens said. But despite his pedigree, he claimed Bonds did not get special treatment. Stevens actually said he had not realized who Bonds' father was until a month into Barry's first varsity season. This seems hard to believe, since Bobby Bonds had starred for a baseball team just a few miles away from where Stevens worked. One would have thought that every high school coach from San Francisco to San Jose was drooling over the chance to get Bonds. Private schools can recruit and give scholarships to players. Public schools are supposed to get just the students who live in their districts, but that rule is badly abused.

Bonds lived in the batting cage, Stevens recalled.

"He wanted to learn everything there was about the game," Stevens said. "He wasn't cocky in a sense that he thought he knew everything, and I think that's why I was able to challenge him so much. He was receptive.

"He had tremendous drive that he wanted to be the best at everything. I think that desire to excel is what has set him apart. Once he crossed the white line, he came to play."

Bonds played center field and batted *leadoff* at Serra, hitting .404 in three seasons on the varsity.

"Except for that instance with the wooden bat, most of the balls Barry hit were like they were shot out of bazookas," said Stevens. Bonds hit one home run more than 400 feet off the Mitty High gymnasium in San Jose, and blasted another more than 450 feet at St. Francis High in Mountain View that landed in a parking lot across the street. "One of the first things I noticed about Barry was he had great balance at the plate and his swing was snap-of-your-fingers quick. You didn't have to do much fine-tuning.

"I have pictures of him at home at bat and they don't look very different from the way he steps in the batter's box today."

McGwire is not a guy who gets jealous. He was not jealous of Barry, not of the media attention or the chance that his record was in jeopardy. When I approached Big Mac (an old friend from my USC days) around mid-season and told him I was writing a book about Bonds, because Barry had a chance at the record, he wished me luck. He certainly showed no problem with the possibility that the record could fall. Still, he continued to say that until Bonds reached 60, his pace should not be taken seriously.

He had earlier been asked what player was most likely to break his mark, and his answer was not Bonds, Griffey, Sosa or Vladimir Guerrero.

"He's probably not even born yet, to tell you the truth," he had said.

McGwire is a self-effacing man. He had turned down an opportunity to write an authorized autobiography after the 1998 season, reportedly for a $1 million advance, according to a literary agent I spoke to. He told me he would not write a book until "10 years after I retire," and that it would be less about his baseball career, and more about "what I've learned in life."

Bonds acted as if McGwire was the king and always would be.

"Mark McGwire's home run record is not in jeopardy," was his mantra. "Mark McGwire is bigger and stronger than all of us. Mark McGwire hits the ball harder than anyone who's put on a uniform. The balls we hit, we have to hit 'em. Mark McGwire hits 'em 550 feet, upper deck, almost out of the stadium. He mis-hits 'em, they're 402 feet. We mis-hit 'em, the infielders and outfielders are going like this [he waves his hands as if signaling 'fair catch.'] We have to hit 'em to hit 'em 402 feet.

"My wife is tired of seeing me on TV, and so am I," Bonds told assembled St. Louis, San Francisco and national media, about 80 altogether, gathered at a press conference. "I don't even turn on the television anymore. After a while it's just too much. Especially when there's so many more parts of the game that's going on, I think it takes away the whole perspective of the game of baseball."

"I've never received that much attention," joked Bobby Bonilla, just a little wistfully. Bonds seemed to want to use the opportunity to lecture the press a little.

"The media should look into the mirror and see why you are changing," he said. "Because I don't believe that I have changed. I'm the same person. . . . I don't feel I'm any different."

Bonds did admit he wanted to get to 50, a mark Mays had goaded him about

"Truthfully, I just want to get my Godfather off my back," laughed Bonds.

Bobby Bonds had turned Barry around to hit left-handed from the first day he picked up a bat. From his earliest childhood, he had been nurtured to play the game of baseball.

An article in ESPN.com described the kind of influence Mays had on him. One writer described going to Shea Stadium a few years after Mays and Hank Aaron had retired, for an old-timer's game. The writer first got Hammer's autograph, then went to Mays, who refused to sign his autograph because the guy had not chosen him first. The man was thinking on his feet, though. He asked Mays, since he would not sign for him, would he at least say how good did one have to be to get to The Show back in his day. Back then, there were Negro Leagues, and many minor leagues, stretching all the way to Class B, and Spring Training was like an Army camp full of young hopefuls.

"*Three* times as good," Mays had said.

Mays then went into a tirade about being black in America. He was convinced that, no matter their avocation, a black kid had to be *much better* than white kids in order to succeed.

This reminded me of my own first meeting with Mays. When I played college baseball, our team was taken to hear Mays speak. I expected to hear stories about being on deck when Bobby Thomson hit the "Shot Heard 'Round the World", or sentimental remembrances of Leo Durocher.

Instead, for 45 minutes Mays graphically described the South of the late 1940s. His entire talk centered not on his Major League career, but his pre-big league days, mainly his short minor league tenure prior to the Giants calling him up in May, 1951.

He talked about what rednecks called blacks from the stands. He talked about fleabag hotels that blacks stayed in because the nice hotels would not allow them. He spoke of restaurants that would not serve them.

Willie Mays is from Alabama, so he knew about bigotry all his life, although growing up black is different than traveling around with a professional team while black. He saw things when he ventured out from his little world in Fairfield that stuck with him all his life. He was *bitter*.

Once, a man found himself on an airplane, sitting next to Mays. Mays kept to himself, as did the man, who recognized him. At some point in the flight, the man had occasion to request something of Mays. Not an autograph, or tickets. Some kind of request that one passenger might make to another sitting near him during the course of a flight.

"Fuck you," Mays is supposed to have said. The story eventually made the rounds of the sports radio circuit.

Once, Barry Bonds entered the dugout, and found a sportswriter talking to his father, then the Giants' batting coach.

"Get the hell out of here," Bonds barked at the writer, who looked at Bobby. Bobby just gave him the, "What can you do?" look.

Did Willie Mays influence his Godson, and in what ways?

In *Ball Four*, Jim Bouton revealed, or at least was the first to publicly talk about, the "double standard" in sports. He pointed out that among the league batting leaders, a large percentage were black. However, the percentage of blacks among the league's statistical leaders was much greater than the percentage in the league overall.

This confirmed Bouton's premise that you had to be better to get to the Major Leagues if you were black than you were if you were white. If it was close, the white guy would get the nod.

Bouton is so liberal, some of his more Neanderthal teammates thought he was a Communist, but he had a point, and Mays had confirmed it at Shea Stadium in the 1970s.

Some blacks call baseball a "white man's" game. Basketball is the game in the hood. There are not many good baseball facilities in the inner cities, but you can play hoops on any outdoor court.

Here it is, straight up. Blacks are the best athletes in the world. Period. End of argument. Aside from all the evidence available by looking at baseball, basketball, football, and now even sports like tennis, golf, and volleyball, the evidence is out there every day. Just look around and do your own sociological study.

Take Marin County, California, where I grew up and played high school baseball. Marin is an affluent, upscale, liberal suburb of San Francisco. For those reasons, it is not a gold mine of prep sports talent, like its gritty, across-the-bay neighbor, Oakland.

That said, there have been some good athletes from Marin. My senior year at Redwood High, we were ranked number one in the nation in baseball, "mythical" National Champions.

In Marin, 75-90 percent of the populace is white. Ten percent is black, if that. Half of the best athletes ever to come from Marin are black.

Get the point? Next time you go to the health club, look around. If I had a nickel for every time I was in a gym that was 80 percent white, but the biggest, strongest, most physically impressive individual—in essence, the guy (or gal) who looked like the best athlete—was black, I would be a hundredaire.

Many contend that to discuss such things is not politically correct. Some blacks think it is racist to suggest that they are *naturally* the best athletes, implying that they do not measure up in the area of hard work, discipline and mental courage.

Let me state right now that not only has it been my experience that blacks *measure up* in these areas, I think they often exceed their white counterparts? Why? Mays hit it on the head. They feel they need to be better.

Are they hungrier to succeed in sports than whites? Maybe, although the whites who get to the top level, like everybody else at that stage, is a different kind of animal. The drive, competitive desire and ability to handle pressure of the big league athlete is not normal. The longer a pro plays, the more they hone these innate abilities.

So stating that blacks are the best athletes is just a fact.

The Boston Red Sox gave Mays a try-out at Fenway Park in 1949. *Willie Mays*! He knocked 'em dead, of course. Read some of the old stories of scouts and players who saw Mays as a kid, for the first time. Unless he had a broken leg or pneumonia, Mays was going to be Mays and Ray Charles could see it. The Red Sox sent him packing without could so much as a "hello, good-bye, shit or go blind." Ten years later they hired their first black, a dud named Pumpsie Green. The Red Sox Curse has nothing to do with Babe Ruth.

Want to know who Barry Bonds' biggest influence is? Willie Mays. You had better believe that in their many quiet moments, Mays told these stories to his young protégé.

Oh yeah, and his father, Bobby? *His* biggest influence had been Mays. It was no accident that Mays was Barry's Godfather.

How about cousin Reggie Jackson? Reggie had plenty of stories of racism in Baltimore, where he lived much of his youth. Baltimore had been the antebellum South, a Confederate stronghold only about 40 miles from Abe Lincoln's residence during the Civil War. Jackson was probably the best young prep athlete in the nation in the early 1960s, but colleges were not exactly beating a path to his door. He went to Arizona State, at the time not the high-powered school it is today, and starred in football and baseball.

In 1967, Jackson played for Oakland's Class AAA Birmingham Barons. The A's owner, Charlie Finley, was from Birmingham, and one day brought his friend, Alabama football coach Bear Bryant, to see Jackson play.

Afterward, Finley took Bryant into the clubhouse to meet the strapping, bare-chested Jackson.

"Now this here's the kinda nigger we could use on my football team," Bryant said to Finley in front of Jackson.

"It was a funny thing," Jackson, who is a philosopher, later recalled. "I knew Coach Bryant meant it as a compliment in his way, and that's the way I took it."

Four years later, Bryant's Crimson Tide was killed in a home game by USC, led by a black sophomore fullback from Santa Barbara, California named Sam "Bam" Cunningham. Bryant asked USC coach John McKay if he could "borrow" Cunningham. He marched Cunningham into the 'Bama locker room, stood him in front of 70 downcast, beaten white kids, and announced, "Now, this here's a football player."

The next day, Jim Murray of the *L.A. Times* welcomed Alabama into the Union.

Then there is McCovey, a stoic gentleman and one of San Francisco's most popular players. McCovey and Mays had both played for Alvin Dark. Dark was from the Deep South, and had been friends and teammates with Mays in New York. A deeply religious man, Dark would come to grips, eventually, with his racial views, but not after he got in trouble with the press, suggesting of blacks that "they a different kine" from whites.

McCovey would come to view white attitudes toward him with a certain amount of cynicism. He knew whites invited him to their golf tournaments and banquets not because they loved blacks or him, but because he had thrilled millions on the ballfield. He also knew that there was a certain liberal guilt factored into the equation.

Therefore, Willie Mac had no problem asking for money to attend the golf tournaments and banquets. In a way, it was payback for social inequities, and there are plenty of guilty whites willing to pay.

"A man a my statue, don' atten' no events of this natchure without being remunerated," McCovey once told a man inviting him to attend a charity event at the Meadow Club in Fairfax, California. The man taped the conversation.

Bobby Bonds came to the big leagues from Riverside, California, about 40 miles east of Los Angeles. Now, Riverside is relatively multiethnic and is a bedroom community full of L.A. commuters, drawn to its open spaces and less-expensive housing.

In the 1960s, Riverside was more rural, and a black kid was going to deal with a certain "redneck element." Still, it was a nice place to grow up in, like the sprawling San Joaquin Valley that produced Olympic star Rafer Johnson and his Hall of Fame football brother, Jimmy.

Bonds came up to the Giants in 1968, and was a hit right off the bat. He was a budding star, the heir apparent to Mays, and popular with the fans.

Within a few years, however, he had become difficult to deal with. His performance on the field did not live up to his promise. He had personal problems and drank too much. There came a time in which his public drinking binges became a running joke.

Bobby became distrustful of everybody, especially writers and general managers. He felt the general managers did not pay him what he was worth, and listened too closely to the writers who ultimately suggested that he be traded, which he was almost every year after a while.

So Barry Bonds was surrounded by some serious pieces of work in the form of his father, Mays, McCovey and Jackson.

He grew up watching these giants launch bullets during batting practice. He heard them laugh, cry, moan, and complain. He surely must have known secrets of their love lives, tales of debauchery, sex and drunkenness. These were human beings, not gods, subject to all the oddities of daily life like the rest of us.

Mays had been considered a very eligible bachelor. One day he arrived in the clubhouse and announced, with a smile, "Hey, fellas, I just got married."

Nobody knew anything about it, but they all smiled and congratulated him.

"You all know her," Mays then said. "Marguerite."

There was stone silence in the room. Many of the players did know her, and they did not consider Mays' marriage to her to be a happy thing for Willie. Their skepticism would prove correct.

Barry Bonds was married young, too, to a light-skinned Swedish émigré babe who had moved to the swinging city of Montreal. Montreal is a French-Canadien province known for its beautiful women and wild strip clubs. Sun Bonds was said to be friendly with many National League ball players who visited the city when in town to play the Expos. She was a woman with a past.

That marriage produced children, but not much happiness. Bonds himself publicly acknowledged that his wife was not faithful. Predictably, the union ended in one of the messiest public divorces of the past 10 years.

Athletes are *incredibly* sexual beings, and their peccadilloes are well known. Athletes and strippers go together, in the words of talk show host Jim Rome, like "peanut butter and jelly." In Atlanta, the owners of the Gold Club arranged for high-profile athletes to engage in fantasy sex with beautiful strippers.

They also have a fascination with group sex, usually involving a lot of them with one, or just a few, women. These women are often referred to as "freaks." The National Organization for Women must really love hearing this stuff.

One top athlete decided to marry a stripper who had a notorious reputation for having sex with many high-salaried athletes who came by her club when they were in town.

The player then made a round of phone calls to these star athletes, asking them that, as a favor to him, uh, he'd really appreciate it, uh, if they'd, well, not screw this girl anymore because, well, he was gonna marry her.

"Bad move," one of the "other" players, who prefers anonymity, said. "Guys were callin' around, and like it was, 'Did'ja hear what so-in-so's doin'. He's gonna marry that ho. He's gotta be wack.'" Or something like that.

One New York Yankee player married a nymphomaniac in the 1950s. His wife loved New York, because when the Yankees were on the road, she had her fill of Brooklyn Dodgers' and New York Giants' players. Her husband quickly discovered what was going on, but he was in love with her, determined to make a go of it. He asked for and eventually was granted a trade to a city that had no other Major League teams. At first, the marriage seemed to have righted itself, but some girls just gotta have it. His wife eventually found the arms of truck drivers, milkmen and drunks at the local bar, and the marriage ended in divorce.

In his classic 1984 autobiography, *The Wrong Stuff,* Bill "Spaceman" Lee tells of minor league groupies who "did the whole bull pen."

The Oakland A's had to deal with a scandal with one of their minor league clubs in the 1980s. One of their young players, the son of a prominent Major Leaguer, had a real way with the ladies, and began to pimp them to his buddies, only for free. There were two girls involved, 16 years of age, pure jailbait in halter-tops, shorts like those worn by Daisy in "The Dukes of Hazard," and high heels, driving around in a red sports car.

Have you ever seen 30 young men pick their jaws off the parking lot?

One day, the player decided to stage a gangbang in his hotel room. The two girls were arranged on the bed, and groups of two or three guys at a time were brought in the room. The girls serviced the team, one player after the other. Horndogs waited outside the room, and the line stretched down the hall and on to the stairs.

One pitcher swung by, and took a peek into the room. His first baseman was having fellatio performed on him. The first sacker saw him, and invited him to join the festivities.

"Hey, man, c'mon in," said the first baseman, "and get some head. It's free."

The pitcher was no saint, but that day a little angel standing on his shoulder told him to get the hell out of there. He left for dinner. When he returned, the parking lot was filled with the flashing lights of police cars.

One of the girls was the lillie-white daughter of this small town's mayor. Most of the players were black or Latino, which, unlike the girls, did not go down well. At all. Players were getting arrested for everything from statutory rape to unpaid speeding tickets. It was ugly.

One girl in the Appalachian League was called "roster woman" because she slept her way through the Bristol Tigers, and at mid-season moved in on the Johnson City Cardinals, most of whom were living in a place called the Mid-Town Motel. One wing of the motel consisted of players. The other wing consisted of hookers. "Roster woman" had the Cardinals taken care of by Labor Day, and she did it all for free—much to the consternation of the hookers.

Luis Polonia played in the A's organization when I was with them. Luis enjoyed underage girls. He was good buds with one of my friends. One day my buddy confronted him.

"Hey, Luis, why is it you've got four kids with four different chicks?" he asked him. "I mean, it ain't right."

"Hey man," Luis replied without batting an eyelash. "I looove to fuck."

Sexual hijinks are by no means relegated to the professionals. According to one urban myth, a sexy UCLA basketball cheerleader once fainted at a game, allegedly because she had fellated the entire team to completion the previous evening. Legend has it that doctors had to pump her stomach of the Bruins' semen. Everybody has heard stories about high school girls who enter the locker room to take on the whole football team.

Sometimes the sex games go beyond the coeds. The wife of a prominent college coach was notorious for seducing the players on hubbie's team. She wore short shorts and, according to one of the players, "used to shove her titties in your face, ya know." I know. Her exploits became publicly known, and when the team traveled to play a game against a conference rival, a sign was draped for all to see, asking the coach if he knew where his wife was.

Her husband once recruited two players, but they arrived at the campus before their student housing was available, so the coach let them stay at his home. Coach and wifey had to leave for a few days to attend a conference. The two players had the run of the house so, like Curious George, they rifled through Coach's drawers. There, they discovered 8 x 10 color glossies of the wife in various positions of intercourse and oral action. The players, both of whom later played at the highest professional level, could not verify that any of the men in the photos were Coach, leading them to conclude that the couple were "swingers," and Coach, uh, liked to watch.

Whatever floats your boat.

Of course, the question inevitably comes down to, "What do the wives of athletes think of all this?" Good question. Many of the wives are the very girls who made themselves available to the players. Many met them in bars and night clubs, and calculated their efforts to do this very thing. Former player Jimmy Piersall once said they were all just a bunch of "horny broads." However, athletes, for all their crazed activities, are actually still a Puritan bunch. They tend to come from solid families, because a supportive family unit often helps promote their athletic careers. Fathers who coach little league and take the time to practice with their sons. Mothers who sacrifice their time to drive kids to practice.

Therefore, the players are less likely to marry the kind of glamour girls that rock stars and other entertainers tend to hook up with. Wives wait with their kids in a family area outside the clubhouse, and one is struck by the fact that they do not seem to be the bombshells that one might expect these studs to be with. The reason is that the players often marry a "girl just like the one that married dear old dad," after they have let their yah-yahs out for a few years with the more, uh, promiscuous women. The players do not want these groupie-types to be the mothers of their kids. At heart, most athletes are conservative, they tend to vote Republican, and when it is all said and done, they take family values seriously. A fair number of wives are high school sweethearts.

The wives tend to see their lot in life as a compromise. The boys will be boys. The trade-off is that they get to be big league wives and live in luxury, because their husbands make huge money. Sometimes, however, the men go too far. In the 1980s, Boston star Wade Boggs had an ongoing affair with a woman named Margo Adams. Margo went public in a nude pictorial/article in *Penthouse*, stating that most of the Red Sox' players had mistresses, and that their preferred form of contraception was "facial cumshots." Now *that's* an interesting image!

A few years later, Pittsburgh wives had had enough. Some of the guys were flying their extracurricular women to cities on the road, and the wives got wind of it. They started to call hotels that the team stayed in, asking for copies of phone bills, saying they needed them for tax records. Of course, the numbers included calls to many of these "travel girls." One player stayed one step ahead of this effort by having his agent provide him a calling card number on the agent's phone bill, so the calls to his mistress did not appear on *his* hotel, cell or home phone bills.

Baseball players tell these stories all the time. One can only imagine how many of these kinds of tales Barry Bonds heard growing up. It was these kinds of men and this kind of world that shaped Bonds, who laughed when I asked him about his father.

"He used to climb in my mother's window in Riverside," Bonds said, "tryin' to 'get some.'"

As Bonds moved through his career, he chased these ghosts and came to live the stories they had told him. He honored them but he also overcame them. He had to move on, to be his own man, a new kind of man in a different era. His close friends paint a picture of a man who eschewed the wild party scene. Bonds was not a partier. He was not a swinging bachelor. A monk? No, he was handsome and single and opportunities were there, but he did not "line up" the women, or engage in heavy drinking. There has never been a hint of accusation that Bonds has been a heavy drinker, and definitely not a drug user. All indications are that when the groupies and "Baseball Annies" made themselves available in modern orgies worthy of Caligula's Rome, Bonds was more like that pitcher with the angel on his shoulder, telling him to beat it out of there.

The rules, in every way—race, sex, money, free agency—had changed for him, and for the better. In this respect, he also owed the old players who had lived the stories he heard. What must it have been like for Bonds as he moved up the ladder, playing at Arizona State and the Alaska Goldpanners, then in the minor leagues, and finally getting to the bigs? Was it like they had told him it would be? Better?

Once, the lives of athletes had a secret quality, but books like *Ball Four*, Pat Jordan's *False Spring, Semi-Tough* by Dan Jenkins, and *North Dallas Forty* (along with a handful of expository sports films) had revealed the realities of professional sports to the world. The young men entering the ranks were no longer shocked at the hi-jinks; rather, they more often than not looked forward to them. The son of a big leaguer who had arranged the shocking hotel room sex acts for A's farmhands was big league prodigy, too. He probably had been planning these festivities his whole young life, anticipating the day he would be a pro ballplayer. In the case of Barry Bonds, he was a lot of things when he came up, but being a wild fornicator, in the tradition of Babe Ruth, was not one of them. He could have been. The fact he rejected such a lifestyle is to his great credit.

Bonds' love of family and friends goes back to Riverside. His family moved to San Francisco when Bobby broke into the Majors, but it was on the desert-hot fields of Riverside where Bonds first learned the game, and it is Riverside where his grandparents, on both his father's, and mother Pat's side, reside.

"Oh, I still spend a lot of time there," Bonds told me. "I love it there. That's why I love playing the Dodgers. My grandparents come to every game at Dodger Stadium. They came to all my games growing up."

Most San Franciscans have a built-in hate for all those in Los Angeles and environs, but Bonds has roots there. This may explain why he shows no special disdain for the Dodgers, and his signing a free-agent contract with them would not have been out of the question. In some ways, it would have meant coming home.

Would Bonds ever go into detail about his relationships with all the people in his life—his first wife, the icons he grew up with, his father, friends, and family? Did DiMaggio ever do that? When it came to the subject of Joe D.'s wife, Marilyn Monroe, you could not have pulled a pin out of his butt with a tractor.

As spring turned into summer, everybody was speculating on this new American icon, and the continuing effort to find an elusive nickname that would match The Sultan of Swat, The Yankee Clipper, The Galloping Ghost, the Big Train. "Barry Bombs Away?" The suggestions kept coming.

David Schoenfield of ESPN.com became the latest to try to and figure him out.

"Underrated and hated?" wrote Schoenfield. "He is by the fans. In my five years of working at ESPN.com, we've run many polls along the lines of 'Who's the best player in the game?' Ken Griffey, Jr. always wins. Bonds? Never. Doesn't come close to winning. And if we put a poll up right now asking, 'Who's been the best hitter over their career, Bonds or Tony Gwynn?', Gwynn would win in a landslide.

"Which is a joke. Gwynn is a chunky singles hitter; Bonds produces chunks of runs. Gwynn has scored 100 runs or driven in 100 runs a combined three times in his career. Bonds has done it *17* times. Despite Gwynn's higher batting average, Bonds still gets on base more and obviously has more power. Gwynn has played 140 games seven times in his career, just once since 1990. Bonds has played 140 games 12 times. While Bonds is labeled as selfish, Gwynn sits at home all winter watching video of himself hitting, eating ice cream sundaes and getting fat."

Schoenfield pointed out Bonds' .688 slugging percentage in 2000, the best of his career (and higher than any single-season total by Griffey), along with his Gold Gloves and stolen bases. Griffey, he said, was 31 at that time, but had been in a decline since 1997. Schoenfield doubted that Junior would be an MVP candidate at age 37.

Kent's primary reason for winning the 2000 MVP award, Schoenfield said, was his RBI total: 125 to Bonds' 106. However, Bonds had a higher on-base percentage, higher slugging percentage, more home runs and more runs scored. According to Stats Inc., Kent drove in 125 of 1,036 available RBIs (12.1 percent). Bonds drove in 106 of 761 (13.9 percent). Kent had 275 more RBI opportunities than Bonds. In other words, Kent had a huge year because Bonds was on base in front of him so much, giving him better pitches to hit in prime opportunities. Give Kent credit, he came through, but calling him more valuable than Bonds was a token, a bone in order to create some kind of equity of sorts.

"Feared?" wrote Schoenfield. "Ask National League pitchers who they fear the most."

Nick Peters of the *Sacramento Bee* wanted to know why a guy who averaged 21 home runs in his first four years and 25.1 in seven seasons in Pittsburgh could "suddenly" be in the 500 Club and challenging the 70 Club.

"He wasn't a prototypical homer-type guy, but he could do everything," Giants' bench coach Ron Wotus, who outhit Bonds .315 to .311 when they were Class AAA teammates in Hawaii, told Peters.

"Barry was a slender guy, more into speed than power. The Pirates weren't into weight training then, so Barry wasn't nearly as big and strong— but you could see all the talent."

"You can't predict that a guy will hit 500, but with that bat speed and power you always have a chance," first base coach Robby Thompson, also a rookie in 1986, told Peters. "At the time, Barry was slim and more of a gap hitter. But he had a great body, and he's put some muscle on it. There aren't too many guys with his kind of talent."

Bonds was beginning to "embrace the chase" with the media, but he was enjoying his increased fan support, too. After a Friday night 10-5 victory over St. Louis, Bonds went to a nightclub with Bonilla.

"I think everyone in the whole entire club said hello," Bonds told Marcus Breton of the *Sacramento Bee.*

"A lot of people said congratulations, some people said we hope you break the record, others said we hope you don't break it but we congratulate you anyway. But they were all nice and it was a different feeling."

A bruised right wrist kept him out of the Saturday afternoon game against the Cardinals, but "I'm alive and breathing," Bonds told a breathless world. "The circulation is still going. I'll be out there tomorrow, end of story."

San Francisco rallied for four runs in the eighth inning to beat St. Louis 5-2. Bonds could have been used as a pinch-hitter, but Pedro Feliz was used instead. Feliz drove in the go-ahead runs with a bases-loaded single.

Bonds had gone a week without a home run. He was still well ahead of the previous fastest homer pace in baseball history, but hitless in his last 18 at-bats.

He already held the Major League record for homers before the All-Star break, beating the previous mark of 37 set by Reggie Jackson in 1969 and matched by McGwire in 1998. Bonds still had 24 homers in his last 36 games. He had missed seven of the Giants' 80 games this year; most because of the regular days off Baker gave to him.

It was also pointed out that for all the talk about Bonds' pace, McGwire had belted 14 homers in his last 26 games and eight in the last 13 once he broke Maris' record.

The Barry Bonds Love Tour continued, and writers noted that he "was relaxed, congenial and enjoying himself."

CBS came to Pacific Bell Park for a segment on him. ESPN was the "all Barry, all the time" network. A trip to 7-11? There he was on national magazine covers and the front pages of newspapers from Seattle to Miami.

Bondsmania.

"Ants walk to food and whatever's good, they cling on," Bonds had said, with just a hint of his familiar sneer.

Bonds was charming and insightful except when he was not. It was also worth pointing out that Bonds' harshest critics have included teammates and members of the Giants' organization.

Bonds, perhaps taking a trip down Memory Lane to his days with the nuns at Serra High, said he did not want to be "crucified for whatever decision I have to make" regarding his contract situation.

Crucified? That is a pretty strong word.

A peek into Bonds' life occurred when a reporter wanted to know if anything in his personal life had ever distracted him from baseball.

"I guess my divorce was widely known," Bonds said. "I think I handled it pretty good. That was the only thing in my life that was really nerve-racking."

Companies were calling Bonds about endorsements, one of the most surefire signs that an athlete had achieved a high level of popularity. Bonds had always believed he deserved the spotlight, at least on the field, and now he had it, front and center. Most importantly, he seemed determined not to spoil it. He seemed to realize that he needed to help people appreciate him, rather than his youthful philosophy; that his talent would "overcome his behavior," wrote Peters.

Bonds was having more first-half fun than McGwire, who was surly until well into August, 1998. To this day, Big Mac complains about what it was like, reminding everyone that Sammy Sosa did not have to withstand the scrutiny all season. In June, 2001, he still felt that projecting Bonds to hit 70 was "quite hilarious."

The media said Bonds was doing it all by himself, for some reason not giving credence to the numbers being put up in Arizona by Luis Gonzalez. Bonds was occasionally prone to overdoing the situation himself.

It was "the loneliest thing I've ever gone through in my life," he said, claiming that his father, his teammates and his Godfather did not want to talk to him about it. Apparently they were afraid of jinxing him.

Still, that kind statement reeks of melodrama, as if Bonds was a judge weighing whether to send a man to the electric chair, or an elected official considering the consequences of sending young men into battle.

It is still just baseball. The National Pastime.

When every angle in your life is covered, is that lonely? The man who spent $2.7 million on McGwire's 70th home run ball had been tracked down for his opinion. Roy Firestone had raised the race issue. Bonds, hanging out with Bonilla in St. Louis, was mobbed like Kid Rock. His wife did not want to turn on the TV anymore.

Lonely?

Bonds has it all. He had earned $100 million in salary in his 16-year career, $77 million from the Giants, the rest from the Pittsburgh Pirates.

He is happily married, the doting father of three children.

He lives in a house with 19 television sets and drives a silver Jaguar.

He comes from as royal a lineage as any baseball player ever, a man literally groomed to be the best baseball player in the world, like a young, 19th century German prince prepared from birth to lead a nation and its armies. However, such an upbringing comes with pitfalls. Another young prodigy, Todd Marinovich, had been groomed for football stardom in much the same way. He rebelled, turning to drugs, rock music and surfing. Bonds' acceptance of his role is admirable; the way he handled it is something to marvel at. It was not easy. Sometimes advantage works against you.

Bonds has looks and there is talent in his face and personality. He is a member of the Screen Actors Guild, and is very photogenic when he smiles.

He has the body of a 20-year-old. He should be a poster boy for Gold's Gym.

Does he have true contentment?

Bonds tells the story of Eddie Murphy, who was hot stuff when he made "48 Hours" and "Beverly Hills Cop," but did not maintain that level of stardom over subsequent films. Bonds wanted to know why so much had been expected of Murphy, instead of simply enjoying his considerable talent. Bonds seemed to think that there is an underside to fame, based on people's desire to see the great ones fail.

While he may be right, there is a tabloid fascination with failure, it is not, however, a national obsession. Average people care less about such things than he thinks. They take notice when it happens, but do not urge it along. Sometimes a celebrity will show a psychological desire to sabotage himself, like when Senator Gary Hart invited Miami reporters to follow him around and investigate his alleged extramarital affairs.

What followed was "Monkey Business," Donna Rice and a slew of Guess? Jeans ads.

"I never said I was perfect," Bonds told one press conference. "I can be a butthead, but I am not a butthead. Look, I would love to write. I would love to tell a story. But I can't. I flunked English. There are a lot of things I wish I could do, but I can't. But what I can do is play baseball. Why can't people just leave it at that? I don't understand. I just don't understand."

Well, Barry, we are all glad you would love to write and tell a story. I am more than happy to help you, and the result is this book! Heck, I would love to be able to hit home runs, but I cannot, so we all do what we can do.

Bonds has never understood the social contract of fame, the strings that are attached. He simply does not recognize that the money he makes derives not just from his ability, but from the hype of publicity that the media creates. It is no different for the musician, the actor, even the politician who spends money for advertising, and prefers the free exposure that the press can provide. He is free to give up the money tomorrow. Nobody is stopping him.

Bonds told the media April 17 that he "wouldn't be around" long enough to hit his 661st homer, which would put him past Mays. But he will be, and more. That is what Scott Boras' packet would say.

That packet was put together highly, precisely, and for the pure purpose of securing Barry Bonds more money. Bonds did not need to hire Boras. He could have told Boras not to make those kinds of projections. He chose to dance this dance.

"I don't want to set myself up for that," he said of breaking past Mays, but he does set himself up for that. If pressure makes him uncomfortable, then why let his agent present his past and all potentially future employers a virtual book on the records he will set, and why that makes him worth the money they ask?

There is a term for this. It is an old cliché. It is "you can't have your cake and eat it, too."

If it could be said that if Bonds ever was in a slump in 2001, the period from late June into early July, before the All-Star Game, was that time. Going up against Colorado's Mike Hampton, a tough left-hander, Baker decided to switch things around a little bit. He moved Kent to third, and Bonds into the clean-up spot, but quickly moved Bonds back to third. Bonds had not batted cleanup since August 11, 1999.

The columnists by this time—namely Scott Ostler and Ray Ratto—had taken to calling him Barry (no last name required) or The Barry. Bonds had hit a slight funk, at least for him. Of course, he was still playing fine defense, getting on base, and his team was clutching for every win they could get, doggedly hanging within five games of Arizona.

After the All-Star break, after the All-Star break. That is when Dusty Baker teams get on the right track. A crucial series at the BOB loomed after the break. They just had to hold on.

The Giants were a team fighting for the division, a spot in the play-offs, a chance at the Big Dance. Bonds, whether he was hitting home runs or not, represented a major cog in this effort. All their focus was centered on winning.

This club had a shot at winning not just because of Bonds, but because of other key players. On June 26, they beat Los Angeles at home, 14-8. Bonds went 0-for-4, with no RBIs, no runs scored, and two strikeouts. Rich Aurilia made up for him, going 4-for-5 (including a homer), driving in four men, and scoring twice. Jeff Kent was 2-for-5 with one run scored and an RBI. Aurilia was headed to the All-Star Game, batting .349. Shawn Estes was 7-2 with a 2.90 earned run average, and Russ Ortiz sported an 8-5 mark with an 8.51 ERA. At 41-36, they were a game and a half ahead of the Dodgers after beating them in the slugfest.

Lost amid all the hoopla of Bonds' season was an off-hand comment he had made at his June 25 press conference prior to the Dodger game. He said he knew himself better, he was a smarter player than when he had been a younger man. He said that young players think they can do anything, but now he played within his "circle." His key comment was that he was getting more sleep now than when he was a kid.

As a youngster, Bonds had made the club scene. He was an eligible bachelor and lived that life, although as it has been emphasized, he avoided drinking like his dad, and was never a wild man. When he married, it was to an exotic, sexy girl. The two of them did not exactly settle into an "Ozzie and Harriet" lifestyle, but now, he had found true love with Liz, an old friend from his high school days. He was joking about being in bed by eight on a Saturday night because his little daughter would crawl in with them and drift into never-never land.

The man had settled down.

Three thousand miles away, another man named Bonds was trying to find himself. Bobby Bonds, Jr., six years younger than Barry, was playing for Nashua, New Hampshire in the Atlantic League.

Bobby, Jr. looks more like his father than his brother does. For 10 years, he had, like Jalal Leach, a Giant farm hand, beat the bushes, never making more than $3,000 a month. Known as B.B., he had recently divorced and decided to give up the game. He lived with his parents in San Carlos and worked for a paving company in Redwood City, where the hot, gritty work occasionally took him to his brother's house.

He would knock on the door and invite himself in for lunch.

"You're here again?" Barry would jokingly say.

Looking to support his two young children, now living with their mother in Alabama, Bobby had decided to accept a job offer from a shipping and receiving company in Piscataway, New Jersey. Then the Atlantic League called. Maybe the name "Bonds" would sell tickets. He agreed, for $2,100 a month, $700 less than he had made the year before in Somerset. He was living with a couple he had befriended a couple of years earlier.

The Atlantic League is an independent league, not affiliated with any big league clubs. None of the players are prospects, except for the occasional draft holdout who goes there to stay in shape until his agent negotiates a multi-million dollar deal.

Butch Hobson, a former Alabama football player and Red Sox third baseman who had experienced his own personal problems, was his manager, maybe looking for some kind of redemption.

Mitch "Wild Thing" Williams was a sideshow in Atlantic City, where he was a coach. The same thing? This league is in Stephen King country, and many of its hanger-on participants could be characters from one of his novels.

Still, it is a better life than paving roads. One is reminded of Kevin Costner, who plays Crash Davis in "Bull Durham." When told he has been brought to Durham strictly to guide the career of Nuke LaLouche (Tim Robbins), he claims, "I quit," right then and there. The manager and his assistant coach just look at him, nonplussed. They know he will not quit.

The manager says, "Whaddaya gonna do, work at Sears?"

That stops Crash in his tracks.

"I worked at Sears once," says the assistant coach, played by Robert Wuhl. He moves in for the kill. "Ugly work." He shudders at the memory. "Ugly."

The point of this exchange is that the job at Sears very well may have paid as much as Crash, Wuhl or the manager were making with the Durham Bulls. However, given the chance to work at Sears or in baseball, there simply was no choice in the matter.

So Bobby Bonds, Jr., who could have made more than $2,100 a month, and had some security in his life working for a shipping and receiving company in New Jersey, was instead doing—in his way, the only way he knew— the same thing as his older bro.

He was not alone among "sibling all-stars." The league also employed the brothers of Jose Canseco, Barry Larkin and Tom Glavine. Jose had played in the league until getting another shot at the Majors, and he departed ungraciously, calling it a nightmare.

For guys whose other choices are bagging groceries, paving roads or working in warehouses, honorable jobs that count and make this country go, the league was a dream. Maybe not *the* dream, but a dream.

On July 2, the day the Giants lost at Los Angeles, 8-6, Baker announced that he was reducing media access to his star. He was mired in a 4-for-39 slump against the tough Dodger pitching so far. He had hit only one homer in his previous nine games.

There was an implication, whether Baker meant it or not, that the writers were at fault for Bonds' failure to continue hitting like nobody in baseball history had ever hit.

On Independence Day, the Dogs scored three in the eighth before 36,948 at Chavez Ravine, to beat the Gyros by 4-3. Bonds walked twice, but went 0-for-3. On this day, when traditionalists superstitiously predict the standings reflect what they will be at season's end, San Francisco found themselves at 44-39, six and a half back of Arizona, and two behind the surging Dodgers. It was summer time, but the livin' was far from easy.

By this point, Bonds memorabilia was starting to move up in price. Heretofore, his 1987 Fleer rookie card had sold for $20-$25. Now, that card in PSA-10 (perfect) condition was commanding $1,125, and 1986 Topps Traded Tiffany Bonds cards were going for $4,550. Bonds was also moving from the exclusive domain of the *Chronicle* Sporting Green. On Sunday, July 8, he was all over the front page under the heading "VERRY BARRY" in typeface slightly smaller than, say, "FIDEL SAYS COMMUNISM WAS MISTAKE."

Mike Weiss, an award-winning features reporter, wanted to know if he was a hero, prima donna, superstar, recluse–or all four? His conclusion? All four.

Every detail of Bonds' life was getting the treatment by now. He had tied a College World Series record with seven straight hits his sophomore year at Arizona State. He had hit .404 in three years on the varsity at Serra (you mean he had to toil on the freshman team his first year?).

However, a new statistic emerged. Eleven hundred Bay Area African-Americans had registered as bone-marrow donors as part of a leukemia campaign that Bonds sponsored, but did not publicize.

Bonds the philanthropist is a very real concept. Many top athletes have foundations to serve this purpose. Cynics note that they are tax write-offs. In the 1980s, when the big money was starting to roll in and these foundations started to emerge, many were poorly run and ended up getting shut down due to incompetence.

Michael Jordan put his mother in charge of his, but she had no idea how to run this kind of operation, so it folded. Jordan, like most athletes, meant well, but had made mistakes. Now, however, most agents had financial advisors and experts on the "team." Foundations like Barry's were serving a very positive purpose in communities.

When I first approached Bonds about writing a book, it was made very clear to me that any profits he derived would go straight to his charities. This is a complicated character, but he is a man with a very noble streak.

Photos of Bonds with daughter Aisha were often gracing the newspapers, and it was with his kids where Bonds' smile glowed. Still, this was the same man who had made a *Sports Illustrated* writer, who had flown from New York for an exclusive with him, wait for days for the interview. Whas' up with that?

Bonds had by now moved well past Griffey, Cal Ripken, Alex Rodriguez, or any of the previous pretenders for the title "Best Active Ballplayer." He was challenging Mays for "Best Living Ballplayer." Beyond that? Read on.

With the All-Star Game coming up, Fox analyst Tim McCarver created some controversy with remarks about Bonds' so-called "artificiality." McCarver was a Major League catcher for many years. He had grown up in a wealthy family in Memphis, Tennessee during the days of the Jim Crow South. His family employed black servants, and they were the only people of color McCarver came in contact with. He attended all-white schools, and played with and against all-white teams.

He came up with the Cardinals, the same team that David Halberstam used to illustrate a changing America in *October 1964*. Young McCarver was at first uncomfortable with all the blacks and Latinos on the team. However, there was no denying that the leader was Bob Gibson. Gibby is a big, strong, opinionated black man.

Gibson knew McCarver was uncomfortable, so he took matters into his own hands. On the bus one day, he saw McCarver drinking a Coke.

"Mind if I have a sip?" Gibby asked McCarver.

McCarver reluctantly handed the can to him. Gibby took a big old honkin' slug from the Coke can, like Samuel Jackson drinking some of Frank "check out the big brain on Brett" Whaley's "tasty beverage" in "Pulp Fiction." As they say today, McCarver learned to "deal with it," and was never uncomfortable again. In the photos of Gibson's greatest moments, it is McCarver who congratulates him on the mound.

Now, he was considered one of the best baseball minds in the game. McCarver is bright and, obviously, opinionated. He was no stranger to controversy, however. Once, football/baseball star Deion Sanders, angered by McCarver's on-air remarks, had poured ice water on him in the clubhouse.

"To me, it has a ring of artificiality and phoniness that because you're on pace to break Mark McGwire's record that all of the sudden you're trying to be Mr. Nice Guy," McCarver said about Bonds. "That's strange to me. What turns me off is Barry Bonds trying to all of the sudden clean up his media image. There is a problem when you all of the sudden decide to try to be nice with the media. Either you're a nice guy or you're not a nice guy."

McCarver was scheduled to announce the upcoming All-Star Game, and no doubt would run up against Bonds at some point. In the Pac Bell press box, opinion sided with Bonds on this. A number of writers felt it was McCarver who was "artificial" and "phony." Many felt he had gotten big-headed with his success as a national TV announcer, and that McCarver was the one who treated people without respect if he felt they were below him.

"From a reporter's standpoint, whether it's electronic or written, all they expect is civility out of somebody," McCarver had continued to say. "And *en masse* almost, everybody has been treated in an uncivil fashion or in a fashion they deem uncivil from Barry Bonds' standpoint.

"McGwire can be surly, but he gets it. He can play the game [with the media]. Bonds doesn't want to be a part of it. My personal feeling on it is you don't have to be a nice guy and Mr. Congeniality to break a record. If he breaks the record, then good for him. I'll stand there and be ready to hug him.

"That will be a one-way hug, I guarantee it."

On July 9 at Seattle's Safeco Field, the All-Stars gathered for the annual Home Run Contest. Somebody from Major League Baseball must have gotten to Bonds, because he was there with bells on. He just did not win the contest. Luis Gonzales did. Bonds, however, was all over the news accounts of the showcase event, conducting an interview for ESPN with his children next to him.

Bonds was not the only drawing card in Seattle, however. It was now revealed that if any photographer could get into the Mariners' clubhouse and snap a nude photo of Suzuki, the shot would go for $2 million in Japan. What a world!

The Giants were well represented at the game. Bonds started in left, Aurilia at shortstop, and Kent at second. Ripken made it his last hurrah, winning the MVP award in leading the Americans over the Nationals, 4-1. Bonds grounded to pitcher Roger Clemens, whose ass he did not have to kick, in the first inning. He went down swinging in the fourth.

There were no incidents with Tim McCarver.

Interestingly, Bonds would later say that the Home Run Contest had helped him regain the upper cut in his swing. In the second half, that upper cut would be front and center on the national stage. What he had experienced so far was nothing compared to what would happen in the next three months, on and off the field.

The Giants had gone 18-16 in games in which Bonds homered in the first half. He was at .305 with 39 homers and 73 RBIs. He needed 32 to catch McGwire. His team was in third place at 46-42, five and a half behind the D'backs, and three and a half behind Atlanta in the emerging wild-card scenario.

The Chase

The Giants remained in Seattle for an interleague series with Seattle. Bonds' 40th home run was not enough, as the M's, chasing the all-time victory record of 116, set in 1906 by the Cubs, defeated San Francisco, 4-3. Suzuki led the way with his 135th hit of the year.

Away from the good humor of the All-Star Game, reports of friction in the Giants' clubhouse continued to pop up. This is one of the great overused arguments in sports. The 1972-74 Oakland A's had fought and feuded with each other all the way to three World Championships. Cousin Reggie was right in the middle of all of it.

San Francisco closed out with a loss to Seattle, 3-2 on July 14 when Ichiro robbed Kent of a home run. Frustration. They were up against it, but after traveling to Texas, survived 98-degree Texas heat to beat the Rangers, 7-6 in a three-hour, 21-minute character-builder.

A baseball pennant is probably the best sporting experience in the pantheon of the ordinary. A daily feast for fans. A pressure-cooker for the players. Each game does not carry the significance of an NFL game, in which everything is directed toward 16 individual Sundays. Yet, each game is an opportunity to pick up ground, to gain advantage, to create distance. It is war. The combatants of the modern game come better prepared than their counterparts of the past.

In the 1970s, Howard Cosell opined that managing a baseball team required little from the tired old tobacco-chewing men who held those positions at that time. However, that kind of manager had become obsolete by 2001. Perhaps Tony La Russa started the change in Oakland, using computers and charts to step up the preparation process. George Will had written about these changes. No longer were games being prosecuted by "good ol' boy" managers and their drinking buddy coach-friends. The New Game required the kind of scouting, planning and attention to detail, for each game, every day, that the pro football coach had long put into his one-game-a-week preparations.

Managing a Major League team is now, probably, the toughest job in sports. It is not for the weak. It requires a psychologist, a leader, a strategist, and a numbers guy, all in one.

Now, in midsummer, the scoreboard had come into play. While the Giants were battling Texas, the Ballpark in Arlington scoreboard showed that Arizona had lost. An opportunity. It is like an army that sees a chink in the armor of their enemy, and with a concerted push is able to gain a few miles of ground. Would they be able to hold it, or be pushed back tomorrow, forced to pay for the same real estate twice?

July 16, Texas. A kid named Rob Bell looked like Christy Mathewson, pitching 8 2/3 innings to beat the Giants, 2-0. Rob Bell? Go figure.

Meanwhile, in Alabama, the great Henry Aaron told a newspaper that Bonds, who needed 221, had the best chance to catch his record. In the Lone Star State, on that same day, Barry Bonds could care less. The only thing on his mind, and on the minds of his teammates, was how in hell Rob Bell could shut them out?

It was around this time that a story, told by Bonds to the editor of Bay Area nonprofit groups, appeared in the *Chronicle's* "Open Forum." Bonds was pictured surrounded by kids. He had sponsored a learning program for disadvantaged children in poor neighborhoods. Spurred by the progress he had seen in his own son when he received private after-school tutoring, Bonds had decided to help make this program available to other children who otherwise would not have had the opportunity.

It is a worthy effort deserving of praise, yet Bonds had not publicized this effort. The article appeared in the paper not to let people know Bonds was doing it, but to demonstrate its value. Hopefully, others would contribute to similar programs.

Barry Bonds does not sponsor these programs for tax purposes or to improve his image. The same guy who told a writer to "get the hell out of here" does it because he has a lot of humanity. The conundrum.

July 19 in San Francisco was a good night, facing Rockies ace southpaw Mike Hampton. He was 10-0 against the Giants coming in. Bonds went deep in the fourth, but managed to hurt his back in the process. His next time up, he was doing all kinds of gyrations. Hampton delivered, and Bonds tried to *bunt*. Now, surely he was in pain and could not extend. So Hampton came in to his wheelhouse.

"Bye, bye, baby," as Russ Hodges would have said. Opposite field, number 42. The usual full house at Pac Bell went bananas. Bonds tied Mickey Mantle for ninth place at 536, and San Francisco won a rare breather, 10-0.

Friday night, July 21. Arizona in town. It does not get any better than that, and on this night Livan Hernandez revived his heroics of the 1997 World Series to lead his team to a nail-biting, 1-0 win. Three and a half back.

Sunday, July 22. Forget about it. Schilling struck out seven straight. The Diamondbacks won, 9-2. Four and a half out.

On July 24, San Francisco made a big move. Sabean acquired Andres Galarraga from Texas. "The Big Cat," also known as *El Gato*, looked washed up in Arlington, but the prospect of a pennant race was hoped to be the spur that would revive the 40-year-old Caracas, Venezuela-born first baseman. A strong man, he had made several comebacks. In 1993, he had flirted with .400 in Denver. He had missed all of 1999 with non-Hodgkin's lymphoma, but returned to Atlanta to hit .302 with 100 RBIs. Maybe just as important, Galarraga is pure class, a barrel-chested fellow with a smile that lights up a room. If ever a guy was "just happy to be here," it was Andres, the cancer survivor. Would he bring missing joy to a taciturn, veteran clubhouse?

Over in Arizona, Luis Gonzalez hit his 40th to lead his team to an 11-0 win over San Diego. Six and a half back. In his first game, Galarraga was 3-for-5 with two RBIs, after receiving a big ovation from his old fans at Coors Field. The Giants beat Colorado, 9-3. Bonds was given the day off, but was hitless in a pinch-hit performance.

On July 26, Bonds went deep twice in a game that may have been the most important of the season. Down six and a half games, San Francisco arrived in Phoenix, where it was 105 degrees. 33,666 showed up at the BOB ready to bury Frisco. No dice. Bonds' 43rd and 44th ignited an 11-3 win *over Schilling*, and pushed him ahead of The Mick.

Gonzo smacked his 42nd, and at the time of this showdown, believe it or not, the Arizona outfielder was considered the favorite to win the Most Valuable Player award. If not Gonzalez, then Sosa. Bonds? He answered that question with his bat. Five and a half.

On Friday, Bonds cranked his 45th, went 3-for-3 with two runs scored and a walk, to power the Giants to a 9-5 win. Who was that MVP choice again?

On Saturday, the Giants did the thing that Dusty Baker clubs do. They knocked Randy Johnson around for an 11-4 win before 47,570. Randy Johnson. The guy who would win the Cy Young award and three World Series games. That Randy Johnson. 11-4. Bonds hit a triple. Holy cow. The San Franciscos did it on Sunday, 4-3. Bonds drove in his 85th run, the team scored two in the ninth, and held on with Robb Nen saving his 30th game to give Estes win number eight.

A four-game sweep on the road, two of the wins over Schilling and Johnson. A turning point?

Shortly before the trading deadline, Sabean added pitcher Jason Schmidt, a hard-throwing right-hander from Pittsburgh. On August 1 at home, Schmidt turned in a gem to beat his old team, 3-1. Bonds went yard to thrill the full house and catch Harmon Killebrew.

"Spirits are rising in this town," said Baker. "Spirits are rising in this clubhouse." Scoreboard: Expos 8, Diamondbacks 5. Two out of first, one and a half from the wild card.

On Thursday, August 2, the streaking Giants won their eighth straight game behind Kirk Rueter's one-hit, two-walk performance in seven innings, 3-0 over Pittsburgh. Now they trailed Arizona by a game. Galarraga had 12 RBIs since his arrival, and the next evening added a game-winning homer in a 4-2 win over Philadelphia. It was their ninth straight, and improved their record to 15-7 since the All-Star break. The next day, Bonds lofted a two-run job, but the streak came to an end, 12-2 to the Phillies. He was on pace to hit 69, although he had two more dingers than McGwire at the same point. With the Mets' win over the Diamondbacks, San Francisco stayed within a game.

Half a country away, another Serra High School star athlete was inducted into the Pro Football Hall of Fame in Canton, Ohio. Lynn Swann was an All-American wide receiver at Southern Cal, and Terry Bradshaw's favorite target in Pittsburgh.

What was it with Serra High and Pittsburgh?

In Cooperstown, New York, the Baseball Hall of Fame announced they were revamping their selection process. They had decided to elect Bonds to the Hall right then and there, while still playing, before the season was over.*

Cincinnati gets hot in the summer like no place else. Barry Bonds hits there like no place else. Entering the Giants' series opener, he had a .339 average there with 30 homers, the most of any visiting player (ahead of Mike Schmidt's 29). Cinergi Field, or whatever it is they call the Ballpark Formerly Known as Riverfront Stadium, is an Astroturfed mistake of the all-sport variety, built when those monstrosities were built in the 1960s and '70s. In the summer, the plastic grass gets so hot players cannot stand in one place for more than a few seconds. Outfielders look forward to diving for line drives as much as getting a needle in their arm. How about the Bengals, getting tackled during hot exhibition day games in August? Bad yard.

That said, Cincinnati is a great baseball town with a rich history. The Big Red Machine was one of the great dynasties ever assembled. Bonds was a

*Just kiddin'.

big part of Cincy baseball history. On August 7 he added to that history. In a 3-3 extra-inning game, Bonds touched Danny Graves for his 48th. It unlocked the door, and the Giants scored six in the 11th to win it, 9-3, before 23,588.

The Cincinnati writers, stuck with a 46-65 team, mired in fifth place in the Central, finally had something fun to write about. Bonds' homer made him the fastest to 48 ever (113 games). Babe Ruth had gotten there in 114 games in 1921.

"So, Barry, talk to us."

" . . . anybody who talks about home runs, I'm walking away," Bonds told the professionals doing their jobs to feed their families.

What were they going to ask him about, the Intifada? Would Barry Bonds have the slightest clue what the Intifada is?

Watching Bonds deal with the press, I came to realize why I always felt uncomfortable working as a journalist around professional athletes. It was not just Bonds. No way. I had seen it for several years; baseball, basketball, football, tennis players. I had seen it in Los Angeles, where I had a magazine column, and had written for the *L.A. Times*. Now I was seeing it in San Francisco, where I wrote a column for the *Examiner*.

The professionals had it bad, but the college kids were working on it. There was even a select group of very talented high school athletes who had it. "It" was attitude. Arrogance. Everybody knows athletes have "it." It gets spoken about regularly. But breaking down what it was, the dynamics of attitude and class structure in professional sports, that was something I had not seen written about. So, I will try to put my finger on it here.

I had felt from the beginning that pro athletes would never intimidate me because I had been one myself. True, I had only played a few years of minor league baseball, but you would be amazed how much minor league baseball players think of themselves. You have to be on the inside, where they drink, gamble, bum chewing tobacco, and screw their women to see it. They want to be like the big leaguers. Playing like the big boys is difficult. Emulating their chauvinistic attitudes toward women, or their arrogance towards the press, is easier.

Take a guy like Matt Williams. If Williams did not play baseball, he would be an accountant, a real estate guy, maybe the man who delivers your FedEx packages. He would be very normal, which is what he is. He would smile and be very nice, and he would be considered one of the most dependable, likeable people in your neighborhood.

"Where are the kids, honey?"

"Over at the Williams's."

"Oh, okay."

Maybe he would still be married, instead of divorced, but that is not something I can say I know about. I just know what kind of guy he is. The media like Williams because he is accessible and gives good interviews.

Still, there are stories about Williams occasionally flying off the handle, yelling at people, and making himself hard to like. My point is, those aspects of his personality have a much better chance of publicly manifesting themselves because he is a high-priced, fawned-over, idolized big league baseball player than if he delivered for FedEx.

So, I had been one of those guys, kind of. I knew the drill and was ready for it. Still, I would walk in the clubhouse and not feel quite right. It was not just if I did not know people, those situations do not faze me. It was the social order.

A baseball team has a class structure, and it is not Democratic. It is more on the order of the (Eastern) Indian caste system. The players are the Untouchables. Within their class, superstars, stars, regulars, and scrubs occupied the rungs in that order. However, it is a free market class. Any player can get better, advance, and his earning power can reach the sky.

I have no problem with baseball salaries. They make what they make in a free market, just like actors, singers and other talented entertainers. My problem is with the baseball union. Admittedly, when Marvin Miller started the union, when the big league minimum was around $7,000 a year, the owners were taking advantage of them. Not exploiting them, because everybody was doing what they wanted to do and doing it of their own free will, but taking advantage of them.

The Yankees were notorious for "resting" pitchers for the World Series when they got close to 20 wins, then using the "failure" to be a 20-game winner as leverage in contract negotiations. They also told players what they did not make in salary would be made up in Series shares, which actually had some truth to it.

By 2001, however, the union had badly hurt the game. The players, spoiled children anyway, have come to believe it is their right, not a privilege, to be wealthy beyond the bounds of imagination. Many, many Major Leaguers are interchangeable with minor leaguers, and yet even mediocre players are paid exorbitant sums. Fine, the money apparently is there, but the union wants to codify these salaries, guaranteeing players monies far beyond what is reasonable.

The game is talking about contraction, by eliminating two money-losing franchises. Senator Paul Wellstone of Minnesota probably describes the union mindset better than anyone when he says that to eliminate two unsuccessful franchises is "just so that these business owners can keep from losing money."

Lord in Heaven, what cloud does this guy live on? Baseball players, spurred on by greedy agents and union hacks, think owners do not have a right to avoid losing money. They exist in a profession—American sports—that is the only one (outside the government) that engages in this whacked-out way of thinking.

Operating on a strangely parallel plane is team ownership. Then there is the general manager and the manager. They, too, are free marketers. They have power, they make good money, and have the potential to earn excellent salaries. Still, they are lion tamers, of sorts, whose duty it is to keep the prima donnas from rebelling.

The GM and the manager probably could go out and make a good living doing something else. Not baseball money, but a good living. Most of the players are not at that level, so there is unspoken tension, especially with the GM. Think of the GM as the colonel, and the manager as the top sergeant.

After that, you have the announcers. They are still in the free market, but their situations vary tremendously. Some are free agents who have star power. Others are shills for their teams. Others are media celebrities who work for the cable stations and the news channels. They derive their status from their own careers, and the team is just a part of what they do. They dress better and lord about, in a manner that frustrates the writers, who have to wait until these electronic deadline dudes ask their postgame questions for the 11 o'clock news.

Next are the sports babes. Sports babes work on television. There are women who work for newspapers, and some of them fill a politically correct vacuum, but by and large the female writers are competent.

The TV sports babes are there for sex appeal. No complaints, but that is what they are there for.

When the women first started venturing into the clubhouse, there was a great deal of resentment. In *The Bronx Zoo*, former Yankee relief pitcher Sparky Lyle told about the time at Yankee Stadium when somebody baked a cake in the shape of fully erect male genitalia, just to embarrass some lady reporter. She figured the guilty party was Graig Nettles. She asked him if he was the one who brought the cake and he said, "Naw, I just modeled for it." Today guys are buck-naked and nobody thinks twice about having women in the locker room.

One funny depiction is the "dropped mic" scene in Oliver Stone's excellent football epic, "Any Given Sunday." A female reporter bends down to pick up her equipment and has to twist her neck to avoid the enormous "equipment" of an African-American player, hanging in front of her at mouth level. Players seem to have no problem with it, but it has gotten kind of obvious that some women are there for sex appeal a lot more than for sports expertise.

Now, I know Lisa Guerrero at Fox. I worked with her at *StreetZebra*. Beautiful girl, and smart as a whip. She is a very nice lady. I respect her and am happy for her. But I know for a fact we ran her "One Sports Chick's Opinion" column at *StreetZebra* magazine because we could put pictures of her, wearing a tube top, next to the column. If she were ordinary looking, she would not have gotten the gig.

If she were ordinary looking, she would be successful because she is intelligent and has drive. She would not be on TV.

There is a scene from a film called "Swimming With Sharks" that defines the difference between men and women in sports television. Kevin Spacey, playing a thinly disguised Scott Rudin, a leading producer, explains the meaning of life to Frank Whaley. He is talking about Hollywood, but the words apply to sports TV.

"You can't sleep your way to the top," like a female producer who slept her way to the top, Spacey tells Whaley. "Noooo. Guys like us . . . we gotta fight, and scratch and claw our way up."

I know a lot of women who have slept their way up the ladder. This is an unspoken fact among the media. Well, it is spoken by men to men, and women not only admit it to each other, they brag about it. But men and women do not talk about it to each other, except maybe in code after the man in power has slept with the woman seeking power, and there is some kind of acknowledgment that the act shall be rewarded.

Happens all the damn time. Like Howard Cosell said, it is "telling it like it is."

So the men view the women in media with suspicion because they climb the ladder in ways men cannot. Now, the unfortunate aspect to all of this is that all women do not benefit from this system, only good-looking women. Go to the grocery store and look around. Unless you live in Scottsdale, Arizona, a certain part of Beverly Hills, or it is spring break at Ft. Lauderdale, you will just see ordinary-looking women. Plus, ordinary-looking men. The reason is that people are ordinary looking. Attractive people are relatively rare.

Consequently, ordinary looking, yet talented women do not get the TV jobs they are qualified for. However, the talent pool for jobs in sports media, in general, is larger and more competitive because women are applying for positions they never used to dream of trying for.

Are women on TV more competent than the women who were on TV back when the Christine Craft lawsuit exposed the sex angle (as if anybody did not already know about it)? Take as an example Andrea Thompson.

Thompson was a decent actor on "NYPD Blue," and nice looking. She is abominable as a news anchor, but was placed there for looks and glitter. Thompson has the lips of a porn star, which makes her a great object of fantasy, but creates difficulties when it comes to reading big words off the TeleprompTer. While she is now the exception, brains are still secondary to looks among TV women. Any doubt that this premise rings of Truth can be dispelled by looking at what happened with Paula Zahn.

Zahn is the sexy blonde who was a star at Fox News, then moved over to CNN because CNN needed sex appeal. Now, Paula is no spring chicken, so at least "older" women are getting a chance to work in front of the camera. Of course, she spent $7,000 to highlight her hair and has zero body fat. She is competent, but would not be where she is if she was not still a hottie, whereas many (but not all) of her male associates are not "hunks."

CNN promoted her with an ad that stated she was "just a little sexy," along with the sound of a zipper being opened. The implication, for those of you in Rio Linda, California, is that a significant portion of the viewing audience was not watching her to find out if the Marines were closer to capturing bin Laden, but rather to stroke up some wood.

Zahn, preferring to live a myth, was outraged, so CNN went PC and took the ad off the air. Meanwhile, the men on television continue to often look like Larry King or Aaron Bown, Zahn's average-looking male counterpart.

There is a reality to which "men" get a lot of jobs in media these days, too, and it is not pretty. The corporations that run radio and cable TV stations, which proliferate the sports scene, eschew the experienced journalists in favor of Gen-X boys who will work for much less than the middle class. These people pander to a skateboard mentality that the programmers think sells. It involves, instead of insight, rock music and "shock jock," lowest common denominator humor in the Howard Stern tradition. It is cheap and will not last in the sports genre.

So, around the ballpark, everybody is checking everybody else out, wondering how so-and-so landed such-and-such a gig. It is a real soap opera down there on the field before the game. Not surprisingly, sports babes in LA and New York are better looking than sports babes in San Francisco or other towns.

Then there are the writers. What a group of unshaven ragamuffins. First, you have to get past the characters at your own paper.

Every copy editor and assistant editor has his own little fiefdom, and if ever the term "no good deed goes unpunished" is apropos, it is at the sports desk. Some of these little people will offer their help, then when you take them up on the offer, they use it to stab you in the back, saying that you cannot carry your own weight.

Editors sometimes act like kings, taking exception to employees who know true things about them, or have the temerity to actually remember the words they say and the promises they fail to keep. Unfortunately, the true things about them are not always good things.

Beat guys treat new writers the way northern Yankee veterans on the Tigers treated the Confederate Ty Cobb, when the Georgia Peach came up to Detroit.

I approached one beat writer about membership in the Baseball Writers Association of America when I arrived in San Francisco from L.A. As God is my witness, I was as sweet as honey, and complimentary, too.

He looked at me like I had Ebola. Pure attitude. Then my assistant editor told me this guy, whom he had worked with a few years prior, told him *I* had attitude.

The thing about the writers, and the thing I discovered I did not like about it, was that we are the serf class of the "above-the-line" talent. "Above-the-line" is a movie term, meaning you are one of the people whose name is credited before the film starts—stars, director, producers, writer, cinematographer, etc. All the rest are "below-the-line" people—keygrips, wardrobe consultants, blah, blah, blah.

The writer is an interesting species in the baseball universe. They can hurt the players, or make them. Day-by-day, they have more local influence than anybody does. Still, the players occasionally treat writers like crap in ways they would never act with TV people. Bonds is as nice to Roy Firestone as a boy scout with a little old lady, but he does not give Henry Schulman that respect.

Sometimes race is an issue. Latin players favor Latin writers. A black writer might have a better chance with a black player. It is interesting to note that Bonds and Firestone get along famously, yet obviously Bonds and Tim McCarver did not.

Some columnists have a little star power, but you usually cannot tell one from the other. You might see some grommet walking around, and only when you see him sitting at his assigned seat in the press box, where the name tags are, do you realize it is a writer you always respected.

Bruce MacGowan of KNBR lives by this rule, "Be nice to everyone, and nicer to the people you don't have to be nice to." God bless him, but he is not average.

The problem with the writers, why I have a hard time with it and subconsciously so do the players, is they are not free marketers like the others. A working journalist makes a finite amount of money, even most columnists. They are limited. They are working stiffs, the proletariats of sport. In the framework of newspaper and most magazine careers, the best you can do is make editor and columnist. Neither will pay you what Julia Roberts or Alex Rodriguez make.

The players can make millions. The manager can make millions. So can the GM. The owner already has made his. A few of the TV stars can walk those golden stairs. There are writers who make big dough like George Will, but within the confines of a sports beat, they will not. You have a guy making $50,000 dealing with guys making $15 million.

So, writers being humans, sometimes feel resentment. At first they are just glad to be there, because they are fans and this is a dream job. Big league sportswriting is one of the best jobs you can have, no question. But over time the fantasy fades into reality.

Me, I am an entrepreneur. I never liked that claustrophobic economic feeling you get amongst the writers. The rabble. I have pursued the more lucrative areas of writing, such as screenwriting, political speechwriting, public relations, and obviously the book you are reading.

Then there is the "below-the-line" talent. These are the youngsters working in the club's PR department, usually right out of college. It is a great job and a resume-builder, but they will have to decide between a lower-paying career in team sports media, or to move elsewhere. A lot of them put up with a ton of crap from the players, and unfortunately from everyone else, too.

After that there are the elevator operators, the stadium workers, the gatekeepers who make sure you have your pass. There are the cooks and the press dining room workers, and the clubhouse attendants.

These people are usually union, locked in to a certain wage that will rise only with cost-of-living adjustments, and they can be difficult. Every stadium has them, and you move through them with kid gloves. They are like the lifetime workers of socialism. Some "celebrity" in the media may treat these people with a big smile and a lot of love, but one cannot shake off the feeling they are being condescending. It looks like the king's advisors being kind to serfs.

Being locked in financially is not the sole irritant many writers have. In the old days, writers were guys who ran away from home, and instead of joining the circus, went to work at 16 as a copy boy for the newspaper. Read Budd Schulberg's *What Makes Sammy Run*.

They eventually became writers. Fed all the free booze and food that clubs used to provide, they quickly became alcoholics, reprobates and freeloaders.

Nowadays, a writer majors in journalism at San Diego State, where he wrote for the student newspaper. They are erudite, well-educated people. They have gym memberships, not passes to a speakeasy. However, because they live in the sports world, some of them dumb themselves down to their environment. Like so many of the athletes they cover, some writers tend to lose focus on events in politics and society. However, most of them maintain a good, working knowledge of issues and events. After all, they work for newspapers.

Now, here is the rub. A very large number of the athletes they cover are not very smart. In fact, a good percentage of them can be listed as being members of the Dumbellionite Class.

You know the Dumbellionites. In ancient times, there were the Canaanites, the Israelites and the Mennonites. Those tribes came and, for the most part, went. The Dumbellionites stayed to roam the plains of the Earth.

They are immersed amongst us today in numbers greater than all other tribes. The Dumbellionites.

A lot of baseball players are Dumbellionites. Most do not read books or newspapers. Some cannot read. Their knowledge of things outside how to prepare for and play a boy's game is often nil. The "jockocracy," as Cosell used to say. Many could have developed knowledge, but were slid through school to stay eligible for sports, never finding a need to educate themselves. The college guys usually are decent interviews, but few scholar athletes in college are scholars. They were the guys who chewed tobacco, spit in cups and left it in class, then got the girls at frat parties. Those guys.

Every writer knew those guys in high school and college. Most resented them, although it did not stop them from kissing their butts. Now, they are doing the same thing, only getting paid (a lot less than the jocks) for it.

Then there are the foreign players, who usually come from impoverished backgrounds. The Americans, being Americans, have enough moxie acquired through osmosis to make a living for themselves even if they were not baseball players. Of course, instead of being paid $7.2 million guaranteed for two years, they would be making $45,000 unguaranteed with no contract. The Latin players, particularly the Dominicans, might be able to make a living coaching and scouting in their home country, but outside of the game, their prospects are dim (outside being a player) if they are not born in the U.S.A.

The recently retired Stan Javier, a Dominican, played with me. He has some education because his father played in the Majors and raised him with prospects outside of the game, even though he signed with St. Louis at 15 or 16. Miguel Batista of Arizona admires Albert Einstein and quotes poetry, but he is as rare as rare can be.

Unfortunately, the writer lives in a one-bedroom flat with a Bunsen burner, if he can afford City rents at all. The player lives on a hill with 19 TV sets. On the road, the writers stay to themselves. In the old days, the scribes would drink with the players, and sometimes even get some of their "left over" women. Nowadays, the players go clubbing, but not with writers. The writer just looks on in envy while the players get all these porn-star types. Then he goes back to his room and calls for phone sex.

In every single walk of life in most civilized countries, the educated people make more money than uneducated people do. What a concept. This reminds me of the joint Harvard-Yale study that took two years and cost $1 million. All these academics determined that people with a college education who possessed specific job skills earned more money than people without a college education who did not possess specific job skills.

Except for pro athletes, and baseball players are the least of the species. Not that playing football at the University of Miami guarantees knowledge.

Remember Jerome Brown? Prior to the 1987 Fiesta Bowl, an Army fatigue-clad Brown stood up at a banquet involving Miami and Penn State players, and said the following:

"Did the Japanee [*sic*] siddown to dinna with Pearl Harba before dey bombed him? *No*. Fellas, let's go." The Hurricanes followed Brown out of the room. At least football and basketball players go to some kind of college, though. Baseball players often sign out of high school, sometimes before they finish high school if they went to high school. If they went to college, they usually sign after their junior year, or out of a community college. Basketball and football players rarely sign out of high school or JC. Football players are much more likely to go in the draft after their senior year than their junior year.

Of course, playing sports really well is a heck of a job skill. Still, the writers are placed in this position of cow-towing, sniveling around, and kissing up to these uneducated dudes who, in any other walk of life, would not likely be in their social or economic class. It is a real upside-down world. It goes a long, long way to determining the reason there is tension between athletes and writers. Writers do this knowing there is a complete ceiling, and this is no glass ceiling, but a thick, impenetrable one, that separates their lot in life from the players. This is their destiny, unless he makes a daring break for the land of David Halberstam, Tom Clancy or Aaron Sorkin.

If an athlete can complete a sentence, he is pronounced "articulate." If he does not swear at the writers, he is spoken of in reverent tones as if he were Gandhi. There is this politically correct dance that everybody thinks about, but nobody comments on.

The writer, or the broadcaster, interviews the player. The media person asks intelligent questions, but is careful not to stray into territory that would show the player's lack of smarts. At the same time, the interviewer tries not to be condescending.

The player opens his mouth. Sometimes you cannot tell what the hell he is saying. If this were a job interview, he would not get past the first round, because people do judge you by the words you use. Players are likely to have no idea how to use the English language and have no grammatical structure.

It is changing. There are some refreshing interviewees, and Jim Rome is great at bringing the best out of them. Rome is tops because he has broken out of the mold and is "one of them" financially, so the players "get with him." His big bucks bring him respect.

Mostly, though, the interview ends, the interviewer thanks the athlete profusely, and the athlete walks away. The interviewer then just sighs to himself.

Me? I am not concerned with the intelligence of the athletes. They are living the American Dream and God bless 'em for it. What always bothered me, and I now can put my finger on, is that the baseball clubhouse is not free market enterprise. So, I have made that break for the land of Halberstam, Clancy and Sorkin.

In recent weeks, Arizona had gone cold. Los Angeles and San Francisco were hot. The Dodgers led the division now by a game over the Giants and one and a half over the D'backs.

On August 9, the two great scions of baseball matched each other with long balls. Bonds and Griffey hit big flies, and San Francisco won, 6-4. Two days later Bonds joined Mays and Johnny Mize as the only Giants to reach 50 in a year, as his team defeated the Cubs at Wrigley Field, 6-4. Mays got a morning phone call, waking him up after he had flown in from New York the previous evening. It was John Shea telling him that his Godson had reached 50.

"Oh, he did?" Mays said. "That's a little history for us."

In the musical chairs that had become first place in the West, the Diamondbacks had crawled back up by half a game over both the Giants and Dodgers. The division race was shaping up to be the best since the "wild, wild West" race of 1969, when Atlanta edged out the Giants, Reds, Dodgers and Astros to win it.

On August 14 at home, the Marlins fell, 13-7 when Bonds tied Mr. Mays, with a grand slam off Ricky Bones. He also walked three times and raised his average to .308. It was back to front-page headlines in the *Chron* after "Bonds blasts past Mays" for his 53rd homer in an important 5-3 victory over Florida.

"It's like being with Patton after the Bulge," I told Bonds of the experience of covering his run at history.

"I'm not that talented," he replied. I am still not sure if he knew George Patton from George Will, but the smile on his face said he *was* enjoying himself.

Bonds' McGwire pace had not yet caught up with the redhead on the auction block. McGwire's record-setting home run ball was estimated at $3 million, while experts were saying that if Bonds got there, his ball would only be worth a million. Hey McFarlane, are you listening? The comic bookmeister apparently was not, since he never did sell his ball. He would be left with a deeply devalued piece of horsehide when Bonds broke it.

A Bonds autographed bat was said to be worth $300, compared to McGwire's $713 asking price.

Bonds smashed number 54 off Jason Marquis on a sunny Saturday, August 18, before 41,722 at Pac Bell, in a 3-1 loss to Atlanta. It tied him with Mike Schmidt at 548. He now had 107 runs batted in to go with a .310 average. The pace was for 71, and McGwire only had 47 up to that point in

1998 (123 games). In the up-and-down West, San Francisco found themselves two and a half behind Arizona. Slumping Los Angeles trailed by four and a half.

The incredible thing about Bonds was that, unlike almost all other sluggers, he was a contact hitter. His career strikeout ratio was one every 6.2 at-bats. Cousin Reggie twisted himself like a whiffing pretzel once every 3.8 trips to the plate. Joe DiMaggio had been a tremendous contact hitter, but he did not have Bonds' power, albeit many of his drives fell short in the pre-remodeled Yankee Stadium's notorious "death valley." With 121 bases on balls, Bonds was making a run at the all-time record in this statistic, too. Would Jim Tracy, Bruce Bochy, Larry Dierker and Bob Brenly, West Division managers who would be facing him over the next month and a half, let him swing?

After hitting a pinch-hit, game-winning home run off Graeme Lloyd at Olympic Stadium to beat the Expos, Bonds had made the front page again. The article appeared just above photos of Congressman Gary Condit and missing intern Chandra Levy. It was a slow "hard" news summer, although that would all change on September 11.

The August 27 issue of *Sports Illustrated* hit the San Francisco Giants like a bombshell. Rick Reilly, one of the most-respected sportswriters in America, had this to say:

"In the San Francisco Giants' clubhouse, everybody knows the score: 24-1.

"There are 24 teammates, and there's Barry Bonds.

"There are 24 teammates who show up to pose for the team picture, and there's Bonds, who has blown it off for the last two years.

"There are 24 teammates who go out on the field before the game to stretch together, and there's Bonds, who usually stretches indoors with his own flex guy.

"There are 24 teammates who get on the players' bus at the hotel to go to the park, and there's Bonds, who gets on the bus with the broadcasters, the trainers and the manager who coddles him.

"There are 24 teammates who eat the clubhouse spread, and there's Bonds, whose nutritionist brings in special meals for him.

"There are 24 teammates who deal with the Giants' publicity man, and there's Bonds, who has his own clubhouse-roving PR guy, a freelance artist named Steve Hoskins, who turned down George Will's request for an interview with Bonds because Hoskins had never heard of him.

"There are 24 teammates who hang out with one another, play cards and bond, and there's Bonds, sequestered in the far corner of the clubhouse with his PR man, masseur, flex guy, weight trainer, three lockers, a reclining massage chair and a big-screen television that only he can see.

"Last week, after Bonds hit his 51st home run in a 13-7 win over the Florida Marlins, most of the players stayed to celebrate the victory, and at least one was gone before the press arrived in the clubhouse: Bonds.

" 'That's Barry,' says San Francisco second baseman Jeff Kent. 'He doesn't answer questions. He palms everybody off on us, so we have to do his talking for him. But you get used to it. Barry does a lot of questionable things. But you get used to it. Sometimes it rubs the younger guys the wrong way, and sometimes it rubs the veterans the wrong way. You just hope he shows up for the game and performs. I've learned not to worry about it or think about it or analyze it. I was raised to be a team guy, and I am, but Barry's Barry. It took me two years to learn to live with it, but I learned.'

"If you get the feeling that Kent, who's in his fifth season with San Francisco, wouldn't spit on Bonds if Bonds were on fire, you might be right. Maybe it has something to do with last year, when Kent and Bonds were running neck and neck for the National League MVP award. The week before the award was to be announced, Bonds had a member of his entourage call the commissioner's office to try to find out who had won. We've got to know, said the stooge, because if he's not going to win, he can get out of town.

"Perfect! No staying around to congratulate Kent. Or going to the press conference to shake his hand. Just, 'If it ain't me, I'm outta here.' The commissioner's office didn't know the results of the voting. Kent won.

"Someday they'll be able to hold Bonds' funeral in a fitting room. When Bonds hit his 500th home run, in April, only one person came out of the dugout to greet him at the plate: The Giants' batgirl. Sitting in the stands, you could've caught a cold from the freeze he got. Teammates 24, Bonds 1.

"Bonds isn't beloved by his teammates. He's not even beliked. He often doesn't run out grounders, doesn't run out flies. If a Giants pitcher gives up a monster home run over Bonds in leftfield, Bonds keeps his hands on his knees and merely swivels his head to watch the ball sail over the fence. He's an MTV diva, only with bigger earrings.

" 'On the field, we're fine,' says Kent, 'but off the field, I don't care about Barry and Barry doesn't care about me. [Pause.] Or anybody else.'

"Bonds will be a free agent after this season, and if he decides to sign elsewhere, will the Giants be devastated? Kent grimaces. 'See: Seattle Mariners,' he says, walking away."

When Bonds arrived in New York for a four-game series at Shea Stadium, the New York press was all over him. Some said Bonds' breaking the record so soon cheapened it. Billy Crystal's HBO movie "61*" suggested that there should be nostalgia for this record, but Bonds was heading for it with all the subtlety of Sherman marching through Georgia, with the ink barely dry on McGwire's new record in the books. Some said Bonds deserved the record because he was a great player having a great year, as opposed to Maris, a good player who had a great year. Comparisons were made with Luis Gonzalez, a good player having a great year. Was McGwire a great player? He was a great home run hitter, but he could not hold Bonds' jock strap, as they say, as an all-around ball player.

Others argued that McGwire and Bonds had "earned" the right to chase the record, since they were already members of the 500-homer club. Maris had not even hit 300 career home runs and will not make the Hall of Fame.

The season-long argument that Bonds neither had the support, nor endured the scrutiny endured by McGwire in 1998, was brought up. He lacked "charm." He was not the "rightful heir" to the record. Sosa was.

Bonds' gap between his previous high, 49 and a potential record would be similar to Maris' 39-to-61 jump. Bonds, however, like Aaron, had four 40-homer seasons, six 30-homer seasons and the kind of consistency that enabled Hammer to reach 755.

In an article called "Bonding With Barry", *New York Daily News* sports writer John Harper said "no matter what Barry Bonds does, his remarkable run at history was never going to resemble the feel-good story that Mark McGwire and Sammy Sosa authored in 1998." He continued with the New York theory that the mystique surrounding baseball's single-season home run record disappeared along with Maris' name from the record book.

"But now, as Bonds brings his 54 home runs to center stage in New York tonight for a weekend series with the Mets," wrote Harper, "he is being portrayed nationally as a player so selfish that his teammates can barely tolerate him."

The spacious quarters apart from his teammates in the Pac Bell clubhouse that included a recliner and a big-screen TV for his personal use were brought up as "evidence" that makes Bonds "easy to dislike, and perhaps difficult for America to embrace…"

Mike Piazza at one point shared a superstar status on a par with Bonds, yet he could not be more different in personality. He blends in easily among teammates. Piazza thought it "absurd" for Bonds' superstar trappings to be such an issue.

"Me, I don't like an entourage," Piazza told Harper. "If I'm going to go shopping, I just go. I don't need any special treatment. In here, I like being one of the guys, hanging out.

"Barry Bonds may be different, but if he's getting results, I don't care. The locker room stuff, I think that's so overrated. You don't have to be the best of friends with everybody in the locker room. You don't have to take guys out to dinner.

"Don't get me wrong. I think it's good when you have good guys on a team, but it's sort of a bonus. There's nothing Barry Bonds can't do on a baseball field, so as far as I'm concerned, I want him on my team. I don't have to be his best buddy."

Piazza was also probably frustrated by the Mets' disappointing season, and was thinking about the run production Bonds would bring to his club, plus the fat pitches he would see with Barry hitting in front or behind him. Piazza was astonished that anybody on his own team, in the middle of a pennant race the Giants were in the thick of, would take shots at their star player.

"How can you criticize a guy who's carrying you to the playoffs?" Piazza asked. "If Barry Bonds was a nice guy, very gracious, cheery, outgoing, a breath of fresh air—great. But he's not, at least not all the time. I don't think he's a bad guy, but hasn't he been this way his whole career?

"Why all of a sudden is this coming out now? Because he's having the year he's having?"

In the wake of Reilly's piece, Kent insisted his quotes were "doctored up pretty good," and accused Reilly of bearing a grudge because Bonds turned down an interview request from him the previous week.

"He wanted to pull the trigger big-time," Kent told the press. "It sounds like he did."

"What do they think, that we're supposed to be break-dancing in here?" Bonds had said. The controversy added a little excitement to Bonds' home run chase as he arrived at Shea, a place in need of some pizzazz in this down year for the home team.

"If he does hit 70, wow, I can't even think in those terms," Piazza said. "I don't have a problem celebrating it. I think it'd be a cool thing."

The *Associated Press* had this to say during the Mets' series:

"He doesn't care whether fans like him. He doesn't care whether teammates like him.

"Winning a World Series, that he does care about.

"'Is it important for you to be liked be your colleagues?' Bonds asked Friday at a news conference at Shea Stadium. 'Yes. But what can you do if they don't? That's life. You can't change it. You pray for these people.'"

Bonds arrived in New York with 55 homers, needing 15 in San Francisco's final 35 games to tie the season record

"I don't feel I have a bad relationship with Jeff," he said. After games, Bonds said, "we all go our separate ways. That's normal. He has his family and goes his way and I have my family and I go my way. . . .

" . . . If he wants to go out to lunch with me, I'd love to go. If he wants to ride motorcycles, we'll ride motorcycles."

So is Bonds a "lone wolf?"

"That's between us," Baker answered when asked that question.

"I don't want to get into that, I really don't," owner Magowan said.

Magowan, wearing a Giants cap, sat on an end of the third row for the New York news conference but didn't ask any questions of his biggest star, who earned $55.2 million in his first nine seasons in San Francisco.

Bonds, who frequently claimed he was misquoted or taken out of context, was making himself available primarily in group interviews, where there is taped evidence of the exact words.

When McGwire and Sosa chased Maris, they generated a "warm, fuzzy feeling among many fans," said the *AP*. "The impression Bonds has left is of distance and coolness, which he says is created by a media unhappy with him.

"Bonds, who is black, didn't give a direct answer when asked if he thought racism played a part in the reaction to his chase.

"'Does the KKK exist?' he answered. 'Sure. Probably. I don't know. Is it affecting me? No. Does it bother me? No.'

"It hasn't changed drastically," he continued in reference to the racism faced by Aaron in 1974.

"There are still people don't like people of all kinds of races," said Baker, who played in the latter part of Aaron's era. "One thing I've noticed: The lack of fans of color in every ballpark."

"I think about Hank Aaron," Bonds said in a telling remark. "Babe Ruth is second. I don't think about second place. I've been there before."

ESPN commentator and former Hall of Fame second baseman Joe Morgan wrote a special article for ESPN.com.

"It's shocking that pitchers continue to pitch to Sammy Sosa when he is on one of his home run binges," wrote Morgan. "Hitting three home runs in a game twice in one month is an amazing feat. By comparison, Barry Bonds barely gets three at-bats in a game.

" . . . Every Major League pitcher has pride in his ability when he faces Sosa or Bonds. A pitcher is not supposed to be afraid when he is standing on the mound. He must always believe in his ability to throw his pitches and retire the hitter. If he doesn't, then he gets hit."

Morgan recalled something another Hall of Famer, reliever Rollie Fingers, once said: "Sometimes you tame the tiger. Other times the tiger eats you for lunch."

"This guy just had an ax to drop on Barry," Kent told the writers, who would not drop the subject of Reilly's article. "People seem to have a phobia that I have a problem with Barry . . . but it's not an issue with us. It seems to be an issue with reporters."

Bonds had not seen the column, so he simply went over to Kent's locker and asked him about it. Kent told him to read it. Bonds was then given the gist of it by the media horde. He shrugged. He is, to his credit, not excitable.

"Do you have friends everywhere?" he asked the writers. "I'm supposed to have friends all over the world all the time? What's the point? Doesn't it seem kind of strange?

"I've got friends in the game of baseball, but I don't have 700 of them."

The subject of a Ray Ratto column was Kent, who said his quotes were somehow accurate, doctored and out of context. He had told Bob Nightengale of *USA TODAY* essentially the same thing for several years, only now Bonds was bigger news than allegations that a Democrat Congressman had murdered his possibly-pregnant lover.

On Friday, August 24 at Shea Stadium the Giants experienced *déjà vu* all over again, losing to their October tormentors of the 2000 playoff, 4-3. New York was virtually out of the Eastern race, where surprising Philadelphia was challenging old-standby Atlanta, but on this evening they muted San Francisco's offense just as they had in two postseason Shea wins a year prior.

Bonds endured the New York media, along with East Coast-native Peter Magowan, and again was a top-of-the-page front section *Chronicle* headline, eclipsing another one: "Condit's bid to answer critics called 'disaster,'" after the politician's poor showing with Connie Chung.

Bonds indicated that he might be willing to give a hometown discount to the Giants in contract negotiations. On the field, things did not go well for San Fran. They lost three of four, barely escaping a four-game sweep with a 6-5 Monday afternoon getaway win, in which Bonds slammed number 56. The Phillies beat Arizona, so the Giants picked up one of the games they had lost over the weekend, to stay within shouting distance in the late dog days of summer. Two and a half games, and at .557, they were positioned three percentage points ahead of Chicago for the wild card.

Bonds had put together his usual complete game against New York—3-for-4, two runs scored, one RBI, one walk, to up his average to .314. Talk of Gonzalez and Sosa for MVP was fading, and everybody knew September is Bonds' month.

Any hope of repeating the heroics of their earlier four-game sweep in Phoenix were removed the next night at the BOB, when the Big Unit, Randy Johnson, mowed them down, 4-1.

Gonzo showed he was still a force to be reckoned with when he helped his team jab the knife into Baker's team, and twist it around. His 50th homer ignited a 2-0 win before 31,990 over Frisco, but they stayed alive in the series finale, 13-5.

On Saturday, September dawned with a 2-1 Giants victory at home against Colorado. Baker sat Bonds. To many, this seemed unthinkable. The team was in a heated race, and he was chasing ghosts and legends. Baker knows his man better than anybody. He always argued that resting Bonds meant he would have more when it counted later. Bonds was adept himself at keeping his tank from running empty, even if it occasionally meant pulling up after a weak ground ball to second base.

A big Saturday crowd may not have appreciated Baker's move, but the team plays Saturday day games exclusively, and the plan was to sit Bonds in day games after night games. Bonds did pinch-hit, which gave his team a psychological lift in an important 3-1 win that sent away the home folks' happy.

On September 5, the *Chronicle* put Bonds back on the front page (Gary Condit was relegated to page two). This time, science writer Carl T. Hall used a comprehensive scoring system called the Total Player Rating to determine the greatest baseball player of all times. Apparently, Bonds was such a star they needed a guy who usually covers NASA to describe his greatness.

The statistics covered all aspects of the game, including offense, defense and pitching, and took into account a player's performance vs. his contemporaries, not just raw numbers. Entering 2001, Bonds had ranked sixth with a TPR of 89.4. By Labor Day, however, he had passed Walter Johnson, Ty Cobb, Nap Lajoie and Mays to firmly ensconce himself into second place, at 97.4. Only Babe Ruth, who had picked up points under the system for his pitching record with Boston from 1914-19, was ahead of him at 126.1. After Bonds, Mays was at 95.9, Cobb at 92.1, and Aaron at 89.1.

Bonds was also on pace to finish with the second-best season ever, behind Ruth's 1920 performance. Many people think of Ruth in 1927, when he hit 60 homers, and the Murderer's Row Yankees won 110 games, swept the World Series, and were considered the greatest team ever assembled. However, Ruth's best years were 1920 and 1921.

In 1920, Ruth was sold to New York. Red Sox owner Harry Frazee was looking for funding of his Broadway play, "No, No Nanette," so he took Yankee owner Jacob Rupert's money and sent The Babe, along with Hall of Fame pitcher Herb Pennock, to the Apple. Thus, the so-called Red Sox Curse.

Boston had won the World Championship in 1918 behind Ruth, the best left-handed pitcher in baseball. He set a Series record for consecutive scoreless innings that lasted until 1961. He was traded after the following season, and the team has never won the Series since, losing three heartbreaking seven-game classics by virtue of various freaks worthy of Greek tragedy.

Think of Johnny Pesky holding the ball while Enos Slaughter scored in 1946 and Bill Buckner letting Mookie Wilson's grounder go under his legs in 1986. The Curse?

New York did not win the 1920 pennant. They played at the Polo Grounds, where they were tenants of John McGraw's mighty New York Giants. They had only recently changed their names from the Highlanders to the Yankees and had never won the AL flag. They would not play at Yankee Stadium, the House That Ruth Built, until 1923.

In 1920, Ruth hit .376 with 54 homers and 137 RBIs, 148 walks and an .847 slugging percentage. Ruth broke his own home run record of 29, set in 1919 when the Red Sox finally switched him permanently from pitcher to outfielder. His 29 had come in the "dead ball era," in which the ball was mushy and did not travel well, and pitchers were allowed to throw spitballs, Emory balls, grease balls, licorice balls, and scuff balls.

In 1919 the "Black Sox" scandal hit. Eight Chicago White Sox players threw the World Series against Cincinnati. They were actually acquitted toward the end of the 1920 season, but the new Commissioner, Judge Kenesaw Mountain Landis, banned them all from baseball right after the trial.

Seeing the excitement that Ruth's power produced, baseball felt that the game needed a jolt amid gambling allegations involving not just the Black Sox but rampant over previous years throughout the game. Highlander first baseman "Prince Hal" Chase openly bet on baseball, and was said to manipulate games on the behest of gambling influences.

In "Godfather II," Hyman Roth (based on Meyer Lanky) tells Michael Corleone he loved baseball ever since "Arnold Rothstein fixed the World Series" in 1919.

Baseball powers, looking to create excitement that would deflect attention from gambling and corruption, decided to tighten and harden the baseball, producing longer flight, beginning in 1920. They also outlawed all the trick pitches like spitballs and Emory balls, except for a small number of identified pitchers who had relied on these pitches throughout their careers, like Burleigh Grimes. These pitchers were allowed to use these pitches until each of their careers eventually ended.

Ruth actually out-homered every other American League team in 1920, and his performance is monumental. However, in comparing him to Bonds, one must consider certain factors. First, he was the first hitter to really emphasize power, and therefore the only batsman in 1920 to truly take advantage of the new, livelier ball. He played in an eight-team league that traveled by train, no further west than St. Louis, played no night games, and he saw no sliders, split-fingered fastballs, blacks, Cubans or Dominicans.

In 1921, The Babe hit .378 with 59 homers and 171 RBIs, 171 runs scored, 144 walks (his Major League record for walks was 170 in 1923), and an .846 slugging percentage. His team won the pennant before falling to McGraw's Giants in an all-Polo Grounds World Series.

His statistics eclipsed the rest of baseball in a way no other athlete has ever done in any sport. It says here that he was the best athlete of the 20th Century, no matter what ESPN said about Michael Jordan.

However, statistics aside, it also says here that Bonds was in the process of having an even better season in 2001 than Ruth in 1920 or '21. It also says here that Bonds has it within his ability (and Scott Boras agrees) to break records that will make him the greatest player ever.

The only thing that may hold that title back from him, and from anybody else, was Ruth's pitching record. That is The Babe's trump card. However, in his day pitchers-turned-hitters were not as unusual.

"Smoky Joe" Wood won 34 games for Boston in 1912, and after injuring himself became an outfielder. George Sisler came up as a pitcher out of the University of Michigan, but switched to first base and hit .420 en route to the Hall of Fame. Stan Musial was a pitcher before switching, as was Ted Williams.

By Barry Bonds' day, however, specialization had crept into all areas of the game. High schools have used the designated hitter for years. The same thing in football, where you almost never see "two-way" players in college or the pros. So the comparison of Bonds and Ruth has to be viewed from this lens, like comparing Lawrence Taylor with Chuck Bednarik. For purposes of comparison, consider that Ruth's pitching career just would not have happened after World War II.

Baseball is the only sport in which old-timers are considered to be as good as modern players. Nobody thinks Red Grange is as good as Barry Sanders. Few believe Sammy Baugh to be the equal of John Elway. Stanford's Hank Luisetti was possibly the best basketball player in the country in 1940, but would he be able to handle Michael Jordan or Kobe Bryant?

Uh uh.

Look at other sports with quantifiable statistics, like track and swimming. Even a 1972 Olympian like Mark Spitz has seen his times eclipsed, and no records stand very long in these sports. Factoring in the travel, population growth, internationalism, night games, sliders, splitters, societal evolution and racial progress, it says here that Bonds has a legitimate shot at being Number One!

Number one hit number 59 in a 5-2 loss to Arizona on September 4.

Speaking of The Babe, Bonds tied him by joining the 60 homer club on September 6, hitting it off Arizona's Albie Lopez to spur a 9-5 home win, and pull his team to within one and a half games. Of course, this meant he was back on the front pages of the *Chronicle* and the *Marin Independent Journal*, neither of which, thankfully, mentioned a word about Gary Condit or Chandra Levy in the entire section. He finally admitted "anything's possible" when asked about his chances at 70. He would need 10 in 21 games. *Chronicle* sports editor Glenn Schwarz, an Age of Aquarius kind of guy from Mill Valley, went to the old Sonny and Cher card with the headline, "I got you, Babe."

Maris' family was now being trotted out, just as they had been for McGwire's chase. They announced plans to attend an upcoming Giants-Dodgers series in Los Angeles.

"I didn't think it would happen again this quickly, but Barry has a shot at the record," Roger Maris, Jr. told John Shea. " . . . I hope he does it. It would be good for the game."

On Sunday afternoon, September 9 at hitter-friendly Coors Field in Denver, Bonds put on one of the greatest offensive displays in history. Maris' family should have figured he would not wait for them, and he did not. In the first inning, he tied Roger when he drove a 3-1 Scott Elarton fastball 488 feet out.

Four innings later, he took Elarton *deeeeep* for his 62nd, and in the 11th inning, given an extra at-bat, he crushed his third of the game off rookie Todd Beilitz. The Colorado fans, like Atlanta fans in May and fans all over the country throughout the summer, chanted "*Barr-y! Barr-y!*" San Francisco's 9-4 win allowed them to take a one-game lead over St. Louis in the wild card, and stay one and a half back of the D'backs. They were one and a half ahead of the Dodgers in the wild, wild West.

Bonds' 3-for-5 performance also included three runs scored, five driven in, a walk, and he lifted his average to .319. The MVP award was now his. Baker remarked that he overheard some fans near the dugout express disappointment that they had missed Bonds' first homer, " . . . but they got to see the second one. Then they left early and missed the third one. They learned their lesson about leaving early."

Naturally, Bonds' "three-feat" warranted front-page headlines on September 10, and again Condit was nowhere to be found. The rest of the page, however, left readers wondering what kind of world they lived in.

"Attacks leave eight dead in Israel" left the Mideast peace talks in shambles. "Sacramento rampage—four shot dead," and "Family of four found slain in S.F. home" also heralded unpleasant doings. Little did we know, it was our last day of innocence.

9/11: Everybody knows where they were on certain dates in history. Most Americans probably did not hear about Abraham Lincoln's assassination until the slow-moving news reached them. Older folks certainly recall the news of Peal Harbor on the date that lives in infamy, December 7, 1941. Bill Lee's aunt, playing in the All-American Ladies Professional Baseball League, was busy throwing a no-hitter on June 6, 1944. Asked if she remembers anything else about that date (like D-Day), she replied that she was pretty focused on the days she pitched.

My father was on duty in the Navy, in San Diego, when Bobby Thomson hit the Shot Heard 'Round the World on October 3, 1951. The Walter Cronkite age was upon us by November 22, 1963, when John Kennedy was assassinated.

I have a routine in the mornings. Coffee, the newspaper, breakfast, work. On September 11, 2001, I was into that routine. The phone rang. I have no idea who it was, but the person said to turn on the television.

Terrorists flew two planes into New York's World Trade Center, bringing them down. Another landed in the Pentagon. A fourth plane was headed toward the Washington, D.C. area, probably aiming for the White House, or perhaps Camp David. Terrorists had control of that plane, but they had underestimated the courage of ordinary Americans. The Americans, superior human beings as opposed to the terrorists, who were scum, thusly prevented the plane from blowing up their targets by fighting back. Everybody died. The Americans ascended to Heaven. Satan is now poking red-hot pokers up the terrorists' butts.

The Giants were waking up in their hotel in Houston, having traveled from Denver on their Monday off day. None of them slept in. Phones were ringing there, too, and TVs were getting turned on.

September 11, 2001 will live on just like the other days mentioned. It will shape the politics of the first half of the 21st century. It says here that it will be found to be a date in which the people trying to hurt us will discover that the very essence of the *opposite* of what they were trying for has happened. Why factions, nations, and despots of any kind think they can take us down is a mystery. A little history lesson ought to dissuade these people—Admiral Yamamoto waking the "sleeping giant," and perhaps 1991 images of smart bombs turning the Republican Guard into fire simply because some American decided to do it, and touched a button.

In subsequent months, Americans decided that terrorists would die, and so terrorists died. The struggle, of course, will go on in complicated forms, but within short order, President George W. Bush began the process of achieving victory.

However, in those first hours, days and even weeks, there was no flush of military conquest, no occupying forces restoring order where chaos had reigned. Many Americans felt beaten.

"They got us." It felt that way at first. Victory just *looked* a long way away, and grown men cried.

Baseball did not matter. Bonds' home run pace did not matter. Numbness overwhelmed all feelings. Bonds said as much when asked. Mark McGwire said the same thing.

Baseball teams scattered all over the United States stayed where they were, then eventually braved intense security and long waits to fly back to their home cities. All sports—Major League baseball, the NFL, college football—cancelled their games.

Within days, President Bush and New York Mayor Rudolph Giuliani had lifted American spirits in Churchillian fashion. Baseball decided to resume on September 17. All the games would be made up in October, and the postseason would be pushed back a week.

Sports Illustrated's cover on September 24 showed an American flag draped over an empty seat, and stated "The Week That Sports Stood Still."

Bonds was in shock, like everybody else. Because of his status, he was sought out to air his feelings, and the poor guy frustratingly tried to say something that could have meaning.

He simply had no emotion left for baseball. There is a time when a person's sincerity is in his face, worn like clothes, unable to hide. This was Bonds. He was in deep pain for this beautiful, wounded nation.

God bless him, and God bless America.

In 1942, Jimmy Doolittle was leading his raids over Tokyo. Admirals Nimitz and Halsey were orchestrating a Naval victory at Midway. Americans were getting beaten in their first time at bat against the Germans at Kasserine Pass. An argument ensued that baseball should not be played.

President Franklin Roosevelt took it under consideration, then said that no, baseball should go on, for the sake of the country's morale.

So, Stan Musial led the Cardinals to the 1942 World Championship.

For many of the same reasons, the National Pastime returned on Monday, September 17. Players wore "FDNY" and "NYPD" hats to honor the Fire Department of New York, and the New York Police Department, because so many officers and particularly firemen had perished in the heinous attack.

Teams had American flags sewn on their caps. "God Bless America" would be sung during the seventh-inning stretch of every game the rest of the season.

When the Giants played again, on Tuesday at home against Houston, at first there was little to care about. Mike Krukow, Ted Robinson and Jon Miller, announcing the game, were subdued, not sure how to handle it. San Francisco lost when Nen gave up two runs in the ninth.

Something strange happened at some point either Tuesday or Wednesday, however. The games began to have some meaning again. It did not take away from the numbing loss of life in New York. At first, it was believed that 20,000 people had perished. Thankfully, those figures gradually came down to around 6,000, and by November, in news that pierced the black hearts of the pissant-terrorists, it was announced that less than 3,000 souls had actually been lost.

The thing about the games was that it allowed America to take the first baby steps toward regaining normalcy. The world is changed forever, but life does go on. Baseball helped lift morale, beginning on September 17, and Barry Bonds would be a big part of that.

Images of ballplayers running on the field with American flags lifted spirits. One image showed Bonds standing at attention during the National Anthem, holding a small flag.

The networks would eventually run commercials that said, "Baseball means nothing . . . and yet . . . " then demonstrated the heart-lifting power of this game.

In "Field of Dreams," James Earl Jones (playing a thinly disguised J.D. Salinger) gives a dissertation on the game, how American history is "erased like a blackboard," only to be rewritten again. Yet, as Jones says, the "one constant is baseball," which stands for something good. He tells Kevin Costner that "people will come," and in September and October, 2001, people did come to get away from the news, the tragedy, the awful depression of it all. They came for baseball, to stadiums with tight security and checkpoints, and with threats of planes or Anthrax or any number of catastrophes hanging, literally, over their heads.

In so doing, American baseball fans did substantial damage to the terrorists, whose main goal was to disrupt, to change our way of life. The fans, by showing up, thumbed their nose at the scum, as if to say, "Look at us, you have not changed us. Because we choose to live, to love, to laugh, *we win.*"

In a bit of very strange timing that falls under the "life goes on" category, California state Senator Sheila Kuehl saw her prenuptial agreement bill signed by Governor Gray Davis on September 12. The law had been sparked by Bonds' divorce. The law now bars a court from finding that a premarital agreement is valid unless the affected party was represented by an attorney or had waived that representation in writing.

The agreement had said that Sun was to be given $10,000 per month in child support for each of their two children, and she had been given $10,000 per month in spousal support, ending in 1998.

Kuehl, a liberal lesbian who represents a district called the "People's Republic of Santa Monica," where many Westside elitists are divorced, had taken up Sun's cause, and after pushing the bill through the process, Democrat Davis signed it.

Sun had recently been to court asking for more money, and in baseball circles Bonds, interestingly, was viewed sympathetically in this soap opera. The effects of the bill on Bonds' future payments to his ex-wife were still undetermined, although Bonds' attorney, Bob Nachshin, later said the bill did not have any affect on his client. No doubt on September 12 Bonds was too distracted by world events to really think about Kuehl's bill.

The Giants were not winning when play resumed. Bonds homered on Thursday, but it was not enough to prevent a three-game sweep at the hands of Larry Dierker's Astros. At the time, because of the nature of things, the sweep did not permeate the baseball consciousness like it normally would have. However, in a postseason analysis of the year, it would prove to be the fatal blow.

It was also reported that Barry was donating a large sum of money for every homer he hit to the 9/11 relief fund, said to be as much as $10,000 for every one he hit.

There was still a lot of baseball, and a lot of history, to be made in the mean time. For the Giants, and for many baseball fans, Sunday afternoon, September 23 was a turning point, when the game regained some of the importance that it had lost. In Oakland, Mark Mulder won his 20th game of the year, and the A's clinched a wild-card berth. Art Howe's team had sobered up after the Giambi Spring Party Tour of the Scottsdale bars. After their 8-18 start, this young, talented, exciting squad turned it on and sprinted back into the race. At this point, despite Seattle's run on the 1906 Cubs' all-time victory mark, Oakland looked to be as good a bet to win the World Series as anybody. It was turning out to be one of the best baseball seasons in Bay Area history.

Down in San Diego, the Camp Pendleton Marines were given the day off and arrived wearing fatigues at Jack Murphy Stadium. They got a standing ovation from 35,247 on a sun-splashed Southern California afternoon, plus some history.

This was the day Bonds turned it on and put himself in a place where the record would fall. Before the game, he conferred with the guru Tony Gwynn. Afterward, Bonds would tell reporters that Gwynn gave him helpful hitting hints that he used to beat the Pads.

Gwynn smiled and said that was not so, they had just chatted each other up as fellow superstars are wont to do. On the field, Bonds hammered a 2-1 changeup from Jason Middlebrook over the center field fence. His next time up, he followed Aurilia's 35th homer with an opposite-field shot off Middlebrook.

San Diego was out of the race, and Bruce Bochy had elected to challenge Bonds, although the nature of the game was what really dictated strategy. Bonds went 3-for-4 with three runs scored, two RBIs, and a walk, to raise his average to .320. He now had 66 home runs, tying Sosa for the second-highest figure ever, to go with 127 runs batted in and 155 walks against only 91 strikeouts. He was now on a pace to hit 71, and was four games ahead of McGwire through 150 games, needing five to break the record in the remaining 12 games.

The Giants' 11-2 victory put them at 82-68, and kept them within two games of Arizona (84-66), and three behind St. Louis (85-65) for the wild card. Unfortunately, the Diamondbacks had beaten Los Angeles (80-70). An interesting phenomenon had developed that would continue the rest of the way. When San Francisco won, Arizona, willed on by their two aces, Schilling and Johnson, would win, too. The Dodgers' defeat had dropped them four back of the Diamondbacks, and five behind the Cardinals. The Dodgers took some more bad news on this day, when they learned that star pitcher Kevin Brown was out for the season with a torn flexor muscle in his elbow.

For all practical purposes, the West was a two-team race from this point on.

The next night at Dodger Stadium, the glitterati came out to see Bonds, Barry Bonds. Baseball's superman was licensed to kill the Dodgers, slamming his 67th off James Baldwin before 38,849 (including Farrah Fawcett). That provided the razor-thin margin in San Francisco's 2-1 victory. He had entered the game hitting .122 with two homers (none in LA) and four RBIs in 49 at-bats against the Dodger staff.

Still, Bonds likes playing in L.A. The fans have usually booed him, but now they were cheering him. The events of 9/11 had changed many people's perceptions of things. The "hated" Bonds was now a patriotic American and he was pursuing a record we could all share in. United We Stand also meant love for our fellow baseball players. A guy who was occasionally standoffish to the press and did not always have time to sign every autograph was a much better person than Osama bin Laden.

Even Boston fans, who usually sport signs that read "New York sucks," or worse, were displaying "We love NY" placards.

Barry's Riverside folks visit with him when plays in Los Angeles. His wife, Liz, likes to shop on Beverly Hills' Rodeo Drive. Barry is not the kind of guy who hits the Sunset Strip until three in the morning, though.

"I've never done that," he said, but he enjoys seeing Sheffield, his grandmother and family members. It is old home week for him.

Arizona was idle, so now the orange-and-black were within a game and a half.

"I played with Willie Mays, and I played with Roberto Clemente," Dodgers batting coach Manny Mota told John Shea, "and I see in Barry the same ability I saw in Willie and Roberto. I see a guy who trusts himself at the plate and in the field. If I managed against Barry, I wouldn't let him beat me. I wouldn't give him the opportunity."

The next two nights, in which the teams split games two and three, the Dodgers did not let him beat them.

"I'm pulling for Barry," former Dodger manager Tommy Lasorda told Shea, "just not here." In San Francisco's 6-4 rubber game win on Wednesday night, they walked him three times.

The weekend brought San Diego and more history. Baseball may not have pushed the war on terrorism out of people's minds, but Bonds and the game had an elixir effect that allowed people to embrace the joy of the National Pastime.

It was a Hall of Fame extravaganza for Pac Bell fans, but not just because of Bonds and his 67 dongs. Gwynn was making his final appearance in the City by the Bay, and Rickey Henderson was closing in on Ty Cobb's career record for runs, as well as his 3,000th hit. He would eventually get both marks by season's end.

Henderson, truly one of baseball's all-time greats, had never received very good press, perhaps because he makes Bonds look like a brain surgeon, and Gwynn a nuclear physicist. Now, the Barry Watch overshadowed his great achievements.

In Tempe, Arizona, Todd McFarlane, who had not sold his McGwire ball while it was hot, was sweating it out. While Bonds' upcoming 70th, or whatever would be his last of the season, was not said to be worth more than $1.5 to $2.5 million, according to Doug Sprague, a Bay Area collector, the value of McFarlane's ball would plummet if Bonds got there.

By this point, Bonds had taken to raising his arms and saluting God in Heaven whenever he hit one out. He did on Friday night, September 29 off of poor Jason Middlebrook, who by now must have been contemplating whether he should have used his Stanford education to pursue another line of work.

The Giants rolled, 10-5, but Bonds' salute to the sky meant more than usual. In a pregame press conference, tears welled in his eyes when he revealed that Franklin Bradley, his longtime friend and bodyguard, had died of complications from routine surgery the previous day. The 37-year old Bradley had worked with Bonds for a decade.

"Dude, it's hard," Bonds responded to a question, then revealed what had happened. "Right now, I'm just trying to relax. One of my friends, I lost yesterday. Right now, I have a lot emotions about everything that's gone on for me off the field, and there have been distractions for all of us.

"Every time I have the opportunity to exhale or breathe, something has come up that has been difficult for me. I had a very disappointing article come out [in *Sports Illustrated*], what happened with the tragedy and I lose one of my best friends yesterday. I really haven't had any time to do anything, and anytime I want to enjoy it for a minute something else happens."

Baseball is a mythic game. Babe Ruth, according to legend, once hit a home run for a sick boy he had visited in the hospital. He had promised the kid he would do it, if he would cheer up and get better. The deal was struck, Ruth had delivered, and supposedly the boy made it. Apocryphal? Maybe, but the game has always fed itself on legends, creating a series of real-life heroics worthy of "The Natural."

Now, Barry's friend had died. This was real life. He had hit a homer for Franklin, which of course would not bring his pal back. But it did allow the press to memorialize Franklin, and further mythologize Barry Bonds.

By now, circling the bases with tears flowing down his cheeks, this man was Larger Than Life.

On Saturday afternoon, number 69 fell. It was his 563rd career home run, tying him with cousin Reggie for seventh place all-time. He had seven games to go. This one broke a 1-1 tie before 41,383 fans on a perfect day. San Francisco weather is as odd as The City itself. Mark Twain once said, "The coldest winter I ever spent was a summer in San Francisco," but summer was now past. Fall is the best time of year in the Bay Area. From Labor Day until shortly before Thanksgiving, this is the time when bikini-clad girls lie in the sun, roller bladders traverse the Marina Green overlooking the Golden Gate Bridge, and joggers inundate the roads of the Presidio.

It was also, in 2001, the Season of Barry Bonds. It was a thrilling spectacle, the greatest athlete on the face of the Earth pursuing the biggest sports story of the young century. This time, the victim was left-hander Chuck McElroy, and Bonds' clout gave his team a 3-1 win. Unfortunately, the victory simply meant treading more water, for Arizona also won.

"I did something for a friend," Bonds said of Franklin Bradley, "and I was able to let it go after that."

There was no crying in the dugout like the previous evening. He was all smiles, soaking in the fans' adulation.

On Sunday, the Padres went "wild." Pitcher Jose Nunez plunked Bonds in the elbow, eliciting a moment of fear before it was determined that Superman had not encountered any Kryptonite. They also walked him twice, and San Diego got out of town with a measure of dignity left, 5-4. Los Angeles staved off elimination with a 2-1 victory in Phoenix, so the Giants' held ground, but the pressure was mounting.

Sports Illustrated was there, and this time there was no controversy, just history of the highest order. Bonds graced the October 8 cover, following through on a home run swing. It read, "Smashing! Home runs are only part of Barry Bonds' record-busting season." Bonds had reached 69 on 2,479 pitches, 854 swings, hitting a home run on 34.5 percent of his cuts, one every 12.4 times he took a swing at the ball. McGwire had required 2,692 pitches, 1,064 swings, a 39.5 percentage that averaged a homer every 15.2 long balls during his 70-homer 1998.

Now it was on to Houston, to play the games that had been cancelled after 9/11. Bonds' entourage was almost Presidential in size, and included his father, who said that his son was not feeling any pressure. Bobby said that, left to his own devices, Barry did not even talk about the record, preferring to converse about the things he always speaks about—his wife and his kids.

"If he talks about anything," Bobby told the writers, "it's 'Can we catch the Diamondbacks?'" Bonds' friends are not usually baseball people, and they normally do not even talk about baseball. His family tends to stay off the subject, and Mays had ceased to converse with him, fearing a jinx.

"I see Barry work out in the winter until there are tears coming out of his eyes," revealed Bobby. "I don't think he's any different than he was at Serra High."

Bobby noted that Franklin's death "devastated" his son, who had taken care of all the funeral arrangements. Franklin had died during a routine surgery for cosmetic enhancement of his abdomen, a procedure paid for by Barry.

Bobby also revealed that the trademark ear ring wore by his son, thought by many to be a fashion statement, is in fact worn in remembrance of Bobby's father.

Bobby Bonds expressed a love and pride for his son, and he told the media that this was based not on his Barry's assault on a baseball record, but because of his growth and success as a man.

"All the things in society, all the drugs," he said, "Barry fought against that and handled himself pretty well. He's successful as a man. That's pretty important."

Barry *had* disdained the drugs and temptations so available to him. ("I never did that," he had said of all-nighters on the Sunset Strip.) His father, too, had grown. Once bitter, oft-traded, oft-criticized, considered to have been less than his potential, now Bobby Bonds was an elder statesman of baseball, and a joyous insight into his son's personality.

There were mixed feelings at Enron Field during this series. Everybody wanted Bonds to break the record, but they also wanted to see him do it at home. On October 3, the 50th anniversary of Bobby Thomson's Shot Heard 'Round the World, Dierker directed the 'Stros to pitch around the slugger. Houston was battling St. Louis for the Central crown. They were playing to win, and there would be none of the "challenging" that San Diego had directed at him.

Bonds was 1-for-2 with two walks and a hit-by-pitch, but Aurilia got his 200th hit of the season to lead the Giants to a 4-1 win.

"They didn't challenge me at all," Bonds said afterward. His daughter, Shikari, sitting in the stands, was now carrying a sign that read, "Pitch to our Daddy #25."

Dierker paid no heed. On Wednesday night, his charges walked Bonds three more times, breaking Ruth's 78-year-old record in that category. Jeff Kent made them pay big time by going 3-for-5 with three runs batted in to power an 11-8 victory before a frustrated crowd of 43,630.

The Astros were showing no respect for Bonds' teammates.

"This is not right," he said of the situation.

Bonds was also back in the non-sports news when an op/ed piece by Madison Schockley, titled "The importance of playing ball," addressed the value of his home run chase in relieving the psychological damage of the terrorist attacks on the minds of Americans. Schockley said that each home run Bonds hit helped us get "back to normal," and the article resonated with much truth.

On October 4, Houston again offered very little to Bonds, and it was the same story as the previous two nights: They paid dearly.

Bonds was walked three more times, including an intentional pass with the score 8-1, San Francisco, before 43,734 booing fans. Kent was up to the challenge, making Dierker and pitcher Dave Mlicki pay with a home run and three RBIs.

San Francisco ran away with it, and in the ninth inning, at 9:21 p.m. Central time, with the Giants leading 8-2, Houston ran out of excuses. Twenty-two-year old Wilfredo Rodriguez, a hard-throwing Venezuelan, worked Bonds to a 1-1 count, and then delivered a 93-mile-an-hour fastball right down the middle.

Bonds powered it 454 feet into the second deck in right-center, where 38-year-old Houston real estate agent Charles Murphy was in the right location to catch it. Barry's teammates mobbed him at home plate, along with Nikolai, and the Houston fans, who stuck around in hopes of seeing just this, gave him a standing ovation.

Baker had told the press that he had seen it coming, and predicted more of the same against the Dodgers over the final weekend. There was not a lot of time after the game for the press to dissect what had happened, since the team faced an all-night flight to San Francisco. The Dodgers and Chan Ho Park (15-11) waited for them the next evening. Bonds, who had shown great joy rounding the bases, seemed to have had a large weight lifted off his back. He did meet with the media for a little while.

"I just felt grateful to share something with someone I have a lot of respect for," he said of McGwire. "I felt proud to be in the same level with Mark. I just felt proud. I don't know how else to explain it. I . . . just felt proud."

"I don't wonder about the great things Barry can do," said Kent. "I just sit back and watch." The Giants' second baseman, if he ever was a rival of Bonds, or felt antipathy towards him, was now in full-blown "fan mode." He also verbalized why his latest achievements were different for his teammates.

"We weren't part of 500," he said. "We were all part of 70. Some of us still don't understand 500. Heck, they brought his family out on the field for 500, and they didn't do that this time. Just the teammates."

The 10-2 victory kept San Francisco two games behind Arizona who—surprise!—also won, beating the Rockies, 5-4. The three-game sweep was a terrible blow for Houston, who now entered a season-ending series against St. Louis, who had defeated Milwaukee, 10-3, to take a one-game lead in the Central.

San Francisco would go into the last weekend of their Quixotic season, hoping to chase not windmills but a beachhead, a niche, an invite to the dance. They could not do it themselves. Their eyes on the prize would not just be focused on beating LA, but on events in Milwaukee, where the D'backs were, and St. Louis.

San Francisco was at 89-70, and Arizona was 91-68. In the wild-card hunt, they trailed the Astros, also 91-68, by two games. They would have to win. Either Milwaukee would have to step up and upset the Arizona apple cart, or St. Louis would have to knock off the slumping Houstons.

Would the Dodgers pitch to him? We would find out.

CHAPTER
EIGHT

73

The Dodgers did pitch to Bonds, and history had been made (see chapter one). Now, there was the rest of the weekend to play. This was a chance for Bonds to add to his record. Beyond that, there would be endless speculation about Bonds' contract, and his ranking among the game's immortals.

On Saturday afternoon, the exhausted Dodgers defeated the exhausted Giants, 6-2. Bonds, like everyone else, had not gotten to bed until the wee hours. Normally the home team arrives at the park around 10 a.m. for a 1:00 o'clock game, but Baker gave everybody a break from batting practice and the usual pregame work. Throughout the season, he had often rested Bonds in day games after night games, a practice that had been utilized with Mays when he got well into his 30s.

Some had criticized Baker for doing this. For one thing, Saturday afternoons are assured sell-outs and many fans can only attend games on weekends. If Bonds does not play on Saturdays, they miss their chance to see greatness. Baseball is a fun game, and being a big league ball player is a wonderful way to make a living. However, it is not easy. The schedule, the travel, the demands—the life of a Major Leaguer is one that requires tremendous discipline and work ethic. The mental strain is greater than the physical aspect.

Baker, a former star with the Braves and Dodgers, understands this well. Throughout the season, he patiently explained to the press that Bonds would be better off to rest and revitalize, and like clockwork Bonds would always come back better and stronger.

Over 41,000 fans packed Pac Bell on Saturday. Many had bought tickets in advance hoping this would be the day, and they were further disappointed when Bonds sat out, although it was understandable. In the ninth inning, Bonds pinch-hit and, after a standing ovation, singled.

The "Will he stay?" question hung as heavily over the stadium as the "Will he do it?" question that had dominated the previous months. Fans and writers were looking for a parsing of Bonds words like Ken Starr when he went after Bill Clinton.

"I'm proud to wear this uniform," Bonds had said at his ceremony. Would he be just as proud to wear pinstripes in '02?

"He talks a lot," said Mays, a man who is probably the greatest influence on Bonds' life, "but he backs it up. He belongs here in San Francisco."

Bonds' teammates, hardened professionals who had just gone through a grueling, pressure-packed campaign, are still fans at heart and recent events had left them talking like little kids.

"What's there to say?" said Aurilia, a decent-but-not-great player from New York City who had been elevated to All-Star status by virtue of the pitches he saw hitting ahead of the man. "To witness this first-hand as a fan of the game and a teammate of Barry's is unbelievable."

Long-time Bay Area sports columnist Art Spander had grown up in the Los Angeles area and understood the Giant-Dodger rivalry as well as anyone. He wrote that Bonds' two Friday shots were even bigger than Thompson's drive off Ralph Branca in 1951. He also noted that Kent, reputed to be a redneck with a surly streak who "supposedly wants nothing to do with Barry, could be seen pounding on the mass of humanity, enjoying the home run as much as anybody, and as much as Bonds, belying all the contentions the Giants are individuals and not a team."

Kent can go from unapproachable to a teddy bear when he is with his kids, or kids in general, and after Friday's game held Bonds' little daughter, Aisha, battling to stay awake past her bed time, bless her. The look on his face told it all: There was love in his heart.

There was wistfulness to Bonds, a combination of everything that had come down.

Spander pointed out that rather than being seen as selfish, his teammates were viewing Barry as having grown as a man. Bonds had kept insisting that his primary goal is to win a World Series, and his attitude after breaking the record reinforced that view.

"I told them," Bonds told a press conference, "if it's meant to be, it's meant to be. Let's just win." The Giants had given it all they had, winning five of six prior to the Dodger series, including the awesome three-game road sweep of a very tough Astro team.

Spander also reflected the view that Bonds' home run chase had been a welcome relief after the events of September 11.

Baker was queried about Bonds' future.

"I don't negotiate contracts," he said. "The same guy who signs my checks, signs his. Whether you like it or not, sometimes in life things change. Some things can remain the same. It's going to be a pretty touchy situation. What to do? How much it's going to cost? How many years? Can you not replace him? Can you replace him? There's a lot of things there. Now is not the time to address that."

"It's amazing what he's doing given the limited number of pitches he's given to hit," Gary Hughes, director of scouting at Cincinnati, told Dave Albee of the *Marin Independent Journal.*

Baker also told the writers that early in the season he had spoken to Tony La Russa about how to handle the media crush he foresaw. Baker understood the media well, having been a teammate of Aaron when he went after Ruth's career home run mark in 1973-74. In recent weeks, the Giants had arranged for Bonds to handle a press conference on the first day of each series, reducing the crowd in the clubhouse. Baker had also been known to entertain 35-minute dugout media sessions that helped lessen the pressure on his star and his teammates.

"You don't even understand what you did," Bobby Bonilla told Bonds.

"You know what, Bobby?" replied Bonds. "I'll understand it later. Right now, I just want to not lose three games to the Dodgers. We can talk about it in the off-season."

"You're not ready to go home yet," said Baker. "You're not ready to pack up your office. It's the same every year. The season's not over until the World Series. That probably will be the hardest part—explaining to my son why there's no more baseball here, they're still on TV. Why am I watching baseball at home with him?"

"I'm on a hot seat—we all are—and you can't avoid that," Magowan said. "I fully support the fans' interest in trying to get that guy back."

Magowan had saved the San Francisco franchise in the early 1990s when they were virtually relocated to St. Petersburg, Florida. In a series of almost miraculous moves, he coalesced the group that kept the team in San Francisco, brought Dusty Baker on board, and signed Bonds. These moves generated excitement and success on the field, but now he was facing the age-old sports question, What have you done for me lately?

"Barry really does want to be here," said Magowan. "Everything being equal, we'd love to have him back. So we start off with that. I think that gives us an advantage."

Despite the Boras factor, which is about greed and getting the highest bid from the highest bidder, other things would influence Bonds' decision. First, he wants to win, and that means going to the team with the best chance to win. The Yankees, who lost the seventh game of the 2001 World Series, obviously were the team with the money, the talent, and the capability of getting back to the Series.

Arizona, the team that beat New York, had not entered into the free agent equation. Atlanta was mentioned as a team with the money, good available talent, and the likelihood of being a consistent contender. St. Louis, too, was frequently brought up as a club with the money, a great fan base, a player-friendly environment, and the tools to stay on as a contender. La Russa, however, was not considered a "Bonds guy."

The Giants were giving lip service to the notion that they were a "small market" team lacking the financial resources to handle Bonds' salary demands. However, after two years of sell-outs playing in one of America's glamour cities, that concept lacked the full ring of truth. The big question that Bonds would have regarding his team was whether they would improve enough to get over the hump in the next couple years.

The other factors involved location and family. Bonds is from the Bay Area, and his friends and family live here. He lives in a gorgeous mansion in Hillsborough, the preferred residence of San Francisco sports superstars like Jerry Rice, as well as Silicon Valley tycoons.

One team not mentioned was the Oakland A's, winners of 102 regular-season games and, very possibly the favorite to go to the Series in 2002. Oakland was looking at losing MVP first baseman Jason Giambi, but if Bonds would be willing to sign for less than market value, he could play on a surefire winner in the area he grew up in, and go home to his house and family every night, too.

In 1997, McGwire had been traded by Oakland to St. Louis. The A's felt they would not be able to sign him. They wanted something in return. That off-season, McGwire signed on to stay with the Cardinals. Money was not the biggest factor in his decision, either, although there was some question as to what it really was. A product of Claremont in Los Angeles County, McGwire had been an All-American and *The Sporting News'* College Player of the Year at Southern Cal. At USC, he met his wife, Kathy, an Orange County lass who was a batgirl for the Trojan baseball team. His son, Matthew, was born on the last day of the 1987 season, causing the rookie to miss a chance at hitting home run number 50 because he left to be with his wife.

The storybook romance did not take, however, and a few years later the two were divorced. McGwire entered a relationship with another girl he had known at USC, but they broke up, too. That failed relationship was reported to be the reason for depressions that led to a significant dip in his career, which hit its low in 1991 when he batted a mere .201. McGwire would regroup, inspired by his own efforts when he returned to weight training with renewed vigor throughout the 1990s.

Matthew stayed with his mother, who would remarry, in Orange County. McGwire would reside in nearby Huntington Harbor in the off-season. While it is only an hour and a half flight from L.A. to Oakland, anybody who knows about the demands of Major League baseball realizes that separation from a child 400 miles away means just that, separation.

After the 1997 season, McGwire had a chance to sign with the home-town Anaheim Angels, who had just been purchased by Disney. The Angels were penurious and did not meet McGwire's value in the marketplace. At that point, he had firmly established himself as baseball's top slugger, and Maris' record was constantly mentioned in connection to him.

Still, had McGwire been willing, he could have been an Angel. At some point, a man has enough millions, and the difference between, say $19 million and $42 million is, oddly, less than the difference between $100,000 and $500,000.

McGwire opted to sign with St. Louis, spurred by the enthusiasm of Cardinal fans, probably the best all-around baseball people in the world. He would be with La Russa, a manager he had always been associated with, and while St. Louis was a contender, they were by no means a big favorite to win the 1998 World Series. He could have signed with Anaheim, continued to be a millionaire, and for the first time worked in a place near where he lived and could see his son any time he pleased.

Summer time is well and good, but it passes quickly, and it is not as easy as it sounds for a kid to visit his dad all summer, since road trips constantly break up the calendar.

Matt Williams went crazy after divorcing his wife and being separated from his children, even though he made it to the World Series with Cleveland in 1997. He made his agent figure out a way to get him a deal with the Diamondbacks so he could be near his children's Phoenix home.

Big Mac, a man of some enigmatic qualities, had chosen to sign based on neither money nor geographical proximity to his only son. Fan support seemed to have been what drove his decision. What would motivate Bonds' decision on who to sign with?

Boras had negotiated Alex Rodriguez's 10-year, $252 million contract with Texas the previous year.

"We were all just blown away by that," Magowan said. Rodriguez relative youth was a deciding factor in his getting so much money, and despite his heroics, nobody was actively predicting that Bonds could command that kind of money.

Still, with Boras, who operates out of Irvine, California, one never knows. He was well known for hard-balling teams, and also for gobbling up top amateurs prior to the annual draft. One of his clients, outfielder J.D. Drew of St. Louis, had been selected second in the 1997 draft by Philadelphia following an All-American career at Florida State. However, following

Boras' advice, Drew continued to hold out against the Phillies' offers, all the while echoing his agent's "greedy" tactics with inflammatory comments of his own. That helped inflame passions not only against him but also against Boras.

After playing for an independent pro team, Drew reentered the draft and was selected by St. Louis, who had pre-negotiated with Boras, in 1998. To his credit, he had learned to keep his mouth shut after engendering bad feelings from other players.

On the other hand, Bonds had said earlier in the season that, "Boras works for me, I don't work for him," giving rise to speculation that pure dollar signs were not his driving motivation. Of course, Bonds had said all of this prior to completing the greatest season in history, and breaking the game's most hallowed record. What many fans fail to understand about contracts is that while players may never live long enough to spend all the money they make, they do view their salaries as a source of pride in the pecking order of greatness. They are a way of comparing themselves to their peers in a highly competitive environment.

In the Rodriguez negotiations, Boras had squeezed the highest offer from his last employer, Seattle, then used that as the starting point for all bidders. The word around the campfire was that he was looking for a contract in the $20 million per year range.

"I don't want to get into what his strategy is going to be or what our strategy is going to be and we're going to do our damnedest not to talk about it frankly in the press," Magowan said. "I do feel that hurt everybody concerned last year on the Alex Rodriguez thing."

In Dave Albee's October 7 column, he added the Orioles and Red Sox to the mix of contenders in the Bonds Sweepstakes, and predicted a Yankee-Met bidding war in the Big Apple.

Magowan also had to be considering the value of the publicity splash that resigning Bonds would do for his organization. After all, it was that very kind of "splash" that had kept the team above water in 1993.

Albee also predicted that the offers for Bonds would not be as high as some were predicting, and that a "wait and see" approach by San Francisco was their best strategy, foreseeing Bonds' "gravitating" back to his first choice after testing the waters.

The "money isn't an issue" factor, however, would take a hit in Bonds' first postseason national interview with Roy Firestone on ESPN. He addressed the question of whether the Giants were credible in calling themselves a small market club that could not afford to match the large contract offers to ensue.

Bonds rejected that notion, saying that San Francisco *is* a large market, and Boras had often pointed to the financial success of so-called small market teams who had built new stadiums and reaped great benefits. The baseball fan in him also was apparent when he showed enthusiasm over the prospect of playing for the legendary Yankees.

Albee's Sunday column concluded with a Mick Jagger quote that rings of Pure Truth. "You don't always get what you want." The question would be, would they get what they needed?

Chad Kreuter again found himself in the spotlight after Friday's game.

"I told him [Bonds] a fastball was coming," he joked with the media. Of course, since Boras represents Park as well, maybe a deal was struck to give him a fastball. Just kidding.

"Once he hit it, it was no big deal," said Kreuter, who had either seen a little too much history up close or just lacked a feel for great drama. "It was 5-1 at that point and we're going to pitch to him."

Kreuter had signaled for a hard one on the inside, but "I went to catch it and my glove came back over the plate."

Good-bye, Mr. Spaulding.

Two innings later, revealed Kreuter, he had signaled for a backdoor slider that Park, obviously not on top of his game, left hanging.

"His eyes got as big as saucers on that one," Kreuter said. "It's phenomenal that someone can be locked in like that. It was fun. You can't say it in any other way. It was very electric. The noise was deafening. I soaked it all in and had fun with it."

Another Marin County product would be a footnote of this historical weekend, the opposite of Bonds, if you will.

"Yeah, who was the guy who replaced Barry Bonds on the day after he broke Big Mac's single-season home run record?" asked the man who is the answer to this trivia question, Jalal Leach.

In doing so, Leach made his first Major League start on Saturday. Leach was, however, no ordinary rookie. At 32, he had broken into the league as a September call-up after having played in the minor leagues since 1990. A 1987 graduate of San Marin High School in Novato, he had followed Kreuter to Pepperdine, then gone on to be the Crash Davis of baseball. Davis was the Kevin Costner character from "Bull Durham."

The post-homer letdown was appropriately captured by the public address system playing "Boulevard of Broken Dreams" when Bonds emerged from the dugout prior to Saturday's game, only to be met by golf legend Arnold Palmer, who stopped by to congratulate him.

Sadness would be mixed in with awe, too.

"This is a man," said Santiago, "who did something that nobody can do."

" . . . Bonds didn't just have a brush with greatness," wrote Jenkins. "He knocked down the door, plopped down on the sofa and put his feet up." Jenkins also seemed to capture the Bonds duality when he wrote, "Through it all, Bonds' personality was split in half. Friends and family always knew of his soft, pleasant side, the man who's good to his kids, stays out of trouble and gives willingly to the community. Nobody ever saw that at the ball park, where Bonds lived in a self-contained world, trusting no one, separating himself in ways that seemed both selfish and immature."

Bonds, however, had changed in the weeks leading up to the record. He had embraced the effort. Perhaps his decision was calculated. It was definitely wise. He would often be seen in the company of his very, very cute children, smiling and disarming his critics, who really were searching for reasons to like him.

He would cry, his tears shed for Franklin, but also moved by the weight of circumstance and spiritual connection with a game that transcends the American consciousness.

Sunday, October 7, marked the final day of the season, and history again hung in the air like a towering Bonds home run. The play-offs were all set, but Bonds would play and the fans came out to see him add to his legend.

Knuckleballer Dennis Springer replaced Terry Mulholland, who had had about as much success against Bonds as a batting practice pitcher. It did not matter. In the first inning, in front of 41,257, Bonds sent number 73 into the arcade. This would be his last, and the "73" would be the number that resonated through history.

In 1998, much fanfare had surrounded Big Mac's 62nd against Chicago at Busch Stadium. Sosa, his foil all year, was there to give him a hug. His son, Matthew, who bore a resemblance to the lovable batboy in Robert Redford's "The Natural," was there to extend a big hug for his old man. A Cardinal employee had caught the homer and dutifully given it to McGwire.

However, when the dust cleared in '98, it was not "62" that people remembered, it was "70". Felipe Alou had ordered his Expo pitchers to challenge McGwire in that last weekend, and with nothing riding on the games for either team, Big Mac had gone yard five times.

In the off-season, quirky comic book producer McFarlane had purchased the ball for $3 million, plus several of the balls McGwire had hit out leading up to his 70th.

McFarlane, a native of Canada, is a baseball fanatic who had played at Eastern Washington State University. At Eastern Washington State, he had met a black second baseman named Al Simmons, and they become fast friends. In the summer of 1980, he and Simmons had played for a fast collegiate summer team in Kamloops, B.C., the host of a then-prestigious amateur tournament. Upon graduation, Simmons would go on to a short minor league career in the Mariners organization. McFarlane, a bench scrub, never realized pro aspirations, but he did have artistic talent, and went to work for Marvel Comics.

In the late 1980s, McFarlane made a fateful, gutsy and entrepreneurial decision that is, at its core, the essence of the American Dream. Instead of staying at Marvel, where he had created a number of popular characters and had a secure position, McFarlane started his own company on the strength of an idea that he called "Spawn."

Spawn was Simmons, who had accepted McFarlane's offer to become his right-hand man at McFarlane Productions, located in Tempe, Arizona. The storyline McFarlane developed was that "Al Simmons" was a black CIA officer whose wife had been murdered by the forces of evil. Somehow Simmons gets involved with the supernatural and ends up in hell, but instead of roasting in the flames of eternity, he is chosen by an evil general to lead his forces of darkness in an earthly war intended to give the balance of military power to the bad guys.

Simmons is converted into Spawn, complete with burned skin and muscle development that is a cross between the Incredible Hulk and a big snake. You can take it from there.

The character was a hit, and McFarlane became a multimillionaire, with the real Simmons tagging along for the ride. Eventually, Hollywood came calling and the movie "Spawn" was produced starring Martin Sheen, who leads it off by looking into the camera and saying, "Al Simmons is the best."

Naturally, this line is, to Al Simmons, the equivalent of Humphrey Bogart telling Ingrid Bergman, "Here's lookin' at you, kid." The film is no "Casablanca", although John Leguizamo's turn as a perverted clown is a *tour de force*. Video renters are fed a post-film interview with the vainglorious McFarlane, who addresses the social importance of his creation in a serious manner worthy of Orson Welles dissecting "Citizen Kane."

In the interest of research, "Spawn" is worth viewing, but watching the sequel? Let us not go there, okay?

McFarlane paid far more than the market would normally have brought to get McGwire's ball. Big Mac himself had demonstrated disdain for the guy, who had then taken it on a tour of all big league stadiums in 1999, using as his front man the outrageous, gravel-voiced sportstalk shock jock, Scott Ferrall.

Ferrall was known for "pouring beers" for his listeners, and often prefaced his commentary with something like, "I'm in the foulest of moods possible." You have to hear it to get it.

As Bonds got closer and closer to the record in 2001, McFarlane had gotten as nervous as the shell-shocked soldier that George Scott slaps in "Patton." He continued to make pithy comments about Bonds, trying but not succeeding to make light of the fact that his investment was becoming almost worthless.

McFarlane was contacted after the end of the season and asked about his feelings on the subject of Bonds, and the ball he still held on to.

"Maybe I'm more fair minded, but I don't really know the man, so I have no reason not to like him," said McFarlane. "Sometimes people have it in their minds that somebody should feel a certain way, when that's not a correct perception. I've not been witness to any of the supposedly bad things Barry's done, so I can't say anything about that.

"I was around him at card signings. At one he was sitting off to the side and he was signing and I was signing, but we were rushed. We just waved to each other. I was near him at a home run hitting contest that he lost.

"The media's always looking for easy sound bites. To be honest, in a perfect world he does not break record, duh, of course. I didn't want him to break the record, but I don't control any of it. The media was more concerned than I was, if he does it I don't control it, but given I have the 'record' ball, I would have preferred he not have done it.

"You have to take into account, at that time [when I was asked about the record-breaking possibilities], this was after the delay from the time off after the attack, and it was less of an issue to me. I still can't get worked up about my ball given the other things in life.

"It's like, whatever. I was applauding him at the end. People were looking for feel-good stories.

"Absolutely, I don't spend that kind of money if you think the record will be broken, but Bonds' ball won't get what I paid for McGwire's. Three years from now somebody could break this record, although it's hard to fathom 74.

"The other thing, to be clear, people seem to blur the idea of an investment. It was never bought in the true sense of an investment. Ownership of the ball has value in and of itself, even if you can't put it on a spreadsheet.

"What's it worth? Obviously less, but it's still a moment frozen in time that's still there. I'm not saying I would never sell it, if my companies went bankrupt then I never say never, but it was never my willing intent to sell the ball, that's irrelevant to me. Ten million or $10, I have no plans to get rid of it, so I don't worry about the value of something I never intend to sell.

"I bet I can get my money back in other ways, by making a profit from being the minority owner of a sports franchise, etc. People take me more seriously, that leads to future deals, and what portion I attribute back to buying the ball is bigger than zero."

McFarlane had parlayed his notoriety into deals with Hollywood, and as an NHL owner, so he had a point. He was asked if he had ever spoken to McGwire.

"McGwire was underwhelmed by my buying that ball," he said, "but nobody understood what I was gonna do with it, which was to display it at stadiums all season [in 1999]. I did see him at an event once, but didn't have the nerve to talk to him. Just because I spent a lot of money on that ball doesn't mean I have more access to McGwire. I don't push myself on the athletes. I'm on the other side of being a celebrity, depending on who you talk to."

The fans sitting beyond the outfield fence no doubt knew how much McFarlane had paid for number 70, and the result was an ugly scramble for this one. Three million was high, but collectors were saying that the ball would net a $1 million asking price.

It was the first inning, and nobody could guarantee it would be the last of the season, but if it was it would be a moneymaker. The ball landed in the glove of 37-year-old Alex Popov, who had borrowed his girlfriend's mitt for the day. The fact that a man borrows his girlfriend's mitt is commentary on American society in the 21st century, but for another day.

"I tucked the glove in my stomach, and I hit the ground in a protective mode," the San Francisco resident told the media. KNTV's television crew captured it, as did photographer Josh Keppel.

However, the ball "snow coned" on the top of his glove, like Joe Rudi's famous catch of a to-the-fence drive in the 1972 World Series. A dog pile ensued, and Popov lost the ball. It was picked up by another fan named Patrick Hayashi.

"It was ugly," said eyewitness Kathy Sorensen, who did not know Popov. "Then I saw this guy bend down and just pick up the ball."

"Is this the ball?" Hayashi asked MLB officials, who had focused on the melee and not seen him casually pick it up.

Hayashi was ushered away to a secure room, where the ball was identified, then returned to the man. Popov and his witness, like bystanders after a car crash, then protested to Giants officials. Despite Popov's pleas, it was determined that the melee was not much different than what happens on most home runs hit into crowds, and stating that "Possession is nine-tenths of the law," senior vice president of ballpark operations Jorge Costa deemed that Hayashi was its rightful owner.

Hayashi declined to do a postgame press conference or identify his hometown, but Popov told reporters that he expected him to "do the right thing." The following day, apparently Hayashi had not done the "right thing" yet, so Popov went on a Bay Area media blitz of radio and TV stations. He began the American-as-apple-pie process of taking legal action to recover damages. God bless this country.

"Today's home run, I felt more in shock," Bonds told reporters. "Your chances of hitting a home run on someone who throws that slow are so slim, and when I did it, I was just, 'What else can you give me, God? What else can you give me?'"

San Francisco won the season finale, 2-1, and Bonds also finished with a .515 on-base percentage, the highest in modern history. Of all the singles hitters of the 20th century, guys ranging from Honus Wagner to Ty Cobb to Pete Rose to Tony Gwynn, none of these people had reached base more consistently than Bonds. He had done it swinging for the fences instead of play-ing "Punch and Judy." He hit one out a big-league record once every 6.25 at-bats. He drew his 177th base on balls, another all-time mark.

While the home run record was an insane accomplishment, historians and statisticians will point to his slugging percentage as the most unbeliev-able record set by Bonds. His .863 obliterated Babe Ruth's .847 set in 1920. That alone does not tell the story.

Ruth was the only player ever to slug over .800, having done it twice. Nobody else ever did it; not Gehrig, Foxx, Williams, Mantle, Mays, or any-one. Except Barry Bonds!

"Soon the Babe's not going to have any records, is he?" Baker asked, having recovered the ebullience that Friday's loss had robbed him of. "I think it's awesome. This was one of the greatest years—no, it was *the* greatest year – I have seen from a single person."

History is not everyone's favorite subject. The mystique of Ruth and even Mays overshadows their actual accomplishments. Many were not see-ing Bonds' season for what it really was, the greatest season in the history of baseball by a player who, when it is all said and done, may be the best ever. Bonilla was on the case, but it says here that when the dust clears and the record is examined with a fine-tooth comb, the Greatest Ever tag, not just the Greatest I've Ever Seen moniker, will hang around Barry Bonds' neck.

Bonds came out of the game in the eighth, having gone 2-for-4 with an RBI and a run scored. The home nine pushed a run across in the bottom of the seventh, right after hearing "God Bless America," which was now be-ing sung during the seventh-inning stretch at all the games, in honor of what people were now calling the 9/11 Tragedy, to win it 2-1. Bonds finished at .328, and his club's final record was 90-72, two games behind Arizona. They finished three behind wild-card St. Louis, who had blown their finale to the 'Stros, 9-2.

A 2002 season-ticket ad appeared in the paper showing a photo of who else, but Barry Bonds. Eric Davis retired after a star-crossed career in baseball, and had nice things to say about his year in The City, stating that he had played with "the best player in the game." Aurilia finished with 206 hits and a .324 average to go with his 37 home runs and 97 RBIs out of the two-spot.

Jim Tracy told the media he thought Bonds could have hit *100 home runs* if he had not been walked 177 times.

"I'll take 73," Bonds said, apprised of Tracy's remarks, and when asked if thought the record could be broken, replied, "No, I wouldn't be surprised. I'll tell you one thing: If you break 73, I don't know anyone's ever going to break whatever the new number is going to be, because that's a lot of home runs."

The homer record is one thing, the slugging percentage mark is something else again.

John Shea was one of the few journalists who had expressed the opinion that Bonds was a pretty nice guy even before his assault on the record and accompanying efforts at rehabilitating his image. This may have something to do with Shea being more or less in Barry's age range. The older writers tended to get down on him.

Ron Bergman of the *San Jose Mercury News* said Bonds was an "arrogant jerk." Bruce Magowan of KNBR, one of the nicest guys in the media, said he never had a problem with Barry because he didn't take his slights personally. However, when sitting in San Rafael's Flatiron sports bar, he told Giants mega-fan Pat Quinlen that Bonds was among his "top 10" toughest guys to deal with.

Shea's October 8 *Chronicle* column was entitled, "Barry is caught being kind again," citing Bonds' emergence on the postgame field despite having been taken out, instead of packing it in to the clubhouse. Shea might have been reaching by calling such a minor thing an act of kindness, but he definitely had been a better man than in the past, although Barry insisted that he had not changed.

"The more scrutiny, notoriety and pressure he was under this year, he became more open," Shea quoted Kent, who refused to dislike Barry no matter how hard the media tried to paint him that way, "and that's very uncommon for an athlete, especially for Barry, who's been a closed-type person."

Bonds' had given commemorative bats to his teammates after he hit his 500th homer. After hitting his 61st (a symbolic number) he gave the clubhouse attendant who fished it out of a fountain at Denver's Coors Field a motorcycle. Bonds let outsiders in, made curtain calls, granted interviews, and not just at press conferences. Most important, he did not snap when asked stupid questions.

This may very well have been a lesson he had learned from Baker, one of the best, most patient interview subjects in baseball.

"I think every week he became more open," Shea quoted Kent. "I think he's been better with you guys, too. I was surprised. I thought he'd blow you guys off and just focus on home runs. I wouldn't have had a problem with that. But, heck, he's been open with you guys and open with teammates both in the locker room and on the field."

Kent could probably take some lessons from Bonds. During the season, he gave of himself by granting a weekly radio show on KNBR with Ralph Barbieri and Tom Tolbert, and was always gracious and full of "goldarns" and "heck yeas," but away from the mic Kent can hector print journalists with an array of four-letter epithets. For the most part, Bonds did not swear, he just blew off. The Patrick Swayze effect.

"I saw him smile a lot more than he did in the past," said Aurilia. "It was good to see him do that. I think he tried to enjoy what he went through this year." Of course, one does find incongruous that a man could do what Bonds did and not *enjoy* it, but Aurilia's point is well taken. At mid-season, some had speculated that because he is not as popular around the league as Arizona's Luis Gonzales, San Diego's Tony Gwynn, or the likeable McGwire, he would not get the pitches to break the mark.

Of course, they did deny him as many pitches as possible, but that had nothing to do with his personality. The "universally likeable" McGwire image is a myth, too, and perhaps leads one to consider that race is an issue when it comes to Bonds' perception, at least when making the comparison with Big Mac.

McGwire loves children and has a heart of gold, but so does Bonds. Like Bonds, though, McGwire does not suffer the slings and arrows of celebrity easily. At USC he was serious about baseball, with a touch of the rogue. One of his best friends since childhood in Claremont, Randy Robertson, was a pitcher for the Trojans and a ladies man of the first order. Robertson lived in an off-campus apartment on Hoover Street called the Hoover House with three teammates. They included pitchers Phil Smith and Tony "Bruno" Caravalho, and outfielder Mark Stevens. Without getting into details, these fellows liked to, uh, entertain the attractive coeds that make up a large segment of the SC student body. Some of the "events" of the Hoover House are nothing less than legendary. McGwire, who lived in a nearby apartment with third baseman Craig Stevenson, was a frequent party guest who did not necessarily indulge in the more graphic sporting activities, but had a definite *voyeuristic* streak.

Throughout his ascension through Oakland's minor league system, he was a happy-go-lucky fellow who frequented Trojan games before leaving for Spring Training. He maintained a self-effacing way about him despite everyone's high hopes for his future. In his rookie year, McGwire canceled an autograph-signing session at a cigar store in San Francisco at the last minute after he discovered that the store sold pornography, which is interesting when one considers the activities he enjoyed observing at the Hoover House.

In his first few years in The Show, McGwire stayed in touch with his old pals, holding friends' children in dugout photo sessions. He always returned phone calls. Over time, however, he seemed to lose touch with those once close to him, even good friends like Robertson and Stevenson. At one point they would be invited to his Huntington Harbor home in the off-season, but eventually that stopped. Any efforts to get ahold of McGwire had to go through his agent . . . without good results.

One ex-teammate, Terry Marks, a Trojan pitcher who has risen to a spot near the very top of Coca-Cola's corporate hierarchy, is an important person in his own right. He tried to contact his old friend for an autograph on behalf of his son, a baseball fan. McGwire never got back to him.

"That's just not a part of my life anymore," McGwire said of his All-American years playing under Rod Dedeaux at USC, the most prestigious college program in the nation. When asked about the names herein mentioned, he expressed little knowledge or interest in how any of these people were doing, and in some cases did not even remember them. This may even shed some light on why he had fled to St. Louis instead of signing with Anaheim in 1998.

McGwire is busy, but so is Bonds. Both men have reached the rare status of Jordan-like celebrity. Bonds may be a lot of things, but his friends from high school and college consider him very loyal. Playing in his hometown is helpful in this regard. If Bonds is comfortable with somebody who asks about old pals or family, he smiles and finds time to talk about them. Of course, if he does not feel like it, he will look right through you. Again, picture Swayze in "Ghost."

The questions about his friends break the monotony of the same old "Can you do it?" questions. McGwire winced when asked about his old friends, as if they were a bad memory. Go figure.

McGwire tolerates the media, but has a very testy side. In '98, he virtually shunned the press when they tried to cover what was obviously a legitimate, beginning-to-end race for Maris' record. What did he think these people were doing? He was making history, and the very essence of the press is to cover and write about just that. McGwire acted like they were nothing but pests instead of professionals doing a job, and serving a need that the public demands! He called the scene a "zoo."

Finally, when he got to 50 prior to Labor Day, McGwire acceded to the concept that he had a chance to break the record. Of course, everybody in America had known he would break it long before that. When he started doing press conferences, he smiled and opened up, showing intelligence and grace. Everybody fell in love with the Great White Hope, but the reality is that he was no Tony Gwynn, who is the very face of Class, every day, year in and year out.

Human beings are greedy. That is their natural state. Professional athletes are no different. However, pro athletes almost always have been treated specially and given things all their lives. By the time they become professionals they accept is as rote. Fans like to give them a hard time because they are spoiled and selfish. However, it is just not reasonable to take people, already blessed with extraordinary natural gifts, serenade them like gods, and expect anything else out of these (wo)men/children.

The same with entertainers—actors, rock stars. Divas all.

They want as much as they can get. Take the money and run. If they get hurt, they take the *cashe*, as Jim Rome calls it. If they play lousy, they take the money. If they get fined, they appeal. There is very, very little pride, integrity or honesty among professional athletes when it comes to money. They do despicable things. Ninety percent of us would do the same thing given the chance.

Jack Nicholson gets $20 million to do a picture, but if it stinks up the joint, does he give the money back? Heck, no. Athletes are entertainers like Nicholson or Britney Spears, but they generally do not get paid as much.

Two things are relatively true about athletes' pay: They reap what the marketplace bears, and most are overpaid.

In the early days of free agency, 1978, Lyman Bostock was a .300 hitter. He signed a big contract with Gene Autry and the California Angels. When he started the season in a bad slump, Bostock offered to *give the money back*. Autry would have none of it. Free agency was new and the big money had everybody up in arms, but the point is that this was one guy, 23 years ago, who showed some honor in this area. Very rare.

What did Bostock get for being honorable? Shortly thereafter a jealous husband shot him to death. *Niiiice.*

Mark McGwire went Bostock one step further in 2001. The Cardinals had a standing $30 million extension on the table. All he had to do was sign it. He never even went public with it, but La Russa revealed toward the end of the season that Big Mac could have the dough with the stroke of a pen. He was holding off on it because he was unsure if he would play another season.

On November 11, citing nagging injuries and stating that he could not give his team the kind of value they deserved for the money, McGwire retired. Never having signed the extension, he got nothing.

Any other player would have signed that deal. Then they would have had their agent go to the team for a severance package. Or they would half-ass it through another year or two, injured and not at 100 percent. They would cash every check along the way (actually, they are automatically deposited in the bank nowadays).

McGwire is like Bonds, a man of dual personality. He is the guy who loves his kid "with a passion," but chose to relocate a couple thousand miles away from him when he could have played at home. He is the guy who called the media a zoo but then gave them his time and energy. He is the guy who seemingly forgot where he came from, yet performed an act of integrity and honesty almost unheard of in recent history.

Yes, it was the right thing to do. There are plenty of people in public life who would have done it. It is just that few of them are athletes. Former UCLA basketball coach John Wooden, now 90 years old, comes to mind as someone who would have done what McGwire did. Maybe Dodger broadcaster Vin Scully might have done it, too.

It is not tantamount to Albert Schweitzer or Mother Theresa. McGwire is still a set-for-life millionaire with a bright future in or out of the game. But it was darn noble, and it freed a huge windfall of Cardinal money for a talented free agent to replace McGwire. Would that free agent be Giambi, or Bonds? In the end, it would be neither. Giambi would sign with the Yankees, and Bonds would sign with the Giants.

Some stated that McGwire's injuries, which kept him from getting to 600 homers, were "heartbreaking," which brings us to another example of overused hyperbole in sports. A person losing a loved one to cancer is heartbreaking. A father having his daughter ripped away from him when his ex-wife moves a couple thousand miles away, *that* is heartbreaking.

Others "feel sorry" for a relief pitcher who gives up a game-winning homer in the World Series, or a receiver who blows a winning touchdown pass in a bowl game. These are young, healthy men at the top of their game, pursuing their dreams at the highest level of competition. There is no place for sorrow, just *joy de vivre*. Feel sorry for the paraplegic, the Alzheimer patient, the lonely old lady with no one to visit her.

Priorities are not always in order. Mark McGwire is a rare man who seems to have a firm grasp on where his priorities lie, at least most of the time.

So what about Barry Bonds? Would he do what McGwire did if he could no longer perform? He has publicly stated that you can "forget the money," that he would retire if he felt he was no longer a productive player. If so, he would be in the minority. Bonds, like McGwire, is a contradiction sometimes. His teammates and opponents do not always like him, but there is a sense that they *want* to like him.

Bonds himself has raised the race issue, which is troubling, yet somehow this remains a legitimate issue. It is not, however, an issue with teammates and opponents. In today's environment, white racism towards minorities is spotted, exposed, and not tolerated.

"They're not pitching around him because they don't like him," Larry Dierker had said. "They're pitching around him because they want to win games."

"Since I've been here, he's been a great teammate," said pitcher Jason Schmidt, who had come over from Pittsburgh in July. "I've definitely come across worse. He wouldn't make my top 10 list of bad teammates."

Is that a compliment?

Bonds takes criticism for a number of things that set him apart from teammates.

Bonds' personal trainer works him out with a special, individualized routine that is reported to be very intense. He has a personal chef who prepares meals for him at the ballpark based on his particular dietary needs.

Bonds does not usually stretch with his team and has been known to miss team photos. It has been reported that he does not stay at the same hotel as his team on the road. What really happens is that he stays under an alias so fans cannot call him or find his room. This is understandable, in fact necessary. He usually does not take the team bus.

Many players miss team stretching and prepare on their own. Baseball pregame is a day-in, day-out routine subject to variation. Half the team usually takes cabs or makes other arrangements instead of taking the bus.

Can anybody argue that Barry's workouts and diet have not paid huge dividends that benefit his team tremendously? Should he have been in the team photo? Yes, he should have. Should he run out every ground ball? Yes, he should. Is it a big deal? No.

His performance over many 162-game seasons is *not* subject to debate.

"You guys are like ants," Bonds had told the media in July. "You see something sweet and crawl towards it." The media has always been subject to these kinds of put-downs. Air force fighter ace Chuck Yeager used to call them "root weevils" when they covered the first U.S. astronaut program in the early 1960s. As somebody pointed out in Tom Wolfe's *The Right Stuff*, those "root weevils write history."

The fact is, most of the major media, the guys and gals who really matter in the Opinion Game, are polished professionals who have beaten some pretty heavy odds just to get the jobs they have. How many people think they could cover sports and try to do it? Just about everybody, it seems. If somebody writes for a major metropolitan newspaper or a national magazine, pens successful books, is on-air talent for a network, or overcomes all the competition for a gig as a big league broadcaster, they are to their line of work what a big league ballplayer is to theirs. We just do not get paid the same way.

"I don't think I've changed at all," Bonds said as the season progressed. "I think you guys are just nicer this year. My teammates, we have fun. I think it was because when you're doing so well, you're a part of it and the whole team is a part of it. There's joy with everyone."

"Every year, we gain more respect for one other," said Kent, who may have done more changing than Bonds or the media. "The perception is we hate each other, and we don't. In fact, I think we have a working relationship that's probably stronger than just about anybody else's in this locker room. It's because of how we work together."

The Monday, October 8 *Chronicle* featured a special section devoted to Bonds. The cover was a dominant, full-page photo by Carlos Avila Gonzalez, showing Bonds following through on his historic homer. Leading it off, Bruce Jenkins stated that there was an "arrogance" to Bonds playing style. Getting Freudian, Jenkins surmised that this was the result of his family's always being forced to prove something. Jenkins used statistics to make the case that Bonds' season was one of the greatest ever.

According to Jenkins, relations between father and son turned "sour" when Barry was 11 in 1975, after Bobby was traded to the New York Yankees and "tossed around like an old suitcase" over the succeeding years. Bobby would play for numerous teams, showing offensive prowess but never living up to his full potential, and being discarded mainly because he exhibited a bad attitude.

Some weeks earlier, Barry had given no credence to a question suggesting that he was distrustful because of this experience, calling those years "wonderful" because he was able to travel the country and see various Major League stadiums first hand. To quote a "Saturday Night Live" skit on Freud, "sometimes a banana is just a banana, Anna."

Would Bonds' record mean less because he broke it so soon after McGwire? Some media were saying it, but this is an argument that does not hold up. Jenkins hypothesized that Bob Beamon's long-jump record meant more because it stood for a long time; that Wilt Chamberlain's single-game scoring mark of 100 is more awesome because it has not been broken. After playing devil's advocate, Jenkins concluded that Bonds' record is everything it seems to be and more.

One can also make legitimate note that Beamon set his record in the high altitude of Mexico City. Chamberlain faced comparable pygmies. Babe Ruth did not play against comparable competition. Right field at Yankee Stadium is 290 feet away, and Lou Gehrig hit behind him. Maris played with the same short porch with Mantle as his shadow.

How did Bonds become the player *he* is?

"He could always hit," Bobby Bonds told John Shea, but photos of him as a Pittsburgh rookie are pictures of an unrecognizable individual, a thin kid—athletic, yes—but not a picture of power. Some hitters have done it without brute strength. Aaron, in particular, hit off the wrong foot and generated his homers through sheer wrist-induced bat speed. Bonds is the product of weight training, diet and supplements. Does he use steroids? Many think he does, but it is not a given. An athlete can get to where he is through hard work, and good genetics.

Like Aaron, Bonds was a power hitter throughout his career who did not put up insane numbers. He would hit his 35 homers, over 40 in a good year. He did it consistently. In 2000, when the team moved to Pac Bell, he upped it to 49. Is it the park? It helps, but it would not be a logical assumption that a stadium makes *that* much difference. Besides, he hit an all-time record 36 on the road.

McGwire is the guy who broke the psychological barrier, like Roger Bannister running the four-minute mile, or Chuck Yeager exploding through the sound barrier. When Big Mac hit 70, it was "Katie bar the door." If anybody had the mental make-up to do such a thing, it is Bonds, and this has always been his advantage. Bonds has accepted challenges since high school.

In the spring of 1982, Bonds' led Serra High School into a West Catholic Athletic League game in The City vs. St. Ignatius High. The game was played at West Sunset Playground, a sweet yard overlooking the Pacific Ocean. It is not far from the beach. It is a place where many legends have played over the years.

In a story that has been retold many times, a scout who knew Bonds hit well using aluminum bats asked him to switch to wood. Just to see what would happen.

"Yeah, sure, dude," Bonds replied.

"He hit the longest homer I've ever seen by a high school kid," said his coach, Dave Stevens. They are still talking about it at Serra, a school that has produced numerous big leaguers. Stevens built on the Bonds years to develop a powerhouse that challenges for the California Interscholastic Federation—Central Coast Section championship regularly, and has also competed for the "mythical" National Championship.

"The wall was 300 feet from the plate and 10 feet high with a six-foot cyclone fence above it," Stevens recalls of The Bomb at the Beach. "And the ball landed in the sand dunes beyond the fence. The ball exploded off his bat. Everyone gasped. I went home and told my wife I saw something I had never seen before."

The *Chronicle* rated Bonds' home run record as the third-greatest single-season record ever set in sports. Their list, printed on October 8, was as follows:

1. Joe DiMaggio's 56-game hitting streak (1941)
2. Wilt Chamberlain's 50.4 scoring average (1961-62)
3. Bonds' 73 homers (2001)
4. Oscar Robertson's averaging a triple-double (1961-62)
5. Hack Wilson's 191 RBIs (1930)
6. Byron Nelson's 18 tournament wins (1945)
7. Wayne Gretzky's 92 goals (1981-82)
8. Rod Laver's tennis Grand Slam (1969)
9. Orel Hershisher's 59 consecutive scoreless innings (1988)
10. Eric Dickerson's 2,105 rushing yards (1984)

"What he's done, it's absolutely phenomenal," McGwire said from St. Louis. "It's in the stratosphere. It's almost like he's playing T-ball."

"He talks a lot, and he backs up what he talks about," said Mays. "I am one he made a liar out of because I didn't think he could do it."

"I hope everybody here has time to realize what has happened," opined Aurilia on the night Bonds broke the mark. "One of the great sports records of all time was broken tonight by one of the greatest players of all time."

"All of us who were here tonight have seen two moments in a baseball game we will never forget," Peter Magowan had said in the early Saturday morning hours.

"It's unreal," Terrence Long of the cross-bay A's said. "I'm so happy for him, especially the way he did it, because people wouldn't pitch to him."

"I think it's great," said teammate F.P. Santangelo. "Barry was always great to me, great to my family. I'm proud to say I played with him. People always ask me what he's like, and when I say 'He's a great guy,' they look at me funny, but he's always been nice to me."

The *Chronicle*'s Mark Camps specializes in a column called "By the Numbers," in which he uses statistics to make his points. Unlike some of the others, who probably were so awed by what they saw that they could not put it in historical perspective, Camps pointed out that by combining Bonds' slugging percentage and on-base percentage, his numbers add up to 1.378—.863 slugging and .515 on-base.

The only player ever to post better numbers was Ruth—1.379 in 1920. Nobody else ever topped 1.300.

Bill James uses a stat called "runs created." Bonds' 231 trails only Ruth's 239 in 1921. Bonds also struck out a mere 93 times. From 1966 to 2000, 14 times a player hit 50 or more homers, and only Albert Belle (1995), Luis Gonzalez (2001) and Bonds were under 100.

His 107 extra-base hits were third highest in history, tying Philadelphia's Chuck Klein's National League record set in an offensive crazy year, 1930, in which *baseball* hit .303! Ruth held the big-league record of 1,119, set in 1921.

Bonds' 107 extra-base hits included 73 homers, 32 doubles, and two triples.

His 494 career home runs were the most ever by a player prior to his first 50-homer season.

Still, Bonds failed again to win a World Series, in this case not even making it to the postseason. For all of his greatness, he still needs to lead a team to the Promised Land. He needs a Ring.

He had been quoted that he was "scared" in the postseason, tantamount to admitting that he "chokes." Until he wins the Big One, this is something that will haunt him.

"Now, I've probably figured why I don't hit in the play-offs," Bonds had told Henry Schulman. "The spotlight. It's tough."

CHAPTER
NINE

Other Voices

CHARLES SCOTT

When researching celebrities, whether they are athletes, entertainers, politicians, or the like, all the research, press conferences and "up-close" TV interviews yield little information about the "real" person compared with what you get from their true and legitimate friends—or enemies.

Charles Scott is one of Barry Bonds' very best and closest pals. By pure coincidence, he and I have been casual buddies for 10 years. We played a few years apart for competing high schools, and have known each other socially. I found greater enlightenment on Barry from Scott than from any other source.

Charles Scott is an excellent example of how great one has to be to make it in professional sports. He is 6-5, 225 pounds, a magnificent multi-sport athlete who was a superstar pitcher at Terra Linda High School near San Francisco, and at Arizona State. He pitched in the Cleveland Indians and Minnesota Twins organizations from 1985-92. He reached Class AAA and knocked on the door for years. He played winter ball in Mazatlan and Venezuela. He never got the call.

For an athlete of Scott's great skills—natural talent, work ethic, intelligence and desire—not to ascend to The Show is proof positive that the men we see playing in big-league arenas are truly special. For every Major Leaguer, there are 200 Charles Scotts; great stars who dominated every level from little league on, but did not permeate the SportsCenter consciousness.

For many, to come so close and yet so far would be intolerable. Scott never let it get him down. He finished up his schooling (playing basketball at Dominican College in the process), then got into scouting. He is one of the architects of the World Champion Arizona Diamondbacks, and must be considered a potential future general manager.

Scott played high school ball a few miles north of Bonds, at the same time that Barry prepped at Serra, yet they never faced each other. They met at fall practice at Arizona State in 1982. Scott was interviewed by ESPN for their "Sports Center" feature on Bonds. For an hour, he gave them the same things he gave me, the truth about Bonds—most of it positive. When the show aired, all of that was cut out in favor of a sound bite of Scott calling Bonds "big mouth Barry" because he had stood up to Arizona State coach Jim Brock. This says a great deal about the reality of sports journalism.

"I asked Barry about it beforehand," said Scott, "and he said, 'Hey, dude, just tell 'em the truth.'

"He doesn't need anybody to validate him. He doesn't need to appease anybody, plain and simple."

The first subject was Jim Brock and his wife, Patsey.

"I can't stand Patsey or Jim Brock," said Scott, "and I don't know many people who have good things to say about them, and I don't care if you print that. Both of them were manipulative and evil. That said, Brock was successful, and you can probably say the same things about Barry Switzer or Steve Spurrier or Bobby Knight. Nobody can dispute their success. But my personal experiences with Coach Brock were not very favorable, and his wife was just as bad as he was. She did a lot of secretarial work in the program, and if you weren't in the 'in crowd,' or weren't really helping the program at that time, she was just really rude to you. I spent three years with them, and I'm just telling you, they're not good people.

"I know Coach Brock died of cancer, and that's horrible, but honestly I think maybe that was God's way of dealing with him for the way he was with people. I'm not sad he's gone."

Scott observed the Brock's playing "power trips" on young players like Bonds and himself. They moved up the ladder from being lowly freshmen, and then found the couple to be receptive to them.

"When he needed something from you, he tolerated you more," Scott recalled, "and he needed Barry. Barry was a very productive player from day one. He brought a lot of prestige to the program, he put up huge numbers all three years there and was a first round draft pick, so obviously he fell into a different category than most, so he could get away with more than most. If you're a valuable commodity, you're gonna be able to get away with more than others.

"Barry just made light of it. But for others, when a new class replaced a graduating class, now he [Brock] needed us and we got treated better as we moved up."

The conversation then centered on Patsey Brock and some well-known rumors (which I have chosen not to discuss herein) that had circulated regarding her during those years. The rumors had nothing to do with Bonds, and Scott addressed what Bonds' reaction would have been had the stories been printed in his biography.

"I can tell you, when Barry reads this," Scott said, "I can tell you how Barry thinks, and if you're trying to—he's already got enough negativism around his name alright, and he's not afraid of that, he's not hiding from that, but I can tell you how we as athletes feel about certain things, and we'd just look at this as something that's really just out of context...

"You're gonna have enough bad things to put in this book about Bonds without this. If I were him, I'd take it personally, like 'What's this doing here?'"

Of course, Scott may be missing the point of a book, which is not about catering to what its subject wants it to be. The point of a book is to entertain readers and, the shame, to sell as many copies as possible, all while telling the truth and providing fair, balanced coverage of the subject matter. If there are side anecdotes that are funny, amusing, titillating or informative, as there are in this work, then the book is what it should be.

Scott grew up a Giants fan, and therefore he was a fan of Bobby Bonds when he got the chance to meet Barry's ballyhooed father. This was shortly after Bobby's Major League career came to an end.

"The only thing I could tell you about Bobby Bonds," he said, "and this is the God's honest truth, is he was an unbelievable player, and when I first met him, it was like, 'Oh, my God, that's Bobby Bonds.'

"My freshman year, Bobby would make trips down, and I would just sit in the room, quiet, and just look at him, because he's frickin' Bobby Bonds, you know, so my impression of Bobby Bonds is that he's someone who's high up on a pedestal for me, just because I grew up in the area and followed the Giants and really admired the things he did on the field.

"As far as his off-the-field antics and things like that in those days, I don't know much—I don't know anything to tell you the truth. When I was with Cleveland, I had to fly to Cleveland for arm surgery. They brought me to a big-league game and into the clubhouse, and obviously Bobby was their hitting coach at that time.

"He knew me from Arizona State and we went out to the hotel bar that night, and I remember Bobby giving me total words of wisdom which I recall to this day, about how this game works. He says, 'Charles, there is no need for you ever to go out to bars, chasing women and doing all these type of things when you're in the minor leagues. When you get to the Major Leagues, then you will have earned the right to do these things, and nobody can tell you what to do.' These were probably the strongest words *any* coach at any level has ever given me and it came from Bobby. So, as far as his off the field antics, the drinking thing, the family thing, and all that, and even Barry being embarrassed by that, I never ever saw that or could feel that. I was shocked to hear him talk about it on 'Sports Century.'"

Regarding Barry's assertion on the show that he was afraid to have his father even show up because he might be drunk, Scott said, "I think those were more part of his high school days. I don't ever recall. Barry's not a real open person about his personal life, and even to this day, Barry's not the type of guy whose gonna just sit down with you and spill out his heart. He's just not like that.

"He's not gonna hide things, but he's not gonna give you information that just doesn't matter at this point, things that you can't change, and if he can't do anything about it, he's not gonna volunteer you that stuff. And I'm not one to ask those kinds of things."

Now, we start to see what makes Barry tick, by seeing what traits he values in a friend.

"'Hey, Barry, what about this,'" mocks Scott. "I don't give a shit what happened. All I care about with Barry is the way we interact with each other. If he treats me like an asshole, I'm gonna tell him he's a fuckin' asshole. If he treats me with respect, I'm gonna treat him with respect, so our relationship is built on basically how we interact with one another, and it's not based on a lot of 'Well, what happened when your dad did this?' or 'What happened with this?'"

When Brock made Bonds and Scott run because they broke curfew in Hawaii—my, what an outrage!—Bonds ended up running about 20 miles, as compared to Scott's five. That was because Bonds had protested, saying other players were out, too. Bobby Bonds did not like his son being singled out for embarrassment, and to paraphrase a term lawyers use, "ripped Brock a new asshole."

"One incident that stands out in my head was Bobby defending Barry," said Scott. "When Brock made Barry run all those miles for the Hawaii thing, Bobby found out about it and flew down . . . and *snapped!* It was before a game, and we were all coming out of our clubhouse onto the field. There were fans all around, and Bobby had Brock back against the fence, and was airing him out for making Barry run all those miles.

"Now, we were all happy to see Brock getting chewed out, first of all. It was kind of like finally somebody sticking up for us. I think Bobby was definitely sticking up for his son, which he should. If that were my son and somebody had humiliated him that way—especially with the articles about the team vote, and kicking him off the team—and made him run 20 miles, I wouldn't have been happy."

It was true the team had voted Bonds off, but "still, even to put it to the team like that was not fair. Brock wouldn't a done that with anybody else. He would have taken a team vote with anybody else. If I'd a gotten in that much trouble, I'd a just been kicked off the team. If Don Wakamatsu had gotten in that kind of trouble, he would have kicked him off the team without taking a team vote, for whatever he felt was right."

Brock, it turns out, "brainwashed us. I got kicked off the team like six times my freshman year. Getting kicked off the team then was having your locker cleared out, and scaring the shit out of you, you'd go the to the field and your locker'd be cleared out. It was little things—the thing was you did somethin' wrong, you didn't sprint to the friggin' batter's box or somethin' like that—you might go the field the next day and your frickin' locker was cleared out. He played mind games with you."

Brock was a martinet who would leave notes saying "'See me in my office on Monday.' It'd happen on Friday and that whole time your wonderin', 'What the hell's goin' on, am I frickin' done?' You'd go to the office on Monday and he'd say, 'You're going to the JV team for a week.' You're wonderin' what the hell's goin' on.

"It was a total power trip," Scott continued, but the suspensions "never" happened if you were a starter the week of a big game. "By the time you were a junior and he really needed you, you didn't make those kind of mistakes because you were petrified of what had happened the previous two years."

Scott agreed that the whole act, which was orchestrated not just by Jim Brock but by his wife, was basically a Bill and Hillary Clinton-style cabal, designed to keep the players under their thumb. Getting back to Bobby's tirade on Brock, Scott said, "I can assure you, 90 percent of the other players on that team would have been kicked off hands down, no doubt, you're done. But he needed Barry, plus Bobby was right, and Brock was pretty much mortified by it, he really had nothing to say about it. I stood there for awhile and watched it because it was so nice to me to see somebody giving him what he deserved. He never spoke a word back to Bobby. Bobby was in his face like this [Scott indicates face-to-face, Leo Durocher to Harry Wendelstedt-stye], and he never even spoke a word back to Bobby."

Brock's power trip was "not a racial thing. Not at all. Brock was like that with everybody. It didn't matter whether you were white, black or green. He's got a Master's in psychology and was good at that stuff, but he did get the most out of his players, but not in a positive way. He did it out of fear.

"Five years ago, me, Doug [Henry] and Barry were all talkin' about going back for the alumni game, they were gonna, but we all said we didn't like to go back because we didn't like Brock. We didn't go because Barry was getting married, I think Barry went back when they retired his number. I think Brock's methods were wrong. From a parent's standpoint, I'm a parent now and have my own children, and if I'd known somebody purposely treated my son the way he treated us, I'd not want him to play for that person."

The subject switched over to Bonds' marriage to his Swedish immigrant first wife, Sun, and Bonds' reaction to the public perception of his performance as a husband.

"I heard the rumors that others players have been with this woman," said Scott. "She's no angel. As cocky and as arrogant and as hardheaded as Barry is, it's kind of laughable that he'd care what anybody thought. You know what kills me about Barry, and people's perception of Barry, is people look at him and say 'he's this and this and this,' he'd never put himself in a position of asking for approval or opinion.

"Barry's been the same way his whole life. He's never changed. He's been the same since day one. Barry's personality never changed when he became a superstar. Barry's the exact same person today he was the first day I met him at fall workouts at Arizona State. He's the exact same person. His fame, his stardom and accomplishments have not changed his approach toward people, towards himself, his family, he's the same guy. I could see him jumpin' on someone and fighting them over something, but he'd never ask for approval ahead of time.

"I do recall when Barry met Sun, and he told me this girl had changed his life, and he was in love. Big time. I remember him saying that. He said, 'Charles, this girl makes me feel like nobody's ever made me feel.' He was in love, and that marriage was made public and trashed, but it was real love when it started out."

Bonds was a good-looking guy "and still is. But the one thing I know about Barry is that sometimes Barry just deals with people the way he sees fit. But he's not the kind of guy to think, 'I'm this and I'm that. I'm good-looking and I can have any girl I want.' He doesn't think like that. He's not the type person to think of himself like that.

"He's moody and it all depends on the moment. If he's had a bad at-bat, and if you ask him a question when he's in a bad mood, getting a direct answer . . . or asking him a question when he's in a good mood and getting this charming, great-to-be-around-type guy. . . .

"The same thing with women. He doesn't really look at the fact that this girl is beautiful or sexual. Right at the beginning, first impressions with Barry are huge. He's into one-on-one, and he's as direct and honest as anyone I've ever known to be.

"I think he didn't perceive himself as that way [a playboy] and he didn't care to be. He didn't see himself that way, I don't think he cared to be that way, his personality isn't that way.

"Barry alienates himself from a lot of people. He's not the most likable person. He's never had a lot of friends. He has a select few friends that he's close with. But he's always really had just one single woman in his life."

With friends, "The most important thing with Barry is, if he doesn't respect you he will *chew you up*. He's very, very direct and to the point, and if you're not a strong individual who can deal with that, and counteract that, then you're not gonna be able to spend any time with Barry Bonds."

Scott then addressed Bonds' mood swings.

"Barry's like that with me," he said. "That's just Barry's personality. It's not like he's trying to play this game with people. No, it's not like, 'I'm Barry Bonds and I can get away with that.' That's not the way Barry is. Barry's like that with everyone, including his dad. He's like that with everyone, except maybe his kids. I do know he's a gaga unbelievable guy with kids. But he's like that with everybody, even guys he trusts, just everybody. It's not personal. I mean, I'll go in the locker room sometimes, Trav, and it's like, '*Chas*,' hugs, kisses, frickin' jumpin' all over me. Then I'll go there another time and it's like, [subdued] 'Hey, whas'sup' You know, like we just talked last night."

People in the media hate this aspect of him.

"You see, that's my point, that's other people's insecurities," continued Scott. "Barry doesn't just do that to people in the media. Barry doesn't care what they have or what they are. It doesn't matter if you're frickin' Michael Jordan, he's just gonna do that, and that's the way he is. He don't give a shit if you understand him or you don't, and that's what I really love and respect about him so much, is that he really is so much his own person and has been ever since I met him as a freshman at Arizona State. He's been the *exact same way*. That's a rarity. I've learned over the years to respect that a lot more than when I was rooming with him and we were friends in college. I respect him so much more now for being that way and staying that way."

Regarding other celebrities who have changed, Scott said, "It's amazing, somebody like me, whose inside the game, I've known Mark [McGwire], I know Randy Johnson, I've played against these guys, and I know their personalities and how the media perceives these guys. Then I look at a guy like Barry whose really been true to his friends and has been throughout his career, and yet he's villainized so much because of that, whereas *these other guys*, who really lost reality over who they are and who they should be and who they were associated with before, are kind of almost painted in this beautiful picture because they know how and what other people want, and they know how to give it to them, whereas with Barry, he knows what you want, but he's not gonna bring himself to that level."

The question of race is brought up. Charles is, like Bonds, a black man who grew up in a mostly white suburb. I asked if he felt this was something that attracted them to each other.

"It never once was mentioned," he replied, "it was never talked about, but yeah, there are advantages that both Barry and myself have from being black and having the closest people to us be black. I consider myself very fortunate, because not only do I have this black side of me, which I love, because I have this history and this heritage and it's made me the strong individual that I am, but I'm also fortunate enough to have moved to a place where everybody did have a mom and a dad and a house and drugs weren't sold on the corner, and went to a high school where I was a minority, based on the fact I was a black person at a white school, and I've had all those different types of elements added to my life, to where I can communicate on that level also, and I think Barry's the exact same way.

"Barry has black folks in his family," continued Scott, referring to his early years and extended family in Riverside, "and the Christmases that Barry experienced were not white Christmases, they weren't going to Tahoe on, you know, ski week and stuff like that. I mean, he was with black people and celebrating in Riverside, and that's his childhood.

"So Barry is very black, which is what I'm trying to get to, just as I am. But yet, we do have, and it's really a society thing where we can communicate on both levels, but Barry's comfortable either way, because of the way he's been brought up."

What about Gary Sheffield and Bobby Bonilla? They are a couple of "boys from the 'hood." Does Bonds seek some kind of affirmation of his African-Americanism through his friendship with them?

"Check the personality on those two guys," answered Scott. "Very outspoken, in your throat, if you like it, this is what it is, fuckin' take it, if you don't like it, whatever. That's what I'm talking about. When you talk to Barry, it's all about mutual respect. If you're not a guy he respects, you won't get respect. Eric Davis is another guy who he really likes. Those are the reasons why. Barry gravitates towards people who are real. Those guys don't have any bullshit. If Sheffield feels he's being underpaid, he says it.

"Once again, I don't think Barry sees any kind of advantage to associating with these guys, and he doesn't say to himself, 'These guys can solidify my position in the black community.' I think he likes those guys because they are real and direct and to the point and he respects that. "

Friendship with him is "an understanding of where he's coming from and an understanding of where they're coming from, and if he doesn't respect you because he thinks you're associating with him to get something that's not real, you're not going to get close to Barry, plain and simple.

"I can just sense the kind of mood he's in. I'm not gonna kiss his ass. If I sense he's in a quiet mood, it's, 'Hey, Barry, I'm not here to kiss your ass, I'll holler at you later, I'm outta here. See ya.' You know? And never ever has Barry said, 'Hey, man, you disrespected me, I'm Barry Bonds, you know, you gotta kiss my ass.' Bullshit. You know?

"I recall one time I went down there, I hadn't seen him in a while, and we were sittin' there, chitchatting, and I said, 'You know Barry, one thing I really respect about you is the fact you are the same person that you've always been.' And later that evening he did something in the game, and they were interviewing him after the game, and it was on the radio, and the guy asked him, 'Hey Barry, do you think that you've changed?' and he said, 'That's funny that you asked me that, because I was just talking to one of my good friends, Charles Scott earlier, about this exact same thing, and he said I haven't changed at all, and I'm the exact same person.' And that's my point. *Barry is the same person.*

"Like this year, I hadn't seen Barry in eight months, I'm covering [scouting] the Giants. I walk down to left field, Eric Davis is out there, Barry's out on the field, all scouts and media, and I told Eric to tell Barry to look over here, and Barry looks over and sees me, and before he even gets me to he says, 'Where's Marcy at? [Marcy is Charles' wife and former childhood sweetheart]. Bring her out, I want to see Marcy.' Before he says 'hello,' before he says 'kiss my ass,' before he says anything. He does charity things for Marcy. He signed a bat last year, we auctioned it off at a little league boys thing, it brought in a thousand dollars for the school. He loves Marcy. This year he said he's coming to the school and coming to the auction to do whatever Marcy wanted him to do, so that you know she could raise more money for the school.

"Barry is down for his people. He's really, I mean he's a very giving person like that. I was at the game that day, he said, 'Bring Tyler [Charles' son] to the game tomorrow. I want to see Tyler tomorrow, bring Tyler to the game. I haven't seen Tyler. I want Tyler in the locker room tomorrow. Bring him to the game, it's three or four years, I wanna see how big he is.' I bring Tyler down there, he signs Tyler's posters, he's very, very giving.

"Now, he doesn't have to do that type of stuff, and he's not doing it because he cares about what others think, he's doing it to do it, he's showing me that type of respect because he respects me, you know what I'm saying? He's not doing it for other people to see and know or any other reason because nobody sees or knows that anyway, and that's what I love about Barry, and that's why Barry's my friend, and that's why I stick up for Barry the way I do."

Scott told all of this to "Sports Century." They cut out all of it and left Scott hanging with his "big mouth Barry" sound bite. It should also be noted that Jim Rooker said that in Pittsburgh, teammates would ask Bonds to sign things, and he would refuse. Go figure.

"You know, Barry knows these things," explained Scott, in reference to media manipulation. "I don't worry about how that interview was perceived because Barry knows there's no bullshit in me. I'm not gonna say something to them that I wouldn't say to him. Just as when I asked him if there was anything he wanted me to get across, he said, 'Hey, dude I know what you're gonna tell him, you're gonna tell him the truth, I *want* you to tell 'em the truth.' And Barry is a big mouth, he's gonna speak his mind, I'll tell that to his face. I mean, I'm not hiding anything about the way I think or feel about Barry or kissing his butt. Barry's got a real abrasive side, which he'll show to anyone—not just you, the media; to me, his friend, to his dad, to his wife, all right to his best friend, Bobby McKercher. He's got that abrasive side that he'll definitely show when he's ready to shop it. But at the same time, he's got that real giving side. I saw that whole show to be very negative. It's not personal.

"I have a strong-willed personality, so a lot of things Barry is likely to do or say, I'm likely to do or say myself. So I think from a friendship standpoint I can tolerate him a little more so than other people. I'm still to this day, I'm proud of what he's done, I love what he's done for my family, I think he's done a lot of good things, but he's not a guy that I could freaking hang out with on a daily basis."

Now we are getting something interesting.

"I can't put up with the ups and downs of his mood swings," he said.

Could Bonds have a chemical imbalance?

"I won't go that far to say something like that," answered Scott, "but you can walk into him on certain days and he's wonderful. On other days he's not, and that's the media perception, but it's the same with us. He does the same with Garry Sheffield and Bobby Bonilla. If he's in a bad mood, he's like that.

"Basically what you're asking is your trying to put Barry in a position that you're not willing to put the rest of society in. I'm sure people who write for the *Examiner*, some guy whose a guru, he gets away with things. . . .

"Now, if you're asking if I'm going to like him . . . Cal Ripken and Michael Jordan have hang-ups and don't stay at the same hotel, if you're that much of a draw, you're entitled to do those things, you can't be expected to be accountable to the same things. He deserves the lounge chair, the reason there is complaint is because it is different."

(Randy Johnson of Arizona has a lounge chair at his locker at Bank One Ballpark. I know, because I have sat in it. Mike Morgan and Matt Williams goofed on me for sitting in it, offering me a beer and a sandwich as if they were waiters, but Johnson knew me from USC and told them, "Us Trojans stick together.")

"The media put themselves in a higher position than where they put Barry in," Scott said, now firmly on a roll. "They feel they have the power and ability to make or break his career and they've felt like that through the history of time, but when you get a guy like Barry who doesn't give a shit, then all of a sudden it's like they purposely do these things to him, that's where those stories come from. He's basically gotta defend all this stuff that's bullshit. Does Cal Ripken ever have to defend himself? Do you ever hear Michael Jordan defend himself? You never heard people get on them about things that don't mean shit, who cares if he's got a lounge chair. Ninety percent of the guys stay in hotels under an alias. Rich Aurilia probably stays under an alias. Does Jordan abide by the same rules and come in the same doors? That's my point, why vilify him for not playing the game?"

I told Charles my theory about the players owing the media, because the publicity helps generate the dollars that make them rich.

"I'm gonna disagree on that," he respectfully said. "I'm gonna go back 50 years ago and say these guys are still superstars. Joe DiMaggio and Babe Ruth were still making millions then compared to what everybody else was making, and there was so *Sports Illustrated*, no ESPN, there wasn't all of these things to glorify them, but the National Pastime has always been what it is. I don't think you're right, these guys would still be icons in their field."

I pointed out that Babe Ruth made $80,000 in 1929, which was more than President Herbert Hoover. When told this, Babe replied, "I had a better year." However, $80,000 in 1929 still does not translate to the multimillions of our modern day. While his contract was in Hoover's "ball park," George Bush makes about half a million a year, and that salary has only recently been raised. That is a utility infielder's salary in the Majors.

"In fact, there's a huge market out there that doesn't even read your newspaper or watch TV," said Scott, "because they don't wanna hear all that bullshit. And I'm one of 'em. When I played, I stopped reading all the articles, even the good articles, because I didn't want to know what they were saying. It really doesn't matter. The only thing Barry really cares about, he doesn't care what you think, because you didn't even play in the big leagues. I'd say 95 percent of the guys who are writing these stories never even played. A lot of 'em, Trav—I mean, you're probably a freakin' hero in your business because you played professional baseball, but how many pencil-neck geeks do you think can answer the question, 'Did you ever play?' and that's my point. To talk to a guy like Barry whose accomplished the things he's accomplished, would you bow down to a guy who fuckin' got beat up every day in school?"

Scott was asked about the pay scale of the media vs. the athletes.

"There's a certain respect based on money," he replied. "A lot of these guys grew up in not-so-good situations, and that's all they respect. When you have the pencil-neck geek that used to get beat up writing unfavorable things about things you can't change; it's not the athlete who thinks that way. If I take you to the hood, and you write about the way people conversate, then they write about the way you conversate, you're gonna look pretty bad, too. I mean, it's really a matter of perception, and the majority of the people you are reaching don't understand where these guys are coming from. Barry did grow up in a white neighborhood, you know, and he does know how to conversate, and he does know how to pronounce his vowels, he knows how to talk.

"The true of the matter is guys from the Dominican Republic may live in poverty if they were not in baseball, but they *are* in baseball, and they make a lot of money, and they are great at what they do, so you taking that and saying, 'if it wasn't for baseball this fucking guy would be here, so I'm better than him so I can use that to put him down'—you can't do that, because they're doing what you wish you could do and what everybody sitting in the stands wishes they could do. It's respect. You gotta give it, as hard as it is to bow down and say that, you gotta give it to that athlete for being able to do what we all believe is such a tremendous accomplishment.

"It takes tremendous talent, work ethic and a lotta luck. When I got hurt I was the number-one pitching prospect of the Cleveland Indians the year we were picked to win our division. I went from being the number-one prospect to never making it in the big leagues. There's not a whole lot of guys in the big leagues who can do half the things I could. Your peers, the people you play with, that's a respect that athletes give to each other, because that's something you can do, regardless of whether you capitalize on it and become this millionaire or not, but there's a certain amount of respect that athletes give to athletes."

Scott twice went to Omaha to compete in the College World Series with Bonds. Both times they came up empty-handed.

"You're talking about single- and double-elimination tournaments, and unless you've got [Curt] Schilling and [Randy] Johnson, that's how we [Arizona] won the Series this year, anything can happen. Talent-wise, my junior year, 14 guys got drafted. Anything can happen in those kinds of series, and against [Texas pitcher Roger] Clemens, mistakes are maximized. Both years we were ranked first, we had talent, but whether it be the College World Series or the World Series, it's about pitching and defense.

"Barry was a 20 homer/20 steal guy who hit over .340, and that's a projected first-rounder. A definite star player in the bigs, the guy who gets the money that first rounders get. Oddibe [McDowell] was better in college, but he didn't have a body like Barry's, and he didn't have his mental make-up. Bonds had height and the kind of frame that could expand and handle weight, so he was able to gain strength as he got older that's made him utterly explosive."

The seemingly unavoidable subject of race comes up again.

"It's there with me," said Scott. "It's not about trust. Certain people are out to do him [Bonds] worse because he's black. It's not equal. General managers, managers are 95-99 percent white. Owners, 100 percent white.

"Mays was a huge influence, one of the few people Bonds looked at and says, 'Holy shit,' he's got tremendous respect for him. Sure, Willie did tell him about the 'black experience,' as did Bobby, but all blacks go through it. I did, my mom told me stories about growing up in St. Louis. That's what we do, we reach out to people and pass on stories. It's part of history, part of what makes us strong. Barry knows about it and understands, but it's not an issue with him."

Regarding Barry, women, sex and his personal sense of charisma, Scott had this to say.

"Barry never partied, he's not into interacting with people, he'd rather be one-on-one. His psychology is more feminine; he's a momma's boy, not confrontational. He doesn't know what his potential is. He'd rather be in a sports bar with a few people. I've been in Johnny Love's' with him, and here's Johnny pulling up a special stool at the bar, and I've seen the women lining up for him, and he doesn't notice. He doesn't think of himself that way. At ASU he never went out, and that's the ultimate party school."

This helps explain Bonds' second marriage, to an old friend from his high school days, instead of a glamorous actress, singer or model. I then got into some other interesting areas. What if Barry had been hurt in 1985, and never made it to the Major Leagues?

"I think Barry'd be the exact same person he is right now, doing something different," he said. "Barry would do well, he'd never be on a corner selling drugs, he's too strong for that." Then Scott said some something that is worth noting.

"He's a friend and I respect him," he added, "but if he was not a player I would not hang out with him."

Charles actually admitted that if Barry Bonds were not a celebrity athlete, he would not "tolerate" him. Scott felt that Bonds' greatness as a player gave him the right to treat people differently, and he was willing to accept that because of Bonds' elevated position. He also said he would not take the time to be friends with a guy who acts like Bonds, if he were not a star. Interesting.

Scott was asked about Bonds' siblings.

"People say Bobby [junior] had better baseball instincts," he said. "Rickey was the wilder one. Maybe had some problems with alcohol. He's a nice kid, more outgoing than Barry. Barry's a wait-and-see type. Neither brother is as moody as Barry. Rickey had the least success in sports.

"Barry was not coachable when he was young, he never worked hard. Now he's matured incredibly. He talks about stocks and bonds. He has a trainer. He never would have listened to a trainer for a second. At first it was about strength, but he's learned patience through a trainer, whose taught him to concentrate on a muscle and take it slow. It takes him longer, but he reaches and exceeds the strength level he would have had he been doing it his own way. The same with stretching. His training methods are a reflection of his new patience as a player, an understanding of himself."

BOB NACHSHIN

An honors graduate from Bucknell, earning his juris doctorate at the prestigious Columbia University School of Law, Bob Nachshin was recommended to Barry Bonds when Bonds needed an attorney to handle his divorce from Sun Bonds in the early 1990s. Nachshin, known as family law's most noted expert in the area of prenuptial agreements, was recommended by Bonds' old agent, Dennis Gilbert of the Beverly Hills Sports Council, who retired from the agents business a couple of years ago. Nachshin works at a tony firm and has one of the best business addresses in Los Angeles, the 11000 block of Wilshire Boulevard.

"Barry's case was groundbreaking," said Nachshin, "because it was decided by all nine of the California Supreme Court Justices, and they decide very few family law cases. In the trial before a judge in 1994-95, it was decided that the prenuptial agreement that Sun Bonds signed was a valid document.

"Right now, we're in the driver's seat," he explained. "She [Sun] went to the court to appeal, and there was a bitterly worded dissent that decided with Barry. All nine justices on the Supreme Court said the Court of Appeals majority was totally off base.

"The issue was what constituted voluntariness. They tried to create a new law, and then hold Barry retroactively to it. Sheila Kuehl's new law doesn't affect Barry. That only affects prenuptials signed after the law went into effect. I think it's crazy. I think it gives family law judges new power to set aside prenuptials. It treats women as if they don't know what they're doing, but that's not applicable to the women I know, and it's not true of Sun Bonds. She is bright and knew what she was doing, and was capable of handling herself in all areas of her life. She was not the least bit reticent to sign that agreement, and did so voluntarily.

"The new law implies that women are unequal to men. People who are adults can't sign agreements without an attorney after the law, and there are just a lot of agreements people can competently sign without an attorney.

"Sun waived her rights, according to the trial judge in San Mateo County and the California Supreme Court. Sheila Kuehl's bill is political, and based on her constituency as a perceived hard-line feminist.

"Sun and Barry settled the case, and as part of the settlement, neither they nor their representation can publicly make negative comments about the other. Therefore, I have nothing to say publicly about Sun.

"What I did find remarkable about Barry was his ability to stay focused on baseball when all this was going on. He was subject to public ridicule, and it was very stressful, but he was able to handle it.

"I agree with the assessment that Barry's workout regimen is not just good for him physically, but has a Zen quality to it that allows him to stay patient and focused. I was at Barry's marriage to Liz, who he's known since high school, and she's just a great fit for him.

"I think it's incredible to win four MVPs and beat Ruth's and McGwire's records, and be a winner before the Supreme Court, all in the same year. To me, he's won a real Triple Crown."

RUSS BERTETTA

Russ Bertetta is the director of alumni relations at Serra High School, and he knew Barry well when Bonds was a student there.

"I was the U.S. history and English teacher, and I also coached the 'B' basketball team, although Barry played for the 'A's' as a freshman before moving on to the varsity for the rest of his Serra career. I know him pretty well. It's not like he calls me up and asks, 'Hey, man, how ya doin?'—I wish he did—but I know him and have stayed in touch with him over the years.

"Frankly, I'm leery of talking for this book. I gotta be real careful, because Barry's had a real good relationship with the school, but we don't want to make him mad by doing or saying anything that would get us in trouble with him.

"I have no personal problems with Barry. It was always pleasant and continues to be to this day. He was pretty much a regular kid who was a great athlete. Others were jealous of him because of that, but he's the same way as he always was. He's guarded with people he doesn't know, because what he does is so magnified. The way he is depends on his mood.

"Basically, there's no great difference in the way he is today and the way he was then. I was disappointed with ESPN when they did that show on him ['Sports Century']. They came out here and asked us a whole bunch of questions. We told them what our experiences with Barry were, which were positive, but they were looking for negative things, stuff about his relationship with his dad that we didn't know anything about. Nobody does, except probably Barry and his dad.

"Out of all the things everybody said, they pulled just the critical things and used that. I knew the stuff I said on ESPN was not going to be used because I had nothing bad to say. He was in my history and English class. My father coached him a little in little league, but they just wanted to know about Barry and his dad.

"You can tell he wanted to be his own man, not Bobby Bonds' son. It was kinda like they wanted us to analyze him on this point.

"In history class, the things that interested him were African-American history or black history. He had ripped his finger, his ring got caught on a doorjamb as he was swinging around, he ripped the tendons, so he couldn't play a few weeks and had some time to work on an oral report on Harriet

Tubman. It was not an 'A' report, but he was interested in the subject and put effort into it.

"That's the type of thing he was interested in. In English as a sopho-more, he was not into reading 'Romeo and Juliet,' that was not his favorite. I'm not sure he was ready to study, say, the writings of Frederick Douglas. But maybe just a little bit he was looking to find his roots from a racial perspec-tive.

"He went to a private junior high school, but I don't think he was Catholic when he got to Serra. His second marriage was in a Catholic Church to a girl who is local [Liz Watson], but I'm not sure if that was because of Barry's religion, her religion, or both.

"When he was here, we had three or four priests, and it's a disciplined atmosphere, the rules are there, but I don't think he ever had a problem. He's pretty straight arrow, that's why his career is so good, because he knows what it takes. I never saw him under the influence or have any major discipline problem.

"Unfortunately for Barry, he is basically a great athlete who's underappreciated because the press doesn't like him, but he's never been ar-rested, he doesn't do drugs, I don't even think he's a drinker.

"He's moody like a lot of people, except his moods are publicized and he doesn't disguise his moodiness. He deserves better treatment. He could make it better, but he's not a bad guy. He's led a decent life, we're all proud of him for what he's done, and he's brought no shame to Serra. We all hope he sends Nikolai here."

No shame? Barry has brought only pride and distinction to what was already an honorable learning institution.

BRUCE MACGOWAN

Bruce MacGowan is one of the most respected veteran radio sports journalists on the West Coast, as well as being a heckuva nice guy. If everyone in the world were just like Bruce, we would not need police, the military or a court system. He is honorable and ethical, and wears his opinions on his sleeve. Throughout the Bonds Watch, he and I often sat together in the Pac Bell Park press box. In between one-upping each other on film quotes and occasionally-not-so-bad imitations of Marlon Brando, William Devane and Burt Lancaster, we watched history unfold together. For this reason we be-came members of a wonderful, and thankfully not-too-exclusive baseball club. I asked the popular KNBR AM/68 sports personality to say a few words about what watching Bonds meant to him.

"The 2001 baseball season was one of the most remarkable in the history of this grand old game. As a sportscaster, it has been my good fortune to have witnessed in person, many exciting and noteworthy moments involving our Bay Area teams, but the remarkable campaign of 2001 will always occupy a special place in my treasury of memories.

"While the Giants and A's battled in their respective divisions for the top spot, something even more exciting was taking place. When Barry Bonds first gave indication that he was going to experience an almost supernatural season, there was an almost audible murmur of excitement heard within the usually cynical circle of the sports media.

"While Bonds was never and has never been a favorite among reporters, virtually everyone who covered his exploits during that memorable season had to admit that they were a bit awed by what they were seeing.

"Each of us who covered those fateful days will take with us to our dying moments some very distinct images of that record-breaking drive. One of my favorites involves an interview I was doing in the Pac Bell press box with baseball broadcaster Joe Angel during a game that summer. The San Francisco native and former Giants' radio play-by-play man and I were engaged in a discussion about the season while a game unfolded below us on the field. As we continued our conversion we noticed that Bonds had stepped to the plate, and I pointed this out as the crowd could be heard in the background responding with a hearty ovation. No sooner did Angel begin answering a question I had just asked him when suddenly an unmistakable 'CRACK' of a ball striking a bat could be clearly heard in the background. Suddenly interrupted from his train of thought by a laser-like blast over the arcade in right field, Angel made a spontaneous but seamless transition from our discussion into a quick play-by-play description of the home run.

"Two months later in early October as I roamed the outfield bleachers while wearing a remote headset, ready to give a firsthand report to our broadcasters on KNBR, should Bonds bash record-breaking homer number 71, I was swept up in the energy and excitement of the scene surrounding me. Fathers with their young sons, teenage couples on dates, and middle-aged men wearing caps and carrying gloves were among the many who stirred restlessly throughout the bleachers and surrounding walkways in anticipation of the big moment. Beyond the right field wall in McCovey Cove, a huge flotilla of boats of all types, large and small, surfboarders, intertubers, even a few swimmers clad in wet suits enjoyed the festive atmosphere while awaiting the roar of the crowd.

"When Bonds parked his record-breaking 71st just in front of the brick wall above the seats in right-center field, a glove reached down from the arcade to snare the ball in brilliant fashion. As Bonds circled the bases, fireworks exploded overhead and the cheers seemed to linger in the air for a good

10 minutes. Three years after Mark McGwire had electrified the baseball world, Barry Bonds had done him one better.

"Bonds would hit one more homer that night in a wild four hour-plus game that the Giants finally lost to the rival Dodgers 11-10, a loss that I should emphasize, knocked the Giants out of the pennant chase. Later an exhausted Bonds and his Godfather Willie Mays rewarded those who stayed well after the midnight hour by sharing their thoughts in a postgame ceremony on the field.

"Barry Bonds is certainly one of the most fascinating, enigmatic, and least popular superstars in the game's history, and yet it should be noted that some of the game's other greats, such as Ted Williams and Ty Cobb were both reviled by fans, the media and in some cases, even teammates. Be that as it may, Bonds clearly proved that he is not only one of the game's elite, but at the advanced age of 37 still probably the best player in the game today.

"Having had the opportunity to watch him play on a near-everyday basis for nearly a decade has been a pleasure and a privilege. While Bonds cherishes his privacy and maintains a somewhat aloof manner with most of those at the park, I was also pleased to see how well he handled himself under the constant scrutiny of the media and fans. Bonds got far less coverage and credit for his feat in 2001 than McGwire did in 1998, yet number 25 was much more accommodating and agreeable to all requests for interviews than McGwire had been. Big Mac always seemed ill at ease and even bothered by the attention until the final weeks, while Bonds scarcely seemed fazed by all of the hoopla.

"Because he is one of the big names in our pro sports scene today, and since he has shattered a record that was only broken three years ago, it's appropriate that my good friend Steven Travers has chronicled Bonds' amazing season. But hopefully the reader will find even more interesting, Travers's rare look at this reluctant superstar.

"Bonds trusted Travers enough to open up and share some private thoughts with him, about his life as an athlete, as a kid growing up and watching his dad Bobby play in the Majors, and some of his opinions regarding our turbulent society.

"Rarely do we get a chance to watch something quite as remarkable as Bonds' record-breaking home run chase. Rarer still is the opportunity to read firsthand about the man who authored such a feat. Read and enjoy this book about an unusual athlete and an incredible season. I think you'll not only enjoy yourself but learn a few things that you didn't know about Barry Bonds. And perhaps you'll come to realize as I have, that he's not only a great ballplayer, but a most interesting person."

EPILOGUE

Will Barry Bonds Retire the Greatest Player in Baseball History?

In the aftermath of the 2001 baseball season, Barry Bonds' incredible performance was viewed as the Great Distraction from the events of 9/11. He had done for America what Joltin' Joe did during World War II, the Sultan of Swat after the Black Sox scandal. He had turned himself into as big a Bay Area hero as Mays, DiMaggio, Montana, Walsh, Jackson, Bill Russell, Ken Stabler, Rick Barry. His reputation with the fans and the media had turned full circle, like Williams in Boston and Mantle in New York. He had performed on-field heroics of mythic proportions that put him in a class with Lou Gehrig.

He had completely eclipsed the names of Rodriguez, Griffey, Giambi, and Juan Gonzalez from any of the usual "Who's the best player in the game?" discussions. Bonds had warded off the MVP aspirations of Sosa and the relative newcomer Luis Gonzalez. He had made people forget the likes of Michael Jordan. He had forced Tiger Woods and Shaquille O'Neal to wait their turn at the title World's Greatest Athlete. He had placed himself in the position of frontrunner for all the Player of Year awards.

If Mays had been the Greatest *Living* Ballplayer, his Godson had come along and symbolically said, "MAYBE I AM." If Ruth were the greatest player ever, Bonds had entered the campaign that someday may place that moniker alongside his name, not the Babe's.

No name in sports was larger than Bonds' name now. Not Wilt Chamberlain, Kareem Abdul-Jabbar, Hank Aaron, Ty Cobb, Jim Brown, O.J. Simpson, Johnny Unitas, Pete Sampras, Rod Laver, Pele, Wayne Gretzky, Bobby Orr, Gordie Howe, or Dale Earnhardt.

No record was greater or more sacred. The single-season home run record is the greatest in sports. Next is Aaron's 755 home runs, and Bonds is after that now just as surely as the U.S. is after Osama bin Laden.

Other records pale in comparison when it comes to luster. Not Eric Dickerson's rushing record or Chamberlain's season points-per-game average. Not other big-time baseball records, such as Cy Young's 511 career victories, Pete Rose's 4,256 career hits, Rogers Hornsby's .424 single-season batting mark, DiMaggio's 56-game hitting streak, or Cobb's .367 lifetime average.

What does Bonds need to do to attain Greatest Player Ever status?

1. Win a World Championship.
2. Break Hank Aaron's home run record (and, for good measure, Japanese star Sadaharu Oh's all-time mark) while making a run at 800.
3. Get 500 career steals, which will happen in 2002.
4. Get 3,000 career hits, which according to Scott Boras' calculations is attainable.
5. Hit .300 lifetime.
6. Approach all-time records for bases on balls and runs batted in.
7. Win a batting championship, and for good measure, a Triple Crown.

All of these goals are absolutely attainable.

The 2001 postseason would be one of the most exciting in recent baseball history. Along with Bonds' breaking the record, the games served as a tremendous tonic to the post-terrorist malaise. While the games were being played, President Bush began a successful bombing campaign against Taliban terrorist enclaves in Afghanistan, which also started to lift spirits.

The big story was the New York Yankees. Every game at the Stadium was an event, complete with Presidential security, and featuring Mayor Giuliani. He had emerged as a national hero to America, and a folk hero in the Big Apple.

The fans simply responded, to the exciting play of their team, and to their own indomitable spirit. Would-be terrorists saw the enthusiasm of these people. These were the residents of a city they had tried, and failed, to bring to their knees. They had to realize that they had engaged in acts of futility.

In a different way, it would be like the Japanese, who thought they had destroyed the U.S. fleet at Pearl Harbor, only to be thoroughly defeated by that fleet a few months later at Midway Island.

First, the Yankees beat Oakland in an unbelievable five-game series. After losing two at home, their backs against the wall, the Bombers took two in Oakland, and the decider at home. Then Seattle fell in five.

In the National League, Arizona moved through the process in far less dramatic fashion. Johnson, and particularly Schilling, put on a performance similar to the Koufax-Drysdale duo that propelled Los Angeles to World Championships in 1963 and 1965.

The World Series between the Diamondbacks and Yankees was one for the ages. Bonds threw out the first ball in the opener and sat next to "61*" director Billy Crystal. Controversy did not elude him. There were reports that he had been irritated over delays in security and seating arrangements.

Arizona won the first two at home, but heading back East, the general consensus was that the thing was even. It was not. New York had the edge. They won three straight, including two consecutive ninth-inning comebacks.

Back in Phoenix, Johnson won his second game to force the Series to a deciding seventh. Schilling pitched his heart out, but trailed. Johnson was brought in in relief with zero days' rest and held the Yankees. In the last of the ninth, Luis Gonzalez' bloop single against a drawn-in infield against the great Mariano Rivera gave the World Championship to the D'backs.

The Giants have been in San Francisco since 1958. They have been to two World Series, and lost them both. Their last World Championship was in 1954, when Mays roamed the Polo Grounds. Arizona came into the league in 1998, and they face speculation that they will eventually be switched to the American League. Still, because of free agency and money in the New Economy of baseball, like Florida in 1997 they were able to go all the way.

The Giants, sitting at home and watching on television, had to be kicking themselves, particularly over the three losses against Houston at home, right after the cancellations. They had finished two behind Arizona in the West and three behind wild-card St. Louis.

The World Champions had lost four straight to them in Phoenix after the All-Star break. They had the two best pitchers in the game, but lacked offense and sported a very shaky bullpen. They could have been had.

There was an added element to the questions running in the minds of the Giants' players and management. If they had the greatest player in the game, who had the best season ever, but they still could not win with him, could they afford to keep him? It is a modern baseball question, not faced by Branch Rickey or John McGraw.

Bonds had not planned anything for October because he had hoped to be playing baseball. He did have a vacation set for November, and he told the media and the Giants he did not want to concentrate on his contract until he got back. He reportedly told Boras not to call him until he got back.

He did begin to appear on Wheaties breakfast cereal boxes, and a marketing firm began the process of "changing his image from that of a curmudgeon," at Boras' request. The speculation on where he would end up began to build into a fever pitch, and if he was going to give the Giants a "home team discount," it was only after testing his market value to the nth degree. Boras wanted a minimum of $20 million a year.

The Jason Giambi factor came into play. The Yankees wanted the younger man and had decided to go after him. Bonds would have to wait and see what happened with Giambi if he planned to negotiate with George Steinbrenner. Giambi was also rumored to be headed to St. Louis, where McGwire had retired to free up money for him. He had reportedly recruited him, too.

Some talk about Bonds replacing Giambi in Oakland appeared. This made some sense, just as it had for football star Jerry Rice, who was able to stay where he lived when he signed with the Raiders. Rice, however, was well past his prime. Bonds was in the middle of his.

On November 14, Bonds sat down with KNBR sportstalk host Rick Barry, a Hall of Fame basketball player with the Golden State Warriors in the 1970s. Barry and Bonds had a lot in common. They were great athletes who had been criticized by the press, fans and teammates for their prickly personalities.

Bonds revealed for the first time that he had received death threats right after his three-homer game against Colorado on September 9. The FBI had showed up at his door to tell him, and helped maintain a security force when the games resumed after the terrorist attacks in New York. Bonds told his wife and Baker, who had been with Aaron when he received racially motivated death threats during his chase of Ruth's record in 1973-74. Bonds never informed his teammates. He also had deflected some media questions on the subject.

In an announcement that surprised nobody, Bonds won his fourth (and what should have been his sixth) Most Valuable Player award, taking 30 of 32 first place votes to beat out Sosa, 438 to 278. No other player has more than three MVP awards.

The award came on the heels of Boras' 40-page binder projecting Bonds to hit 800 home runs and get 3,000 hits by 2006. Of course it would be nice if these milestones could be accomplished while wearing a black cap that said "SF" on it.

In the meantime, Judge David Garcia ruled that it was unclear whether Alex Popov or Patrick Hayashi should have custody of the 73rd home run ball. Only a trial could determine that.

In Tempe, there was no word on whether Todd McFarlane, holding on to the now greatly devalued McGwire number 70 ball, was waiting to find out the outcome so he could make a bid.

On November 19, Rob Neyer of ESPN.com wrote an article titled "The best seasons of all time." Using various sources, Neyer concluded the following:

10. Rogers Hornsby, 1922
9. Ted Williams, 1946
8. Mickey Mantle, 1957
7. Barry Bonds, 1993
6. Mickey Mantle, 1956
5. Babe Ruth, 1921
4. Babe Ruth, 1923
3. Babe Ruth, 1920
2. Honus Wagner, 1908
1. Barry Bonds, 2001

Barry Bonds' record-breaking season made him, and those associated with him, think just a little bit more about a number of things. Among them was his legacy, race, religion, and life in general.

"I think Barry is trying to prove something this year," Colorado Rockies coach Rich Donnelly, who was a coach with Pittsburgh when Bonds played there, told *The Sporting News*. "Deep down, he wants to prove he's the best player in the game. I know Barry, and he's tired of hearing about everybody else. Enough about those guys, this is my year.

"His legacy means a lot to him. He might say it doesn't, but if you say, 'Barry, you're going to be in the Hall of Fame,' he'll go, 'I know.' If you tell him, 'You're the greatest player who ever played,' he might say, 'What about Ken Griffey or Willie Mays?' but deep down . . . he just wants to be known as the best."

Bonds had given the country something amazing to immerse themselves in all summer, and as the autumn leaves began to fall, he gave them something to take their minds off of brutal reality.

"The only positive thing out of it is it brought this country together, and it's good to see how strong this country is," said Bonds of 9/11. He had pledged $10,000 per home run to the United Way relief fund.

The day he hit number 60, a reporter asked if Bonds could remember the first time he understood Babe Ruth's significance.

"Naw," Bonds said, "but I'll tell you about Hank Aaron. Aaron was my guy. In the true history of baseball, Hank Aaron is the home run king. Babe Ruth is not the home run king, and I wasn't going to slight Hank by talking about Ruth when I don't know that much about Ruth."

Bonds believes some players, the media and fans understand the role of blacks with the glorious game. Blacks never forget that the game excluded them until Jackie Robinson reached the majors in 1947. Therefore, everything before that date is suspect in their eyes.

"I'm African-American, and our achievement is part of what I stand for in this game," said Bonds, noting that eight of the 17 players with 500 home runs are black.

"My heritage is what I need to know and need to talk about. How Jackie paved the way. About the Negro Leagues, from 'Cool Papa' Bell to Josh Gibson and Satchel Paige. Those are my people, the ones who opened the doors to give me the opportunity to play this game. Everyone already knows the American history of baseball. But in the African-American history, and in the American history of baseball, Hank Aaron is the home run king, and that is that."

If Bonds averages 47 homers—as he did the previous five years, from 2002-2006—he would finish with an astounding 802. Bonds has 567 homers, ranking seventh all time.

"He's really at peace with himself," Bobby Bonds said. "He's consistently happier in his life right now, so he's going out and having fun. Things have to go right in your family life, and he's really feeling great about his wife and kids. Everything is flowing the way it's supposed to be flowing."

Ken Griffey, Jr. said that Barry Bonds is the "greatest player of his generation."

Toward the end of the 2001 season, Bonds had been asked if his negative image was because he was black.

"Probably, I mean reality is reality," he told CNN/SI.

Barry's grandmother always talked about the importance of God, and so did his parents. Bobby and Pat taught Barry and his brother to read the Bible.

"My father said it is the most powerful book in the world today," Barry Bonds said.

"While we are talking about my parents, let me say something else about them. My parents are not racists, and they did not raise me to be a racist. They always said that there is reality and you must deal with that. But my parents also said that nothing should stop you in today's era from excelling."

"Black athletes are not supposed to think," teammate Eric Davis once said.

Bonds gets hate mail. Is it racist, or just hateful?

There is an interesting point worth making when it comes to black athletes. It is easy to look at the popularity of African-Americans like Tony Gwynn, Michael Jordan and Kirby Puckett, and conclude that racism is not a factor. How could it, if so many white fans love these guys?

The reality is that most whites love to like blacks. It makes them feel good. It helps convince them that racism is not what it used to be. What is not on the surface, however, is that most whites love to like *certain kinds* of blacks. Barry Bonds has not always been the kind of black athlete that they love to like.

Dave Kingman was an utter pain to deal with. So was Steve Carlton. Had they been black, they would have been perceived much differently. Instead of being viewed as curmudgeons, they would would have been *militants*. White people like folks they can *identify* with. They like smart, personable, media-savvy guys and gals. They do not much care for players who are always reminding them of racism.

Bonds runs a multi-cultural household. His son Nikolai, 11, and daughter Shikari, 10, both by an earlier marriage with Sun, speak Swedish and French, because Sun does.

"It is important for them to learn other cultures," Barry said. He and Liz have a lovely daughter, Aisha Lynn.

Bonds can be a narcissist. He reads the papers and is sensitive to criticism. Watch him observe the Jim Rome Show when it is about him. Reporters would watch him like monkeys staring at a red rubber ball. Bonds would watch them watch him. Other televisions would be on, all centered on a discussion of Bonds' "choking." He used the word himself in describing his dismal postseason record.

Is he a misunderstood superstar or surly loner?

Bonds at the plate stops clocks. He has the effect on baseball fans of a bikini-clad blonde bombshell strolling a beach filled with frat boys. Time stops, an aspect of baseball that is one of its most endearing qualities.

He stands straight, staring at the pitcher like a sniper. He bends his knees slightly. He chokes up on his bat. His hips swivel like a golfer, the way Ted Williams did it. When he swings, it is like a cobra.

When he steps to the plate, crowds roar to life, stadiums sparkle with camera flashes, and the noise takes on a new level of anticipation.

Out of all the people in all the world who have chosen to play this game, first on the sandlots and in the little leagues, and then gone through the great weeding-out process that determines who plays on the high school varsity and who goes to the JVs, finally on to the college ranks, the minors, and the big leap to The Show—of all these people from the United States, Mexico, Canada, Japan, Taiwan, the Dominican, and every place baseball is played—Barry Bonds is bidding to be *the very best of them all.*

He is to baseball what Winston Churchill is to statesmanship, Marilyn Monroe to sex. You get the point. Is the mind yet boggled?

Still, greatness on the field is only half the story. There must be something more. Manny Ramirez of Boston put up numbers on a relative par with Bonds (until 2001), but with all due respect, he is not a very exciting personality. Albert Belle was a gargantuan power threat, but the man was so taciturn and downright nasty that nobody would have written a book about him even if he had banged out 80 homers in a year.

The beauty of Bonds is that some people think of him the way they did of Belle, but they are wrong. There is, to Bonds, substance, intelligence and humor.

The best sports subjects are fascinating people who happen to play sports. Bo Belinsky was a playboy pitcher of the '60s Angels who swung with Frank Sinatra, Hugh Hefner, and J. Edgar Hoover.

His manager, Bill Rigney, was a first-class baseball mind who palled with presidents.

Moe Berg was a no-hit catcher of little note, but off the field his exploits as a spy in Nazi Germany, helping to bring top German scientists to the U.S. after World War II, make him an object of fascination.

Bill "Spaceman" Lee had the normally hard Boston press in the palm of his hand because he was funny and off-the-wall.

"I live on Rural Route One in Vermont," he once told a crowd. "The state told me they were naming the streets, and I could name mine. I told 'em I didn't want people to know where I lived, which is why I live in rural Vermont. They said either you name it, or we will. I told 'em to name it the Ted Kaczynski Memorial Highway . . . I mean, I don't advocate killing anybody, but some of his ideas were pretty good."

Ted Williams, the conservative Republican, infuriated the Kennedyites among that town's "knights of the keyboard" with his views on politics, among other things, but nobody ever accused the man of being boring.

Therein lies the key to Barry. He is never boring. In his own way, he has a unique and interesting personality.

The fact is that Barry Bonds is a college man, an intelligent fellow with a high IQ. He can relate to the same TV shows, music and popular icons that other Americans can relate to. For some reason, mostly because of youth and inexperience, he said some things when he was a kid that led writers to get a negative impression of him. In order to protect himself, Bonds learned to be silent.

It is said that children can tame the savage beast that beats in the hearts of men. Watch Bonds take his place in the on-deck circle, then wave tenderly to Liz Aisha, seated in the stands.

Watch father and daughter exchange waves, then watch dad hit a baseball 450 feet. Bonds is the dual personality. Bonds is the father and husband whose friends away from baseball do not know Dusty Baker from Dusty Springfield. Then there is Bonds whose extended family included Baker and Reggie Smith, who called Reggie Jackson "cuz," the Bonds who some call arrogant.

Bonds never had to ask Willie Mays, his Godfather, to make somebody "an offer they can't refuse" to further his career. Bonds did it all himself, which is the beauty of sports. Between the white lines, who you know, what your address is, or how much is in your bank account; none of that matters. The baseball field is a symbol of true equality.

Adding another name to baseball's immortals, Bonds has put himself on sport's Mount Rushmore.

"Ted Williams is the greatest hitter who ever lived, I don't doubt that," Tim McCarver told Tim Kawakami of the *San Jose Mercury News*. He may have thought Bonds a phony, but his admiration for his play knows no bounds. "But when you're talking about both sides of the ball. . . . Bonds is the best left fielder who's ever played the game."

"He's brought arrogance to the game," Reggie Jackson told Daniel Brown of the *San Jose Mercury News*. "There have just been too many balls he didn't run out, too many times when he didn't run as hard as he could after balls in the field. You know this isn't just me talking. There are certain obligations that come with having a talent for the game like he has.

"I wish he'd enjoyed himself more than he has. I don't know what's going to happen with Michael Jordan now that he's out of retirement. But I'll tell you something about Michael before: He enjoyed the game. He enjoyed being Michael. And he sure as hell enjoyed his greatness.

"I don't get the feeling Barry does."

In an interview with the *New York Daily News'* Mike Lupica, Jackson once discussed Bonds' place in history.

"I was at a signing with Pete Rose the other day," Jackson said, "and we got to talking about Bonds and all the home runs and all, and Pete said, 'At least this time the record will belong to an all-around player.'"

Charlie Silvera is one of the oldest baseball scouts in the U.S. On any given Sunday during baseball season, you can find him at Big Rec. That is the baseball complex in San Francisco's Golden Gate Park, where The City's legends have performed. Prep and semi-pro hopefuls still play this joyous game in the same eclectic surroundings where Jim Morrison, Jefferson Airplane, and the Grateful Dead gave vibrancy to the Summer of Love, back in 1967.

Silvera has seen them all (DiMaggio, Gehrig, and those guys—I doubt he saw The Doors at The Fillmore West). He says that the last guy he saw who was as quick on the inside pitch as Bonds was Gehrig. *Lou Gehrig!*

Another sign that an athlete has reached for new heights is when journalists who normally write about other things, like politics and world affairs, suddenly find you worthy of their prose—and sometimes even praise.

David Halberstam himself had deigned to write about Bonds for ESPN.com during the summer. Halberstam did not have much nice to say. He dredged up Bonds' infamous "get the hell out of here" quote to the writer talking his father, and echoed McCarver's theme, that Bonds' newfound openness was just a facade. It was all orchestrated by Boras to shine his image for the contract run, Halberstam thought.

Thomas Sowell, a black conservative, was more interested in pure baseball history.

"In personality, Bonds seems much more like Roger Maris than like crowd-pleasers such as Willie Mays or Babe Ruth. Maris was a private man, respected by his teammates, but not appreciated by the media, who like more colorful players like Sammy Sosa or Bunyanesque figures like Mark McGwire. It is very unlikely that the kinds of quotes attributed to Yogi Berra will ever be attributed to Barry Bonds.

"None of this should matter when judging a baseball player. Barry Bonds has as much right to be Barry Bonds as Sammy Sosa has to be Sammy Sosa or Babe Ruth had to be Babe Ruth."

Baseball is a simple game, filled with complex characters. Take Ty Cobb. They say he was racist, and he was, but he set up college funds for numerous African-Americans in his hometown in Georgia. He believed in separation of the races, but he was not a redneck advocating lynch mobs.

When he saw Willie Mays play, he finally came around to believing the game was better off integrated. It is kind of funny, he lived in Atherton at the end of his life, and that is where Willie moved in. In a way, that says a lot about America.

What about Jackie Robinson? He was his own man, a Connecticut Republican who backed Richard Nixon. Bonds has said he never would have stood for all the racist crap and death threats, but people never really know what they would do until actually confronted with the situation. One can imagine Branch Rickey asking Bonds if he was "man enough not to fight back," and he would have said something like, "Are you kidding? I'm gonna kick some ass." In Bonds' view, he would have been a lot more like Jack Johnson than Jack Robinson.

Christmas came early for the fans of San Francisco when, on December 19, 2001, Bonds accepted arbitration with the Giants. Eschewing free agency, Bonds put himself into the position of getting a $90 million, five-year contract, which he signed in January, receiving a $10 million signing bonus to be paid through April, 2004. He got salaries of $13 million in each of the next two seasons (2002-03), $16 million in 2004, $20 million in 2005 and $18 million in 2006. Bonds also got a no-trade clause.

Just when it looked like Bonds' image had changed with the media, the lovefest receded over the winter when *Sports Illustrated* made reference to Bonds' charities. An article appeared with a photo depicting bored Portland Trailblazers basketball players standing around yakking on cell phones during a charity event with kids—except the kids did not seem to be capturing their attention. In the article, there was reference to money raised by Bonds, ostensibly for his varied charities. According to the piece, however, the money was not going to charities, but to his mother.

On the field, there has never been a question. Bonds seemingly had won every award there was to win. In 1996 he had been named to the All-Time College World Series Team. Three years later, he was named the left fielder on the Giants' All-Century team. The 2001 awards kept piling up for the 6-2, 226-pound superman throughout the off-season. In addition to the MVP, Bonds, who had been named Player of the Month in May when he set a Major League for home runs in that month, was also named *USA Baseball Weekly, The Sporting News, Baseball America and Baseball Digest* Major League Player of the Year. He won the NL Hank Aaron award, recognizing the best overall hitter in the league. The *Associated Press* named him 2001 Male Athlete of the Year.

In another interesting development, Tim McCarver, who had been so critical of Bonds in his pre-All-Star Game comments, was hired by the Giants to announce approximately 25 televised games on San Francisco/Oakland's local Fox affiliate, KTVU/2. Because Jon Miller does ESPN's Sunday night telecasts with Joe Morgan, the Giants need a fill-in when Jon is on the road, and it was McCarver they chose.

Finally, in a one of the most telling signs that Bonds had "broken through" the barrier of major national popularity, he starred in a national television commercial that aired during the 2002 Super Bowl (where Serra's Tom Brady was MVP in leading a team, appropriately named the Patriots, to the championship). In the commercial, for San Francisco-based Charles Schwab & Co., Bonds takes batting practice while a "Field of Dreams"-type voice warns him that he should not pursue the all-time career home run record. Bonds turns and faces the announcer's booth, and it is revealed, to comic effect, that the voice belongs to Hank Aaron.

Baseball is a wonderful, thrilling game that provides lasting memories for the many fans who sample its wonders. One thing is for sure. Barry Lamar Bonds has been giving baseball aficionados in Pittsburgh, San Francisco, and throughout the world, special thrills since 1986. In 2001, he gave them, arguably, the finest individual performance of all time.

He will continue to do so for years to come, and when it is all said and done, he may be—arguably—the Greatest Baseball Player of All Time.

Do not bet against him.

BARRY BONDS' LIFETIME STATISTICS

Full Name:	Barry Lamar Bonds
Number:	25
Born:	7/24/1964
Birthplace:	Riverside, CA
Height:	6-2
Weight:	210
Bats:	Left
Throws:	Left
College:	Arizona State
ML Debut:	4/20/1986
Experience:	16 Years

SEASON/TEAM		G	AB	R	H	2B	3B	HR	RBI	TB	BB	SO	SB	CS	OBP	SLG	AVG
1986	Pirates	113	413	72	92	26	3	16	48	172	65	102	36	7	.330	.416	.223
1987	Pirates	150	551	99	144	34	9	25	59	271	54	88	32	10	.329	.492	.261
1988	Pirates	144	538	97	152	30	5	24	58	264	72	82	17	11	.368	.491	.283
1989	Pirates	159	580	96	144	34	6	19	58	247	93	93	32	10	.351	.426	.248
1990	Pirates	151	519	104	156	32	3	33	114	293	93	83	52	13	.406	.565	.301
1991	Pirates	153	510	95	149	28	5	25	116	262	107	73	43	13	.410	.514	.292
1992	Pirates	140	473	109	147	36	5	34	103	295	127	69	39	8	.456	.624	.311
1993	Giants	159	539	129	181	38	4	46	123	365	126	79	29	12	.458	.677	.336
1994	Giants	112	391	89	122	18	1	37	81	253	74	43	29	9	.426	.647	.312
1995	Giants	144	506	109	149	30	7	33	104	292	120	83	31	10	.431	.577	.294
1996	Giants	158	517	122	159	27	3	42	129	318	151	76	40	7	.461	.615	.308
1997	Giants	159	532	123	155	26	5	40	101	311	145	87	37	8	.446	.585	.291
1998	Giants	156	552	120	167	44	7	37	122	336	130	92	28	12	.438	.609	.303
1999	Giants	102	355	91	93	20	2	34	83	219	73	62	15	2	.389	.617	.262
2000	Giants	143	480	129	147	28	4	49	106	330	117	77	11	3	.440	.688	.306
2001	Giants	153	476	129	156	32	2	73	137	411	177	93	13	3	.515	.863	.328
Career Totals		2296	7932	1713	2313	483	71	567	1542	4639	1724	1282	484	138	.419	.585	.292